Advance Praise for *Improving the User Experience through Practical Data Analytics*

Mike Fritz, Manager of Usability, PeopleFluent, Massachusetts, USA

Paul D. Berger, Visiting Scholar and Professor of Marketing, and Director of the Master of Science in Marketing Analytics (MSMA) program, Bentley University, Massachusetts, USA

"It is only fitting that a statistics book written for UX professionals keeps its users in mind, and Mike Fritz and Paul D. Berger do that masterfully in *"Improving the User Experience through Practical Data Analytics"*. Readers will find mastering statistical techniques approachable and even enjoyable through the authors' use of case studies, applied examples, and detailed instructions for analyzing data using both Excel and SPSS in each chapter. A great resource for UX professionals who desire to increase their statistical rigor."

–Nicholas Aramovich, Ph.D., Assistant Professor, Organizational Psychology Program, Alliant International University, San Diego

"Improving the User Experience through Practical Data Analytics by Mike Fritz and Paul D. Berger is a handy-dandy desk reference for all usability professionals. Too often usability reports either don't include necessary statistics, or worse, provide the wrong statistics. With this easy to use guide, now there's no excuse. The book is laid out so that it is easy to map your study in to one of the chapters and find all the relevant tests and formulas to use."

–Bob Virzi, Raver Consulting, Adjunct Professor of Usability Testing at Bentley University, Waltham, MA (MS in Human Factors in Information Design program)

"Are you intimidated by statistical concepts? Has your manager asked you if your test results are "significant"? Are you concerned that you are using the appropriate statistical test? Can you use Excel, a tool that you probably already know well, to do statistical analysis of your test data? *"Improving the User Experience through Practical Data Analytics"* by Mike Fritz and Paul D. Berger helps answer these questions with clear explanations of statistical concepts and methods, step-by-step procedures for using Excel as your analysis tool, case studies, tips on how to avoid common errors and biases, and a good dose of humor. Each chapter in the book describes a method, ranging from paired-samples t-tests to regression analysis, using a case study to put the method in context – an extremely useful and user-friendly approach. I recommend this book for all designers and researchers who are trying to understand both what method should be used and how to use that method."

–Chauncey E. Wilson, UX Architect, USA

"This book stays above statistical detail by posing realistic business scenarios, then clarifying the concepts of data-driven design for usability students and practitioners, giving this growing profession the objectivity and repeatability that VPs seek. Choosing the applicable method and particularly interpreting the analysis for a business problem is emphasized while illustrated computer applications handle the numerical load."

–Charles N. Abernethy, BSEE, PhD, CHFP

Improving the User Experience through Practical Data Analytics

Improving the User Experience through Practical Data Analytics
Gain Meaningful Insight and Increase Your Bottom Line

Mike Fritz

Paul D. Berger

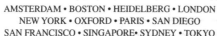

AMSTERDAM • BOSTON • HEIDELBERG • LONDON
NEW YORK • OXFORD • PARIS • SAN DIEGO
SAN FRANCISCO • SINGAPORE• SYDNEY • TOKYO

Morgan Kaufmann is an imprint of Elsevier

ELSEVIER

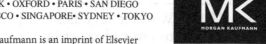

Acquiring Editor: Todd Green
Editorial Project Manager: Kaitlin Herbert
Project Manager: Punithavathy Govindaradjane
Designer: Maria Inês Cruz

Morgan Kaufmann is an imprint of Elsevier
225 Wyman Street, Waltham, MA 02451, USA

ISBN: 978-0-12-800635-1

British Library Cataloguing-in-Publication Data
A catalogue record for this book is available from the British Library

Library of Congress Cataloging-in-Publication Data
A catalogue record for this book is available from the Library of Congress

For information on all Morgan Kaufmann publications
visit our website at www.mkp.com

Working together
to grow libraries in
developing countries

www.elsevier.com • www.bookaid.org

To Mary, the love of my life
  – Mike

To my wonderful wife, Susan
  – Paul

Contents

Preface

The book will help you utilize both descriptive and predictive statistical techniques to gain meaningful insight from data collected employing traditional UX research methods, including moderated usability studies, unmoderated usability studies, surveys and contextual inquiries.

However, the analytic methods we described can easily be applied to data collected in a myriad of other UX research methods, including focus groups, live Web site analytics, card sorting, competitive research, and physiological testing like eye tracking, heart rate variance, and skin conductance.

This book is a how-to guide, not a treatise on statistics. We provide practical advise about which methods to use in what situations, and how to interpret the results in a meaningful way.

In addition, the book provides lots of easy-to-grasp tutoring for those who have a limited knowledge of statistics. We hope the book makes many of the calculations—such as calculating a simple correlation coefficient—seem almost effortless, while providing all the necessary "hand-holding" when utilizing a more complex method, such as logistic regression.

WHY WE WROTE THE BOOK

Over the past 5 years, excellent books have been published regarding collecting, analyzing, and presenting usability metrics. Arguably, the best ones in this category are the **Morgan Kaufmann** books, including *Measuring the User Experience* by Tom Tullis and Bill Albert, *Beyond the Usability Lab* by Bill Albert, Tom Tullis and Donna Tedesco, and *Quantifying the User Experience* by Jeff Sauro and James R. Lewis. These books do an outstanding job of instructing the UX professional how to choose the right metric, apply it, and effectively use the information it reveals.

And yet, as we surveyed the UX research literature landscape, we saw there was currently no book that urges UX professionals to use predictive and other advanced statistical tools in their work. (The current books on usability metrics leave out the techniques often used for data analysis, such as multiple regression analysis.) But these statistical tools—which begin with basic correlation and regression analysis—are now fairly easy to access. In fact, if you have Excel, you probably have most of these tools already at your fingertips!

At the same time, we recognize that many UX researchers come to the profession without formal statistical training. As a matter of fact, usability studies, contextual inquiries, surveys, and other UX research methods are sometimes performed on an *ad hoc* basis by designers, information architects, and front-end coders who have had no formal training in these methods, let alone training in the statistical tools used in the analysis of the data collected through such methods.

Because of these realities, we start with an introductory chapter on basic statistical fundamentals. Then, we proceed gently into basic means comparison and ANOVA models. Then we move into basic correlation and more advanced regression analyses. Throughout, we strive to make techniques such as means comparisons, correlation, and regression analysis so easy to understand and apply that you will naturally turn to one of them after collecting your data. Armed with the meaning of the results, you will be able to make design decisions with authority and the backing of empirical evidence.

HOW THIS BOOK IS SPECIAL

- We show the real-world application of these techniques through the vignettes that begin and close each chapter. By seeing parallels between the problems introduced and resolved in each chapter and your own work, you'll easily be able to ascertain the right statistical method to use in your particular UX research project. In addition, our hope is that you'll find the vignettes, and the accompanying illustrations, entertaining. All characters appearing in this work are fictitious. Any resemblance to real persons, living or dead, is purely coincidental.

- We provide clear insight into the statistical principles without getting bogged down in a theoretical treatise. But, we provide enough theory for you to understand *why* you're applying a certain technique. After all, understanding why you're doing something is just as important as knowing *what* you're doing.

- We minimize the amount of mathematical detail, while still doing full justice to the mathematical rigor of the presentation and the precision of our statements. In addition, many of our numerical examples use simple numbers. (This is a choice we consciously made, and it embraces a question posed by Ching Chun Li, Professor of Biometry at the University of Pittsburgh (1912–2003), which the authors took to heart and have incorporated into their writing: "How does one first learn to solve quadratic equations? By working with equations such as $242.5X^2 - 683.1X - 19428.5 = 0$, or with equations like $X^2 - 5X - 6 = 0$?") Our belief is that simpler numerical calculations aid the readers in the intuitive understanding of the material to a degree that more than offsets any disadvantage from using numbers that don't look "real."

- We focus on how to get the software to do the analysis. There are a few exceptions, in those cases where Excel does not provide a built-in solution, when we show you how to use other Excel commands to duplicate, as closely as possible, what Excel would do if the technique were a built-in available one. Also, we provide end-of-chapter exercises that encourage, demonstrate, and, indeed, require the use of the statistical software described. By the way, we do not apologize for writing our chapters in a way that does not insist that the reader understand what the software is doing under the hood!

- We've provided additional explanatory commentary through sidebars. The information contained in the sidebars is not essential to the task of applying the analytics to the research problem at hand, but we believe they add richness to the discussion.

THE SOFTWARE WE USE

We illustrate the use of statistical software packages with Excel and SPSS (Statistical Package for the Social Sciences). There are a large number of displays of both software packages in action.

The Excel displays illustrate Excel 2007 for the PC. There is a specific module within Excel, named "Data Analysis," that needs to be activated. We show you how to perform this activation. Once you are using "Data Analysis," there is no difference at all between the Excel 2007 and Excel 2010. Since there are some minor—and not so minor—differences between the PC and Mac versions of Excel, we've provided a Mac addendum at the end of the book that shows you how to complete the same tasks step-by-step on the Mac version.

Most of our displays of SPSS illustrate SPSS Edition 19. In the later chapters, we illustrate SPSS using SPSS Edition 22, the most recent version. For purposes of the techniques and analyses discussed and performed in this book, there is no meaningful difference between the two editions in how the techniques are accessed, and the resulting output format. (If you purchase SPSS, make sure that these techniques described in the book are available in your version before you buy; there are many different versions with different prices.)

WHAT YOU NEED TO ALREADY KNOW

Nothing! For the statistical beginner, we provide a chapter dedicated to some basic statistical concepts. We wrote this chapter assuming that a reader has not studied the subject matter before, but we believe that the vast majority of readers, even if they have studied the material before, will benefit from at least a cursory reading of this first chapter. The two key topics that we emphasize in the chapter are *confidence intervals* and *hypothesis testing*. We also provide some background for these two topics, centering around discussion of the bell-shaped (i.e., normal) probability distribution. A few other useful topics from a typical introductory statistics course are reviewed on an *ad hoc* basis.

The principles and techniques discussed in this book transcend the area of their application to the UX field; the only difference from one application area to another is that different situations arise with different frequency, and correspondingly, the use of various techniques occurs with different frequency. Still, it is always helpful for people to actually see applications in their area of endeavor, and thus, we never forget that the aim is to illustrate application of the techniques in the UX area. After all, many people beginning their study of predictive analytics and statistical techniques "don't know what they don't know;" this includes envisioning the ways in which the material can be usefully applied.

We assume a modest working knowledge of high school algebra. On occasion, we believe it is necessary to go a small distance beyond routine high school algebra. But, we strive to minimize the frequency of these occasions, and when it is necessary, we explain why, in the most intuitive way that we can. These circumstances exemplify how we aim to walk the fine line noted above: minimal mathematical presentation without compromising the rigor of the material or the precision of our statements.

ORGANIZATION AND COVERAGE

Our goal was to write a book that covered the most important and commonly used statistical methods employed by UX researchers. We have strived to keep the scope of the book at a level that is compatible with what most UX researchers can handle without great difficulty. At various points in the book, we refer to areas that we believe are beyond the scope of the book. However, these are not areas in which a lack of knowledge will materially hamper a cogent analysis and allow meaningful conclusions to be drawn from the methods demonstrated.

We have made attempts to be consistent in our ordering of the topics and the references from one chapter to another. For example, in the six Chapters, 2–7, we essentially present three different techniques, devoting one chapter to the case of independent data and the other to the case of a "repeated-measures"/"within-subjects" design. Both of these situations arise frequently in the UX world, and we believe that it is important to not only know how to handle each case analytically, but to be able to recognize which case is applicable in a given situation, and how to "design" each situation. With this view, Chapters 2 and 3 go together, as do Chapters 4 and 5, and also Chapters 6 and 7. A special highlight of our book is the extensive coverage of the topic of correlation and regression analysis. We have three separate and extensive Chapters (9–11) on simple regression, multiple and stepwise regression, and binary logistic regression.

EXERCISES AND SUPPLEMENTARY MATERIAL

Each chapter (except for the introductory Chapter 1) has Exercises at the end of the chapter. The data for these exercises, in both Excel and SPSS (except in a few cases where Excel does not have the necessary functionality), and the corresponding output in Excel and SPSS, are available on the book's companion Web site (booksite. elsevier.com/9780128006351). Also present on the Web site, on a separate file for each exercise, is a discussion of the solution based on the software output. The Exercise section of each chapter provides the exact names of the aforementioned files.

About the Authors

MIKE FRITZ

Mike Fritz has been helping businesses make their products both more usable and useful for over 20 years. An ardent proponent of the user-centered design process, he's helped to maximize the user experience for Verizon, Monster, GlaxoSmithKline, Lilly, Windstream, Fidelity Investments, Forrester, WGBH (Boston), and PeopleFluent, among others. Mike's specialty is collecting user data through a variety of UX research methods—including moderated and unmoderated usability tests, contextual inquiries, surveys, Web analytics, focus groups, interviews, and more—and making informed design decisions based on meaningful interpretation of that data. Mike's motto of "Test Early, Test Often" has resulted in exceptional user experiences, whether you're installing FiOS or applying for a job.

Currently, Mike is the Manger of Usability at **PeopleFluent**, the leading provider of total talent management software and services. Mike is also CEO and Founder of **BigUXData.com**, a user experience research and design firm; the firm's emphasis is on collecting and interpreting data collected from variety of UX research methods to inform designs that will maximize the usability and utility of any product or service.

Mike holds a Bachelor in Arts in Journalism from the University of South Carolina and a Masters in Science in Human Factors in Information Design from Bentley University. In his free time, he plays jazz piano in the Boston area and swims in his beloved Lake Cochituate.

You can reach Mike at mikejfritz@gmail.com.

PAUL D. BERGER

Paul D. Berger is a Visiting Scholar and Professor of Marketing at Bentley University, where he is also the director of the Master of Science in Marketing Analytics (MSMA) program. He earned his SB, SM, and PhD degrees from the Massachusetts Institute of Technology (MIT), Sloan School of Management. He has published several texts, including *Experimental Design: with Applications in Management, Engineering, and*

the Sciences. He has published over 180 refereed journal articles and conference proceedings, and is on the editorial board of several journals, including the *Journal of Marketing Analytics* and *Journal of Interactive Marketing*. He is an active consultant in marketing research, experimental design, data analysis, database marketing, and quantitative techniques in general. While teaching at Boston University, he won the Metcalf Award, a university-wide award for teaching excellence, and the John R. Russell award for excellence in executive teaching.

ABOUT THE ILLUSTRATOR: RICK PINCHERA

Rick Pinchera is an illustrator and graphic artist who lives in Boston with his wife and 3 children. He has contributed his talents to many great projects over a 20 year career, focusing on educational media, visual storytelling and character development. He finds inspiration for his work in comics, retro design and science fiction. To see more of Rick's work, visit: rickpinchera.com.

Acknowledgments

First we'd like to thank Meg Dunkerley from Elsevier, who recognized the need and importance of this book, and who provided us with the encouragement and support that got us started. We'd also like to thank the other great Elsevier team members that provided support and guidance, including Heather Scherer, Todd Green, Punitha Govindaradjane, Amy Invernizzi, and Maria Inês Cruz.

Many people have been helpful in shaping the scope, organization, and review of this book. The thoughtful comments and suggestions of the following reviewers are gratefully acknowledged: Bob Virzi, Chauncey Wilson, Jim Lewis, Nick Aramovich, Charles Abernathy, Susie Robson, and Bill Gribbons. We're especially grateful for the advice of Bruce D. Weinberg, Professor of Marketing and Marketing Department chair at the Isenberg School of Management at the University of Massachusetts, Amherst.

MIKE

First and foremost, I thank Paul Berger for agreeing to coauthor this book. Quite simply, I couldn't have done it without you, Paul. The breadth and depth of your statistical knowledge is astonishing, but your willingness to share it with me and all of your lucky students is priceless.

I'd like to thank Mary Myers for her unwavering support and encouragement during the entire process, from my very first thought of writing this kind of book, to the bitter end, with countless love and affection every step of the way. I'd also like to thank the entire Flynn family for their support and encouragement during the writing stage of the book.

I'd like to thank my current PeopleFluent colleagues for their encouragement, support, and suggestions: Jim Bowley, Stephen Bruce, Charles Jones, Mark Munzer, Rex Palmer, Stacy Soley, Nick Aramovich, Jeff Basile, Wilson Kapanga, Keng Qui Procter, Alan Sloan, Mark Rudden, Ajay Babu Raj, Selmon Shewit, Jeanne Caraglia, Barbara Bean, Sam Higgins, Joseph Boughan (go Cougars!), and Michael Sakowich.

I'd like to also thank former colleagues and other friends who provided moral support and guidance: Lou Susi, Charles Abernathy, Becky Burd, Scott Gieske, Andy Celley, Jean Monahan, Kate Pullano, Rick Buchanan, Pat and Trevor Bartram, Corey and Andrea Polonetsky, and Eric Kachel. Heartfelt thanks to Edwin Wheihe, PhD, for early encouragement, Noreen (Nonie) Wheihe for always providing good vibes, Julie Norton for support and laughter, and Kate and Tom Myers for the "young and hip" perspective. Special thanks to my old WGBH buddy Rick Groleau for putting me in touch with illustrator Rick Pinchera.

I'd like to thank and congratulate illustrator Rick Pinchera for bringing my vignettes to life though his amazing illustrations. As our deadline loomed, Rick stepped up to the plate big-time. He interpreted each chapter's character in astonishing and wonderful ways, interpreting the scenes with flavor and detail that I could only imagine. To see more of Rick's amazing work, visit rickpinchera.com.

I'd like to thank Paul and the entire staff at Mel's Commonwealth Diner in Wayland, Massachusetts for keeping my coffee cup always full as I researched and wrote this book. Never-ending coffee means never-ending productivity. There's no better diner in MetroWest!

I'd like to thank my sister Kathleen M. Fritz, PhD for her encouragement and support throughout the entire process.

Finally, I'd like to thank my parents Capt. Ernest S. Fritz (USN) and Eugenia Balzano Fritz for their love and support and for instilling in me a lifelong quest for knowledge. Case in point:

When I was 12 years old, my father informed his family gathered around the dinner table that he was taking a night course. As a petulant adolescent, I was baffled that my father, a graduate of the United State Naval Academy who also held a Master's degree from the Naval Post-Graduate School in Monterey, California—and had risen through the ranks as a naval aviator to become a Captain—should need to take any further classes.

"You're already very successful, and you've got plenty of degrees." I stated. "Why are you taking a class?"

My father looked me right in the eyes. "Because, Mike, you never stop learning."

Truer words were never spoken.

PAUL

I wish first to thank Mike Fritz for getting me involved in what has turned out to be a very enjoyable process, and for being an understanding and thoughtful coauthor. I also wish to thank Bentley University for its support in terms of encouragement and staff assistance.

Susan Berger would patiently wait for her husband to tear himself away from his computer in his home office to join her for dinner, and would wonder at times whether he was aware that she was in the house!!

Introduction to a variety of useful statistical ideas and techniques

1.1 INTRODUCTION

In this introductory chapter, we present several basic statistical fundamentals that will help get you ready for the techniques that begin in Chapter 2. If you're already familiar with these fundamentals, you may prefer to skim this chapter or proceed directly to Chapter 2. But we believe that it will be worth your time—even for the busiest UX (User Experience) researcher—to spend a little time with the ideas in this chapter. We have made a concerted effort to try to make this background material easily digestible.

1.2 THE GREAT NORMAL CURVE IN THE SKY

There are many phenomena in nature that are determined by the probabilities associated with a *normal curve*. The normal curve is also called the "bell-shaped curve," the "bell curve," and by engineers, often, the "Gaussian curve."

In fact, we can also explain a lot of unusual phenomena by what is inferred or predicted by a bell-shaped curve. Indeed, professors teaching statistics will often refer to pure luck—the purposeless, unpredictable, and uncontrollable force that shapes events favorably or unfavorably for an individual, group, or cause—as governed by the "Great Normal Curve in the Sky." We're so enamored with the normal curve that we requested that one appear on the cover of this book—and the good folks at Morgan Kaufmann made it happen.

So, what is this normal or bell-shaped curve? When you construct a histogram with a large number of data points (basically, a bah chart—oops, sorry, the Boston accent crept in—a bar chart), the result, when smoothed out a bit, will be a normal curve if the contour of the curve has a certain shape, indeed, referred to as a normal curve.

The normal curve is based on a complicated mathematical equation that we don't really need to know and has a basis in the physics of our planet, Brownian motion, and lots of other stuff that none of us may want to even think about. Well, at least not right now. May be a picture is the best place to start to describe the normal curve. A set of normal curves is pictured in Figure 1.1.

The normal curve (and now you can see why it is also called the bell-shaped curve; it looks like the outline of the Liberty Bell in Philadelphia) is really a *family* of curves. It can center at any point, but that point is always its mean, median, and mode. The normal curve

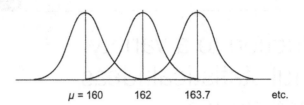

$\mu = 160$ 162   163.7   etc.

FIGURE 1.1

A family of normal curves.

is symmetric around this center point (i.e., the left and right sides of the curve are mirror images of one another) a fact that allows us to more easily interpret other points within the curve. This center point is always denoted by the Greek letter, μ, which is referred to as the "Greek m." In English-language countries, it's usually pronounced "myu."

The key interpretation of a normal curve (or even a curve with a different shape) is that *the area under the curve between any two points on the horizontal x axis equals the probability of getting a result in between these two points.* So, finding the area under a normal curve between two points is the same as finding the probability that you will get a result between two points. This notion holds true for all kinds of data, including all kinds of UX metrics like task completion times and satisfaction ratings.

A normal curve is determined not only by its center, but also by how tall and thin or short and fat the curve is. The area under the curve must always equal 1— although we don't specify the units of the "1." This means, essentially, that 100% of the data possibilities are represented under the curve. But a normal curve has the same area being taller and thinner or shorter and fatter. An analogy is that a man weighs 160 pounds, but can still be either tall and thin, or short and fat, or any inter- mediate combination. Of course, to keep a constant area of 1, any curve that is taller must be thinner and, if shorter, must be fatter.

This flexibility of a normal curve is very useful for a number of reasons. First, if a curve is relatively taller and thinner, it represents a situation where there is relatively little variability in the result that comes out—nearly all of the area is near the center. On the other hand, if the curve is relatively shorter and fatter, it represents a situation where there is relatively more variability—more of the area is farther away from the center. In responding to a Likert-scale question, larger variability would represent the fact that there is less agreement among the respondents (whether the pattern of responses was bell-shaped or not).

Second, different phenomena have more variability than other phenomena, but the normal curve can accommodate these differences. For example, the time it takes to perform certain usability test tasks will vary from person to person to a different extent from task to task. But the normal curve has the flexibility to accommodate all the different degrees of variability.

Traditionally, we measure how tall and thin or short and fat a normal curve is by a quantity called the "standard deviation." Don't let the term intimidate you. It's similar to, but not exactly the same as, measuring the average distance of all your data points from the mean. It's always denoted by the Greek letter, σ, which is the "Greek s."

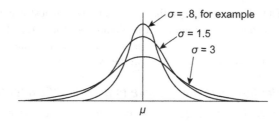

FIGURE 1.2

A family of normal curves with different values of σ.

Figure 1.2 illustrates different normal curves, all centered at the same value, and all having the same area of "1," but being different degrees of short and fat and tall and thin. That is, each has a different value of σ, where a larger value means more variability among the resulting outcome values. Conversely, a small value means less variability within your data set (e.g., more agreement/similarity among the respondents' results). Compare the curve with a standard deviation of 0.8 to the curve with a standard deviation of 3. The former is taller and thinner—thus having less variability—than the latter.

So, to summarize, a normal curve is determined by its "μ" and its "σ," and

smaller σ ↔ taller, thinner curve
larger σ ↔ shorter, fatter curve

SIDEBAR: THE NORMAL CURVE FORMULA

OK, so returning to the normal curve, we feel obliged as UX research professionals to tell you that there is a mathematical formula for a normal curve, but, happily, we generally don't need to know it! But…maybe you're curious. We'll show it to you, but first you need to promise not to let it intimidate you into not reading the rest of the book!! Promise? OK, here we go… The normal distribution mathematical function, $f_N(x)$, given values of μ and σ, is depicted in Figure 1.3.

$$f_N\left(x \middle| \begin{matrix} \mu \\ \sigma \end{matrix}\right) = \frac{1}{\sqrt{2\pi} \cdot \sigma} e^{-\frac{1}{2}\left(\frac{x-\mu}{\sigma}\right)^2}$$

FIGURE 1.3

The mathematical expression for the normal curve.

It isn't pretty! Even the exponent has an exponent; but, it is what it is. Luckily, you don't have to think about this formula for the rest of the book.

1.2.1 FINDING PROBABILITIES OF COMPLETION TIMES OR SATISFACTION LEVELS, OR ANYTHING ELSE, ON A NORMAL CURVE

We mentioned earlier that finding an area under a normal curve between any two points is the same as finding the probability that you get a result (satisfaction value, time to complete a task, etc.) between the two points. The easiest way to do this is to use an Excel command—a command that is already built into Excel and is easy to use. But, before we get into the calculations, let's provide a scenario that will help you see the value of doing the calculations in the first place. ☺

1.2.1.1 Vignette: how long does it take to hook up DSL Internet service?

You're the UX researcher at a gigantic telecommunications company that provides broadband service to hundreds of thousands of customers in the United States. You're part of the user experience team that is dedicated to improving the user experience for those broadband clients. One of the key projects you're working on is trying to decrease the time it takes for a typical new customer to install DSL Internet service. (In the past the company sent out technicians to complete the installation, but has recently gone to a "customer self-serve" model of sending out DSL installation kits. The cost savings have been dramatic.) Shorter installation times usually indicate higher satisfaction, and fewer calls to technical support, which means significant cost savings. During home visits to watch folks installing DSL, you take many measurements—time to download necessary software, time to activate the account, etc.

But one of the most important metrics is simply the time to hook everything up. That is, plugging a phone line to the modem, plugging the modem to the computer, filtering the existing phone line, etc. Obviously, the shorter the better for the customer, but for the company as well, because it means fewer calls to the customer support center in Mumbai, India—they're already swamped.

Your collected data indicates that the average time, μ, to hook everything up is 160 seconds (2 minutes, 40 seconds), and that the variability factor (which, remember, is a measure of how different the time required is from person to person), is represented by a standard deviation, σ, of 20 seconds. You know that the "hook up" time is viewed historically as around 180 seconds (3 minutes) and, to beef up the report—and anticipating the question during your presentation—you decide to calculate the percentage of the users who will require less than 190 seconds to hook everything up.

OK, so we have the average task completion time value (μ) = 160 seconds with a standard deviation (σ) of 20 seconds. And we assume that we have a set of data that follows a normal curve (although not every process in the world follows a normal curve; more about the prevalence of the normal curve later), and a picture of what we want is the shaded-in area of the normal curve in Figure 1.4.

The letter, X, here represents the time to hook everything up. In essence, X is a traditional statistical symbol; statisticians would refer to it as a "random variable." We would now find the shaded-in area (i.e., the probability that the time to hook everything up is less than 190 seconds)—or percentage[1]—by using the following Excel command:

$$= \mathrm{NORMDIST}\,(X\,,\,\mu\,,\,\sigma\,,\,1)\,,$$

---

[1] Actually, we need to multiply the value by 100 and add a percent sign to get the answer as a percent. The command provides the value from 0 to 1, in essence, a probability or a proportion.

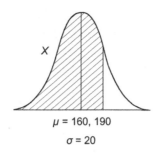

$\mu = 160, 190$

$\sigma = 20$

FIGURE 1.4

A depiction of the area under a normal curve.

which tells the user the probability that the result is less than X, when the mean and standard deviation are the values they are. The "1" in the last position is simply always a "1" and is there for technical reasons that need not concern us—in a sense the "1" is simply indicating a "left-tail cumulative." (See the "How Many Tails" sidebar in Section 1.4.) We denote this as:

$$= P\left(\text{result} < \left[\text{specific value of}\right] X\right).$$

Filling in the actual values, the formula in our current scenario becomes:

$$= \text{NORMDIST}\left(190, 160, 20, 1\right),$$

In our example, we have both the command above and the answer, depicted in the Excel spreadsheets in Figures 1.5 and 1.6, in a random cell (J7).

	Home	Insert	Page Layout		Formulas	Data	Review	View	Get Started			

Paste — Cut, Copy, Format Painter — Clipboard — 11 — A A — B I U — Wrap Text — Merge & Center — General — $ % — Number

SUM ▾ X ✓ *fx* =NORMDIST(190, 160, 20, 1)

	A	B	C	D	E	F	G	H	I	J	K	L
1												
2												
3												
4												
5												
6												
7										=NORMDIST(190, 160, 20, 1)		
8												
9												
10												

FIGURE 1.5

Excel spreadsheet showing the command in cell J7 for finding the area under the normal curve in Figure 1.4.

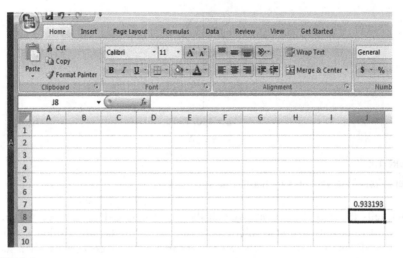

FIGURE 1.6

Illustration of the probability of obtaining a result under 190.

SIDEBAR: SOME EXCEL BASICS

To find a sample mean of data set (say, 100 data points in the first 100 cells of column A of an Excel spreadsheet), we use the Excel command:

$$= AVERAGE\,(A1:A100)$$

This command can be typed in any cell on the spreadsheet, and after you press "Enter," the command is replaced by, indeed, the average you are seeking. The same is true for finding a standard deviation, except that the command is now:

$$= STDEV\,(A1:A100)$$

In the commands, you can use capital letters or small letters; it does not matter at all. Every Excel command starts with an "=" sign; this tells Excel that a command is coming.

Excel also has very handy type-ahead feature. Simply enter the first couple of letters of your command, and voilà, all possible commands starting with those letters appear. Roll over each command, and descriptive text appears:

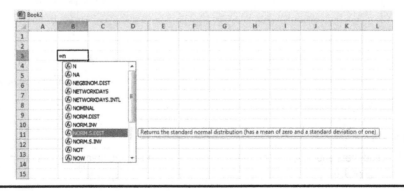

After pressing the enter key, we see the probability in Figure 1.6.

The probability is 0.9332, or, to answer the question specifically posed, 93.32% of the users will hook everything up within 190 or less seconds.

If we wanted to find the percentage of users who would require *more than* 190 seconds to hook everything up, we would simply subtract 93.32% from 100%, to get 6.68%.

1.2.2 FINDING COMPLETION TIMES OR SATISFACTION LEVELS, OR ANYTHING ELSE, ON A NORMAL CURVE

Pretty cool so far, right? Ok, now, let's stay with the DSL installation example, but choose another task: the time it takes to open up the installation kit and verify that all the necessary installation components have been included in the kit. Again, we assume that we have a normal distribution (curve) of times required to complete the task. We know the mean equals 69 seconds and the variability factor, as measured by the standard deviation, is 3 seconds. This indicates that there is relatively little variability, meaning that the times are somewhat similar from person to person. It also implies that there is not a lot that the user can do to affect the task completion time, but that the primary determination of task time is how easy it is to open the box and find all the parts needed.

Now, to again beef up the report and anticipate the question about how long it takes most people to open the box and find all the parts, you decide to determine the range of values that 95% of the users will require (symmetric around the mean of 69 seconds) to open up the box and find everything. In essence, you want to find two values of X, $x'0$ *and* $x0$, along the horizontal axis (such that the area under the curve between the two values equals 0.95), as depicted in Figure 1.7.

SIDEBAR: GET USED TO THE HEAVY SYMBOLS

We have labeled the two unknown values of X by the somewhat ponderous symbols of $x'0$ and $x0$. This is based on traditional notation—and is often more onerous than need be.

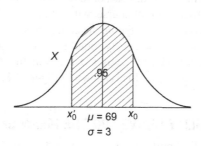

FIGURE 1.7

Depiction of values sought on a normal curve, given the value of the area.

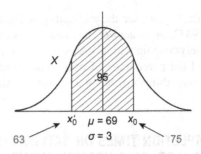

FIGURE 1.8

The range of values determined to be from 63 to 75 seconds.

In any event, here's the Excel command that is tailor-made for the above problem:

$$= \text{NORMINV} (p, \mu, \sigma)$$

This command finds for us the *value* of X (again, here, the time to complete a task) so that "*p*" proportion of the time (or, with probability = *p*) the result will come out under X.

This time, you're going to have to use the ole noggin a bit more. Due to the symmetry of the normal curve, each white (i.e., *not* shaded-in) corner of Figure 1.7 is 2.5% (or, 0.025). With 95% in the middle, the white must add to 5% (remember, the total area under the curve must be 1, or, 100%), and hence, each corner is 2.5%. So, the total area below x'_0 is 2.5% and the total area below $x0$ is 97.5%. Therefore, the answer to our question can be determined by the commands:

$$= \text{NORMINV} (2.5\%, 69, 3)$$

and

$$= \text{NORMINV} (97.5\%, 69, 3)$$

The probability values (in the first position in the above commands) can be entered in percentage terms, as is the case, or in decimal terms—the values would be 0.025 and 0.975, respectively, and of course, without percent signs.

The values of these commands—typing the commands into any cell of Excel and then pressing the enter button—are easily found to be 63.12 and 74.88 seconds, or roughly, 63–75 seconds. So, 95% of the user task completion times will be between about 63 seconds and 75 seconds. This is shown in Figure 1.8.

1.2.3 THE PROBABILITY CURVE FOR THE MEAN OF MANY RESULTS

Having fun yet? Up to this point, we have depicted the role of the normal curve to find the percentage of time that a result will come out below or above some specified value, X. We also depicted the reverse or inverse problem of specifying a probability/percentage of time a result comes out less than "X," and determining what the value of X is.

We need to add one simple aspect to what we have already discussed. Up to now, we've been inquiring about probabilities for an individual user. (When we make a statement such as, "95% of the users will have a time between 63 and 75 seconds, we are referring to 95% of the *individual* users.") But, what if we wish to inquire about the *mean* of a specific number of users from the same population? That is, how do things change if we wish to ask about the behavior of the *mean of n users' completion times*? For example, suppose that we ask, "If we have a sample of four users independently (i.e., separately) completing a task, what is the probability that the *mean* completion time exceeds some value?"[2]

To answer the question, let's go back to the problem posed in the previous section in which the average time of hooking everything up for the Internet installation (for the whole population of users and potential users) was 160 seconds and the standard deviation was 20 seconds. We showed that the percentage of individual users who would require a completion time less than 190 seconds was 93.32%.

To answer the question about the *mean time of 4 users* being less than 190, we use the same NORMDIST(X, μ, σ, 1) command, but adjust the standard deviation to reflect that we are now asking about the behavior of a mean of a sample of "*n*" (4 in the specific question), and not the behavior (i.e., time) for just an individual person. It certainly is a different question to ask what the time will be *on average* for four people and what the time will be for an individual (one) person.

The adjustment is simply to replace the value of the standard deviation, σ, which is known to be 20, by what we can call the "adjusted standard deviation" (officially called "the standard deviation of the mean") which is the original standard deviation (i.e., for one person/time), divided by the *positive square root of the sample size comprising the mean*—here, the sample size equals 4. So, the adjusted standard deviation is 20 divided by the positive square root of 4, which equals, of course, 2.

The resulting adjusted standard deviation is, hence, 20/2 = 10. Now we use the same Excel command we used earlier, but with a "10" instead of a "20." We repeat the earlier command for reference, and then the new, revised command:

$$= \text{NORMDIST} (190, 160, 20, 1) = 0.9332 \text{ or } 93.32\%$$

$$= \text{NORMDIST} (190, 160, \textbf{10}, 1) = 0.9987 \text{ or } 99.87\%$$

In other words, one user's time has a 93.32% chance of being less than 190 seconds, but the average of four users' times has a (gigantic!) 99.87% chance of being less than 190 seconds.

---

[2] Any time that we take a sample, the reader should assume that it is a "random sample," unless indicated otherwise. A random sample is one in which every possible sample of the "population" from which the sample is drawn has an equal chance of occurring.

SIDEBAR: SO *THAT'S* WHAT THE LAW OF AVERAGES REALLY MEANS…

The numbers in this chapter exhibit the principle that when we average *more*, rather than *fewer*, results, we tend to have a higher chance of getting a resulting sample mean nearer to the true (population) mean. Actually, this is an intuitive way to explain the often heard, not so often understood, phrase, "the law of averages." Honestly, we realize that nobody needed this book to intuitively know that the more values averaged, the higher the likelihood of obtaining a more accurate result—and a more accurate result equates to a result that is more likely to be nearer to the true (population) value we wish to get an idea about. But, sometimes you need to state the obvious!!☺

1.2.4 THE CENTRAL LIMIT THEOREM

There is another concept that needs some explanation, since it is the primary reason that the normal distribution is so important—probably 100 times more important than whatever shaped curve is in second place!

We're talking about the "Central Limit Theorem." It says, in simplified terms, that for any data you would ever see, as we average a larger and larger number of sample values, the resulting sample mean, denoted "X-bar," converges to follow a normal curve, *no matter what the shape of the individual X curve before we take means.* (Technically, the data values need to be independent and from the same distribution, but this is usually the case in UX work, anyway.)

SIDEBAR: X-BAR

A bar over a quantity is traditionally used to denote a sample mean. We'll write "X-bar" in this text, and actually write $\overline{X}$ in equations.

For example, if we were to take many groups of 10 data values, each—that is, $n = 10$—and take the mean of each of these samples, and then draw a histogram of the means, it would look very much like a normal curve, *regardless of what the histogram would look like if we drew a histogram of the individual values* (*which may or may not be a normal curve!!*).

We do need to clarify that if the sample size is only 10, the resulting histogram for the means may deviate somewhat from a normal curve, since $n = 10$ is not that large a sample, even though it is what you may be dealing with as a UX researcher; i.e., usability studies are usually conducted with a sample size of 5–8. However, as a practical matter, you should assume that the mean, even for $n = 10$, will follow a normal distribution/curve, since the difference from a normal curve is unlikely to be material.

SIDEBAR: THE NOT-SO-MAGIC NUMBER 30

Statisticians, being on average (pun intended) a conservative lot, suggest that if the sample size is at least 30, then there is no need for much worry about applying the central limit theorem. In fact, there is a common belief that it's impossible to obtain meaningful results with a sample size of less than 30. Indeed, many statistics instructors have used 30 as the "magic number"—the number you need to obtain any meaningful result about anything.

In truth, for most of the probability distributions/curves that you will encounter in a UX research setting (say, using data from Likert scales), the curve of the sample mean will converge fairly quickly to what is very close to a normal-shaped curve, even for sample sizes less than 15. So, even with a sample size of 10, or even 5, you should apply the central limit theorem and assume that the probability curve for the mean, X-bar, is bell-shaped, or close enough to it for any practical purpose.

By the way, if anybody insists you need a sample size of 30, ask him/her if $n = 29$ is OK! After all, nobody would *ever* say that you get great normal convergence at $n = 30$, but not that good at $n = 29$. Although we all want larger sample sizes to increase the accuracy of our predictions, there is really nothing magic about the number 30.

So, since we so often deal with means—as we shall see in subsequent chapters—the normal distribution/curve is the basis of nearly everything we do in this book, even if the connection is not directly visible.

1.3 CONFIDENCE INTERVALS

One very important statistical technique is the calculation of a "confidence interval" for an unknown quantity. As background to the concept, consider the simple idea of an "estimate." We think you'd agree that our best "estimate" is much more useful—and believable—if accompanied by a measure of the uncertainty in the estimate! This measure of uncertainty is best (and most often) conveyed by a confidence interval. Put simply, a confidence interval is an interval, which contains a population value, such as the population mean, with some specified probability, usually, 0.95 or 95%.

SIDEBAR:

In the field of data analysis, we never use the five-letter "dirty word," *guess*. We never guess!! We estimate!!

In practice, confidence intervals are extremely useful—and even critical—to any UX researcher. Here's why. You're often dealing with small sample sizes in UX research. For example, in usability testing, you're typically testing with 5–8 participants. (You can usually have confidence that you're finding the major usability issues with that sample size. See Chapter 4 for a deeper dive into this very important assertion.) But when these same 5–8 participants complete the typical posttest Likert-scale ratings, you're entering a land mine of potentially weak confidence. Simply reporting a mean from a typical post-usability test Likert-scale with a sample size of 5–8 *without* a confidence interval can be viewed as unprofessional at best and extremely misleading at worst. The typical small sample sizes often yield wide confidence intervals (we discuss this further later in this section), and we'd argue that it's your professional duty to report them. Without them, you're just not telling the full story.

SIDEBAR: PROBABILITY VERSUS STATISTICS

The topic of *confidence intervals* is often considered a "sub heading" of what we call "interval estimation." In turn, interval estimation is one of two topics under a major heading of what we call "statistical inference." This refers to the basic idea of being able to infer what we can about the true mean (or other true quantity, such as the true standard deviation), based on the data.

When we predict what is likely to happen if we assume a known value for the mean (and perhaps the standard deviation), indeed, this is the field of *probability*—for example, when we assess the probability that X comes out above 160, or below 180, etc. When we "turn it around," and assume the true (population) values are the unknowns (which is the heart of data analysis and predictive analytics), and use data to make inference about the true values, we enter the world of *statistics*.

SIDEBAR: POINT ESTIMATES AND THE PITFALLS OF USING THEM ALONE

A point estimate is just a fancy name for a single value as an estimate; for estimating the true mean, μ, the best point estimate (based on various criteria to define the word, "best") is the sample mean, X-bar. There are times when you need to go forward with your best estimate (i.e., a single value), even though you know it is not the exact true value. However, most of the time, you should not stop with knowing only the sample mean. Using only a point estimate is rarely the best thing to do.

After all, it would be like the consultant (or "best qualified statistics person" at the company) saying to Bill, the boss, "OK, Bill, our best estimate of the mean time it takes to complete the task is 37.5 seconds, but, of course, even though it's our best estimate, it's not the true mean! Have a nice day!"

Not wanting to subscribe to such silliness is why we need to determine not only a point estimate (remember—for us, a fancy word for X-bar), but also an interval estimate, which is a confidence interval. This usually amounts to providing a range of values (an interval) that has a probability of 95% of containing the true population mean, μ.

1.3.1 THE LOGIC AND MEANING OF A CONFIDENCE INTERVAL

To determine the confidence interval, we start by reporting the sample mean, X-bar, but we also report an interval:

$$\overline{X} - e \ \text{ to } \ \overline{X} + e$$

where "e" can be (for the moment) called "error" and

$$P\left(\overline{X} - e < \mu < \overline{X} + e\right) = 1 - \alpha.$$

This says that the probability ("*P*" stands for "probability") that the interval $(\overline{X} - e)$ to $(\overline{X} + e)$ contains the true value, μ, equals $(1 - \alpha)$. By tradition, industry generally uses 0.95 (i.e., 95%) for the value of $(1 - \alpha)$. "Alpha" is the amount of probability *outside* the confidence interval. So, if the confidence level $(1 - \alpha)$, is 0.95, then $\alpha = 0.05$. We will see this "0.05" used more directly in the next section.

Here's an example. Suppose that after running a usability study with 4 participants, we have these 4 data points on a 5-point (1–5) Likert-scale question for the satisfaction of a new design: 2, 3, 4, 3. The sample mean, X-bar, is, of course, $(2 + 3 + 4 + 3)/4 = 3.0$. As can be determined (we'll see how, very soon), we get a 95% confidence interval for the true mean of 1.70–4.30. The interval has 3.0 as its center; it is pretty wide (in practice, we always prefer a narrower confidence interval, since it means we have homed in more closely to the true mean), but that is primarily because we have sampled only four satisfaction values, and there is a fair amount of variability in the four results.

In more practical terms, we can say:

We have 95% confidence that the true mean satisfaction of all people who have experienced the design is between 1.70 and 4.30.

SIDEBAR: CONFIDENT ABOUT THE INTERVAL, NOT THE TRUE MEAN!

Keep in mind that the true/population mean does not vary. It is what it is, albeit we do not know what it is, and may never know what it is. What is subject to variation is the interval—the lower and upper confidence limits themselves. Therefore, a theoretician may argue that the definition of a confidence interval should always read, "…95% confidence that the *interval* contains the true mean…," and never, "…95% confidence that the true mean is in the interval." In other words, the subject of the sentence, that which is subject to uncertainty, should be the interval, not the true mean.

This is equivalent to saying that, "If we constructed a large number of 95% confidence intervals from a large number of replicates of a given experiment, 95% of these intervals would contain the true mean."

Now, this statement is accurate—but it probably won't get you any bonus points with your design team, since the confidence interval is so wide. As we noted, the small sample size, combined with the amount of variability in the four results, has resulted in a wide confidence interval, which doesn't seem useful at first glance. (We acknowledge that you may feel uncomfortable stating that the true average is "almost for sure in the interval, 1.7–4.3.") In fact, it *is* useful: the confidence interval mandates great caution in what you claim for the result. (And trust us; you'll gain credibility by including the confidence intervals and lose credibility if you ignore them.)

Now, if the data had been 3, 4, 4, 4 (still, only four data points, but less variable from one to another!!), the 95% confidence interval would be much narrower (which we like better!), and would be,

$$2.95 \text{----------} 4.55,$$

centered around the X-bar value of 3.75.

If the data consisted of eight data points: 3, 4, 4, 4, 3, 4, 4, 4 (purposely having the last four data points duplicating the first four data points, for comparison's sake), the X-bar still is 3.75, but the 95% confidence interval is now:

$$3.36 --------- 4.14.$$

Now, this is an interval that is less than half the width as when there were four data points, meaning more than twice as accurate! Getting better all the time! (Thanks Lennon and McCartney.) You can see that, *ceteris paribus*, the confidence interval gets narrower (more accurate) as the sample size increases.

The formula for finding confidence intervals depends on three different things: (1) the sample size, (2) the variability among the data values, and (3) your chosen value of (1-α), or level of confidence, usually 0.95 by convention, and its corresponding value on a normal curve.

SIDEBAR: THE OMNIPRESENT NORMAL CURVE

Confidence intervals are a good manifestation of what we alluded to much earlier in the chapter about the normal curve, or distribution, being at the core of many of the data analysis and predictive analytics we do, although the connection may not be directly evident—especially, of course, when you use statistical software to analyze your data.

1.3.2 FINDING A CONFIDENCE INTERVAL USING EXCEL

OK, here's how to calculate a confidence interval using Excel. Suppose that we have a sample of 12 satisfaction-rating values for a design, each provided by a (different) user, and the values are on a 1–5 Likert scale (1 = very unsatisfied, 2 = unsatisfied, 3 = neutral, 4 = satisfied, 5 = very satisfied), and we enter the 12 values into column C in Excel—see Figure 1.9.

SIDEBAR: FOR PC USERS ONLY: FIRST ACTIVATE "DATA ANALYSIS"

To do *any* statistical analysis (beyond finding the mean, standard deviation, etc.), you need to first activate a module in Excel called "Data Analysis." It exists within Excel but you would not necessarily know about it unless you are told about it. Aren't you glad you got this book? Refer to the Addendum to this chapter to learn how to activate "Data Analysis."

SIDEBAR: MAC USERS ONLY

Throughout this book, we show examples in the PC version of Excel and SPSS. The differences between the PC and MAC versions of SPSS are very minor, but there are some minor—and not so minor—differences between the PC and MAC versions of Excel when using the statistical techniques explained in the book. If you're a MAC user, refer to the addendum "For MAC Users Only" in the appendix when our illustrations differ dramatically from what you're seeing in your MAC version of Excel. We'll get you back on track.

To find a confidence interval for the true (population) mean, we click on Data Analysis, and then highlight Descriptive Statistics and click "OK." See arrows in Figure 1.10.

This provides us with another box, into which we enter the required information—the data we want analyzed. (Indeed, Excel, as good as it is, is not a mind reader!) See Figure 1.11.

We now fill in where the data values are in the "input range" section, C1 to C12, (see fat vertical arrow in Figure 1.12), and we check off "Summary Statistics" and "Confidence Interval for Mean" (which has a default of 95% (although, of course, this confidence level is changeable), confirming what we indicated before, that, traditionally, 95% is the choice used very often in industry); see the two horizontal arrows in Figure 1.12. Finally, (see dashed arrow in Figure 1.12) we fill in "New Worksheet Ply" by an arbitrary name—Wolf. We always prefer to get the analysis results on a separate worksheet (i.e., page)—just to ensure the results are not mixed up with our data!

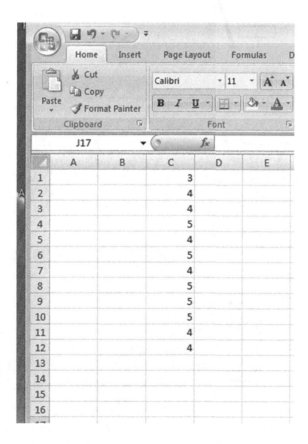

FIGURE 1.9

Illustrative data for determining a confidence interval.

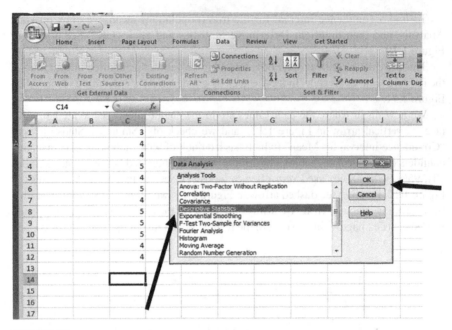

FIGURE 1.10

The first step in using the Data Analysis module to find a confidence interval.

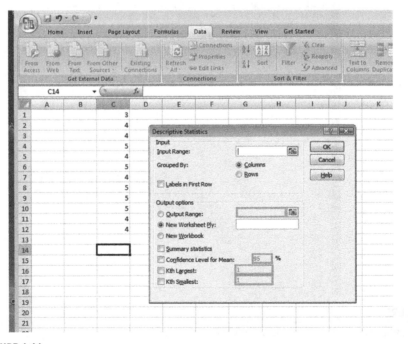

FIGURE 1.11

Continuing the process of finding a confidence interval using Data Analysis.

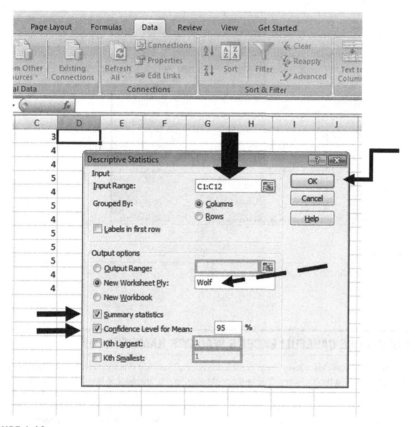

FIGURE 1.12

Getting specific in using Data Analysis to find a confidence interval.

We now get out output (our answer!) by just clicking on OK (see bent arrow in Figure 1.12). Drum roll please! See Figure 1.13.

The output has a lot of information. However, to find the confidence interval, only the first value ("Mean"—in row 3, column B) and last value (confidence level (95%)—row 16, column B). The first value is X-bar (as we know, this is the center of our confidence interval), and the last value (row 16) is "e" the amount we add and subtract to X-bar (with the accompanying note that it, indeed, is a 95% confidence interval). So, our confidence interval is calculated by some basic arithmetic:

$$4.333 - 0.414 \text{ to } 4.333 + 0.414$$

or

$$3.92 \text{ } - - - - - - - - - - - - - - - - 4.75.$$

Thus, we can be 95% confident that the interval, 3.92–4.75, contains the true mean satisfaction with the design; in looser terms that may sound more satisfactory to many people, "We have 95% confidence that the true mean satisfaction is between 3.92 and 4.75."

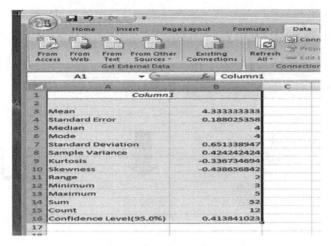

FIGURE 1.13

Excel output for finding a confidence interval.

SIDEBAR: BE CAREFUL! EXCEL'S WACKY'S NAME FOR "e"

Be aware that "confidence level" and "confidence interval" are *not* synonymous. Excel's "notation/language" can be a bit confusing. The number obtained in the "confidence level" row (row 16 of Figure 1.13, for example) is the "error"—what above we labeled as "e." There is no one standard name for "e." It is referred to as the "precision," and also the "accuracy" (both correctly so!), or, indeed, sometimes simply by the more general term, "error." When your chosen confidence level is 95%, which, as we noted earlier, is most often the case—based on tradition, "e" is quite often called "the margin of error." This term is especially prevalent when reporting results of a poll. As indicated in this section, when you add and subtract "e" to the X-bar—in effect straddling the mean—you've now produced a confidence interval.

SIDEBAR: HOW TO DISPLAY CONFIDENCE INTERVALS ON A BAR CHART IN EXCEL

As much as we'd like to hope that any audience for UX research would immediately grasp the idea of a confidence interval, our experience tells us that it's far from a "no-brainer." ☺ As is often the case, a picture can really help. Therefore, we always like to augment any bar chart of means (either alone or against one another) with "error bars" to represent the confidence intervals. Here's how to do it in Excel:

1. First, calculate your different means and values of "e" or "error"; this is the value identified in your Excel data analysis output as "confidence level," and the one we will add and subtract from the mean to form a confidence interval.

SIDEBAR: HOW TO DISPLAY CONFIDENCE INTERVALS ON A BAR CHART IN EXCEL—cont'd

2. Set the values from Step 1 in a simple table in Excel. Here's an example using a simple data set

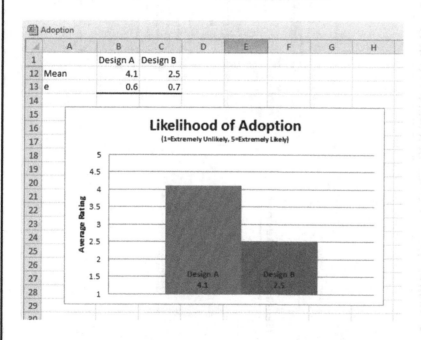

of likelihood of adoption ratings for two different designs:

3. Create a standard chart of just the means and associated column headers:

4. Select your means column. Then, click on the "Chart Layout" tab. From the "Error Bars" dropdown, choose "Error Bars Options." In the results dialog box, click on the "Custom" radio button option in the "Error Amount" section; then click on the "Specify Value" button. In the "Custom Error Bars" pop-up, enter the same value for both the positive and negative error values. In both cases, these will be the "e" you previously calculated. (You can either type in the value or navigate to the value in your spreadsheet using the standard Excel selection control.)

Continued

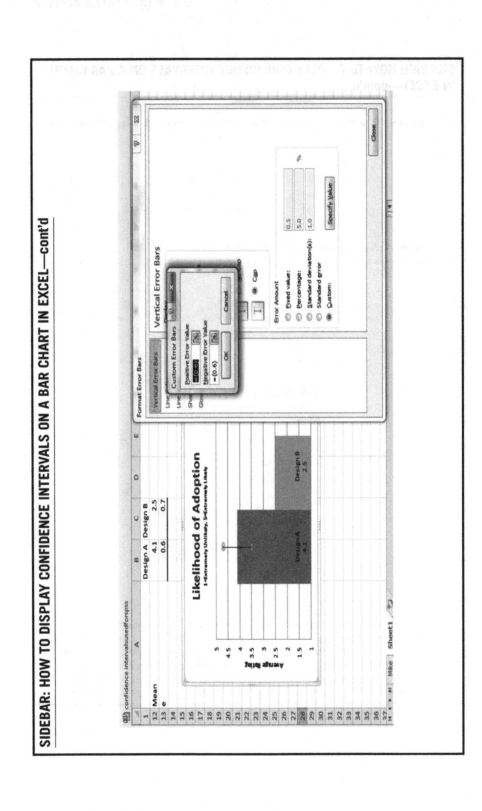

SIDEBAR: HOW TO DISPLAY CONFIDENCE INTERVALS ON A BAR CHART IN EXCEL—cont'd

5. Repeat Step 2 for any other means you have. Close both windows and your error bars should be on the graph.
6. Make sure you indicate on your finished chart the confidence level you've used. In this case, it's the typical 95%:

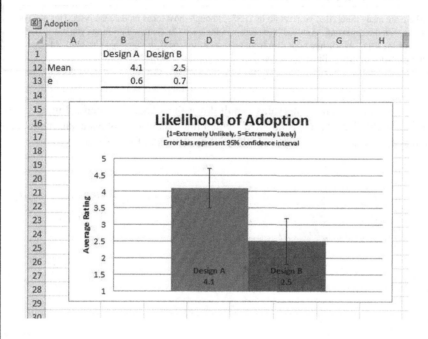

You're done!

When you present your findings, these error bars will help your audience quickly comprehend how accurate your means are, and as a consequence, how different they are.

1.3.3 FINDING A CONFIDENCE INTERVAL USING SPSS

When using SPSS (Statistical Package for Social Sciences), there is nothing to activate! You simply open the software and you're ready to go. You type in the data, or open a file that already has the data in it, and ask for the confidence interval. When you open up a blank SPSS page, what you see is depicted in Figure 1.14.

It looks a lot like a standard Excel page, but, instead of listing the columns according to the alphabet, it simply numbers them as variables ("VAR"). If we enter the data we used in the Excel example in the first column (or, had it been there when we opened the file), we get the picture in Figure 1.15, where "VAR00001" (variable one) automatically replaced the grayed out VAR, to indicate that data values are in that column.

SIDEBAR: THE UBIQUITOUS "DATA ANALYSIS" IN SPSS

There are many things that you can do in SPSS, although most focus on data analysis. This always starts with the command "Analyze" (see arrow in Figure 1.15). Some other things you can do is to recode the data (say, change your data from minutes to seconds), or view some graphs, and other things. Some of these will be illustrated later in the book.

To find a confidence interval, we pull down the "Analyze" menu (Figure 1.16), and highlight "Descriptive Statistics," which immediately displays a sub menu, and on this sub menu, we highlight "Explore." See arrows in Figure 1.16.

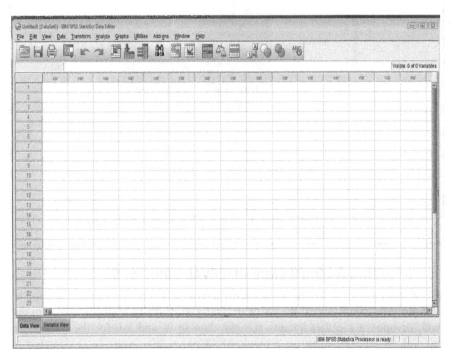

FIGURE 1.14

SPSS when first opened—no data yet entered.

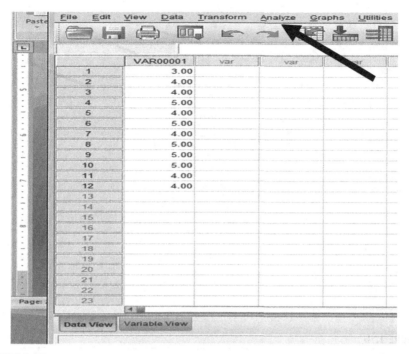

FIGURE 1.15

SPSS with data entered.

We now simply click on "Explore," and we get a dialog box that says "Explore"; see Figure 1.17 and its arrow.

SIDEBAR: SPSS—A WORLD OF BOXES

It is worth taking a moment here to note certain aspects of the dialog box that are common to all of the statistical analysis tools we will use in SPSS. We have already noted how it is labeled "Explore;" had you clicked, for example, on "Frequencies," then, of course, that would have been the label on the box. Also noteworthy is that on the left, you get a list of all the variables (columns) for which there are data values—here, only VAR00001; were there 100 columns with data (yikes!!!), all 100 would be listed from VAR00001 through VAR00100. We can also easily change a generic name such as VAR00001 to a "real name" such as "Satisfaction." (We'll illustrate that [aesthetically-oriented] operation in a later chapter.) You can see other rectangles within the box. There will always be lots of them (e.g., the rectangle labeled "dependent variable"), but they differ by what statistical operation you are doing. Finally, there are little boxes that can be clicked to get selected further detail, such as "plots," and there will always be an "OK" choice available to actually implement the analysis. The OK option is grayed out in Figure 1.17 only because there are no elements in the "Dependent List" rectangle.

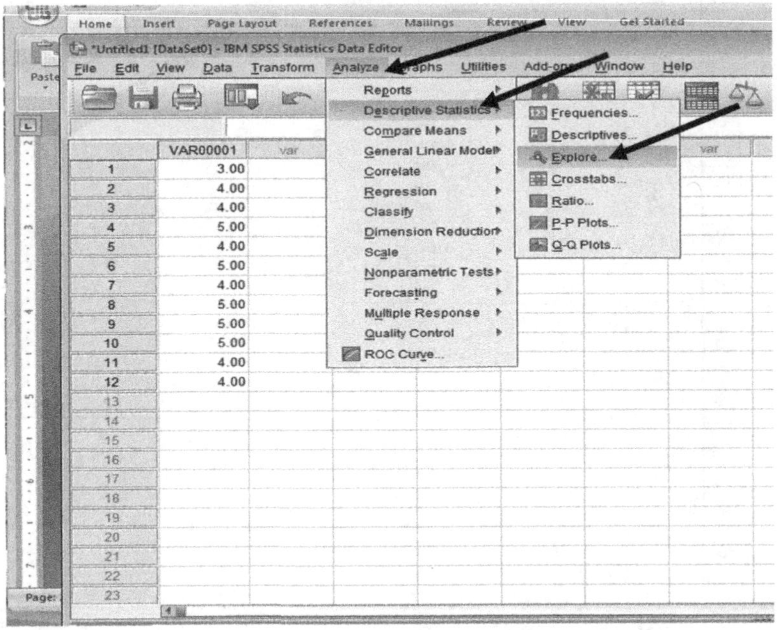

FIGURE 1.16

SPSS after analyze, descriptive statistics, and explore.

Now, to operate on VAR00001, we highlight it in the left large rectangle (it's highlighted in Figure 1.17) and click the arrow next to the Dependent Variable rectangle, which drags VAR00001 into that box. See Figure 1.18, and notice how the arrow, which was pointed toward the Dependent Variable rectangle (indicating something needs to go there), is now pointing away from it. (Perhaps later you will wish to replace VAR00001 [highlight it and click arrow to place it back to the list of variables on the left] by some other variable.)[3]

In our current situation, all we need to do now is to click the OK box (notice—no longer grayed out!!) Doing so produces the output in Figure 1.19.

---

[3] Actually, if you had two variables and wished to find a confidence interval for both of them, you would not have to do them separately, but would drag both variables into the Dependent Variable rectangle and receive output results for both variables in one overall output box.

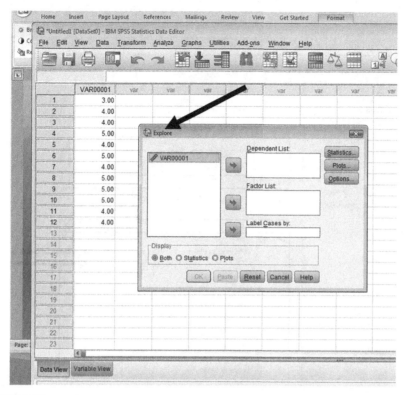

FIGURE 1.17

Dialog box for the command, Explore.

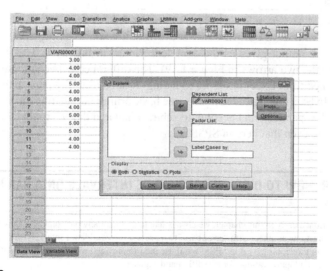

FIGURE 1.18

VAR00001 dragged into Dependent List rectangle.

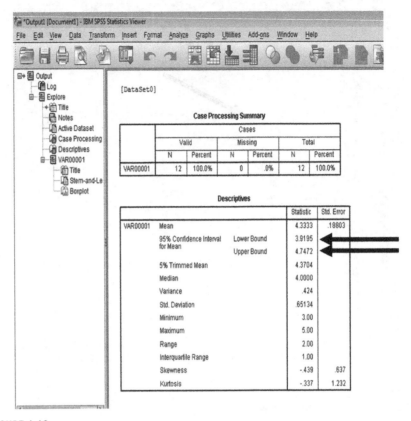

FIGURE 1.19

SPSS output for Explore, with confidence interval "arrowed."

The above output gives us the confidence interval directly. It is 3.9195--------4.7472 (see the two arrows in Figure 1.19). The difference between these value and those obtained from Excel is simply rounding. From a usability perspective, life just got easier. In Excel, you needed to do some basic arithmetic (getting the values of "e" and "X-bar" separately, and needing to subtract and add the "e" to the X-bar), while we are spared even that here in SPSS.

SIDEBAR: HOW TO DISPLAY CONFIDENCE INTERVALS ON A BAR CHART IN SPSS

As we mentioned early in this chapter, we always like to augment any bar chart of means (either alone or against one another) with "error bars" to represent the confidence intervals. We showed you how to do it in Excel; now try it in SPSS. We'll use the sample data, which is simply a data set of likelihood of adoption ratings for two different designs.

SIDEBAR: HOW TO DISPLAY CONFIDENCE INTERVALS ON A BAR CHART IN SPSS—cont'd

1. First, create or open your data in SPSS:

	VAR00001	VAR00002
1	5	3
2	4	2
3	3	2
4	4	4
5	5	3
6	3	2
7	4	2
8	5	4
9	5	2
10	4	2
11		

2. Go into the Variable View and make sure all your definitions have been entered correctly:

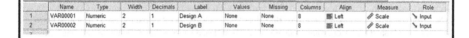

	Name	Type	Width	Decimals	Label	Values	Missing	Columns	Align	Measure	Role
1	VAR00001	Numeric	2	1	Design A	None	None	8	Left	Scale	Input
2	VAR00002	Numeric	2	1	Design B	None	None	8	Left	Scale	Input

3. Choose the Bar chart from the Legacy Dialogs under Chart Builder in the toolbar:

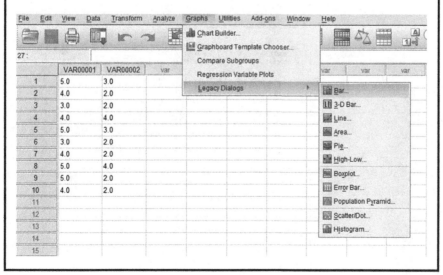

Continued

4. Select the "Simple" bar chart and select the "Summaries of separate variables" radio button:

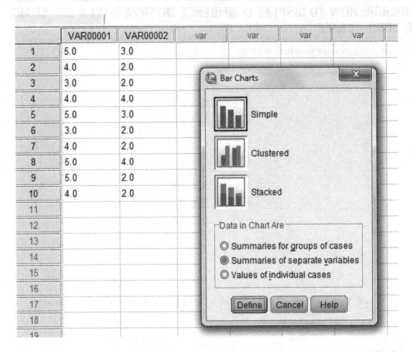

5. Your means should already be in the "Bars Represent" field. Click on "Options" and on resulting dialog box, click on "Display error bar," and select the "Confidence Intervals" radio button. If not, drag both sets of variable data from the left window in the dialog box to the "Bars Represent" dialog box. (Make sure confidence level is set correctly.) Finally click "Continue" and "OK" on the first dialog box.

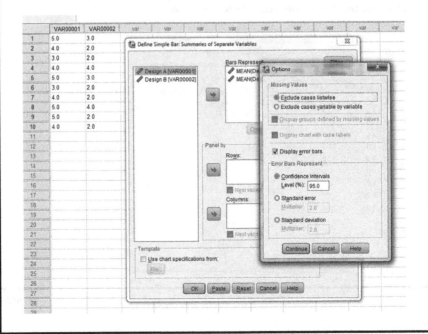

SIDEBAR: HOW TO DISPLAY CONFIDENCE INTERVALS ON A BAR CHART IN SPSS—cont'd

6. If needed, scroll down to the bottom of the viewer to see the bar chart with the confidence levels displayed:

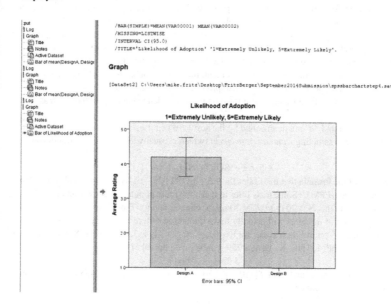

7. To tweak any aspect of the chart, double click directly on the chart, right click and select "Edit content in separate window." This will bring you to the chart editor.

SIDEBAR: DOES ACTUAL POPULATION SIZE MATTER? IT MIGHT! CONSIDER THE NEED FOR THE FINITE POPULATION MULTIPLIER (FPM)

When finding a confidence interval for a mean using Excel or SPSS (or for a proportion, covered in a subsequent chapter), there is an assumption built in that the population from which we are sampling, generally denoted by "N" (recall – the sample size is denoted by "n"), whether known or not, is "large" – at least 20 times as big as the sample size – that is equivalent to saying that we are sampling no more than 5% of the population, or, equivalently, (n/N) > .05. And, probably in 99.9% of the cases, this is the situation.

However, there can be situations when the population size is NOT at least 20 times the sample size. For example, say you have work at a software company that is barely out of startup phase and you have only 20 clients. You send out a survey to all 20, but only 6 respond to the survey. Here, n = 6 and (n/N) is .30, well above .05. We are assuming that the n = 6 is an unbiased (i.e., random) sample of the 20.

Now, there are times when this kind of low ratio of (n/N) will make a difference in both how you calculate your confidence intervals, and the results you get. But before we show you how to do it; we have to introduce the concept of *replacement*. Read on!

SIDEBAR: DOES ACTUAL POPULATION SIZE MATTER? IT MIGHT! CONSIDER THE NEED FOR THE FINITE POPULATION MULTIPLIER (FPM.)—cont'd

There are two basic ways of sampling from a population: sampling *with replacement* and sampling *without replacement*. These two terms have the obvious meanings – *with replacement* means that after we sample one data point, we replace it into the population before selecting the second data point; the key consequence is that we might possibly sample the same data point (e.g., person) again!!

Sampling *without replacement*, on the other hand, means that once we sample a data point, he/she/it is no longer eligible to be selected again – we have not replaced that data point back into the population. The vast, vast majority of sampling that takes place is sampling *without replacement*. In fact, in the rare case of sampling with replacement, this entire sidebar is moot! The reader should assume that in the entire text, all sampling is sampling *without replacement*.

Now, we've provided in this chapter the formula for a confidence interval for the mean as

$$X\text{-bar} \pm e$$

Of course, X-bar and "e" are determined by the software you use.

Technically, when sampling *without replacement* (which is usually the case), the formula you should is:

$$X\text{-bar} \pm e*SQRT\{(N-n)/(N-1)\}$$

The portion of the formula that multiplies the "e" – $SQRT\{(N - n)/(N - 1)\}$ – is called the "finite population multiplier (FPM)." Some texts refer to it as the "finite population correction factor."

Thus, in our example, N = 20 (a *total* of 20 major clients) and n = 6 of these 20, without replacement; the application of the FPM will actually make a material difference! Using this scenario, suppose on a typical 5-point Likert scale, we have data of: 5, 4, 4, 4, 3, 4. We have X-bar = 4.0, and e = .664 without the FPM. Thus, we have a 95% confidence interval of:

$$3.336 ---- 4.664$$

With the FPM, we have $.664*SQRT\{(20 - 6)/(20 - 1)\} = .664*(.8584) = .544$, and a corresponding 95% confidence interval of:

$$3.456 ---- 4.544$$

This is an interval that is about 18% narrower—i.e., 18% more precise! How important this 18% is depends on the specific context, but few would refer to it as totally negligible.

Having said this, the rule-of-thumb generally used is that we ignore the FPM unless we have the somewhat rare case that n/N exceeds .05 (i.e., we are sampling more than 5% of the total population.) The logic behind this rule-of-thumb is that under these conditions, the FPM would not make a material difference to the answer.

By the way, you may be wondering what Excel and SPSS do about the FPM. The answer is: Nothing!! They don't compute a confidence interval incorporating the FPM. The reason follows the above logic that nearly always, including the FPM has a negligible impact.

For example, suppose that N = 10,000 and n = 10. Then the FPM equals $SQRT\{(10,000 - 10)/(10,000 - 1)\} = SQRT(9990/9999) = SQRT(.9991) = .9995$. Well, multiplying "e" by .9995 is surely negligible, and will have not even a remotely material effect on "e" (especially when "e" is likely to be rounded to 2 or 3 digits at most). So, even though we theoretically need the FPM, we hardly ever use it.

Bottom line: If you have a case which *does* require the FPM, first calculate the confidence interval provided by the software to determine "e." Then, multiply "e" by the FPM and then add and subtract the "adjusted e" to the X-bar.

1.4 HYPOTHESIS TESTING

One topic, and perhaps the only topic, that is with us in a major way in *every chapter of this book* is what is called "hypothesis testing." It has several variations in terms of its goals and the specific questions it answers, but, ultimately, it has to do with *deciding whether something is true or not*, based on analyzing the data.

We believe that the topic is so pervasive that it merits the readers' understanding of the "philosophy" or "reasoning" that the topic entails. Indeed, hypothesis testing could be considered "*The* Statistical Analysis Process"—if only one topic deserved that description in the entire fields of statistics, data analysis, and predictive analytics.

An example may help to illustrate the concept of hypothesis testing. Suppose that you're working as a UX researcher at a company where the CEO wants to completely change the design of the company's Web home page. Let's suspend reality a moment and agree that we *know*, for the current Web home page, that the *true* mean (not the "X-bar") satisfaction rating is 4.10 on a scale of 1–5, where 1 = Not At All Satisfied to 5 = Extremely Satisfied.

Recently, the design team has come up with a new home page design. So far, everyone seems to like it, but you want some empirical evidence that the new design is indeed an improvement over the current design in terms of mean satisfaction. You decide to run a 25 person survey, and probe on satisfaction of the new design. You calculate the new satisfaction rating mean (the X-bar) for the new design from your sample of users and get a 4.15. (The true/population mean of the new design is the one, and only one, unknown value.)

SIDEBAR: WHAT IF WE KNOW NEITHER TRUE MEAN?

In Chapter 2, we consider the more detailed, more frequent case, in which we do not know the true mean for *either* design. One home page features a young waif sipping coffee at an outdoor cafe, while another design shows a romantic couple meeting in front of the Eiffel Tower. These are two competing designs in Chapter 2, and, as we noted, we don't know the true mean satisfaction rating of either design. We'll explain how to deal with this scenario in Chapter 2.

Well, 4.15 is obviously higher than 4.10. So the new design wins, right? Or does it? Well, it depends. The true mean for the new design might be 4.00 (notably under the 4.10 of the current design), and *just due to routine variability*, these 25 people happened to give you an X-bar for the new design of 4.15.

SIDEBAR: OMNIPRESENT VARIABILITY

As we've mentioned, variability almost always exists in a data set. Indeed, there is almost always variability in results; in the UX world, the variability depends on who comprises the sample of people. Indeed, when you flip 10 coins, you expect to get around 5 heads (perhaps 4 or 6, or, rarely, 3 or 7), but you might get 2 or 8 heads or a more lopsided result than that.

So, you need to decide—is an X-bar of 4.15 really enough above 4.10 to constitute convincing evidence that the new design has a *true* higher mean satisfaction? Well, since you're reading this book, you're savvy enough now to say "probably not!" (By the way, this is not the same as when X-bar = 4.8. That is a value way above 4.1, with, indeed, little disagreement among the 25 people. If the X-bar is 4.8 out of 5, there just *can't* be a lot of disagreement!).

If 4.15 is not enough above 4.10 to be convincing, is 4.20 or 4.30? The answer depends on the sample size, the variability in the data, and how much chance you are willing to take when stating that the new design has a higher mean satisfaction rating when in truth, it doesn't! This "risk" has a formal name of "significance level," always denoted by "alpha," and is traditionally chosen to be 0.05–1 chance out of 20.

OK, this is where the hypotheses formally come back into the discussion. Our goal is to choose between two hypotheses. Their formal names are the *null* hypothesis and the *alternate* hypothesis. Simply put, the null hypothesis typically states that there is no relationship between one or more things, or that the status quo has not changed.

Let's assume the latter for now. Put another way, you assume that the status quo is still the case, until you can prove that something, often a "μ," has changed. As such, the null hypothesis provides a benchmark against which we can propose another hypothesis that indeed a change has taken place, or indeed, something is now different: an "alternate" hypothesis. In our case, our null hypothesis is that the true mean satisfaction of the new design is no higher than the 4.1 true mean of the current home page design.

Conversely, the alternate hypothesis is *that the new design has a higher mean rating than the 4.1 mean of the current design* (and, hence, we should go with the new design!) The "μ" in the hypotheses below stands for the true mean of the new design.[4] Specifically, we are to choose between:

- H0: $\mu \leq 4.1$ (mean satisfaction rating of new design is *no higher* than 4.1, the mean of the current design; stay with the current design!)
- H1: $\mu > 4.1$ (mean satisfaction rating of new design is higher than 4.1, the mean of the current design; go with a smile with the new design!!)

And, you phrase your conclusion by deciding whether

You *ACCEPT* H0

or

You *REJECT* H0

From a practical point of view, the two hypotheses should be such that *one of them must be true, but both of them cannot be true*. The above two hypotheses satisfy this condition. So, whatever we conclude about H0, we automatically conclude the opposite about H1.

So, how are you going to decide between the two hypotheses? First you will collect some data using the new design, and compute the *sample mean satisfaction*, X-bar. Then, as a function of X-bar, the sample size, n, and the variability in the data (discussed earlier in the confidence interval section), a conclusion will be reached.

---

[4] We know the true mean of the current design, 4.1. We do not know the true mean of the *new* design. We always hypothesize about quantities we don't know—never about quantities we already know!!

SIDEBAR: BEYOND A REASONABLE DOUBT, YOUR HONOR!

The philosophy of hypothesis testing gives H0 the "benefit of the doubt" and imposes the "burden of proof" on H1. You will not reject H0 unless the evidence against it is quite strong! This is a conservative approach, and has some similarity of thought process to a criminal court scenario in which you give the defendant the benefit of the doubt and insist that you find the defendant guilty (i.e., reject H0, the status quo) only when the evidence against the defendant is "beyond a reasonable doubt."

In the UX world, this ensures that the chance is low that we mistakenly adopt a new design, only to find out later that it has the same, or even has lower mean satisfaction than what you knew was the case with the current design.

Keep in mind that the term "accept H0" is really the same as "Insufficient reason to reject H0." After all, if a jury comes back with a "not guilty" finding, it is NOT an affirmation of the defendant's innocence, but, rather, a statement that there is insufficient evidence to convict the defendant. May be Perry Mason should have really been a UX researcher!

Now, common sense would tell you that if X-bar is less than 4.10, there is no evidence that the new design has a true mean satisfaction rating that is higher than the current one, and thus, you (obviously) accept H0. And for a sample mean of 4.15, we noted earlier that this is likely not sufficient evidence to reject H0. But, what about 4.2 or 4.3? It is not clear!

On the other hand, if the mean satisfaction rating of a sample of, say, 25 people is X-bar = 4.8, and nearly everyone gave it a "5"—with a few "4's," then you would intuitively reject H0, and conclude that the new design *does* have a higher true mean satisfaction rating than 4.1.

But, your intuition will only get you so far in the world of statistics. The good news is that software like Excel and SPSS will perform all the calculations that will allow you to *confidently* accept or reject H0. But before we turn you loose, we need to explain the all-important concept of the "*p*-value."

1.4.1 *p*-VALUE

The fact that the software (Excel, SPSS, other statistical software) provides a quantity called "*p*-value" makes the entire process of hypothesis testing *dramatically* simpler. Let us tell you what the *p*-value represents and why it so greatly simplifies what you need to do to perform a hypothesis test of virtually any kind. In fact, it will be a rare chapter in which the *p*-value does not play a role.

The *p*-value, in simple terms, is the probability that you would obtain a specific data result as far away or farther away from what H0 says, assuming that H0 is true. The logic is kind of like a "proof by contradiction" that you may have learned in high school or freshman year in college—although we do not expect you to remember it. We alluded to it earlier in this section when we described how the H0 gets the benefit of the doubt and the H1 has the burden of proof. But, now, we describe the logic more directly:

If the data results you obtain have a very small chance of occurring under the assumption that H0 is true, then, indeed, we conclude that H0 is NOT true!!

As we noted, the traditional cutoff point for "very small chance of occurring" is 0.05. Admittedly, this is an arbitrarily value (see sidebar below), but is it a standard that is used virtually all the time by statisticians. Think of it this way: if any event occurred only 5 out of 100 times, that's a 5% probability. Pretty small indeed. So, the p-value is a measure of the strength of your evidence against H0. Put another way, the null hypothesis fails to account for the "facts" of the case, and those "facts" are the data you collected during your survey, usability test or any other method you used.

SIDEBAR: THE p-VALUE CUTOFF POINT AND THE TEA-TASTING LADY

As we noted, the traditional cutoff point for "a small chance of occurring" is 0.05. This is an arbitrary value, but it is used virtually all the time. It would run contrary to tradition to use a different value, although, of course, you can.

Nevertheless, to a large extent, the reason for using 0.05 is based on an off-the-cuff remark made by a famous statistician at a tea party at a university in England in the early/mid-1900s.

We're speaking of Sir Ronald Fisher (February 1890–July 1962), arguably the most prominent statistician of the twentieth century. He was a bit of a recluse, who to a larger than usual extent, did not "suffer fools," and while not especially well liked, was universally acknowledged as brilliant. Part of his obituary, written by statistician Kendall (1963) in the journal, *Biometrica*, stated, "In character he was, let us admit it, a difficult man." He sometimes wrote pieces on statistical thinking that were hard to understand by other statisticians of the day. Still, his brilliance often shone through.

He wrote a book that began by telling a story. The story was this: a woman entered his office one day and said that by tasting a cup of tea, she could tell if the tea was put into the cup first or the milk was put into the cup first. Fisher built up a complete text, primarily dealing with the ideas of hypothesis testing, based on this example.

How many cups of tea need the woman taste correctly before we should believe her claim? Should there be the same number of cups of tea of each type? What if she got 90% (not 100%) of the assessments right? 90% is, of course, less than perfection, but is so much above 50%, that it is very unlikely to occur if she really had no knowledge of the process of forming the tea based on the taste (Fisher, 1935).

Fisher never formally revealed if the lady was correct in her assertion or not, but it is reported in a book by Fisher's daughter (Box, 1978) that the woman did identify 8 cups of tea correctly, 4 with the tea having been put in first and 4 with the milk having been put in first. This can only happen by chance (assuming that the woman had no discerning skill and knew the (4, 4) split existed) with a probability of about 0.014 (1.4%). This, in effect, is our p-value in this experiment.

In any event, the story goes that at a tea party at a university in England, Fisher was walking by a group of people, in a hurry, when one asked him how low a probability is "too low" to retain credibility, and Fisher kind of waved the question away as he continued his walk without pause (in his all-too-often rude manner) and said something like, "Oh! About 1 in 20!!" Fisher acknowledged this "0.05" value more formally, when he was quoted saying, "If the p-value is between 0.1 and 0.9, there is certainly no reason to suspect the hypothesis tested. If it is below 0.02, it is strongly indicated that the hypothesis fails to account for the whole of the facts. *We shall not often be astray if we draw a conventional line at 0.05.*"

Now, let's go back to our design example and note how the p-value makes the process so simple. But this time, let's assume the new design garnered a mean satisfaction rating of 4.50. Again, for reference, our beloved hypotheses:

H0: μ ≤ 4.1 (mean satisfaction of new design is *no higher* than 4.1, the mean of current design).

H1: μ > 4.1 (mean satisfaction of new design is *higher* than 4.1, the mean of current design).

Suppose that the data values (*n* = 10) are,

5
4
5
5
3
4
5
5
4
5

The 10 data values have a mean of 4.50. Is that enough above 4.10 to reject H0? Let's do the hypothesis test in SPSS and answer the question very quickly:[5]

Type (or copy and paste) the data into SPSS, as depicted in Figure 1.20.

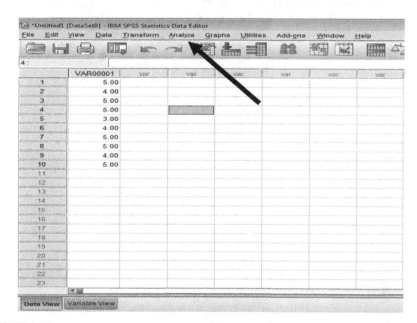

FIGURE 1.20

Data entered into SPSS.

[5] Refer to Chapter 2 to see how to perform the same test in Excel.

Now we pull down the "Analyze" menu item (see arrow in Figure 1.20) and go "compare means" and then to One-Sample T-test; see Figure 1.21 and its arrows:

On the resulting dialog box, drag over VAR00001 to become the Test Variable (see vertical arrow in Figure 1.22) and change "Test Value" from 0 to 4.10, the value stated in H0. See horizontal arrow in Figure 1.22.

This gives us Figure 1.23, which is now ready for a click of "OK" (see arrow).

After you, indeed, click "OK," we get the output in Figure 1.24.

We might first note that the sample average is 4.50 (see horizontal arrow in Figure 1.24).

SIDEBAR: *p*-VALUE = "SIGNIFICANCE" IN SPSS

SPSS does not call the *p*-value, "*p*-value." For whatever reason, even though the *p*-value is the name of a topic in probably 99.99% of introductory statistics textbooks (indeed, using the exact phrase, "*p*-value"), SPSS chooses to use the term "Significance," which is virtually always abbreviated to "Sig." due to space considerations. See the vertical arrow in Figure 1.24. We wonder if the good folks at SPSS conducted any usability testing with target users.☺

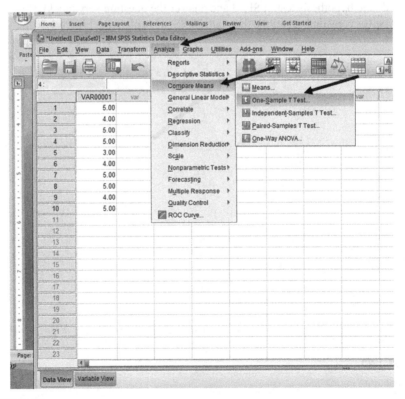

FIGURE 1.21

Implementing One-Sample T-test.

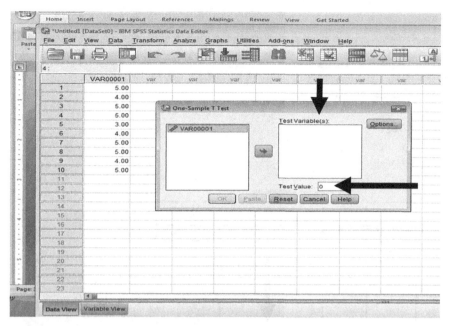

FIGURE 1.22

Implementing the details of One-Sample T-test.

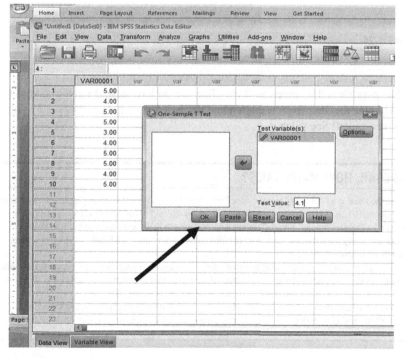

FIGURE 1.23

All set up to go "OK" and get the output.

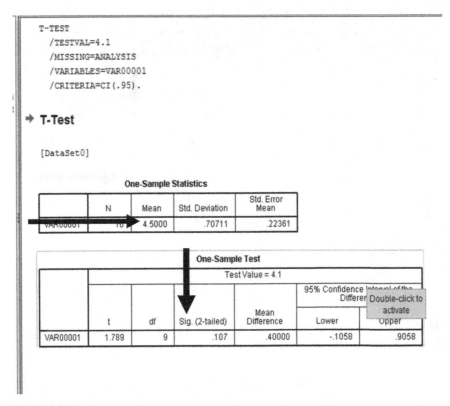

```
    T-TEST
      /TESTVAL=4.1
      /MISSING=ANALYSIS
      /VARIABLES=VAR00001
      /CRITERIA=CI(.95).
```

→ **T-Test**

[DataSet0]

One-Sample Statistics

	N	Mean	Std. Deviation	Std. Error Mean
VAR00001	10	4.5000	.70711	.22361

One-Sample Test

	Test Value = 4.1					
					95% Confidence Interval of the Difference	
	t	df	Sig. (2-tailed)	Mean Difference	Lower	Upper
VAR00001	1.789	9	.107	.40000	-.1058	.9058

FIGURE 1.24

SPSS output for One-Sample T-test.

The *p*-value is thus given as 0.107. But, we do have a slight complication here. You will note that the "Sig." (i.e., *p*-value) is labeled "two-tailed." But our hypothesis test is one-tailed! See sidebar.

SIDEBAR: HOW MANY TAILS?

When the issue is a "not over" versus "over," which is the case here (H0: true average of new design *not over* 4.10, versus H1: true average of new design *is over* 4.10), or, less frequent in practice, a "not under" versus "under" form of comparison, we refer to the hypothesis test as "one-tailed," because the "rejection values," based on common sense, are in only ONE tail of the curve—here, the tail some amount *above* 4.10.

Conversely, when we are testing whether a true mean equals a specific value, versus is not equal to that specific value (e.g., H0: $\mu = 4.1$ versus H1: $\mu \neq 4.1$), that is called a two-tailed test, since we would reject H0 if X-bar is too much in the direction of *either* of the TWO tails.

In the two curves below, the first one illustrates a one-tail (upper tail) test, while the second curve illustrates a two-tailed test. In both cases, the shaded-in region is the region that rejects H0.

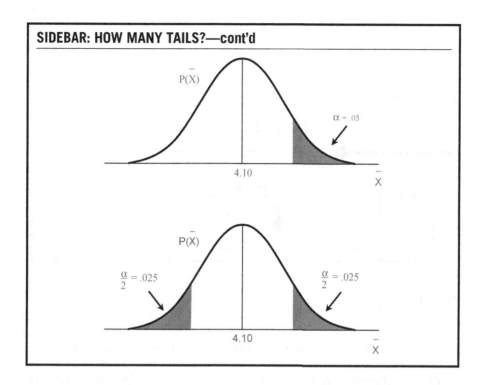

SIDEBAR: HOW MANY TAILS?—cont'd

A *one-tail test has a* p-*value that is half of the* p-*value of the corresponding two-tail test*. We offer this to you without proof; it is the case! SPSS does not know whether we are testing "4.10" as a one-tail test or a two-tail test, and that is why SPSS is careful to tell us that the "Sig." (*p*-value) it is providing is for a two-tail test.

So, the relevant *p*-value for you to consider is half of 0.107, which equals 0.0535, which is a small amount above 0.05, telling us that, if H0 is true, the data we have (with its mean = 4.50, with *n* = 10, and the variability in the data) is *not* (by a tad!!) as rare an event as required to reject H0: $\mu \le 4.1$, when using 0.05 as a cutoff point. Thus we can say that we do *not* have sufficient proof that the true mean satisfaction rating of the new design exceeds 4.10.

Consider a slightly different scenario that yields different results. If we go back to the original data and change one of the 4's to a 5 (say, the second data value) getting data of

$$(5, 5, 5, 5, 3, 4, 5, 5, 4, 5),$$

with sample mean now equal to 4.6, we would get the output in Figure 1.25. It shows that the mean is now 4.60 (see, again, the horizontal arrow), and the two-tail *p*-value is 0.050 (again, see vertical arrow):

So, the *p*-value for you to consider is 0.025 (half of the 0.050), and now, with your X-bar = 4.60, we would conclude that we *do* have sufficient evidence to reject H0, and conclude that the new design *does*, indeed, have a true mean satisfaction rating above 4.10, the known mean satisfaction rating of the current design.

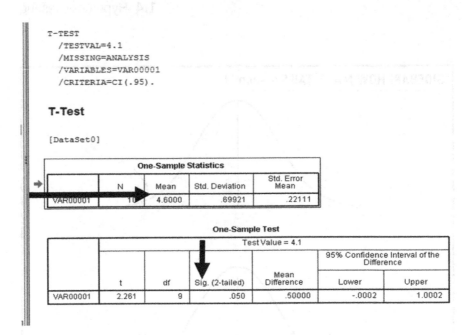

```
T-TEST
  /TESTVAL=4.1
  /MISSING=ANALYSIS
  /VARIABLES=VAR00001
  /CRITERIA=CI(.95).
```

T-Test

[DataSet0]

One-Sample Statistics				
	N	Mean	Std. Deviation	Std. Error Mean
VAR00001	10	4.6000	.69921	.22111

One-Sample Test						
	Test Value = 4.1					
					95% Confidence Interval of the Difference	
	t	df	Sig. (2-tailed)	Mean Difference	Lower	Upper
VAR00001	2.261	9	.050	.50000	-.0002	1.0002

FIGURE 1.25

Revised output.

Keep in mind that this change occurred only because it was a very close case before we changed the one data value, and the sample size was relatively small, and thus, the sample mean changed from 4.50 to 4.60 (25% further above the H0 value of 4.10). In most cases, a small change in one data value is not going to change your conclusion.

SIDEBAR: *p*-VALUE AND STATISTICAL VERSUS PRACTICAL SIGNIFICANCE

Most chapters in the rest of this text will have the *p*-value as an important, indeed, *critical* ingredient in the discussion and decision process. There will be a chapter here and there that does not stress the *p*-value, but only because the practical application involved will be more oriented to such things as the percent of cases correctly classified, rather than the actual statistical impact of a specific variable's role in the analysis. It tells you in a brief moment (by comparing it to 0.05 or whatever value of α is chosen) whether you should accept or reject the null hypothesis, H0. In that sense, the software providing the *p*-value does, indeed, make reaching the ultimate conclusion of accepting or rejecting H0 dramatically easier.

The *p*-value basically "says it all" about whether to accept or reject H0. However, there is sometimes a difference between *statistical significance* (i.e., the rejection of H0, easily determined by looking at the *p*-value), and what we might call *practical significance*. A population mean may be indicated by a hypothesis test, beyond a reasonable doubt, to be higher than 4.10; however, if it is actually 4.12, the difference is probably not meaningful in a practical sense. We would say that the result is statistically significant, but not practically significant. The *p*-value does not say anything at all about the practical significance, while saying it all about the statistical significance.

Yet, a final word needs to be added here: when the sample size is relatively small—and that is often the case in the world of UX research—a result that is statistically significant *will be almost always also practically significant*. It is when you have a relatively *large* sample size that this issue (the possible discrepancy between the statistical and practical significance) may occur.

Still, we should acknowledge that there is a vagueness of sorts in this discussion. Given a specific significance level, say 0.05, there is no doubt when a result is *statistically significant*; however, *practical significance* is very context-dependent, and reasonable people can disagree about whether a result is practically significant.

1.5 SUMMARY

This chapter has explored several basic ideas that you need to know as a UX researcher. First, we introduced the normal curve and discussed how it is actually a very important probability curve. After illustrating how to work with probabilities and values associated with a normal curve, we very specifically discussed how to determine probabilities associated with the mean of several values (e.g., satisfaction ratings) that you may encounter as a UX researcher. We then examined the basic aspects of confidence intervals and hypothesis testing to ease us into their use in subsequent chapters.

1.6 ADDENDUM: ACTIVATING "DATA ANALYSIS"

As we said earlier, to find a confidence interval in Excel, in fact, to do *any* statistical analysis in Excel, beside such routine calculations of a sample mean or standard deviation, etc., you need to first "activate" a module or section of Excel called "Data Analysis." It exists within Excel, but you would not necessarily know about it unless you are told.

The first step is slightly different depending on whether you have Excel 2007 2010 or 2013. In Excel 2007, the first step is to click on the "office button;" using Excel 2010 and 2013, you click on the file menu. Either way, you identify and click on Excel Options (see Figure 1.26).

After clicking on "Excel Options," you get a dialog box, and need to simply click on "Add-Ins" (see arrow in Figure 1.27). At this point, differences among the different versions of Excel disappear.

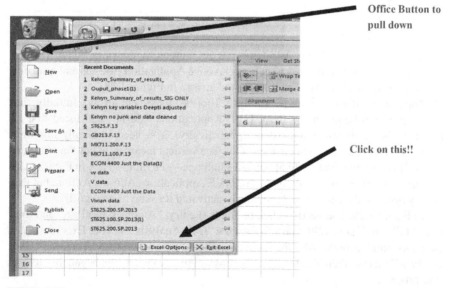

Office Button to pull down

Click on this!!

FIGURE 1.26

Beginning the process of activating Data Analysis in Excel.

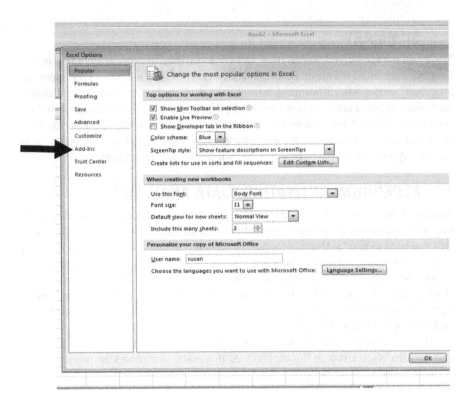

FIGURE 1.27

Clicking on "Add-Ins."

As soon as you click on "Add-Ins," you get a menu as shown in Figure 1.28. In the figure, you see that there is a section of Active Application Add-ins and a section of Inactive Application Add-ins (see dashed arrows in Figure 1.28).

The important application is "Analysis ToolPak" (see bent arrow). Initially, that application will be under the INACTIVE Applications Add-ins, and listed first on that list (the applications are listed alphabetically). You need to simply highlight "Analysis ToolPak" and then click on "Go" (see vertical fat arrow at bottom of Figure 1.28). This will give you the final box—a small one—see Figure 1.29. In Figure 1.28, "Analysis ToolPak" is already in the ACTIVE Applications Add-ins section, but that is only because the authors had previously activated it (many years ago!!).

In Figure 1.29, you need to click on the first entry, "Analysis ToolPak," and then click "OK." In Figure 1.30, you will then see "Data Analysis" on your Excel software (see horizontal arrow), under the main menu item "Data" (see vertical arrow); "Data Analysis" was not there (under "Data" or anywhere else) when you began this activation process.

At this point, Data Analysis is always present and ready to use. Any time you want to use Data Analysis (which will be used frequently throughout several subsequent

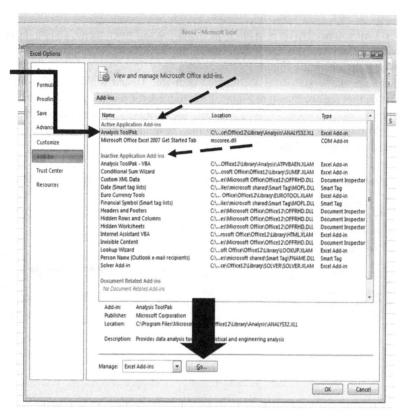

FIGURE 1.28

Continuing the process of activation of Data Analysis.

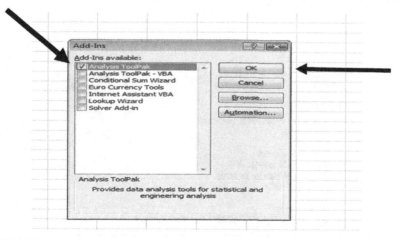

FIGURE 1.29

Final step in activation process.

chapters), all you need to do is to click on "Data" on this main menu, and on the right you will see Data Analysis and you need to simply click on that. After clicking on it, you open it up, obtaining Figure 1.31.

There are many statistical techniques available (listed alphabetically) in this application that are not shown in Figure 1.31. Indeed, the technique in the next chapter (when we discuss a specific type of t-test) does not even show in the figure above, but would require some downward scrolling. Several of these techniques will be illustrated as we proceed through the book.

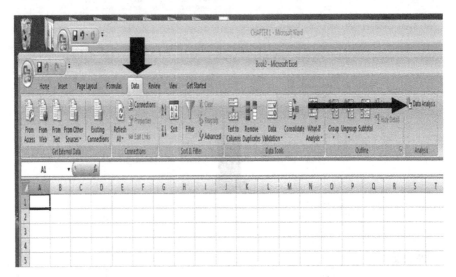

FIGURE 1.30

Showing Data Analysis in the Data menu item.

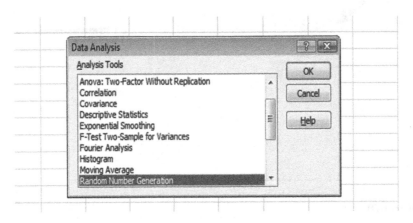

FIGURE 1.31

Data Analysis—opened up.

REFERENCES

Box, F.J., 1978. R.A. Fisher: The Life of a Scientist. Wiley, New York.
Fisher, R.A., 1935. Design of Experiments, ninth ed. Macmillan, London. 1971.
Kendall, W.G., 1963. Ronald Aylmer Fisher, 1890–1962. Biometrika 50, 1–15.

Comparing two designs (or anything else!) using independent sample T-tests

2

2.1 INTRODUCTION

As the researcher on a UX team, you are probably frequently asked to determine which version of a design or feature is more useful or usable (in essence, *better*). In addition, you maybe asked to determine which design is preferable on a variety of attributes, such as aesthetic appeal, trust, emotional connection, and of course, commercial potential.

By "design" we mean alternate versions of lots of things: a Web site home page, the ever-important shopping-cart check-out process, a "wizard" of some type that helps the user accomplish a task, a single important feature, or an entire Web site or prototype. As a matter of fact, this kind of comparison test maybe one of the most common types of jobs you're assigned as the researcher.

Why compare different versions? Lots of reasons. If you're at an agency with outside clients, the client will often ask to see a "couple of different passes." If you're at a company with its own UX team, you may still have "clients" whom you're still beholden to—they're just internal, like the Chief Executive Officer or VP of Marketing. And they want to see a "couple of takes" as well.

And for good reason. Different versions mean that the team has explored different approaches to improve a user's perception of usefulness and usability, and that they're not satisfied with the first approach that someone comes up with. The team wants to satisfy both the clients and themselves that they've left no stone unturned (i.e., considered all alternatives) in their pursuit of the most intuitive design.

So what's the rub? The final design needs to be chosen. And that isn't always easy without further and, perhaps sophisticated, analyses.

2.2 CASE STUDY: COMPARING DESIGNS AT MADEMOISELLE LA LA

You've been hired as the UX researcher at Mademoiselle La La, a high-end online apparel merchant aimed at urbane women from 18–55 years of age with well-above-average disposable income.

47

The La La offices are housed in an old New England mill that has been repurposed for the new millennium; the clanking of enormous looms has been replaced by the incessant click-clack of designers, programmers, IT specialists, marketers and others pounding away at their computer keyboards, feverishly responding to the pontifications that come from upper management. In the basement, young female models—usually close to anorexic—are constantly photographed showcasing the latest fashions that are featured on the Web site. The actual architecture of the office is "dot-bomb chic": exposed brick and beams, cube "pods" that ostensibly serve to increase collaboration, comfy couches, and white boards covering nearly every wall, covered with flow charts, page designs, and random verbiage like "Key Takeaways" accompanied by bulleted lists. There are lots of recreational opportunities as well: foosball and ping-pong tables, pinball machines, and faux basketball hoops with accompanying smurf balls. (Ironically, hardly any of La La's employees can avail themselves of the recreational toys; they're all too busy working.)

Within a couple of days of your start date, you're able to determine the source of the nervous energy that permeates the Creative Group: the rumor mill has it that CEO Massimo Ranieri thinks the home page needs a complete revamp to increase the "sophistication" factor of the brand—and he wants it fast.

As expected, Creative Director Kristen McCarthey calls a team meeting to give out the marching orders. Thin, short-coiffed, over-caffeinated, with a penchant for body piercings, McCarthey has been with "La La" for over 5 years, and has been terrorizing her information architects, designers, researchers, and front-end coders for just as long. Every directive is accompanied by patronizing lectures that are laced with dot-bomb buzzwords: "eyeballs" needs to be "monetized" to find "synergies" in our "click and mortar" world where "push technologies" will decrease our "burn rate," on and on. After studiously taking notes for the first couple of "status meetings," you've given up copying down anything she says, and simply wait for the designers and IAs to take turns updating the group on what they've been working on.

But in this particular meeting, McCarthey has ratcheted up her game, berating the entire group about the "astonishing ineptitude" of the Creative Group. "Massimo is right," she says, "our brand is about sophistication, but we're appealing to bargain basement shoppers in our design!" She glares at the group, as her shrill voice bounces off the exposed brick: "I'm giving you lightweights one more chance with this new website design. Make it sophisticated, make it hip—and make it pop." Grabbing her iPad and *latte*, she heads out the door, but screams one last time: "And I want it by the end of the week!"

"Make it sophisticated, make it hip -- and make it pop!"

The team has its marching orders, and within a couple of days, the designers come back with two designs: Design 1 in Figure 2.1 features a scene of a young *demoiselle* sipping a coffee at an outdoor French café, ignoring the adoring eyes of a nearby young man.

Design 2 in Figure 2.2 features a young couple snuggling together under one umbrella during a shower, with the Eiffel Tower bisecting a slate-gray sky. One version is aloof, mysterious, unresolved, but there's a promise of romance. The other version is resolved, with true love trumping the odds.

FIGURE 2.1

Design 1.

FIGURE 2.2

Design 2.

Invariably, some folks like Design 1 and other folks like Design 2, and they're passionate about their preferences. During multiple reviews, the advocates for each design become more strident and dig in. Consensus is elusive, if not impossible.

During what is supposed to be the "final review," tempers rise, and the two camps are getting increasingly agitated, extolling the sophistication of their design over the other. There are other subplots, because designer Josh Cheysak (Design 1) is hoping his design is chosen to increase his chances of a raise, and designer Autumn Taylor (Designer 2) is hoping her design is chosen because she's bucking for the Creative Director position. Nobody will budge. Think Boehner and Obama during the Great Government Shutdown of 2013.

Just as Cheysak is about to pour his Red Bull all over Taylor's Moleskine sketchbook, you cautiously offer to perform a "head-to-head comparison survey with independent samples."

A hush settles over the room. Taylor finally breaks the silence: "A what?"

You calmly explain that by running a survey featuring two different designs with two different groups of people, you may be able to determine differences between the two designs in terms of perceived sophistication and preference ratings. In other words, you can determine which one is best, based on user feedback. Trying not to sound too professorial, you add that "proper statistical analysis and good survey design can guard against obtaining misleading results."

The attendees simultaneously nod in agreement but McCarthey won't agree to anything without "pushback."

"Where are you getting these participants?" McCarthey asks with skepticism in her voice.

"We can use our client list, and offer them a $25 gift certificate for completing a survey. After all, they are the target audience, but they haven't seen any one of these two designs. Of course, we'll collect demographic data about each participant."

"Will everyone see both designs?" McCarthey asks. "Doesn't sound right."

"In this case, it's probably better that one group sees one design and another group sees the other design. This eliminates any bias from seeing a second design after seeing the first. I can randomize which participant sees which design."

"Hmmm," McCarthey says, staring down at her iPhone, half-listening. "I guess it's worth a try."

Ah, a peaceful resolution is in sight. Before you can say "Camp David Peace Accords," the tension in the conference room evaporates. No more bruised egos, no more subterfuge. Just an easy way to let data do the talkin' and to determine the correct design based on objective evidence, not hunches and egos.

2.3 COMPARING TWO MEANS

In Chapter 1 on basic statistical thought and the role of uncertainty, we covered a topic called "hypothesis testing," and, we discussed how, when data values are collected from a sample of the population, the mean of 10, or 100, or even 1000 people, can sometimes yield an answer that is misleading. Among our examples in that chapter, we considered which hypothesis we should believe about the population mean-satisfaction-level based on what all potential customers would report for a particular design; in essence, whether we should accept or reject a specific hypothesis.

We considered whether to believe that the mean satisfaction with a modified design was higher than the mean satisfaction with the old design, which was 4.1 on a scale of 1 (not at all satisfied) to 5 (extremely satisfied). Formally, we were testing two hypotheses, the null hypothesis (H0) and the alternate hypothesis (H1):

- H0: The true mean satisfaction with the modified design is no higher than 4.1.
- H1: The true mean satisfaction with the modified design is greater than 4.1, that of the original design.

As we noted in Chapter 1, the statistician would write these hypotheses more succinctly, by defining the true mean satisfaction with the modified design as "mu" (the Greek letter, μ)—which, of course, we don't know and likely will never know, and writing:

H0: $\mu \leq 4.1$ (the modified design mean satisfaction is not above that of the original design—weep!!)
H1: $\mu > 4.1$ (indeed, the modified design mean satisfaction is above 4.1; there has been an increase in mean satisfaction—yeah!!)

We noted in Chapter 1 that Excel or SPSS was each able to take the raw data gathered during a typical usability test and put together an analysis that tells us which hypothesis (H0 or H1) to believe. To reach its conclusion, the software performed a "one-sample t-test."

2.4 INDEPENDENT SAMPLES

In this chapter we introduce the reader to an easy extension of the above type example, and present the situation in which we have *two unknown means* that we wish to compare, based on *two sets of data*. The software will still do all the work, and it is likely not a surprise to the reader that what the software would be doing is called a "two-sample t-test."

In the case of Mademoiselle La La, you have to compare the means of two independent samples, and determine the one, if either, that has the higher perception of sophistication. To do so, we will create two hypotheses in an effort to decide between the two:

H0: $\mu 1 = \mu 2$
(The two designs do not differ with respect to mean sophistication)
H1: $\mu 1 \neq \mu 2$
(The two designs do, indeed, differ with respect to mean sophistication)

The software will easily calculate which hypothesis is correct. If the second hypothesis is determined to be true, then we can conclude that the means are indeed different. As a consequence, we can conclude that the mean perceptions of satisfactions are different. Thus, the design with the higher ratings of satisfaction is the winner—and is the one to use for the site's home page.

There are two variations of what the software needs to do in order to correctly assess the situation and tell us which of the above hypotheses to believe. Either way, the software does all the work, but the user does need to inform the software which of the two variations is appropriate. That is, you need to press or check off different buttons to tell the software what is going on. After all, Excel and SPSS are great, but they are not mind readers!

In the case of Mademoiselle La La, we'll be performing a "two-sample t-test for independent samples." This simply means that for whatever comparison we are making, *there are two different groups of people involved, each evaluating one of the two designs.* (Not in this case, but in the general case, the two groups might be evaluating the same design.)

Having two different groups of people is the reason this approach is called "independent samples;" no one person is in both groups, and the mean score for one group of people is totally *independent* from (i.e., unrelated to) the mean score for the other group.

SIDEBAR: WHY INDEPENDENT GROUPS?

At this point, you may be wondering the reason for using two groups in the first place. There are usually two reasons:

First, *our goal may be to compare the two groups* for which one person cannot be a member of both groups—for example, the perception of sophistication garnered from women of 18–25 years of age versus the perception of sophistication of women ranged 26–32 years of age. In that case, there would likely be *one design* that each group would experience. (Of course, we can repeat this test separately for several designs.)

The second reason for having two groups of people would be *to compare two designs with similar groups of people, and it is not appropriate for the same person to experience both designs.* Of course, if it is appropriate for the same person to evaluate both designs, this may be a better choice—we cover that case in the next chapter (Chapter 3).

Why not? Well, sometimes you'll want to eliminate the "learning curve" from having experienced the first design affecting the person, so he/she cannot give an objective evaluation of the second design.

Here's an analogy: in a medical experiment, you have two different medicines, both of which might be a safe and effective cure for a medical problem. Although there are rare exceptions (crossover designs—two or more treatments are applied to the same subject; there is the advantage of needing fewer subjects, but the disadvantage is that there may be a carryover effect from the first treatment administered to the second treatment administered), you would not give the same person each of the two medications to determine which is more effective, since, after a person has taken one medication, his/her medical condition has likely changed.

We realize that we're stretching the analogy a little bit, but not too much! Indeed, if the two designs are like the two medications—in this case, it is the "perspective" or "experience" that has changed and would not allow an independent evaluation to be made of a second design experienced by the same person.

The second variation of comparing two samples, called "two-sample t-test with paired data," represents the case where the same people are evaluating the two designs. As we noted earlier, that is the subject of the next chapter.

2.5 MADEMOISELLE LA LA REDUX

Armed with this knowledge (and this book!) you're ready to jump into action as the UX researcher to determine the winner through a t-test with independent samples. Now, there are lots of ways to collect this data, but probably the most economical and most efficient way to collect the data is using online surveys.

An online survey is one of the easiest ways to collect attitudinal data from your target audience. Typically, surveys contain some combination of open-ended comments, binary yes/no responses, Likert-type rating scales, Net Promoter scales, and more.

In the case of Mademoiselle La La, you'll probably want to construct two different surveys. Each is identical except for the design shown. One will collect basic demographic data (gender, age, income, etc.) and then go on to reveal a new design. The survey will then probe on several different variables: organization of the page, aesthetics, whether the page evokes attributes (in this case, sophistication), and then rate agreement with some kind of bottom line question, like "This home page is sophisticated."

Now, let's look specifically at using Excel or SPSS to perform the independent samples t-test on the data collected from our fictional survey.

SIDEBAR: YOU DON'T NEED THE SAME NUMBER OF PARTICIPANTS IN EACH GROUP

Before we dive in, it's important to note that we do *NOT* need to have the same number of people evaluating each design, although if one were allocating people to each design, it would be most efficient to split the folks in half, or as close as you can get to a 50/50 split.

SIDEBAR: LOW SAMPLE SIZE MAY MEAN LOW POWER

We can use the same hypothesis test framework, and fix the significance level at whatever you wish (usually, 0.05), regardless of the sample size; this controls the probability of rejecting H0 when it is true (called a "type 1 error")—one way an incorrect conclusion can be reached. However, there is another way of reaching an incorrect conclusion, and that is to accept H0, when, indeed, it is false. This is called a "type 2 error." The probability of this happening is one we usually do not control, and cannot even compute unless we pick some very specific H1 scenario that would typically be arbitrary (after all, if we don't even know for sure if the means are equal or unequal, it is very unlikely we would ever know exactly how unequal they are if they are unequal!!). The probability of this type of accepting H0 when it is false decreases as the sample size increases (ceteris paribus). The complement of this probability of incorrect conclusion, which would be the *probability of rejecting H0 when it is false* (a good thing!), is called the *power* of the (hypothesis) test. With a small sample size, the power of the test is often smaller than you might like (and correspondingly, the probability of accepting H0 when it is false, the type 2 error probability, is higher than one might like it to be). Of course, it is difficult to quantify this notion of power when we cannot sensibly determine the actual probabilities. Nevertheless, we repeat the key point of the sidebar. If the sample size is small, it is possible that, although you can still control (say, at 0.05) the probability of rejecting H0 when it is true, you may be conducting a hypothesis test with a low amount of power.

You check your latest survey results and see you have a sample size of 18. That is, 18 people have rated Design 1 on a 1–5 Likert scale, where you ask respondents to rate agreement or disagreement with statements like: "This is a sophisticated design," and "1" represents "strongly disagree," and "5" represents "strongly agree." (The 5-point scale is: Strongly Disagree, Disagree, Neutral, Agree, Strongly Agree). You also have collected a sample size of 20 data points on Design 2; i.e., these 20 people saw Design 2 and responded to the same statement and using the same scale. The data is in Table 2.1.

The (sample) means for the ratings of the two designs (columns of Table 2.1) are 4.22 and 3.40, respectively.

Again, let us remember that there are 38 different people in this study. We are testing the hypotheses:

$$H0 : \mu1 = \mu2$$
$$H1 : \mu1 \neq \mu2$$

where $\mu1$ = the true mean of the sophistication level with Design 1, and $\mu2$ = the true mean of the sophistication level with Design 2. And we believe it is worth

Table 2.1 Illustrative Data from a 5-Point Scale

Design 1	Design 2
4	4
5	5
5	5
2	2
4	2
4	3
4	2
5	4
5	2
4	4
5	2
5	4
5	4
4	5
5	5
2	2
4	4
4	4
	3
	2

repeating: the sample means of the two samples above are almost surely[1] *not* equal to the respective "true means." That is, before we do the analysis, we are not sure whether the difference in the sample means (4.22 − 3.40 = 0.82) is indicative of a real difference in the true means if we could magically collect data from *all* clients of Mademoiselle La La (current and future!). After all, if the true means are indeed equal, the means of the two *samples* will still very likely be different![2]

Thus, we're left with the question of whether the difference of 0.82, given the variability among the values within each group/column and the sample sizes of 18 and 20, is a large enough difference to believe in H1—that there is a real difference!! This is exactly what an independent samples t-test will determine. We will first perform the test in Excel, then in SPSS.

2.5.1 **EXCEL**

First, you go to the "data" tab on the Excel ribbon and click on "Data Analysis" (not shown under the data tab, but on the extreme right at the top, as we saw in Chapter 1)—which you have, indeed, activated as discussed in Chapter 1. Then highlight "t-Test: Two-Sample Assuming Equal Variances." (See arrow in Figure 2.3.) This command in Excel implies the t-test is for independent samples.

Then[3] you click on the highlighted command and consider the dialog box that comes up. Fill in the location of each "variable"—i.e., tell Excel where each column of data you wish to use is located.

From Figure 2.4, you can see that the first design's data ("variable 1") is b2–b19, while the data from the second design ("variable 2") is located in c2–c21. Experienced Excel users may find other, perhaps more efficient, ways to enter the location of the data.

It can also be seen in Figure 2.4 that we have requested that the output be put on a new worksheet (i.e., page!!) that we named "jared"—see the bottom, vertical arrow.

Finally, you click on "OK" in the upper right corner (see "thick arrow" in Figure 2.4). This will provide the output on the "jared" worksheet shown in Figure 2.5.

---

[1] We wish to thank Dr. Robert Virzi for several comments about this chapter and pointing out that the means could possibly be equal, even though it might be extremely unlikely. If we were describing a true normal distribution, in which each data value is theoretically carried to an infinite number of decimal places (assuming, theoretically, there is a measuring device that could do this!!), then the sample mean and true mean would have zero chance of being equal. However, in a case in which the value of a data point is an integer from 1 to 5, there is a chance, likely very small—depending on the sample size and population size—that the two means would be equal. However, the essential thought expressed is still a valid one for all practical purposes.

[2] The same issue arises with this sentence. And, again, the probability that the two sample means are equal is not literally zero. If each sample has $n = 2$, the probability the two sample means are equal is about 13%. It will decrease as the n's increase.

[3] Note that there is another command right underneath the highlighted one that says "t-Test: Two-Sample Assuming Unequal Variances," which is misnamed in Excel (!) and should be "t-Test: Two-Sample Not Assuming Equal Variances." This usually gives a fractionally different result from the test we are doing, one that is rarely materially different, and we shall illustrate this command later in this section.

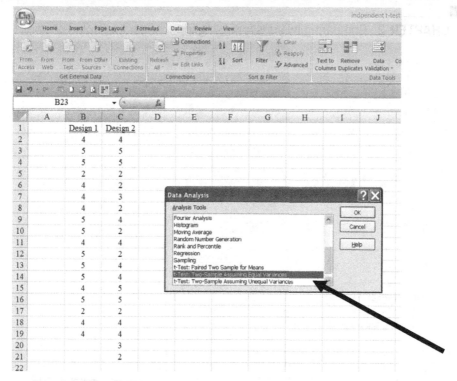

FIGURE 2.3

Opening Data Analysis and highlighting desired technique.

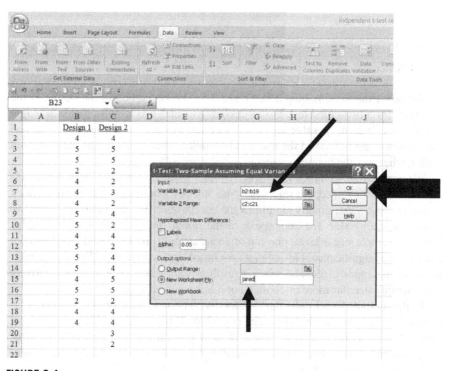

FIGURE 2.4

Opening up and filling in "t-test: two-sample assuming equal variances."

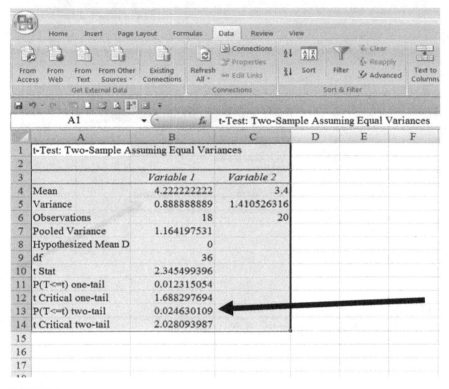

FIGURE 2.5

Excel output.

We now examine this output in Figure 2.5. The key value on the output is the "*p*-value" for a two-tailed test. We discussed "*p*-value" and its importance at length in Chapter 1. Indeed, "*p*-value says it all" was the "mantra" we wished to impart, and we see that again here. And the test was two-tailed—that is automatic, as discussed earlier, whenever the hypothesis test is an "=" versus "≠."

We repeat what we noted in Chapter 1—the "*p*-value says it all" refrain pertains only to whether we accept or reject H0. And, nobody would deny that the software's giving us the *p*-value greatly simplifies the accept/reject H0 decision. However, we agree that the *p*-value does not speak to the *practical significance* of the results. When the sample size is large, one can often get a significant statistical result without any practical significance. However, as we noted, most studies in UX involve relatively small sample sizes, and when a result is significant when using a relatively small sample size, far more often than not it has practical significance also.

In this output, Excel calls the *p*-value by "P(*T* < = *t*) two-tail." See arrow in Figure 2.5. And, we see that the value is 0.0246. This is below 0.05, the traditional standard for significance, so we reject H0 and go with H1, and thus conclude that *there is sufficient evidence to be convinced that the true mean sophistication ratings of the two designs are different.*

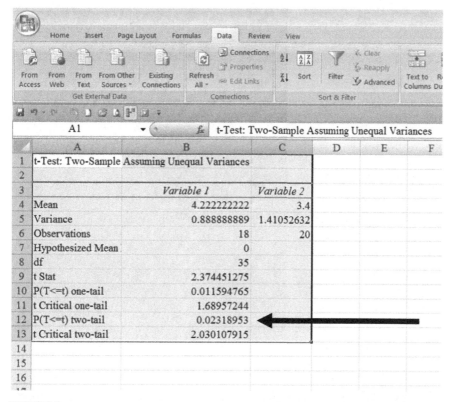

FIGURE 2.6

Alternative Excel output.

If we run the test that is called "t-Test: Assuming Unequal Variances," we get the output in Figure 2.6. If you do not assume that there are equal variances, the test needs to be performed a bit differently, and in some sense is not as accurate (lower value of "power") and the results (i.e., p-value) change. We do not believe that it is fruitful to go into more detail about this. If you want to be thorough, you can run each test. The authors have run many of these tests and, while it is possible, have never found the results to yield a p-value on one side of 0.05 under one assumption and over 0.05 for the other assumption. As we will see, in SPSS, the software indicates which of the two tests is appropriate.

Notice that the p-value is 0.0232 (see arrow in Figure 2.6), as opposed to the earlier 0.0246, a difference of 0.0014, a truly negligible difference.

2.5.2 SPSS

Now, we illustrate the same analysis in SPSS. In SPSS, we must type in the data for both sets of participants into one column, and then designate which data point is garnered from Design 1 and which data point is garnered from Design 2. So, the data would be input as in Figure 2.7.

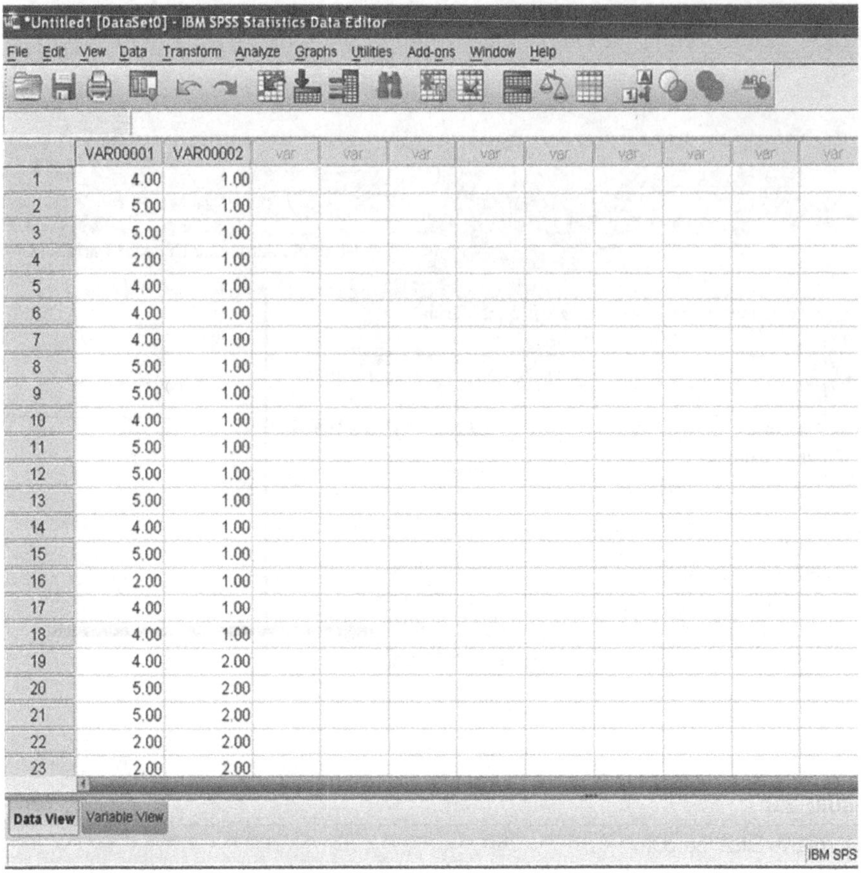

FIGURE 2.7

Data in SPSS format.

In Figure 2.7, the data actually consist of 38 rows (18 for Design 1 and 20 for Design 2), but they did not all fit on one screen. Note that in the "Design" (VAR00002) column, the first 18 entries are "1's"; the next 20 are "2's," although you can see only the first 23 rows.

Next, pull down the "Analyze" menu, choose "Compare Means," and then "Independent Samples t-test," as per the illustration in Figure 2.8. See arrows in Figure 2.8.

Click on "Independent Sample t-test" to produce the dialog box shown in Figure 2.9.

As is always the case for SPSS, and as we have seen, all of the variables are listed on the left. We can enter "Variable View" (in the bottom left of Figure 2.9) and rename the variable 1: Sophistication, and variable 2: Design, or any other names you wish to give.

We now drag "Sophistication" (VAR00001) to the "test variable" box (the variable or outcome on which we wish to know whether there is a difference) and "Design"

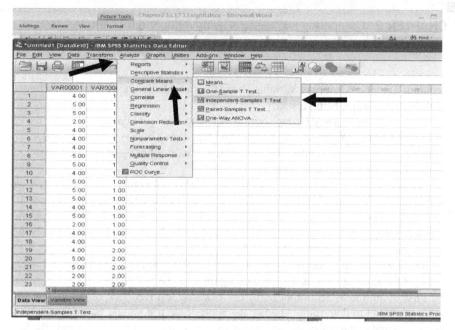

FIGURE 2.8

Performing the Independent-Samples t-test analysis in SPSS.

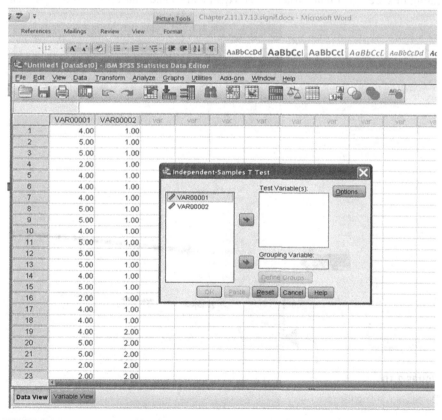

FIGURE 2.9

Dialog box for Independent-Samples t-test.

(column 2) to the "Grouping Variable" box (the variable that represents the different usability approaches being tested).

Next, click the "Define Group" button (see long arrow in Figure 2.10), which will open the "Define Groups" dialog box. Within that dialog box, type in a "1" and a "2" to reflect what we have called the two groups (i.e., designs)—see dashed arrow in Figure 2.10. We called them, indeed, "1" and "2."

Now click on the "Continue" button (curved arrow in Figure 2.10). The question marks next to "design—VAR000002" in the Grouping Variable box will become "1" and "2," the Define Groups box disappears, and we are almost done. Back on the original dialog box, just click the "OK" button (see thick arrow in Figure 2.10). Now, we see the output in Figure 2.11.

There are several things noteworthy about the SPSS output, even though we naturally get the same answer as obtained doing the analysis with Excel.

First of all, the SPSS output performs a Levene test (left side of output, circled in Figure 2.11) to determine whether the appropriate test should be the one which assumes equal variances or the one that does not assume it (n.b., SPSS labels the latter correctly, as "equal variances not assumed."). In this case, the Levene test p-value is 0.046 (recall that SPSS refers to "p-value" as "Sig."), which is under 0.05, indicating that we reject that variances are equal and should, thus, go with the test that

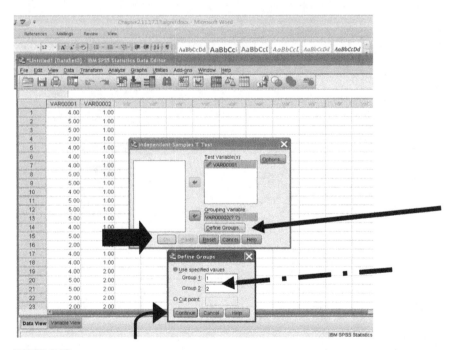

FIGURE 2.10

Details of running the test.

indicates they are not assumed equal. (Of course, as we saw in the Excel output, and see here again, it does not really matter which one we use—there is no material difference between the two *p*-values.)

What the Levene test says is that we should use the "Sig." (i.e., *p*-value) of 0.023 (the 0.0232 of Excel rounded to three digits), instead of the 0.025 (the 0.0246 of Excel rounded to three digits). See arrow in Figure 2.11. (As noted earlier in the Excel section, this is not a material difference.)

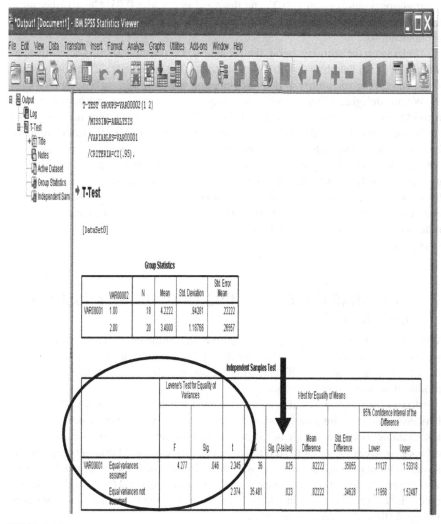

FIGURE 2.11

SPSS output.

And therefore, we reach the same conclusion as we did from the Excel analysis: we reject H0, and go with H1, and thus conclude that there is *sufficient evidence to be convinced that the true mean sophistication values for the two designs are actually different.*

In essence, the *p*-value of 0.023 is saying that a difference of 0.82 (or more) in the sample means of the two designs has only a 2.3% probability of occurring if the true means are, indeed, the same (i.e., if H0 is true).

If you were Perry Mason or Columbo or any lawyer (OK, we're dating ourselves), you might even say that the difference is "beyond a reasonable doubt," since the traditional cutoff point is 0.05 and the *p*-value is under 0.05. Clearly, the direction of the difference is that Design 1 is better (i.e., the design with the *higher* mean sophistication).

Underneath the software hood, the value of 0.023 (or the 0.025) is determined as a function of (1) the observed difference in the means (the 0.82), (2) the two sample sizes, and (3) the *variability* of the sophistication values within each design.

We are delighted that the software does all the necessary mathematics, and provides us the *p*-value, so we avoid doing all the math—with a not-so-simple set of formulas involved. And we also avoid needing to go to a t-table (remember your undergrad stats course?) and finding the critical value for determining whether a "result is significant"—a synonym for a result that rejects H0. By getting a significant result, we have a clear decision about which design should be viewed as superior (as measured by mean sophistication). Ultimately, to get our answer (accept H0 or reject H0), all we had to do is observe the *p*-value and note whether it was above or below 0.05. Thus, again, the "mantra": *p-value says it all.*

2.6 BUT WHAT IF WE CONCLUDE THAT THE MEANS AREN'T DIFFERENT?

What if we did not find a significant result (i.e., a significant difference between the means for the two designs) and thus, the data did not indicate a clear winner between the two designs? And what if increasing the sample sizes with another survey still produced no significant difference?

If there is no clear winner, there's no need to run for the hills with your tail between your legs. Invariably, other factors will help your team make a decision. For example: one design may be cheaper to implement because it contains original artwork, whereas the other design relies on expensive licensed photography. Or one design is more expensive because it will mean 2 weeks of Flash programming work, while the other design requires none. Perhaps you use Design 2 (the couple under the umbrella) because you're launching the new home page in the fall, and you switch to Design 1 (the café scene) come spring.

In any case, you've done your job—and you're ready to unveil the results.

SIDEBAR: CAN I USE A HIGHER ALPHA?

We should at this point note again what a p-value means. If the p-value is, for example, 0.04, this says that assuming H0 is true, the probability of finding the result we found from the data, or a result further away from what H0 says (at the equal to point), is 0.04. We typically set a benchmark of 0.05, and if the probability expressed by the p-value is under 0.05, we call it "significant," and reject H0. However, what if the p-value is 0.20? This would not be called a significant result. Still, it does indicate that if H0 is true, the aforementioned probability is 0.20; some might view this as indicating that there is an 80% chance that H0 is false, and further, view that as a reason to "bet on" H1. This reasoning is faulty for some subtle reasons way beyond the scope of the text, that have to do with Bayesian statistics and prior probabilities. This is why the classical statistics approach of hypothesis testing that threads throughout this text has survived for so long and is routinely utilized as we have described it.

2.7 FINAL OUTCOME AT MADEMOISELLE LA LA

As UX researcher at Mademoiselle La La, you're now ready to confidently announce the winner. After all, the p-value of 0.023 is saying that a difference of 0.82 (or more) between the means of the two designs has only a 2.3% probability of occurring if the true means are actually the same. That's pretty low, so you're able to deliver the news: the higher sophistication mean of 4.22 for Design 1 over Design 2's 3.40 clearly makes Design 1 the better choice for new home page.

That is, "better" from the perspective of sophistication as determined by a sample from your target audience. Your analysis has shown that perceptions for the image of the young girl being adored by the handsome young man are more "sophisticated" than that of the couple in the rain, clutching the single umbrella. The reason for that perception difference is another matter, and perhaps one that you'll be asked to explore. But for now, just knowing the perception difference exists is tangible progress.

At the next creative staff meeting, you're ready for the inevitable question from Creative Director Kristen McCarthey:

"So Sherlock, what did the survey tell us about the designs? You got a winner?"

"Yes," you calmly reply. "I have some reliable results."

You connect your laptop to the projector and show the group some screen shots from your Excel output. You show the sample sizes, individual scores, means, and p-values. You're ready for your short and sweet proclamation:

"What the survey data shows is that Design 1 is perceived as more sophisticated than Design 2 by representative members of our target audience of women ages 18–55 with well-above-average disposable income. Design 1 got a 4.22 compared to 3.40 for Design 2. Furthermore, the low p-value of 0.023 means that we have a statistically significant difference between the two designs. We should launch with Design 1."

A hush settles over the conference room. Your colleagues seem impressed, but McCarthey isn't ready to concede anything yet.

"What's your sample size?" she asks.

"18 for Design 1 and 20 for Design 2," you reply.

"How can you make any conclusions with such a small sample size?" she retorts with a huff.

"The *p*-value of .023 is saying that a difference of .82 (or more) in the sample means of the two designs has only a 2.3% probability of occurring if the true means are, indeed, the same."

She pauses, but has one more salvo: What do you mean by "true means?"

"The true means are the ones we could obtain if we were magically able to poll every customer we have. At last count, our database has roughly 33,000 customers, so it's not likely we'll able to get to them all. Thus, we have to use a representative sample and statistical techniques to make predictions about the true means."

"Hmm...," McCarthey says, staring down at her ubiquitous iPhone. You sense retreat. She punches in a quick text to an unknown recipient, then gets up and bolts for the door, saying: "OK, let's go with Design 1."

As the team streams out of the meeting, Autumn Taylor seems to be taking the news in stride despite the fact that her design lost. She approaches you and whispers: "Hey, I'm really glad we did that survey, for a number of reasons. First, at least I know we're choosing the design based on data and statistics, and not political maneuvering."

"No problem," you reply. "What's the other reason?"

"The fact that you were able to get McCarthey to back down. That's a first!"

2.8 ADDENDUM: CONFIDENCE INTERVALS

We learned in Chapter 1 how to construct a confidence interval for a true mean. We said then (and still believe!) that confidence intervals are very useful. In fact, since a sample mean does not come out equal to the true mean (except in an *extremely* rare case, where the numbers have been rounded and miracle of miracles, we find out later that the sample mean turns out equal to the true population mean), a sample mean is always more valuable to a decision maker if some measure of how far it might be off from the actual population mean is provided. Indeed, the degree of uncertainty is usually provided by a confidence interval.

A good way to provide a description of the potential range of values that the true mean might be is to insert a confidence interval on a bar chart of means, as we illustrated in Chapter 1. As we've noted, you can safely say that means are different if their confidence intervals do not overlap. However, it they do overlap, you cannot assume the means are not statistically different. Sadly, we've seen too many erroneous conclusions drawn regarding the *difference* of means because someone has simply eyeballed overlapping confidence intervals and proclaimed they were the same. We now consider and, indeed, illustrate, how this incorrect conclusion can come about.

Following this incorrect procedure *may* get you the correct answer, but that simply means you were lucky that the confidence intervals did not overlap. It is when the confidence intervals *do overlap* that you cannot be certain if H0 would be rejected by an independent samples t-test or not; conversely, you cannot conclude that H0 is accepted and that the means are equal.

The reason that this method does not work is somewhat subtle. It rests upon the fact that the correct confidence interval for the difference of two (independent sample) means is not the same as the difference in the separate confidence intervals—i.e., the confidence intervals for each mean separately.

Let us review what a confidence interval for the mean is. We will then show you an example in which the aforementioned decision process using the two separate confidence intervals will yield the incorrect answer.

A confidence interval for the mean is a statement about the value of the true mean. We take the sample average/mean and add and subtract an amount, "e," to form the confidence interval, where the software uses the sample mean, the variability in the data, and the sample size, along with the confidence level (which we talked about in Chapter 1 and noted that traditionally, the confidence level is 95%). So, if the sample mean is 4 (representing, say, the mean satisfaction with a design for some sample size), and the 95% confidence interval is 2.8–5.2 (note: the center of the interval is 4), this says that we are 95% confident that the interval 2.8–5.2 contains the *true mean* (i.e., the mean for the entire population of people who might use the design and fill out the satisfaction questionnaire). In looser terms, we are 95% confident that the true mean is between 2.8 and 5.2.[4]

Now consider the following two small data sets, one for each of two designs, with different people examining each design (indeed, making it an independent sample situation):

Design 1 Satisfaction Values	Design 2 Satisfaction Values
1	4
3	6
4	5
2	7

Let us refer to the sample means as (X-bar1) and (X-bar2) for Designs 1 and 2, respectively, and suppose a 10-point scale, 1–10. We have X-bar1 = 2.5 and X-bar2 = 5.5.

The 95% confidence intervals for the true means, $\mu 1$ and $\mu 2$ (we introduced the "μ notation" earlier), are:

---

[4]We note here that the highest value possible is 5. Therefore, you might view the confidence interval as 2.8–5. When the routine formulas for confidence intervals are used, no consideration of the practical maximum or minimum is applied.

$$\text{Design1}: 0.45 - 4.55$$
$$\text{Design2}: 3.45 - 7.55$$

And we can see that, indeed, the two confidence intervals overlap and not just by a tad—there is an overlap of 3.45–4.55. So, you may be prone to accept H0 and conclude that the *true means cannot be said to be different.*

However, when we perform the t-test for two independent samples, testing:

$$H0: \mu1 = \mu2,$$
$$H1: \mu1 \neq \mu2.$$

We get the output in Figure 2.12 from Excel; it would be the same exact results if we used SPSS.

We can see that the (two-sided) *p*-value is 0.0167 (see arrow in Figure 2.12), well below the traditional 0.05 cutoff point (and recall—a 0.05 cutoff point corresponds with a 95% confidence interval), and thus, based on this output, we would reject H0 (and, it's not even close!!), and conclude that *there is a difference in the true means for two designs.*

So, the above example clearly demonstrates that "eyeballing" overlapping confidence intervals and declaring means the same is playing with fire. You've been warned! ☺

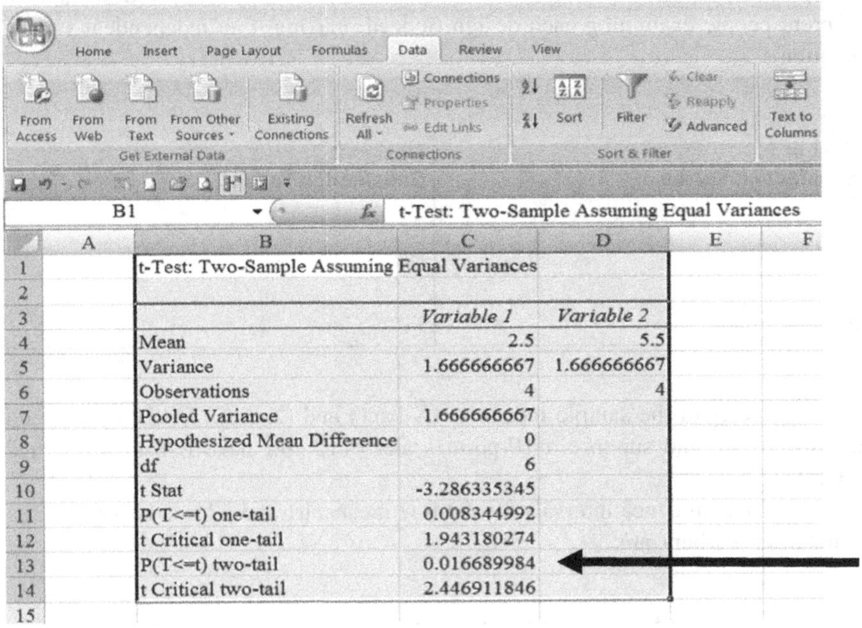

t-Test: Two-Sample Assuming Equal Variances		
	Variable 1	*Variable 2*
Mean	2.5	5.5
Variance	1.666666667	1.666666667
Observations	4	4
Pooled Variance	1.666666667	
Hypothesized Mean Difference	0	
df	6	
t Stat	-3.286335345	
P(T<=t) one-tail	0.008344992	
t Critical one-tail	1.943180274	
P(T<=t) two-tail	0.016689984	
t Critical two-tail	2.446911846	

FIGURE 2.12

t-test for comparison with confidence interval results.

> ### SIDEBAR: CONFIDENCE INTERVALS FOR THE *DIFFERENCE* IN MEANS
>
> There is actually a formula for a confidence interval for the *difference of two means* when you have independent samples. However, this formula is not available in Excel or SPSS.
>
> With this formula, you look at the resulting confidence interval and know to accept H0 when the confidence interval contains the value 0, and to reject H0 when the confidence interval does not contain 0.
>
> The formula exists on pages 70–71 of Sauro and Lewis (2012).

2.9 SUMMARY

In this chapter, we have presented the t-test for two independent samples. This test deals with comparing two sample means when, for our purposes, the two samples are composed of different people and, hence, are independent. We described the circumstances when the test should be used, discussed several situations where it can be used in the world of UX research, and illustrated its use in both Excel and SPSS. We ended the chapter with a cautionary tale and illustration concerning an incorrect use of confidence intervals to duplicate the results of the t-test for independent samples.

2.10 EXERCISE

1. Consider the case of the time it takes to perform a task and testing whether the mean time it takes for one task (T1) is the same as mean time it takes for another task (T2). Data for the times for each task are in data files in Excel (file name: Chapter 2.Exercise 1.data) and in SPSS (file name: Chapter 2..Exercise 1.data). The output in Excel is on sheet 2 and sheet 3 (respectively, assuming equal variances and not assuming equal variances). In SPSS the output is in a file (file name: Chapter 2..Exercise 1.output). All files are on a Web site indicated in the preface to the text.

   Test whether the mean times for T1 and T2 are equal or not.
   A word file (file name: Chapter 2.Exercise 1.discussion) is also provided, which discusses the results.

REFERENCE

Sauro, J., Lewis, J.R., 2012. Quantifying the User Experience: Practical Statistics for User Research. Elsevier.

Comparing two designs (or anything else!) using paired sample T-tests

3

3.1 INTRODUCTION

So, how do you feel, UX analytics guru? Did you blow 'em away with your stats prowess? How many impressed looks did you get when you started to talk "*p*-values?"

Well, don't get too cocky yet. The scenario we introduced with Mademoiselle La La in the previous chapter was pretty straightforward. You just launched a survey with two different designs to two different groups and just sat back to see which one would win.

The reality is that you often don't have the luxury of obtaining even the moderately small sample sizes illustrated in the previous chapter. Why? Because much of your job invariably revolves around conducting good, old-fashioned usability tests.

Standard usability tests are usually conducted with small samples sizes of 5–10 because (1) it's been established that larger samples sizes do not reveal more problems, and (2) conducting traditional lab studies with large populations is both time consuming and expensive.

SIDEBAR: SAMPLE SIZE: HOW MANY PARTICIPANTS DO YOU NEED FOR A USABILITY TEST?

One of the most contentious issues in the usability-testing field has been the appropriate sample size of participants needed to produce credible results. "How many participants are enough?" is an enduring question for practitioners, who often follow their intuition instead of relying on the research. They can hardly be blamed, since the research is sometimes contradictory. As a key decision that needs to be made before recruiting for the test, the sample size debate only muddies the waters when assessing the reliability of the practice of usability testing.

Virzi (1992), Nielsen and Landauer (1993), and Lewis (1994) have published influential articles on the topic of sample size in usability testing. In these articles, the authors presented a mathematical model for determining the sample size for usability tests. The authors presented empirical evidence for the models and made several important claims:

- Most usability problems are detected with three to five subjects.
- Running additional subjects during the same test is unlikely to reveal new information.
- Most severe usability problems are detected by the first few subjects. However, this claim is supported by Virzi's data—but not supported by Lewis' data, or Law and Hvannberg's data (2004).

Virzi's stated goal was to improve return on investment in product development by reducing the time and cost involved in product design. Nielsen and Landauer (1993) replicated and extended Virzi's (1992) original findings and reported case studies that supported their claims for needing only small sample sizes for usability tests.

Continued

SIDEBAR: SAMPLE SIZE: HOW MANY PARTICIPANTS DO YOU NEED FOR A USABILITY TEST?—cont'd

We usually try to have a sample size of at least 8 for our usability studies. Here's why:

1. Although you usually do see the same problems start to repeat after the first couple of participants, there are times when your first couple of participants are outliers. That is, they either zoom through all the tasks without finding a problem or they have difficulty with all of the tasks. In the scenario where your first 2 or 3 participants out of 5 fall into the "unrepresentative" category, you're relying on only 2 or 3 to "normalize" the data. That's a risk we'd rather not take.

    On the other hand, if you conduct the test with at least 8 participants, you have at least some "unrepresentativeness buffer" even if you run into 2 or 3 unrepresentative data points. That is, the impact of the outliers (which you do not know are outliers at that moment) is blunted somewhat by the larger sample size.

2. When you conduct your post task-completion rating scales, you're going to have a much better chance of avoiding the extremely wide (and, thus, not so useful) confidence intervals that can plague a small sample size. That means you're going to be much more confident of the rating scale results you deliver. And, often, we find that those rating scale results can complement the task completion rates, bolstering your case.

    Here's an example. Let's assume that only 2 out of 8 participants are able to complete the task "find a pair of running shoes in your size" on the retail clothing site you're testing. After the test, participants are asked to rate their agreement with the statement "Finding running shoes in my size is easy" on a scale of 1 to 5, where 1 = Strongly Disagree and 5 = Strongly Agree. Let's assume that there was an even split between "1" and "2" (4 each) for an average of 1.5 and a resulting 95% confidence interval for the true mean mating of 1.5 ± 0.45.

    Now assume that you ran the same test with only 4 participants and only 1 out of 4 participants was able to "find a pair of running shoes in your size." (This is the same 0.25 proportion of successful completions as in the example with a sample size of 8.) Again, after the test, participants are asked to rate their agreement with the statement "Finding running shoes in my size is easy" on a scale of 1 to 5, where 1 = Strongly Disagree and 5 = Strongly Agree. Again, let's assume that there was an even split between "1"s and "2"s (2 each). This time, you still have an average of 1.5, but now your confidence interval has more than doubled in size to 1.5 ± 0.92!

    In either case, your post-test rating scale data complement your task completion data, and bolsters the case that you really do have a problem with users finding shoes in their sizes. But, in the above example, with a sample size of 8, your confidence interval size was less than half of that for a sample size of 4, meaning you have, basically, more than *doubled* the accuracy or precision in your result. In a nutshell, you've greatly bolstered your case that users have a big problem finding running shoes in their size.

3. The preparation for creating and preparing a test for 4 versus 8 is almost the same. That is, it's the same amount of work to write up a test plan, define the tasks, get consensus on the tasks, and coordinate the assets for the test whether you're testing for 4 or 8. Admittedly, it's going to take longer to recruit and actually run the tests, but it's probably a difference of only one day of testing. But you will probably be able to report out your findings with much more statistical authority. It's analogous to making a big pot of chili for Sunday's football game; the prep time is the same whether you feed 2 or 8, and you'll invariably have some chili left over.

4. The larger sample sizes will also decrease the binomial confidence intervals for your actual proportion of task completions; you'll learn more about this topic in Chapter 4.

    For an excellent treatment on sample sizes—and specifically how to calculate exactly the correct number you'll need for different types of tests—we enthusiastically recommend "Quantifying the User Experience; Practical Statistics for User Research" by Jeff Sauro and James R. Lewis.

So, we know what you might be thinking: "How can I possibly use these advanced statistical techniques with sample sizes this small?" Well, we acknowledge that having only a small sample size is not ideal. But it's important to realize that, indeed, lots can be done with small sample sizes. The smaller the sample size, the larger the observed effect must be before we view it as a "real" effect, that is, indicative of there truly being an effect. Thus, it follows that when you conduct a test with a small sample size, you should not have an expectation of proving the existence of small, subtle effects. Quite often, in UX work, that's OK, because, like in most all fields, it's more important to find the large effects—which often you can find with the relatively small sample size.

3.2 VIGNETTE: HOW FAST CAN YOU POST A JOB AT BEHEMOTH.COM?

You're a usability researcher at Behemoth.com, an employment Web site. Behemoth. com is aptly named, because it's one of the largest job search engines in the world, with over 1 million job openings at any time, over 1 million resumes in the database, and over 63 million job seekers per month. Behemoth has over 5000 employees spread around the world.

Luckily for you, they realize the importance of usability testing and have built a gleaming new usability lab with all the bells and whistles: dedicated observation rooms, state-of-the-art software and hardware, and a dedicated recruiting team, so you don't have to do your own recruiting (which, by the way, is a royal pain in the neck). The company is located in an old nineteenth-century mill where the US Army made Civil War blankets, but now it buzzes with new millennium dot.com energy. It's a smarter, more pragmatic 2.0 Web; your execs learned the lessons of the late 1990s and aren't going to "get fooled again," to quote the Who. And by the way, all employees enjoy free lunch on Fridays.

Behemoth makes money in lots of ways, but one of the main sources of its income is from employers who (1) post jobs on the site and (2) buy access to its enormous database of resumes to search for good candidates to fill those jobs. (Conversely, most job seekers go to the site to simply look for jobs, and submit resumes and applications to those jobs; they provide no revenue stream for Behemoth.)

As a consequence, you and your UX colleagues are constantly under the gun to minimize the time it takes for job recruiters to post jobs on your job board. Quicker job postings mean more postings. More postings mean more traffic, more resumes, and more searching from paying employers.

The job posting process entails filling out a good old-fashioned form. And despite consensus from everyone on the Design Team that the form is way too long, the very nature of the company business mandates collection of the data. The insatiable database needs to be fed so that the typical job seeker can easily find jobs by location, salary range, minimum requirements of salary, education, work experience, skills, languages, etc. And the company recruiter needs to search resumes by the same criteria and more. In addition, the marketing folks want enough info, so they can constantly upsell (harass?) your current clients. For example, they need the client's industry, size, locations, contact information, etc., for targeted marketing campaigns.

On the one hand, the detailed information that needs to be submitted makes it easier to find a match between a job seeker and an employer. However, on the other hand, you hear from employers about how painfully long it takes to fill out the form practically every time you conduct a usability test with recruiters; they're constantly bellyaching about the "absurd" amount of time it takes to post a job. Even those existing clients with the luxury of prepopulated fields moan and groan. "When are you guys going to shorten this form?" they plead, "It takes me an hour to submit 3 jobs and I've got about 30 to do a day—do the math!"

Bad news travels quickly, and the new UX Director, Hans Blitz, is acutely aware of this condition. Now, he's on the rampage and wants to make sure that no recruiter who visits the site has to spend one extra nanosecond accomplishing his/ her tasks.

Blitz is a recent Hamburg transplant, where he ran UX for the Ottomeyer Group, the second biggest online European retailer, which generates average total e-commerce sales of $7.53 billion annually. Hair cropped tight and high with an intentionally scruffy beard, the double-earringed Blitz has crossed the pond to kick some "UX butt," as he puts it in his thick German accent. He's loud and abrasive, running meetings more like a military operation than a staff gathering. Furthermore, Blitz is skeptical of results produced in the usability lab and your colleagues who work in it; after viewing his first usability session at the Behemoth lab, he proclaimed: "I could train a monkey to run these kind of sessions."

Nevertheless, you're still shocked out of your socks when Blitz charges into the participant room, right in the middle of a usability session! The elderly woman who is the current test participant spins in her seat, befuddled and nervous, as Blitz bangs on the one-way glass between the participant room and the control room, screaming at you at a high volume so that he can overcome the soundproofing.

"Are you on this? Give me a job posting form that smokes!" he screams. "I want a recruiter to be able to post a new job in under 15 minutes!"

"Are you on this? Give me a job posting form that smokes!"

"Easier said than done," you say under your breath as he charges off. After reassuring the startled participant, you continue monitoring the current session, but your mind is elsewhere. "There are just so many mandatory fields…. What can possibly be cut?" you wonder to yourself.

You start to brainstorm with your fellow UX teammates on how to streamline the form. You actually find some fields that you might be able to cut if you can convince your marketing brethren to agree. And, there's always the possibility to make the form one long page instead of the current five-page "wizard." The assumption was that "wizards" helped keep folks on track and helped them understand where they were in the process. In addition, the Web is awash in "wizard frenzy;" every Web shop in town is building some kind of "wizard," whether it's figuring out your interest rate on your dream house or determining your risk of lung cancer. The "wizards" work…but, at what cost in total completion time?

Creative Director Andy Moodboard suggests to your designers that they come up with a one-page prototype of the job posting page. "Kill the five-page wizard, make it one page, don't worry about how long it scrolls…let's just see if it's faster. Let's get the comparison numbers to Hans quick!"

Realizing that "quick" means a standard usability session of 2 days with 10 participants (Moodboard would never give you 4 days to run a test!), you opt to use the hour of each session to time "virgin" participants as they fill out both the current form (the one with the five-page "wizard") and the new "long scroller," one after another. Of course, you'll counterbalance to ameliorate bias. You'll average the timing for each design and see if the new prototype speeds up the job posting process.

One group, two designs: enter the world of paired-samples t-tests.

3.3 INTRODUCTION TO PAIRED SAMPLES

As opposed to the scenario in Chapter 2, the fundamental characteristic here is that each person evaluates both designs. So, in essence, the satisfaction evaluation or the completion times are "paired." One person provides two data points and we know which two came from a given person.

Again, whether we are comparing the mean satisfaction with the two designs or the mean time it takes to perform a task with the two designs, there is no material difference in the analysis. That is, the software does not know, nor care, nor can it distinguish, whether the numbers are representing satisfaction scores, or whether the numbers represent times to perform a task.

Now, it may not be obvious why it matters whether we have independent samples or paired samples. While you can rest assured that it does matter (and the software does the right—but a bit different—process when told whether the samples are independent or paired), we will address this issue in more detail later in the chapter to give you a better sense of why it matters.

3.4 EXAMPLE OF PAIRED (TWO-SAMPLE) T-TEST

When we are comparing two means and the data have the same people providing measurements of both alternatives (the satisfaction rating of two designs, or the time for the performance of some task for two designs), we have what are referred to as "paired data." The term makes sense, in that a data point from one alternative is identifiably "paired" with a data point from the other alternative. As we stated earlier, this makes a difference in the precise way we perform the t-test. The hypotheses are the same as in the previous chapter:

$$H0: \mu1 = \mu2$$
$$H1: \mu1 \neq \mu2$$

Another way to notate the "pairing" of the data is by changing the above notation to

$$H0: \mu1 - \mu2 = 0$$
$$H1: \mu1 - \mu2 \neq 0,$$

and define $D = \mu1 - \mu2$, where D stands for "true average difference" (for the same person using the two alternatives) and writing

$$H0: D = 0$$
$$H1: D \neq 0$$

In other words, is the (true) average difference (D) between the time it takes a person to perform the two tasks zero (H0 is true) or not zero (H0 is false, H1 is true)? Recall from Chapter 1 that if we accept H0 (concluding that H0 is true), this really is saying that there is insufficient evidence to reject H0.

Let's illustrate the "paired-data t-test" using our job posting timing data for design 1 ("The Long Scroller") and design 2 ("The Wizard"). The particular data set has 10 people using each of two designs, and to ensure there is no "learning curve effect," we randomly had 5 of the participants use design 1 first and 5 of the participants use design 2 first. The 20 data points—recall that these data represent 10 participants using each of the two designs—are in Table 3.1.

As you can see in Table 3.1, some of the participants were very quickly filling out the form (e.g., participants 1 and 10, who required relatively little time to perform

Table 3.1 Task Completion Data (in minutes) for Two Competing Designs

Participant #	Design 1 "The Long Scroller"	Design 2 "The Wizard"
1	5.5	6.2
2	8.8	9.2
3	27.2	29.7
4	12.9	13.8
5	13.8	15.9
6	5.1	4.9
7	10.4	15.7
8	15.6	16.3
9	25.6	27.2
10	3.9	3.7
Mean	12.88	14.26

the task using either form type), while some of the participants were somewhat slow at the task (e.g., participants 3 and 9, who required a relatively long time to perform the task using each of the designs). We point this out, since it is related to why there is a difference in the specific way the t-test is carried out by the software, depending on whether the user indicates that it is an "independent t-test"—(as illustrated in the previous chapter) or a "paired t-test"—being illustrated in this chapter.

3.4.1 EXCEL

The means for the two designs are 12.88 minutes ("The Long Scroller") and 14.26 minutes ("The Wizard"). But, as we know from hypothesis testing logic, we do not yet know if this difference in sample means is indicative of a true difference in means. Of course, we might have a strong intuitive suspicion that the difference of nearly 1.5 minutes will indicate that there is a real difference; that the difference is large enough to reject H0. Perhaps; we'll see!

We enter the data as shown, and we open "Data Analysis" in Excel as depicted in Figure 3.1.

Note that the command "t-Test: Paired Two-Sample for Means" (see arrow in Figure 3.1) is directly above the commands examined in the previous chapter on t-tests for independent samples.

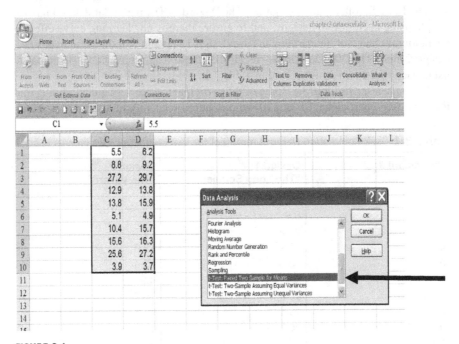

FIGURE 3.1

Opening data analysis to perform a t-test: paired two sample for means; Excel.

We click on the command and enter the location of each column of data (see arrows in Figure 3.2).

We continue to choose to ask for the analysis to appear on a new page (here, arbitrarily named "jared." See next to the last row in Figure 3.2: New Worksheet Ply).

After clicking "OK" in Figure 3.2, we obtain our output in Figure 3.3.

In examining the Figure 3.3 output, we see that the two-sided p-value is 0.0262, certainly less than the traditional $\alpha = 0.05$ (see arrow in Figure 3.3).

Thus, we reject H0, and, beyond a reasonable doubt, we conclude that there is a difference in mean time to post a job between the two designs; design 1 ("The Long Scroller") requires less time than design 2 ("The Wizard").

In other words, if the means for the two designs were the same after we magically tested with everyone on Earth, a difference in means that large $(14.26 - 12.88 = 1.38)$

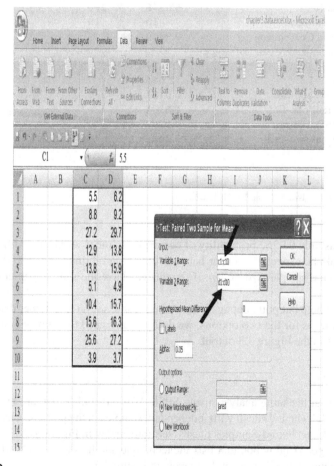

FIGURE 3.2

Entering the location of the two columns of data; Excel.

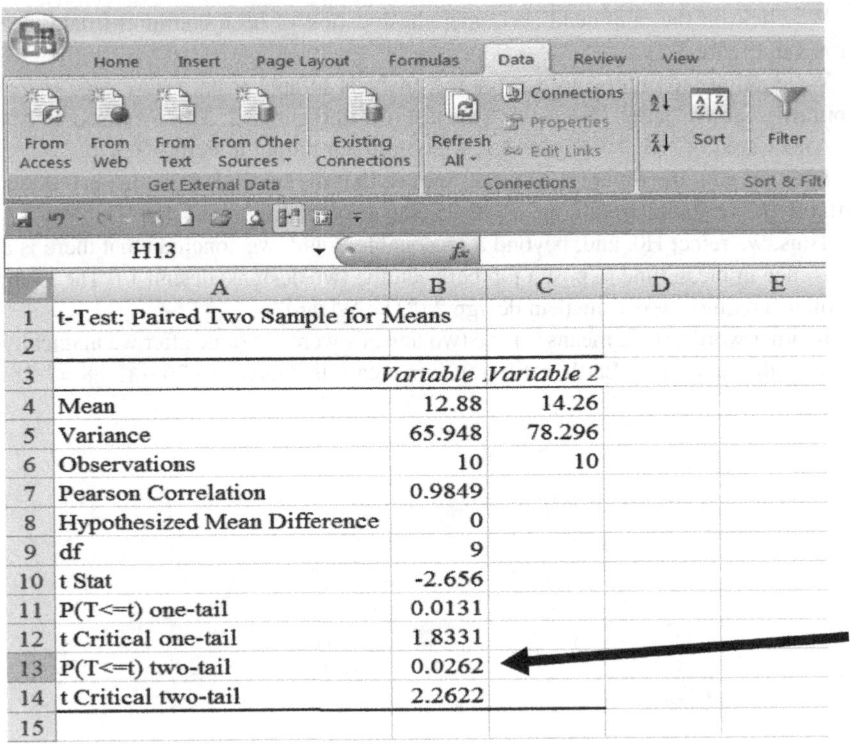

	A	B	C
1	t-Test: Paired Two Sample for Means		
2			
3		*Variable*	*Variable 2*
4	Mean	12.88	14.26
5	Variance	65.948	78.296
6	Observations	10	10
7	Pearson Correlation	0.9849	
8	Hypothesized Mean Difference	0	
9	df	9	
10	t Stat	-2.656	
11	P(T<=t) one-tail	0.0131	
12	t Critical one-tail	1.8331	
13	P(T<=t) two-tail	0.0262	
14	t Critical two-tail	2.2622	
15			

FIGURE 3.3

Output for paired two-sample t-test; Excel.

or larger has only 0.0262 probability of occurring. In other words, this difference in means would be expected to occur between only 2 and 3 times out of 100 attempts (with the same sample size of 10), if the designs have the same mean completion time.

We can't help but point out again how "the *p*-value says it all." Other than the all-important means for the two options, we do not really need to know anything about other values in the Figure 3.3 output.

3.4.2 SPSS

We now repeat the same analysis using SPSS. We start with "compare means," the same as we did when we dealt with independent samples in the previous chapter. But, now we click on "Paired-Samples t test" (see solid arrow in Figure 3.4).

Now we get a dialog box that lists the technique and lists on the left all the variables contained in the data sheet. See arrow in Figure 3.5.

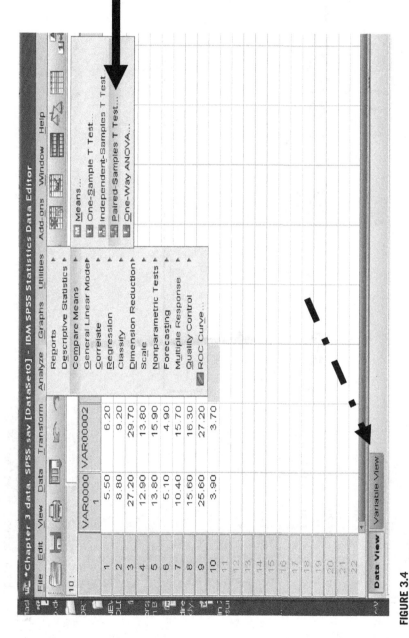

FIGURE 3.4

Opening paired-samples t-test in SPSS.

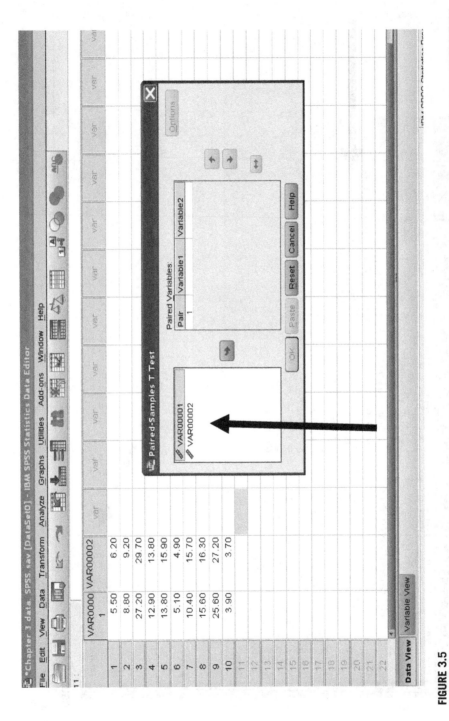

FIGURE 3.5

Dialog box for paired-samples t-test; SPSS.

> **SIDEBAR: USE ANY NAME YOU WISH**
>
> It may be noted that by clicking on "Variable View" (see dashed arrow in Figure 3.4), you can change the variable names to "design 1 time" and "design 2 time" or to "Long Scroller" and "Wizard," or to whatever names you wish. We did not do that here, since this is really an aesthetic issue and we want to keep full focus on the methodology and SPSS analysis process.

We now drag over one of the variables to the "variable 1" slot in Figure 3.5, and the other to the "variable 2" slot in Figure 3.5. Of course, we should keep track of which variable went where! The common sense approach (or "sanity preserver") is to place VAR00001 into "variable 1" and VAR00002 into "variable 2." This gives us the view in Figure 3.6.

Note above the arrows in Figure 3.6 that there is now an opportunity to compare a second pair of variables simultaneously, by placing variables in the second row, under "pair."

So, if we had a third option, we could, with the same set of SPSS commands, simultaneously compare, say, the Long Scroller with this third option. This is efficiency, in that we can perform two hypothesis tests in one fell swoop. Actually, we can compare even more than two sets of hypotheses. Each time you add a pair of

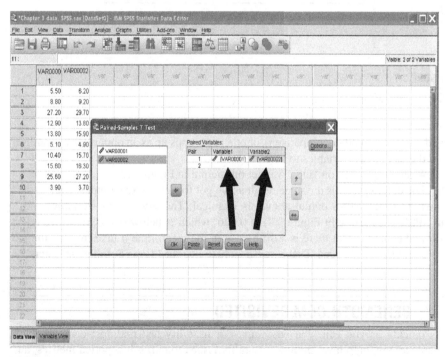

FIGURE 3.6

Entering the appropriate variables into their proper place. See arrows; SPSS.

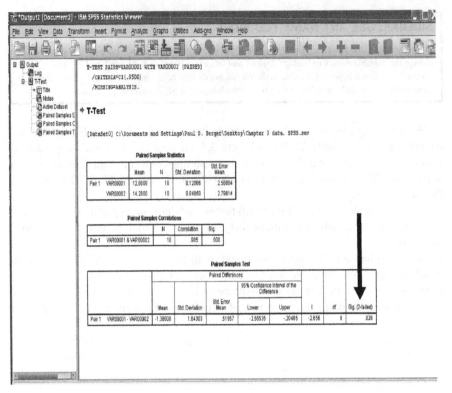

FIGURE 3.7

Output from SPSS.

variables (i.e., another comparison), another row pops up as an opportunity to add yet another set of two variables to be compared.

After we go click on "OK," we get our output in Figure 3.7.

The output gives us the same result as we got from the Excel output. The "T-stat" (just "t" in the SPSS output above) is identical. The *p*-value (as we know, "sig." in SPSS—see arrow in Figure 3.7) is 0.026, which is below α = 0.05, so we reject H0 and conclude that there is a difference in the mean time it takes to post the job between the two designs. That is, we conclude that the "Long Scroller" is faster.

3.5 BEHEMOTH.COM REVISITED

As quickly as you can, you write up your usability test findings: demographics, methodology, high-level findings, usability issues found, self-reported metrics, and of course, recommendations. Most importantly, you cut and paste the SPSS output into the report, circling the *p*-value.

Within moments of sending the report out to the team, Andy Moodboard charges into your cube, clutching the report: "Are you kidding me? The 'Long Scroller' was almost 1.5 minutes faster? That's amazing!"

"Yes," you calmly reply. "As much as we're wed to that 'Wizard,' the task times show the folks really get through the form faster with just a long scrolling vertical page."

"Wow," Andy breathes, "I never would have predicted that. I mean, we always thought the wizard would keep everybody focused, so they could finish it faster."

"Well, the data show otherwise. And that low *p*-value proves there's not much doubt that we would get the same result if we could magically test with our entire client base."

"Yeah, very cool," Andy says. "Listen, I'm gonna schedule a lunch meeting with Hans tomorrow so you can present the results. He's gonna love this stuff! You need any more prep time to finish up your report?"

"No, I'm fine with lunch tomorrow. Can you avoid ordering from that lame faux Italian place?"

"You can name the place from here on out!"

3.6 ADDENDUM: A MINI-DISCUSSION WHY THE INDEPENDENT AND PAIRED TESTS NEED TO BE DIFFERENT

You might wonder why there needs to be a different procedure performed by the software depending on whether we have two independent samples or we have two samples that are paired. After all, the hypotheses being tested are basically the same:

$$H0: \mu1 = \mu2$$
$$H1: \mu1 \neq \mu2$$

The main reason for the two approaches is a bit subtle and is due to the way variability is properly measured for each test. The hypothesis tests we have looked at all have one thing in common; they consider the difference in sample means and they put that difference in ratio to a measure of the variability in the data.

Here's why. The logic of why we consider the difference in means in ratio to the variability is that when there is a small amount of variability, the two sample means are relatively close to their respective "true values," and, therefore, a modest difference in sample means tends to indicate that the true means do, indeed, differ.

However, when there is a lot of variability in the data, the sample means may be quite far away from their respective true values, and it sensibly requires a larger difference in the sample means to be convinced that a real difference exists. By considering the ratio, this concept is accounted for.

So, granting the above, it is crucial to consider the proper measure of variability to use as the denominator. In other words, we need different variability measures to act as the proper denominator against which to compare sample means, depending whether we have independent data or paired data. Why? Read on, dear reader!

Consider the hypothetical case where we are comparing the weights of people before and after an "intervention." The "intervention" has the result that the "before" state is the person's normal weight in pounds and the "after" state is his/her weight a moment later, after picking up a handful of 1-pound weights and putting them in his/her pocket. The "intervention" in this example is a bit silly, but its purpose is to help you understand the issue. We have paired data and, say, $n = 6$ (i.e., 6 people in the study).

Let's assume that the "handful" is between five and seven 1-pound weights, depending on how big one's hand is (we told you it would sound a bit silly, but trust us—the point of the example will be made clear!). Suppose that the data values are as follows:

Before	After	d = Weight Gain
135	140	5
155	161	6
203	210	7
178	184	6
182	188	6
143	148	5

Notice that some "handfuls" were five 1-pound weights, while some were six 1-pound weights, and one person, apparently with larger hands, had a handful consisting of seven 1-pound weights. It is clear from the description of the problem that the true weight gain is not 0, and averages about 6.

So, when we test using the paired-data test, we write

$$H0: \mu1 = \mu2$$
$$H1: \mu1 \neq \mu2$$

which, as we noted earlier, can be "converted" to

$$H0: D = 0$$
$$H1: D \neq 0$$

Looking above at the "d" (weight gain) column, we find that the mean of $d = 5.833$, and there is overwhelming evidence that the true average difference (i.e., D) is near 6 and H0 should be, and will be, rejected. Indeed, the paired t-test output for this example is shown in Figure 3.8.

The result we get is what is expected. The two-sided p-value is extremely small, being 7.5 E−06 ("E" stands for "exponent of 10," meaning 7.5×10^{-6}, or a p-value of 0.0000075), indicating beyond a reasonable doubt that the "before" and "after" true means differ. Again, there's absolutely no surprise here; the sample means differ by 5.833, which is logical, given each person picks up between 5 and 7 pounds of extra weight. There is very little variability in the "d" column, and it's virtually impossible

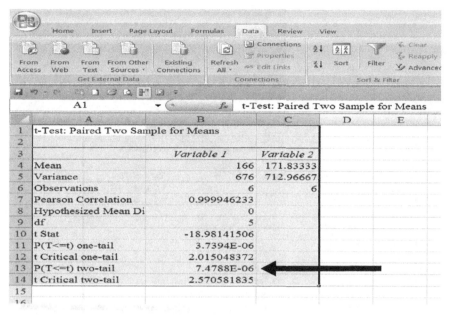

FIGURE 3.8

Output for illustrative example; Excel.

that the true mean could be zero and have every value of *d* between 5 and 7, and more 6's than any other value.[1]

However, if we take the same data and treat them as independent samples, we will get a very different answer! It will still be the case that the sample means differ by 5.833 pounds, but now, looking at the data as two different groups of people (i.e., 12 people, instead of 6 people, in the study), even with the right-hand column of people picking up the weights and putting them in their pocket—the difference of near 6 (i.e., 5.833) will not appear that impressive, given that the weights of individuals within each column vary a lot. So, the sample mean of column 1 is 166, but a 95% confidence interval for that value is 166 ± 27.3 or 138.7–193.3, *due to the large variability in weights of the 6 people in that column*. For the 6 people in column 2, the sample mean is 171.833 (5.833 higher than the 166), with a 95% confidence interval of 171.833 ± 28.0 or 143.833–199.833: again, *due to the large variability of weights of the 6 people in that column*. Given these relatively wide confidence intervals for the true means (and, indeed, they overlap to a larger extent than they don't!), it is clear that the true means could easily be the same. In fact, if we perform the two-sample t-test for independent samples, we get the output in Figure 3.9, with a *p*-value 0.7095 (see arrow in Figure 3.9), nowhere near to being significant.

---

[1] By the way, if you wanted to make the argument that here, it makes more sense to consider the one-sided *p*-value (it's really a case of "Is there an increase or not?"), then we cut the two-sided *p*-value in half, getting even a tinier value: 3.74 E –06.

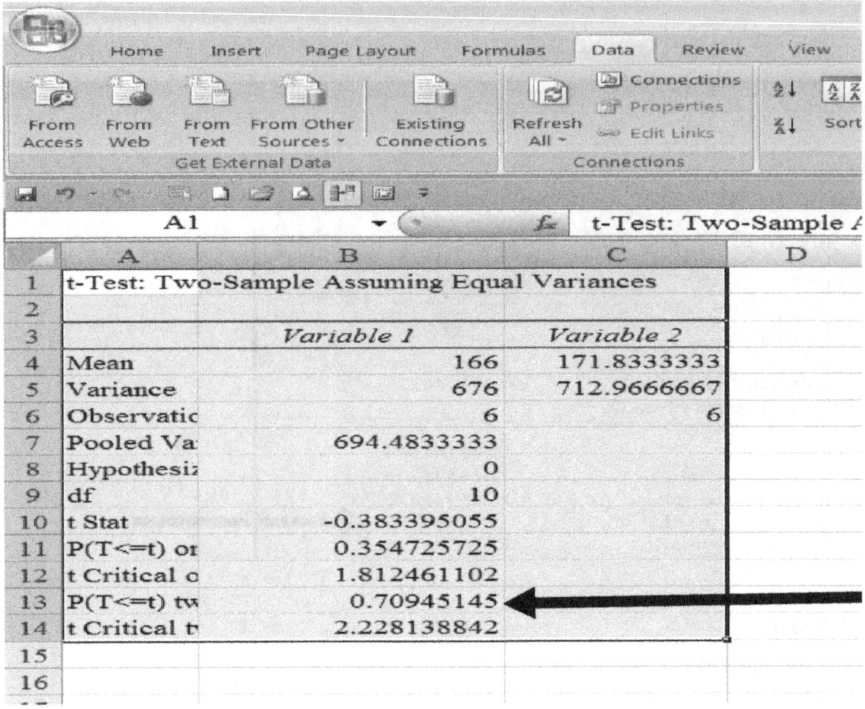

FIGURE 3.9

Output when data incorrectly treated as independent samples; Excel.

The bottom line is that the variability in weights of the individuals before the intervention should not matter if it is paired data, while it should (and indeed, does—in a big way!) when having independent samples.

Fortunately, we don't have to really worry about this detail. All we need to do is to correctly tell Excel or SPSS whether we have independent samples or paired samples—pretty nifty, right[2]?

3.7 SUMMARY

In this chapter we have presented the t-test for testing equality of means using paired data. We described what paired data indicates, how to instruct Excel and SPSS that paired data are being analyzed, illustrated the paired-data t-test in both Excel and SPSS, and

---

[2] By the way, we have not mentioned finding a confidence interval in the context of having paired data. However, finding a meaningful confidence interval and error bar for paired data can be done. It would require first subtracting one column from another, row by row, and finding a single confidence interval and error bar on the resulting difference column.

discussed how to interpret the results. We ended the chapter with an optional detailed discussion of why independent samples and paired samples must be analyzed differently to arrive at correct results.

3.8 EXERCISE

1. Consider the case of satisfaction with a design in a scenario where 20 people each experience two different designs (i.e., paired data). Test whether the average satisfaction is the same for both designs. Data for the satisfaction for each design are in data files in Excel (file name: Chapter 3.Exercise 1.data) and in SPSS (file name: Chapter 3..Exercise 1.data). The output in Excel is on sheet 2. In SPSS the output is in a file (file name: Chapter 3..Exercise 1.output).

A Word file (file name: Chapter 3..Exercise 1.discussion) is also provided, which discusses the results.

REFERENCES

Law, E.L.C., Hvannberg, E.T., 2004, October. Analysis of strategies for improving and estimating the effectiveness of heuristic evaluation. In: Proceedings of the third Nordic conference on Human-computer interaction. ACM, pp. 241–250.

Lewis, J.R., 1994. Sample sizes for usability studies: Additional considerations. Human Factors 36, 368–378.

Nielsen, J., Landauer, T.K., 1993. A mathematical model of the finding of usability problems. In: Proceedings of ACM INTERCHI'93 Conference. ACM Press, Amsterdam, Netherlands, pp. 206–213.

Virzi, R.A., 1992. Refining the test phase of usability evaluation: how many subjects is enough? Human Factors: The Journal of the Human Factors and Ergonomics Society 34 (4), 457–468.

Pass or fail? Binomial-related hypothesis testing and confidence intervals using independent samples

4

4.1 INTRODUCTION

Task success is a fundamental metric for any UX researcher who regularly conducts usability testing. After all, the *sine qua non* of usability testing is tasks. Without them, you don't have a usability test. You painstakingly write them, tweak them, meet about them, get feedback from your colleagues on them, argue about them, try to get consensus, tweak them some more…all the way up until test time. And depending on what happens during your pilot test, they can change *again*.

And for good reason. Although there are lots of variables that go into creating a usability test that will yield good results, the single most important variable is the quality of the tasks. Clear, incisive ones yield meaningful, actionable data; flabby, ambiguous tasks yield garbage. Writing good tasks is one of the most important things you do to prepare for a usability test, hands down. So, it's easy to see that pass/fail is a fundamental metric that you should always deliver for each task. As a matter of fact, the task completion tally should probably go into your executive summary or near the top of your presentation.

SIDEBAR: YOUR CURE FOR A.D.D.!

The audience for your usability test presentation will always sit up and take notice when you present the task completion rates, even if they "multitask" and nod off for the rest of your presentation. It's universally understood and carries immediate impact. You can spend a thousand words describing a particular usability problem or application until you're blue in the face (as our mothers might say), and still get more audience reaction by saying "only one out of eight participants completed the task." In the world of today, where it is harder and harder to get and maintain a person's attention, it's often the only thing an audience member will take away from your presentation.

And as you're probably aware, no usability test consists of just one task. (Well, not in our experience, anyway.) You typically have anywhere from 5 to 15 of them, depending on what you're testing, what you're trying to find out, how much time you have for the test, and how much time you're willing to spend on each task. In our experience, 10 tasks is about the average number of tasks for a 1-hour usability test.

So, multiple tasks mean multiple task success rates, which naturally lead to comparisons. After all, your design-and-development team probably wants to fix the most egregious problems while leaving the less severe problems to fix in a future release. But, how do you discern, for example, whether the result of 7 failures out of 10 for a particular task are really more severe than the result of 5 failures out of 10 for another task? Read on!

4.2 CASE STUDY: IS OUR EXPENSIVE NEW SEARCH ENGINE AT BEHEMOTH.COM BETTER THAN WHAT WE ALREADY HAVE?

Let's return to our favorite employment Web site, Behemoth.com, where you were hired as usability researcher. As we mentioned in Chapter 3, Behemoth.com is aptly named, because it's one of the largest search engines for jobs in the world, with over a million job openings at any time, over a million resumes in the database, and over 63 million job seekers per month. Behemoth has over 5000 employees spread around the world.

You'll recall from the last chapter that one of the main sources of Behemoth's income is from employers who post jobs on the site and buy access to its enormous database of resumes to search for good candidates to fill those jobs. (Conversely, most job seekers go to the site and simply look for jobs and submit resumes and applications to those jobs; they provide no direct revenue stream to Behemoth.)

Because the resume is the lifeblood of Behemoth, as UX researcher you are constantly tasked with improving the usability and usefulness of the resume search engine to keep recruiters happy, which in turn keeps the gravy train rolling. And, as you talk to recruiters and managers during your nonstop usability testing on other projects, the discussion inevitably turns to the search engine.

Basically, the search engine seems to be working fine, but it's much more effective for those savvy recruiters who know how to construct clever Boolean search strings that yield results that get them what they want. For example, a savvy hi-tech recruiter may construct a Boolean string like this:

C++ java -jobs -samples intitle:resume OR inurl:resume

Once he/she has constructed a sophisticated Boolean string that delivers qualified candidates, the recruiter archives the string along with other effective strings, building up a Boolean arsenal. When different requirements are needed for a particular position, the recruiter simply tweaks an existing string to yield good results.

So, what's the rub? The veteran recruiters are good at it, but the newbies struggle.

And when they struggle, they complain to you, since you're in the line of fire. (It's often easier to complain to a UX researcher than a customer rep.) "When are you guys gonna fix the resume search?" they whine. "It takes me *forever* to find somebody decent."

Evidently, the level of complaining has reached a crescendo, because Behemoth decides to improve its search engine asap. But instead of improving what they have, Behemoth top brass has decided to shop for an entirely new engine that is "plug and play." You hear rumblings about the search engine RFP (Request for Proposal) process, but no one bothers to ask UX if they want to conduct some basic usability testing on the search engines the Behemoth brass are considering. The "search for the new search" seems to go on forever, and the trickle down of information is scant.

Finally, you hear through the grapevine that Behemoth has swallowed up a Palo Alto job search engine named Novix—or the mind-warping price of $80 million. Joey Velluci, Behemoth's Chief Executive Officer, calls an all-hands meeting to unveil the new search engine. In a grand ceremony in Behemoth's massive auditorium, he first launches a slickly produced video, where an attractive woman extolls the virtues of Novix's new "Turbo Search." The woman declares that Turbo will fundamentally change the way recruiters search for candidates through its "algorithm that searches for people, not keywords." As Velluci proudly looks on, the woman insists that Turbo's "built-in intelligence provides unrivaled match results based on real life attributes that recruiters care about, such as skills, experience, education, and more."

As the crowd files out of the conference room, you side up to your designer buddy Lou Soosi and ask the elephant-in-the-room question that you were too paranoid to ask during the Velluci's presence:

"Does this mean we're killing Boolean search? We've got lots of clients who rely on it."

"As a matter of fact, we *are* killing Boolean," he says nonchalantly as he carefully pours his steamed milk over his *doppio* at the authentically massive espresso machine. He looks over his shoulder at you and adds caustically: "For 80 million, that new search engine better cook my breakfast."

"For 80 million, that new search engine better cook my breakfast."

"Eighty million?" you gasp. "Should I do a head-to-head usability test to see if the new search does better than our current one before we close the deal with Novix?"

"Too late. Done deal," he says, taking a long slurp of his newly minted *cappuccino*. "But, hopefully, we can make some tweaks before they roll it out. Go for it. Do a head-to-head and see what we find out." "Then tell Hans."

You get a hold of the Novix prototype and start to do some basic searches. You must admit: the interface is slick. It begins with a simple open "title" field that has a type-ahead feature that even accommodates for misspellings. Then, there's a lengthy page of open fields for years of experience, location, skills/keywords, education, maximum salary, and job type. There's even "Willing to Travel" and "Relocation." But, Lou was right: no place for Boolean searching.

Your usability test includes seven recruiting tasks and several post-task Likert scales. You decide to use two different independent groups of 10 participants, 20 participants in all, who try to complete the same seven tasks; group one will try to complete the tasks on Behemoth's current candidate search while group two will try to complete the tasks on the new Novix search.

The 4-day actual testing—five participants per day—proceeds very well. No cancellations, zero no-shows, with articulate and thoughtful participants. (They should be—they all got a $100 Amazon gift card!) Some trends become obvious right away, but the other problematic areas are more nuanced. At the end of the twentieth participant, you're beat and can't really look at the data.

After a good night's sleep, you get to work on analyzing the data. And of course, the first thing you do is tally the task completions in Table 4.1.

The results are troubling, to say the least. Participants were much more successful using the Behemoth search engine on at least four tasks, including pedestrian ones that involved searching for skills, experience, location, and willingness to travel. Other tasks involving searching by maximum salary and education level are much closer. But, overall, it feels like the $80 million price tag is not producing the results Behemoth top brass wanted.

The reasons for the different completion rates are complex, but one of the overarching qualitative findings of the tests is that most of the recruiters automatically tried to use Boolean strings. Of course, on the Behemoth engine, it was business as usual. On the new Novix search, recruiters tried in vain to use Boolean strings, usually in the title field. When that failed, they tried combinations of the Novix fields, with varying degrees of success. Groans of "no Boolean?" were heard during most of the sessions; one recruiter with over 20 years of experience said, "This will make my hair grayer than it already is."

But, staring at the numbers, your analytic brain and statistical savvy kick in. With relatively low sample sizes, is seven completions on task 2 for Behemoth versus two for Novix really statistically significant? For that matter, how about the nine and three difference for task 1? The terrifying question rumbles around your brain as you continue to stare at the numbers: Did CEO Joey Velluci really blow 80 million bucks?

Hypothesis testing using the chi-square test of independence

Table 4.1 Tasks and Number of Successful Completions

Task #	Verbatim Task	Successful Completions on Novix Search Engine (out of 10)	Successful Completions on Behemoth Search Engine (out of 10)
1	Find a Java developer with at least 5 years' experience within 50 miles of Tucson, Arizona.	3	9
2	Find a Web designer with skills using Photoshop, Illustrator, and Flash within 25 miles of San Diego, California.	2	7
3	Find an electrical engineer with a minimum of a Bachelor's degree within 25 miles of Boston, Massachusetts.	1	8
4	Find a business analyst with an MBA. There is no location requirement.	5	6
5	Find a technical writer within 50 miles of Chicago. The maximum your client is willing to spend on the position is $50,000 per year.	7	8
6	Find an intern for a marketing department within 25 miles of New York city. The minimum education level is a Bachelor's degree.	7	9
7	Find a vice president of development who is willing to travel over 50% of the time.	1	9

4.3 HYPOTHESIS TESTING USING THE CHI-SQUARE TEST OF INDEPENDENCE OR FISHER'S EXACT TEST

To put your dilemma into statistical terms, you want to know if there is a statistically significant difference between the task success rates, comparing Novix with Behemoth.

Well, you came to the right place. By using either the chi-square test of independence or Fisher's exact test (depending on your software), we can determine if the results you gathered in your usability test are consistent with what you would theoretically expect to occur, if the task success rates were the same. More simply put, we want to see if there is a significant difference between the search engines on any given task.

Please note that we have "independent samples," as discussed in Chapter 2. The 10 people who attempted the tasks with the Novix search engine and the 10 people who attempted the tasks with the Behemoth search engine are different sets of 10 people, even though each group of 10 are picked from the same population and are, in a sense, "nominally the same"!

SIDEBAR: THE USABILITY OF USING CHI-SQUARE

The chi-square test of independence was referred to a few decades ago as the chi-square–contingency-table test. The latter name, not used very frequently nowadays, derives from the fact that if two entities are not independent (here: having equal success rates), they can be said to "have a contingency" between them.

Both Excel and SPSS perform the chi-square test of independence; however, each software package has its own usability problems. In using Excel, you have to perform what are usually some really simple calculations that Excel could easily have calculated; the calculations are usually not particularly arduous, but on occasion can be, even though they are still "simple." And, in SPSS, the format you need to use to enter the data to implement the test is yet another pain in the you-know-what. Don't blame the authors—neither one of us worked or consulted for Excel or SPSS. But don't worry! We'll hold your hand every step of the way.

Let's begin with task 1, where 9 out of 10 participants were successful using the Behemoth search engine versus the 3 who were successful using the Novix engine.

The hypotheses are now

$$H0: p1N = p1B$$

$$H1: p1N \neq p1B$$

where, of course, N stands for Novix and B for Behemoth.

4.3.1 EXCEL

To do the chi-square test of independence in Excel, on any given task, you need to first specify what Excel calls your "actual range" and compute what Excel calls your "expected range."

SIDEBAR: JUMP RIGHT INTO EXCEL!

The easiest way to compute the "actual" ranges and "expected" ranges is to construct two charts, as we explain on this page. You can do it in Word, Textedit, or any program that you prefer. But the easiest might be to just type the simple tables right into Excel, since eventually you must get those tables into Excel to run the chi-square analysis.

The "actual range" is just the number of successful and unsuccessful completions for each task, using your task completion data (Table 4.1). You need to flesh out the table by adding the failures for each engine. Of course, to accomplish that, just subtract the passes from the total number of attempts (in this case, 10) (Table 4.2).

Next, we need to construct the "expected range" table. The "expected range" is the pass/fail values that would be theoretically expected to occur if H0 is true (even though these theoretical values are unlikely to exactly occur even when H0 is true and the true p's are the same.) An analogy would be that if we flip a hundred 50/50 coins, the theoretically expected number of heads is 50 (along with 50 tails), but the actual probability of that exact result is somewhat small, a shade under an 8% chance!

To construct the "expected range" table, we take the row total of the passes (12) and divide by 2 (number of tasks), getting 6, and for the fails, getting 4. This gives us Table 4.3.

If you haven't constructed these tables directly in Excel, you need to insert them to finish the calculation. See Figure 4.1.

The titles "table of observed frequencies" and "table of expected frequencies" do not need to be entered into Excel. Nor do any of the other words need to be there. We've included the titles just to help explain the process.

OK, let's get to the fun part! In any cell you wish (cell E16 was arbitrarily chosen in this example), type in the CHITEST command. The CHITEST command will prompt

Table 4.2 Actual Range for Task 1

Search Engine	Novix	Behemoth
Pass	3	9
Fail	7	1

Table 4.3 Theoretical Expected Frequencies for the Two-Search-Engines Hypothesis Test

Search Engine	Novix	Behemoth
Pass	6	6
Fail	4	4

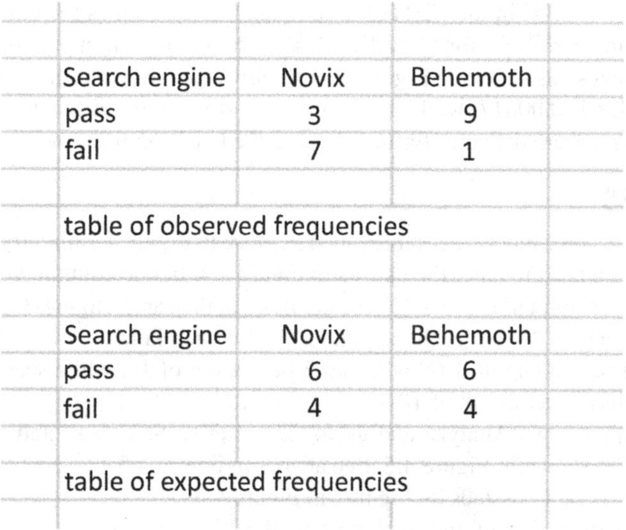

Search engine	Novix	Behemoth
pass	3	9
fail	7	1

table of observed frequencies

Search engine	Novix	Behemoth
pass	6	6
fail	4	4

table of expected frequencies

FIGURE 4.1

Observed frequencies and expected frequencies in Excel.

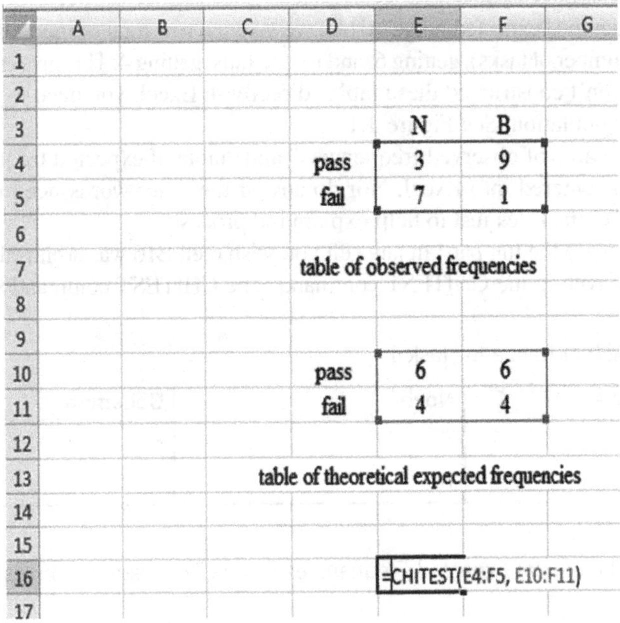

FIGURE 4.2

Excel tables and chi-square test command.

you first for the observed frequencies, then the expected frequencies. Select the appropriate cells to complete the CHITEST command, per Figure 4.2.

By typing "E4:F5" in the CHITEST command, Excel knows the data values are where they are. Similarly for "E10:F11." If we now click on enter, we obtain the p value of the test, as shown in Figure 4.3 (see arrow pointing out the p-value).

The p-value is 0.00617, well less than 0.05, and we reject H0 and conclude that the true pass rates are different for task 1 using the two search engines.

4.3.2 SPSS

Unfortunately, you cannot enter tables such as those in Figure 4.1 directly into SPSS.

Instead, you need to enter the data as in Figure 4.4. In one column, you use a "1" for the Novix search engine and "2" for the Behemoth search engine. In an adjacent column, you enter a "1" for each pass and a "0" for each fail.

Note that search engine 1 (Novix) has 3 passes out of 10, while search engine 2 (Behemoth) has 9 passes out of 10.

We now pull down Analyze and go to "Descriptive Statistics" and to submenu "Crosstabs," as shown in Figure 4.5. See arrows in Figure 4.5.

We now see the Crosstabs dialog box in Figure 4.6.

We bring over one of the variables to the "Rows" box (see dashed arrow in Figure 4.6) and the other variable to the "Columns" box (see bent arrow in Figure 4.6). It does not matter which variable goes to which box. We then click on "Statistics"—see solid (straight) arrow in Figure 4.6. This gives us Figure 4.7.

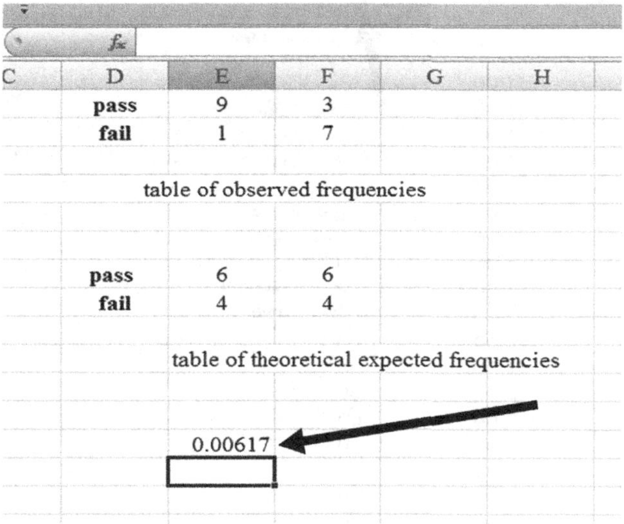

C	D	E	F	G	H
	pass	9	3		
	fail	1	7		
		table of observed frequencies			
	pass	6	6		
	fail	4	4		
		table of theoretical expected frequencies			
		0.00617			

FIGURE 4.3

Output for two-search-engine hypothesis test.

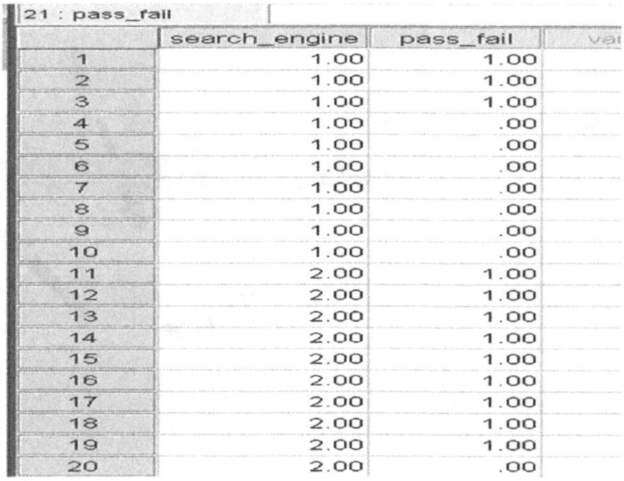

21 : pass_fail			
	search_engine	pass_fail	va
1	1.00	1.00	
2	1.00	1.00	
3	1.00	1.00	
4	1.00	.00	
5	1.00	.00	
6	1.00	.00	
7	1.00	.00	
8	1.00	.00	
9	1.00	.00	
10	1.00	.00	
11	2.00	1.00	
12	2.00	1.00	
13	2.00	1.00	
14	2.00	1.00	
15	2.00	1.00	
16	2.00	1.00	
17	2.00	1.00	
18	2.00	1.00	
19	2.00	1.00	
20	2.00	.00	

FIGURE 4.4

SPSS input for search engine hypothesis test.

You can see in Figure 4.7 that the variables have been "moved to the correct fields in the dialog box." In the Crosstabs: Statistics box, we check off "Chi-square" (see vertical arrow in Figure 4.7) and then click "Continue" (see horizontal arrow in Figure 4.7). This brings us back to Figure 4.6 (with the variables in the Row and Column box (as in Figure 4.7). We now click "OK" to get our output, as shown in Figure 4.8.

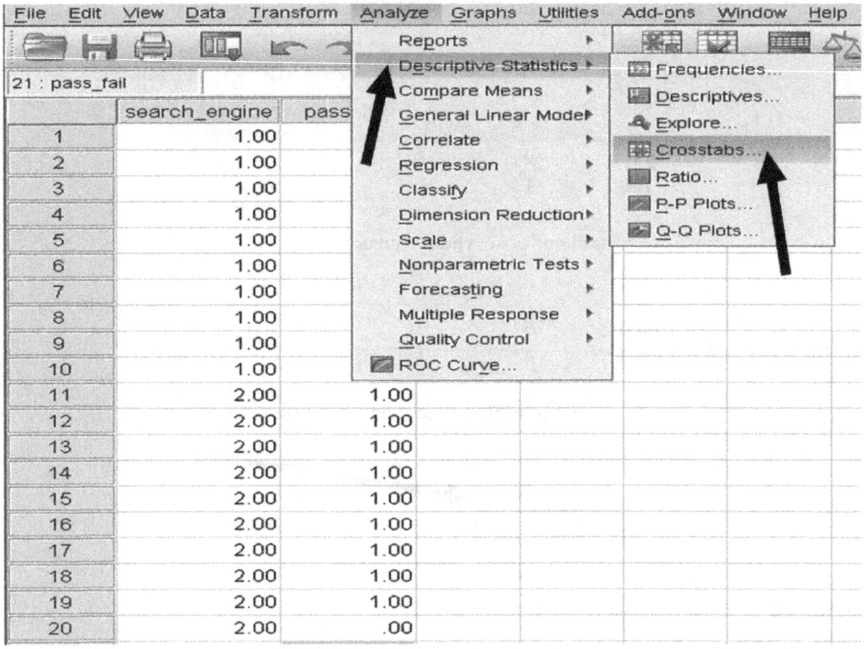

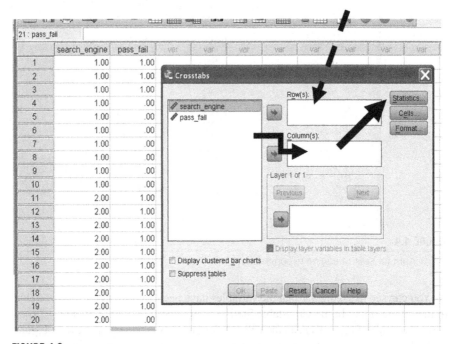

FIGURE 4.5

Menu commands to begin chi-square test of Independence; SPSS.

FIGURE 4.6

Dialog box for Crosstabs Command; SPSS.

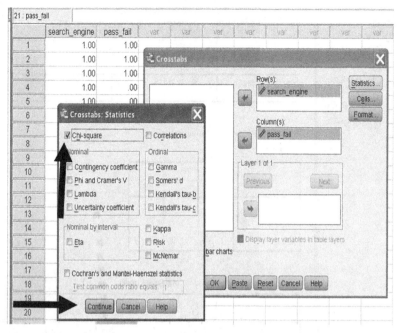

FIGURE 4.7

Crosstabs: Statistics dialog box; SPSS.

The main, and crucial, difference between the result we got in Excel and the result obtained in SPSS is the availability of the Fisher's exact test (see solid arrow in Figure 4.8) in addition to the regular chi-square result displayed (see dashed arrow in Figure 4.8). And you can note that the chi-square p-value is the same 0.006 (here, rounded to three digits) as we obtained doing the analysis in Excel. This, of course, is not a surprise!

SIDEBAR: FISHER'S EXACT TEST

Fisher's exact test was developed by Fisher (duh!), since it was noticed that the chi-square test of independence did not perform as accurately as desired for a 2×2 table. Thus, we use Fisher's exact test only when we have a 2×2 table. As a matter of fact, if you have more than two columns being compared, the Fisher exact test will not even appear as part of the SPSS output. The primary reason why Fisher's exact test is superior to the chi-square test when we have a 2×2 table is that the chi-square is a continuous probability distribution, while the observed frequencies (number of passes and fails that comprise our data) are, of course, integers. This "discrepancy," or "disconnect," is immaterial when we have more than two quantities being compared, but is just material enough to be noticed by Fisher and lead to his developing Fisher's exact test for the two comparison case. In Figure 4.8, the p-value for the chi-square is 0.006, while for the Fisher exact test it is 0.020. This is a small difference (0.014) and leads to the same answer—reject H0—and the same conclusion that the pass/fail rates are different for task 1 between Novix and Behemoth.

We mention this only because Excel does not provide the result for Fisher's exact test (theoretically, a shortcoming of Excel, but *C'est la vie*); in the vast, vast majority of time, the chi-square test of independence and Fisher's exact test yield the same conclusion, as they do here.

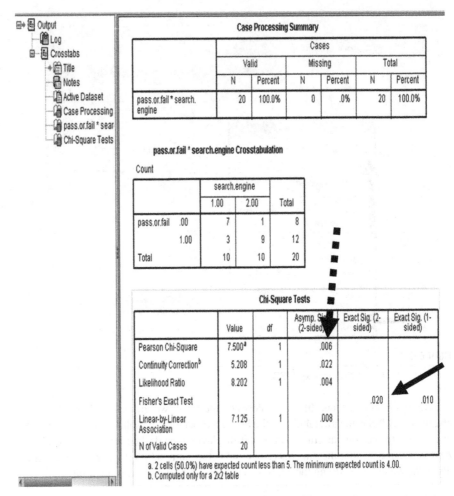

FIGURE 4.8

Output comparing search engines N(1) and B(2) for task 1; SPSS.

So, using the *p*-value of 0.020 (we are doing a two-sided hypothesis test, as indicated by the H0 and H1 being = vs. ≠), and since this is less than 0.05, we reject H0 and conclude that for task 1, the (true) pass rate for Novix is not the same as that for Behemoth.

Now, this is the type of result you might have predicted from the beginning of this chapter. After all, Behemoth had 9 passes out of 10, while Novix had only 3 passes out of 10. But once you've done these calculations, you hold a much stronger hand. *Scientia Potentia Est.* The *p*-value tells you that if the true pass rates were the same for Behemoth and Novix, for this task, the difference we have observed (9 out of 10 vs. 3 out of 10) will occur only 2% of the time, that is, on average, 2 out of 100 times. Since this is below the traditional accepted significance level of 0.05, we conclude that the difference in the pass rates is due to the difference between the search engines and not due to mere chance. Simply put, your current engine does better than the newfangled engine on this particular task.

Table 4.4 Results of Fisher Exact Test for Each Task in Table 4.1, Comparing Novix and Behemoth Search Engines

TASK	Novix—pass	Behemoth—pass	*p*-value
1	3	9	0.020
2	2	7	Not significant, but "close" = 0.07
3	1	8	0.005
4	5	6	Not significant > 0.500
5	7	8	Not significant > 0.500
6	7	9	Not significant > 0.500
7	1	9	0.011

To complete comparisons of all the tasks in your test, you would simply use the aforementioned process in either Excel or SPSS for all seven tasks. The results are summarized in Table 4.4, which shows the *p*-value when we compare each task between the Novix search engine and the existing Behemoth search engine. Remember, any *p*-value below 0.05 is considered statistically significant, and leads to a conclusion that, beyond a reasonable doubt, the pass rates are different. (By the way, the *p*-values you see in Table 4.4 for tasks 4–6 are *not* typos. When the *p*-value is way above .05, it is common to note a higher low limit to give the proper significance impression to the reader. We could have easily used .05 instead of .500 to indicate significance, but .500 tells the user that the different completion proportions for these tasks were *nowhere* near significant.)

If you did the chi-square test, instead of the Fisher exact test (presumably, because you were using Excel and did not have access to SPSS), the results would have been nearly the same. The only material change would be for task 2, where, instead of the 0.07 (as noted, "close," but, technically, not significant—using the Fisher exact test), the chi-square test gives a *p*-value of 0.025, which is significant. So, if you were using Excel and the chi-square test, you would reject H0 and conclude the pass rates differ. However, the "right answer" is 0.07, but since this is so close to 0.05, getting that result would likely lead to reserving judgment on task 2, and just viewing it as borderline one way or the other, thus, not dramatically different from a rejection of H0. As we said a little while ago, the lack of Fisher's exact test in Excel is a shortcoming of Excel.

4.4 MEANWHILE, BACK AT BEHEMOTH.COM

Now that you have the hard, cold facts about "Turbo Search," you sure wish you'd gotten a shot at it before Behemoth spent $80 million making the Palo Alto techno-hipsters rich beyond their wildest dreams. Now, you have to break the news to Hans Blitz.

You write up your findings as quickly as possible. But instead of calling your typical presentation meeting with the entire UX team, you decide you should give Hans a "heads up." You catch him at the espresso machine, and hand him the report. Sipping his iced *doppio*, he skims the high-level findings. His brow furrows in disbelief:

"Are you frickin' kidding me? This is horrifying! The current search engine is doing better, and we spent 80 mil!"

"Yes, but some task completions were about the same. But we definitely have our work cut out for us if we're going to implement the new search."

"You got that right, mister research," he says, flipping through the pages. "I gotta tell Joey about this. He's gonna blow a gasket." He takes another sip. "But tell me something. On task 1, the Palo Alto guys got 3 completions and we got 9. But you only have 10 participants for each engine. How does this translate to a larger audience?"

"Great question. I can calculate the confidence intervals for the pass rates for you; perhaps they will give you more insight about the results."

"Cool. Get me that asap, so I can really deliver the full story to Joey. It's still gonna be a nightmare, but I wanna have our story straight. I don't want to invade if there's no weapons of mass destruction; follow?"

"You chuckle at the Iraq war reference." "Yeah, I got it. I'll get you some numbers by the end of business today."

4.5 BINOMIAL CONFIDENCE INTERVALS AND THE ADJUSTED WALD METHOD

There are a variety of ways you can go about forming a confidence interval for the true "pass proportion," based on a small sample for data. We will focus on what might be called "binomial confidence intervals."

SIDEBAR: BINOMIALLY NORMAL?

In a way, "binomial confidence interval" is an appropriate name, while in another way, it isn't. The underlying data-generating process is a binomial one. Each data point is a "pass/fail" (having two and only two outcomes is the core of the term "binomial"; the prefix, "bi," corresponds with this). There are also other assumptions that go along with having a so-called binomial process. We describe them a bit later. In this sense, the name is appropriate. On the other hand, the method that is considered the most appropriate for determining these confidence intervals does not actually involve using probabilities from a binomial table, but, rather, uses values from a normal distribution table, as we shall describe. This is another example of just how prevalent and useful the normal curve is, and why we spent the time we did in Chapter 1 on the normal curve. Still, it suggests that the name "binomial confidence intervals" is not directly appropriate, even though we are finding a confidence interval for a true proportion.

The method that is considered the most appropriate for finding a confidence interval for a proportion (e.g., the proportion that will use a search engine successfully), when the underlying process is considered binomial (i.e., pass/fail) and sample sizes are small, is the "adjusted Wald method" (Agressi & Coull, 1998; Sauro & Lewis, 2005; Lewis & Sauro, 2006). The theoretical assumptions to have a binomial process are that we have two and only two outcomes to a "trial" (here, successfully completing a task or not), that we have independence between different outcomes (here, in essence, each data point for a given task corresponds with a different person), and last, that the true probability of "pass" (here, the proportion who would pass if we considered the entire population of people who would ever undertake the task, which is, of course, unknown) is a constant for each person, given no information about the person. Since the last assumption may not be strictly true, we are "approximating" a binomial process, but it is more than adequate for our purposes.

We now describe the way to find these confidence intervals, but must say that we lament the fact that neither Excel nor SPSS has built-in modules that will compute them for you (weep!).

The formula that is used for the adjusted Wald method is the standard normal approximation formula for large sample sizes, with adjustments as described below.

SIDEBAR: BINOMIAL CONFIDENCE INTERVALS SHORTCUT

As much as enjoying calculating binomial confidence intervals, we'll admit it can be time consuming. Therefore, you'll find a nifty table at the end of this chapter that speed things up if your sample size is anywhere from 1–15. (Lab usability tests are usually conducted with anywhere from 3–12 participants, so you should be covered.) Simply find your sample size (number of participants) along the top and work your way down that column until you reach the number of successes for a particular task. For example, say you have 6 out of 10 successful completions for a particular task. Work your way down from the "10" column until you reach the "6" row. Find your binomial confidence interval, which is 0.31–0.83.

If you have a sample size over 15 (for example, while running a unmoderated usability study), you can do the calculations as we've explained in this chapter. Sorry; the table had to stop somewhere! ☺

The standard normal approximation formula, with a sample size of "n" and a sample proportion that passed of "p-bar" (analogous to X-bar of earlier chapters) is depicted in expression (1)[1]:

$$\text{p-bar} \pm Z * \text{SQRT} \left([\text{p-bar}] * [1 - \text{p-bar}] / n \right) \tag{4.1}$$

where

n = total number of trials (people)
p-bar = proportion of trials that were successes
Z = the Z-value corresponding to the desired confidence level (e.g., 95%, 90%)

And we will use this formula for confidence intervals when we have large sample sizes. It should be noted that $Z = 1.96$ for a 95% confidence interval, which, traditionally, is the confidence level nearly always chosen. For a 99% confidence interval, $Z = 2.57$, and for a 90% confidence interval, $Z = 1.64$.

However, when you have a small sample size, you adjust the values of p-bar and n (as described below); this is the adjusted Wald method.

The adjustments are as follows:

First, we compute the adjusted proportion:

$$p_{ADJ} = (n*\text{p-bar} + Z^2/2)/(n + Z^2)$$

Then, compute the adjusted sample size:

$$n_{ADJ} = n + Z^2$$

The reader may note that the adjustments make a meaningful difference when n is "small" but make virtually no difference when n is "large." For example, with n = 10 and p-bar = .4,

---

[1] Traditionally, a sample size is considered sufficiently large to use the routine normal distribution formula (i.e., without the Wald adjustment) if both $n*(\text{p-bar}) > 5$ and also $n*(1 - [\text{p-bar}]) > 5$.

$$\text{p-bar}_{ADJ} = .43$$

$$n_{ADJ} = 13.84$$

and we can note that p-bar is increased by about 7% and n is increased by about 38%, a modest increase in p-bar, but a relatively sizable increase in n.

However, if n = 100 and p = 0.4, then

$$\text{p-bar}_{ADJ} = .404$$

$$n_{ADJ} = 103.84$$

and we can note that p-bar is increased by about 1% and n is increased by about 3.8%, both somewhat modest increases that are unlikely to be material (which is why we do not bother with the Wald adjustment when n is large).[2]

Then, we substitute the adjusted proportion and the adjusted sample size into the standard Eqn. (4.1), repeated for convenience:

$$\text{p-bar} \pm Z * \text{SQRT} ([\text{p-bar}] * [1 - \text{p-bar}] / n)$$

OK, let's return to our data from our two search engines. If we consider task 2 using search engine B, in which the sample size = 10, and there were 7 successfully completed tasks out of the 10, then the p-bar = 7/10 = 0.7. To calculate the 95% confidence interval for the true proportion of people who would complete task 2 using the Behemoth search engine (from the presumed large population of people who would or could try task 2 using the Behemoth search engine), we first calculate the adjusted proportion and the adjusted sample size:

$$\text{p-bar}_{ADJ} = (10 * .7 + 1.96^2/2) / (10 + 1.96^2)$$

$$= 8.96/13.84 = .64$$

$$n_{ADJ} = (10 + 1.962) = 13.84$$

Using these adjusted values, and assuming a 95% confidence interval is desired, we simply plug into the Eqn. (4.1). This gives us

$$.64 \pm 1.96 * \text{SQRT} ([.64] * [1 - .64] / 13.84)$$

or

$$.64 \pm .25$$

or

$$.39 -------- .89$$

We can be 95% confident that the interval 0.39–0.89 contains the true proportion, "p," of people who will successfully complete task 2, using the Behemoth search engine. This is not as narrow a confidence interval as would be preferred, but it's what we get, given we have the small (but common in usability testing) sample size of (only) 10.

You calculate the other binomial confidence intervals for all tasks on both search engines, resulting in Table 4.5.

---

[2] It might be noted that if p-bar < 0.5, the adjusted p-bar will exceed p-bar, while if p-bar > 0.5, the adjusted p-bar will be less than p-bar. Since we work with both p-bar and (1 – p-bar), multiplied, this distinction is not material. The adjusted p-bar will exactly equal the actual p-bar when p-bar = 0.5.

Table 4.5 Completion Rates and Binomial Confidence Intervals for Tasks Comparing Novix and Behemoth Search Engines

Task #	Verbatim Task	Successful Completion on Novix Search Engine (out of 10)	Confidence Intervals for Successful Completion on Novix Search Engine (out of 10)	Successful Completion on Behemoth Search Engine (out of 10)	Confidence Intervals for Successful Completion on Behemoth Search Engine (out of 10)
1	Find a Java developer with at least 5 years' experience within 50 miles of Tucson, Arizona.	3	0.1033–0.6077	9	0.5740–0.9999
2	Find a Web designer with skills using Photoshop, Illustrator, and Flash within 25 miles of San Diego, California.	2	0.0459–0.5206	7	0.3923–0.8967
3	Find an electrical engineer with a minimum of a Bachelor's degree within 25 miles of Boston, Massachusetts.	1	0.0001–0.4260	8	0.4794–0.9541
4	Find a business analyst with an MBA. There is no location requirement.	5	0.2366–0.7634	6	0.3116–0.8329
5	Find a technical writer within 50 miles of Chicago. The maximum your client is willing to spend on the position is $50,000 per year.	7	0.3923–0.8967	8	0.4794–0.9541
6	Find an intern for a marketing department within 25 miles of New York City. The minimum education level is a Bachelor's degree.	7	0.3923–0.8967	9	0.5740–0.9999
7	Find a vice president of development who is willing to travel over 50% percent of the time.	1	0.0001–0.4260	9	0.5740–0.9999

Staring at the chart, you're ready to answer Blitz's questions. You insert your latest confidence interval chart into your presentation and send it to Hans. As expected, he pops his head into your office within 15 minutes.

"Thanks, buddy. But what's with the enormous ranges?" That's as precise as you can get?

"It's the nature of binomial data with a sample size so small. Those ranges shrink only as your sample sizes increase.

"English, please."

"Even though the intervals are broad, they hardly ever overlap on those crucial tasks 1, 2, 3, and 7. This further confirms that our old engine really did do better on those tasks."

"Got it. Make sure your phone is on between 10 and 11 am tomorrow. That's when I'm going to show Joey this stuff. I may need you to cover me in the crossfire."

4.6 SUMMARY

In this chapter we studied hypothesis testing for "nominal/categorical" data, more specifically, "pass/fail" data, for independent samples, and the determination of confidence intervals for true proportions. These situations arise primarily when we are assessing the rate (proportion) of successful completions of various tasks, although, as exhibited in this chapter, the key issue was comparing successful completion rates of a task for different search engines. We assume that the underlying probability process is binomial and discuss the assumptions implied by this.

When we perform hypothesis tests to inquire whether successful-completion rates are the same for a task with different search engines, the underlying test we perform is the chi-square test of independence, sometimes referred to as the chi-square contingency-table test. When we are comparing specifically only two search engines (or two "whatevers"), each with the binary result of pass/fail, we recognize that in this one situation, it is superior to replace the aforementioned chi-square test by Fisher's exact test. The hypothesis tests are illustrated using Excel and SPSS. Confidence intervals are not constructed by the software, but details are provided to enable the reader to easily do the construction "by hand" (which expression includes the use of a calculator!). There are online calculators that compute the adjusted Wald confidence interval. One example is www.measuringusability.com/wald.htm).

4.7 ADDENDUM 1: HOW TO RUN THE CHI-SQUARE TEST FOR DIFFERENT SAMPLE SIZES

When we covered how to do the chi-square test using Excel, we gave you a simple rule for computing the table of theoretical expected frequencies (called "expected range" by Excel) of the pass/fail values. As we noted, since we have independent samples, it is possible that the number of people who try each task can be different, whether planned or unplanned. If this is the case, there is a simple, but a bit more tedious, way to find these theoretical expected frequencies.

Consider a revised Table 4.2, which we now label Table 4.6. We have added a third search engine, *Microhard* (M), in this illustration. (This leads us more gently into the next section, Section 4.8.)

Now we have 10 people using search engines N and M, but 15 people using search engine B. To find the table that corresponds to Table 4.3, the table of theoretical expected frequencies, we first find the row totals and column totals and grand total. The row totals are 25 and 10, respectively; the column totals are 10, 15, and 10, respectively, and the grand total is 35 (determined by adding the row totals, or adding the column totals. If those two totals are not the same, it means you made an arithmetic error).

To find the theoretical expected frequency for a cell (row, column combination), you simply multiply the row total of the cell, times the column total of the cell, then divided by the grand total. So, for the upper left cell (the "pass," N cell), the theoretical expected frequency is $25*10/35 = 7.14$. The good news is that you do not need to do this for the "fail" row of N. The total for N must still come out 10, so the fail value = $10 - 7.14 = 2.86$. This easy arithmetic can be performed for any cell. The resulting theoretical expected frequencies are shown in Table 4.7.

You can see that the row totals and column totals are the same as they are in Table 4.6. This will always be the case, no matter how different the numbers of people are per search engine.

Table 4.6 Table of Observed Frequencies with the Number of People in Each Column Not the Same

TASK 1			
Search Eng:	**N**	**B**	**M**
Pass	3	14	8
Fail	7	1	2

Table 4.7 Table of Theoretical Expected Frequencies with the Number of People in Each Column Not the Same

TASK 1			
Search Eng:	**N**	**B**	**M**
Pass	7.14	10.72	7.14
Fail	2.86	4.28	2.86

4.8 ADDENDUM 2: COMPARING MORE THAN TWO TREATMENTS

Now, we illustrate another case where we have a task and there are more than two search engines under investigation. Statisticians would call this comparing more than two "treatments."

Suppose that we have a third search engine under examination, the *Microhard* search engine introduced in the previous section. And, we have another 10 people trying task 1 using that search engine, with the result of eight successful completions. If we use the letter "p1" to stand for the true completion rate for task 1, and "N" for Novix, B for Behemoth, and M for Microhard, we would have a null hypothesis of

$$H0: p1N = p1B = p1M$$

vs. H1: not all three values of p1 are the same

(As a reminder: Task 1 is "Find a Java developer with at least 5 years' experience within 50 miles of Tucson, Arizona.") As another reminder—and we apologize for the repetitiveness of this one—the true successful completion values are those that would result if all people who could ever be performing the task with that search engine indeed performed the task (successfully or not). We can sum up the sample results in Table 4.8.

As we see in Table 4.8, N had three successful completions and seven failures, B had nine successful completions and one failure, while M had eight successful completions and two failures.

4.8.1 EXCEL

To do the chi-square test of independence in Excel, given a table such as Table 4.8, you find the table of theoretical frequencies the way you did earlier, arriving at Table 4.9.

The remaining steps are identical to those performed in Excel when there were only two search engines. You would start with Figure 4.9.

For the observed frequency table, the range is viewed as E4 to G5. Similarly, the range for the theoretical expected frequencies is E10 to G11.

Table 4.8 Observed Frequencies for Hypothesis Test

Task 1			
Search Eng:	N	B	M
Pass	3	9	8
Fail	7	1	2

Ultimately, we arrive at Figure 4.10 and examine the *p*-value.

As can be seen in Figure 4.10 (see arrow), the *p*-value is 0.009559, or just about 0.01. This is, of course, less than our traditional benchmark of 0.05, and we reject H0 and conclude that for task 1 (in Table 4.9), the pass/fail rates are not the same for the three search engines. While the chi-square test does not directly test in a formal way how the pass/fail rates differ (if they do), we can feel very comfortable in this example if we conclude that the N pass rate differs from the other two search engine pass rates, while it is extremely likely that the

Table 4.9 Theoretical Expected Frequencies with Three Search Engines

Task 1			
Search Eng:	1	3	7
Pass	6.667	6.667	6.667
Fail	3.333	3.333	3.333

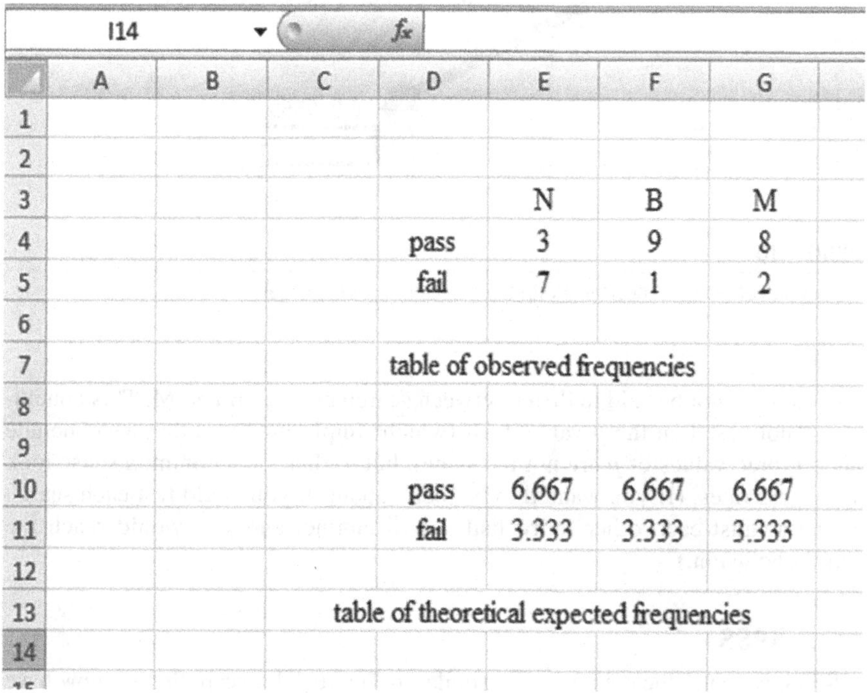

	A	B	C	D	E	F	G
					I14		*fx*
1							
2							
3					N	B	M
4				pass	3	9	8
5				fail	7	1	2
6							
7				table of observed frequencies			
8							
9							
10				pass	6.667	6.667	6.667
11				fail	3.333	3.333	3.333
12							
13				table of theoretical expected frequencies			
14							

FIGURE 4.9

Excel input, three search engines.

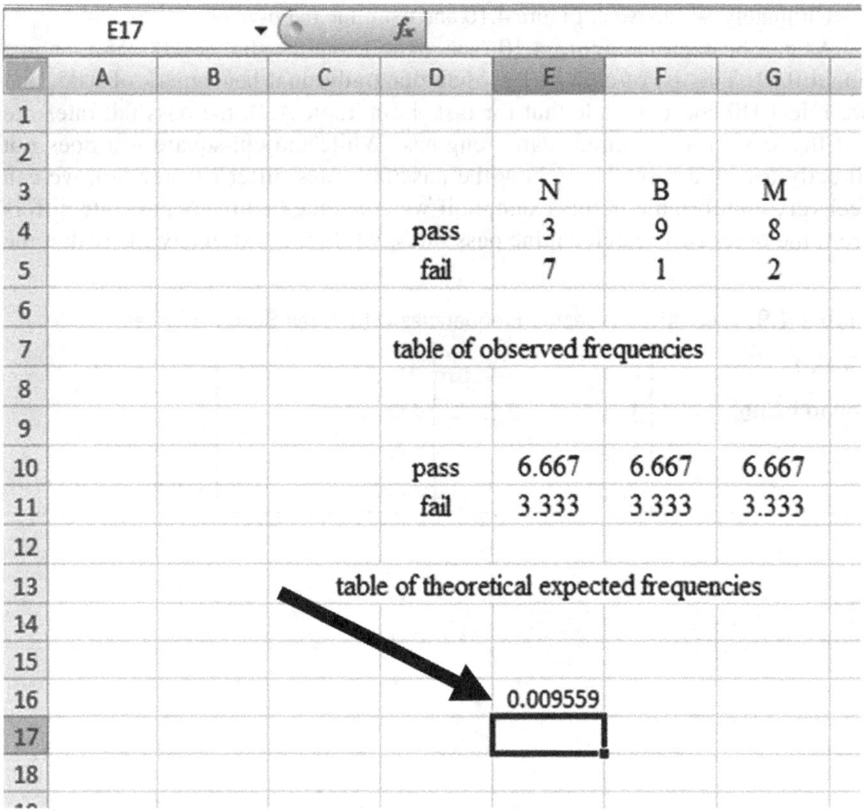

	A	B	C	D	E	F	G
					E17		
1							
2							
3					N	B	M
4				pass	3	9	8
5				fail	7	1	2
6							
7				table of observed frequencies			
8							
9							
10				pass	6.667	6.667	6.667
11				fail	3.333	3.333	3.333
12							
13				table of theoretical expected frequencies			
14							
15							
16					0.009559		
17							
18							

FIGURE 4.10

The p-value of the hypothesis test with three search engines; Excel.

pass rates cannot be said to differ between search engines B and M. This conclusion is not based on the p-value itself (which simply indicates that we conclude that all three values of p are not the same), but, rather, on a common sense look at the pass rates. (If you wanted to be picky about it, you could test each search engine against each other individual search engine, and you would reach the same conclusion.)

4.8.2 SPSS

In SPSS, we enter the data in a way similar to Figure 4.4, except that we now have 30 rows, 10 for each search engine. We let M be denoted by "3" in the search engine column. See Figure 4.11.

	pass.or.fail	search.engine	var
8 :			
1	1.00	1.00	
2	1.00	1.00	
3	1.00	1.00	
4	.00	1.00	
5	.00	1.00	
6	.00	1.00	
7	.00	1.00	
8	.00	1.00	
9	.00	1.00	
10	.00	1.00	
11	1.00	2.00	
12	1.00	2.00	
13	1.00	2.00	
14	1.00	2.00	
15	1.00	2.00	
16	1.00	2.00	
17	1.00	2.00	
18	1.00	2.00	
19	1.00	2.00	
20	.00	2.00	
21	1.00	3.00	
22	1.00	3.00	
23	1.00	3.00	
24	1.00	3.00	
25	1.00	3.00	
26	1.00	3.00	
27	1.00	3.00	
28	1.00	3.00	
29	.00	3.00	
30	.00	3.00	

Data View   Variable View

FIGURE 4.11

SPSS input for three-search-engine hypothesis test.

The analysis process is the same as earlier when we had two search engines. The output is in Figure 4.12, and you can note that the Fisher exact test is not part of the output.

The p-value equals 0.010 ("Sig.," see arrow in Figure 4.12), which, of course, is the same value provided by the Excel analysis, but rounded to three digits. As we noted in the previous section, this is less than 0.05, the traditional cutoff point, and therefore, we reject H0 and conclude that the pass/fail rates are not the same for task 1 for the three search engines.

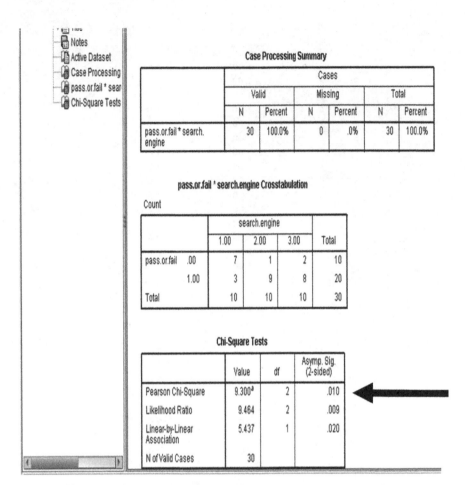

FIGURE 4.12

Output for chi-square test of independence with three search engines; SPSS.

SIDEBAR: ASYMPTOTIC? NOT TO WORRY

Do not concern yourself with the fact that the label for p-value in Figure 4.9 says "Asymp. Sig." This is due to the previously mentioned fact that the chi-square distribution is continuous, while the data values (observed frequencies) are automatically integers. "Asymp" stands for asymptotic, and indicates that the p-value is exactly true only when we have an infinite number of degrees of freedom (we have two degrees of freedom, the value just to the left of the p-value). However, for all practical purposes, we can rely on the given p-value (here, 0.010) to be sufficiently accurate for our needs.

APPENDIX: CONFIDENCE INTERVALS FOR ALL POSSIBLE SAMPLE-PROPORTION OUTCOMES FROM N = 1 TO N = 15, IN TABLE A.1

Table A.1 Confidence Intervals for the True Proportion of Successes, Given a Sample Size (1–15) and the Number of Successes

# Successes	Sample Size														
	1	2	3	4	5	6	7	8	9	10	11	12	13	14	15
0	0.00–0.83	0.00–0.71	0.00–0.62	0.00–0.55	0.00–0.49	0.00–0.44	0.00–0.40	0.00–0.37	0.00–0.34	0.00–0.32	0.00–0.30	0.00–0.28	0.00–0.27	0.00–0.25	0.00–0.24
1	0.17–1.00	0.09–0.91	0.06–0.80	0.03–0.71	0.02–0.64	0.01–0.58	0.01–0.53	0.00–0.49	0.00–0.46	0.00–0.43	0.00–0.40	0.00–0.38	0.00–0.35	0.00–0.34	0.00–0.32
2		0.29–1.00	0.20–0.94	0.15–0.85	0.12–0.77	0.09–0.70	0.08–0.65	0.06–0.60	0.05–0.56	0.05–0.52	0.04–0.49	0.03–0.46	0.03–0.43	0.03–0.41	0.02–0.39
3			0.38–1.00	0.29–0.97	0.23–0.88	0.19–0.81	0.16–0.75	0.13–0.70	0.12–0.65	0.10–0.61	0.09–0.57	0.08–0.54	0.07–0.51	0.07–0.48	0.06–0.46
4				0.45–1.00	0.36–0.98	0.30–0.91	0.25–0.84	0.22–0.78	0.19–0.73	0.17–0.69	0.15–0.65	0.14–0.61	0.12–0.58	0.11–0.55	0.10–0.52
5					0.69–1.00	0.42–0.99	0.35–0.92	0.30–0.87	0.27–0.81	0.24–0.76	0.21–0.72	0.19–0.68	0.18–0.65	0.16–0.61	0.15–0.58
6						0.56–1.00	0.47–0.99	0.40–0.94	0.35–0.88	0.31–0.83	0.28–0.79	0.25–0.75	0.23–0.71	0.21–0.67	0.20–0.64
7							0.60–1.00	0.51–1.00	0.44–0.95	0.39–0.90	0.35–0.85	0.32–0.81	0.29–0.77	0.27–0.73	0.25–0.70

(Continued)

Table A.1 Confidence Intervals for the True Proportion of Successes, Given a Sample Size (1–15) and the Number of Successes—cont'd

# Successes	Sample Size														
	1	2	3	4	5	6	7	8	9	10	11	12	13	14	15
8								0.63–1.00	0.54–1.00	0.48–0.95	0.43–0.91	0.39–0.86	0.35–0.82	0.33–0.79	0.30–0.75
9									0.66–1.00	0.57–1.00	0.51–0.96	0.46–0.92	0.42–0.88	0.39–0.84	0.36–0.80
10										0.68–1.00	0.60–1.00	0.54–0.97	0.49–0.93	0.45–0.89	0.42–0.85
11											0.70–1.00	0.62–1.00	0.57–0.97	0.52–0.93	0.48–0.90
12												0.72–1.00	0.65–1.00	0.59–0.97	0.54–0.94
13													0.73–1.00	0.66 to –1.00	0.61–0.98
14														0.75–1.00	0.68–1.00
15															0.76–1.00

4.10 EXERCISES

1. Consider tasks 6, 7, and 8 of Table 4.1. Test the hypothesis that there is no difference in the true pass/fail rates for the three tasks. The input and output in Excel are in a file named Chapter 4.Exercise 1. In SPSS, the input is in a file Chapter 4..Exercise 1.input and the output is in a file named Chapter 4..Exercise 1.output.

A Word file (file name: Chapter 4.Exercise 1.discussion) is also provided, which discusses the results.

2. Use the adjusted Wald method to find a 95% confidence interval for the true proportion who successfully complete the tasks, if we sample 20 people and four successfully completed the task out of the 20. The answer and discussion are in a Word file named Chapter 4.Exercise 2.

REFERENCES

Agressi, A., Coull, B., 1998. Approximate is better than 'exact' for interval estimation of binomial proportions. The American Statistician 52, p119–126.

Sauro, J., Lewis, J., 2005. Estimating completion rates from small samples using binomial confidence intervals: comparisons and recommendations. In: Proceedings of the Human Factors and Ergonomics Society Annual Meeting, Orlando, FL. Morgan Kaufmann. www.measuringusability.com/papers/sauro-lewisHFES.pdf.

Lewis, J., Sauro, J., 2006. When 100% really isn't 100%: improving the accuracy of small-sample estimates of completion rates. Journal of Usability Studies 1 (3), 136–150.

Pass or fail? Binomial-related hypothesis testing and confidence intervals using paired samples

5

5.1 INTRODUCTION

We noted in Chapter 4 and repeat here that task success is a fundamental metric for any UX researcher who regularly conducts usability testing. Thus, we indicated that pass/fail is a fundamental metric that you should always deliver for each task when reporting your results. In this chapter, we discuss pass/fail data for a within-subject design, or paired data.

5.2 CASE STUDY: CAN I REGISTER FOR A COURSE AT BACKBOARD.COM?

You've just landed a new gig as a UX researcher at Backboard, a learning management system (LMS) company that provides software for the administration, documentation, tracking, reporting, and delivery of online education courses and training programs.

Backboard is barely out of start-up phase, but you're still surprised to find out that no formal usability testing was ever conducted during development of their flagship product Backboard LMS.

During your first week on the job, you run into Bob Buzzkill, the chief technology officer, at the coffee machine. Buzzkill has worked in hi-tech for a long time; he brandishes a pocket protector and digital watch to prove it. Since formal usability testing was rarely if ever conducted during his formative years in the 70's and 80's, he's sceptical of the entire process, but has begrudgingly begun to accept its value. Since you know he'd never introduce himself to a practitioner of a discipline he barely acknowledges, you decide to take the initiative. You introduce yourself, and he sheepishly admits that "our usability was kinda ad hoc," but they shipped the software anyway because they had contracts to fulfill.

"Can we obtain some real usability data asap?" Buzzkill asks. "We're hearing some rumblings about usability problems with our largest customer…. I want them to know we're at least working on it!"

You're off to the races. First, you perform a heuristic review using the persona of a typical company employee-learner who is perusing training offerings, registering for courses, and getting on waiting lists. Based on the review, you have hypotheses of what usability issues exist in the product. Based on those hypotheses you start to create the tasks for a usability test. The tasks seem pretty straightforward, but under the hood you've carefully crafted each one to either confirm or refute your hypothesis about a usability problem.

119

Once you've got a first draft of the test script—which also includes your posttask rating scales—you send it to other members of the UX team as well as to Buzzkill. After collecting and assimilating the tweaks from the UX team on the test tasks, you receive a rather terse e-mail from Buzzkill indicating that "some of the tasks are kinda tough." In particular, he objects to the task involving re-registering for a yearly mandatory safety training session. You ask him for specifics, but never get a response. Unable to get any time on his calendar, and with only 2 days until the test, you finally run into him at the company cafeteria.

"Oh, hi. Sorry I never got back to you," he nonchalantly says as he picks at the last remnants of the feeble salad bar. "Nobody can re-register. Testing it is pointless," he declares as he drizzles his iceberg lettuce with some low-cal dressing.

"Nobody can re-register. Testing it is pointless."

"Ah, OK. But what's your sample size?" you ask.

"Ah…well," he stammers. "I just know everybody complains about it."

"OK," you reply good-naturedly. "Let's test it just to confirm."

"Sure, go ahead; but it's probably a waste of time," he mumbles over his shoulder, heading for the cashier.

You end up with 10 tasks for the test and 6 post-test Likert-style rating scales. You're a little worried that it may be hard to fit in that amount of activity in an hour, but the pilot test runs beautifully, and you're ready to rock.

SIDEBAR: WITHIN = REPEATED

Note that in this scenario we are using a total of 10 people and each one of the 10 people is attempting to complete each one of the 10 tasks. This is a classic within-subject usability test setup; each person provides data for each task, because each person is attempting to do all 10 tasks; we could say that, "each person is repeated [here, 10 times]." This is why another name for "within-subject designs" is "repeated-measures designs."

The 2-day actual testing—five participants per day—proceeds very well. But, at the end of the tenth participant, you're really beat and can't really look at the data.

The next day, you get to work analyzing the data. And of course, the first thing you do is tally the task completions as in Table 5.1.

The results are reassuring in some aspects and very problematic in other ways. You're relieved to find out that the basics of course management—finding and registering for a course—were often easily completed by your test participants,

Table 5.1 Tasks and Number of Successful Completions

Task #	Verbatim Task	Successful Completions (out of 10 participants)
1	"During your annual review with your manager, she described a course that she recently took and enjoyed. She says it might be beneficial for you too. It's a course called Managing, Communicating and Leading. Register for the course."	9
2	"Determine who the training coordinator for the course is."	2
3	"You want to take a financial management course that meets in a physical classroom rather than online. Look for a financial management class that meets in a physical classroom in Montreal and sign up for the course."	8
4	"Suddenly you feel like you're overextending yourself. Drop Managing, Communicating, and Leading."	8
5	Get on the waiting list for "Business Analytics."	6

Continued

Table 5.1 Tasks and Number of Successful Completions—cont'd

Task #	Verbatim Task	Successful Completions (out of 10 participants)
6	"Now, find a description for the 'Analytics for Decision Making' course."	7
7	You recently completed a course called "BA Techniques Program." Rate the course positively and write that "This course was very informative."	3
8	"BA Techniques Program" is a mandatory course that all business analysts must take on a regular basis. You last took it during September 2014. Sign up for the course again."	5
9	You're currently taking a course called "Analytics for Decision Making." You turned in your first homework assignment, but never got the graded assignment back from the professor. You're wondering if anyone else did. What's the quickest way to ask all of your classmates without resorting to e-mail?	2
10	In preparation for your course "Managing Financial Information" (that you just registered for), you'd like to read up on recent trends in hedge funds. Where would you go to find this kind of background material?	2

as evidenced by the high success tally for those tasks. But the more tangential functionality—finding related course material, rating a course, communicating with classmates—doesn't seem ready for prime time, looking at the success tally for the related tasks. And, what about re-registering? Buzzkill said it was in bad shape, but getting on the waiting list looks almost as bad.

"But wait," you think to yourself, "Is there really a significant difference in completion rates between getting on a waiting list (Task 5: 6 completions) and re-registering for a course (Task 8: 5 completions)? Is the difference between 5 and 6 completions really meaningful?" Hmmm! If we knew that the *true rates* of completion were 60% and 50%, respectively, that would be a meaningful difference. But, of course, we don't know this, and perhaps we cannot infer that there is any difference at all in the true completion rates. We'll find out.

The questions rumble around in your head as you continue to write up your test results, adding screen shots, verbatim quotes, and Likert scale results. But you know Buzzkill is going to pop his head into your office at any minute and ask you about the completion rates, and what they mean. You've got to be ready for his questions.

5.3 HYPOTHESIS TESTING USING THE COCHRAN Q TEST

To put your problem into statistical terms, you want to know if there is a statistically significant difference between the task success rates, so that you can confidently make recommendations on what the design team should be working on next. This is basically the same objective as in the previous chapter (with a different setting), but now with a within-subject/paired data design.

Unfortunately, the chi-square test of independence we described in Chapter 4 can properly be used only when we have independent data. For the case at hand, the appropriate statistical test is the Cochran Q test. Excel does not do the Cochran Q test, while SPSS does. However, we will describe how you can easily do the Cochran Q test in Excel.

SIDEBAR: McNEMAR OR COCHRAN?

If there are only two tasks being compared in a within-subject design, the McNemar test is also appropriate. However, the Cochran Q test is appropriate when there are two or more tasks; in essence, the Cochran Q test is an extension of the McNemar test. The McNemar test was first developed in 1947 (McNemar, 1947) and the Cochran Q test in 1950 (Cochran, 1950). Excel does not do the McNemar test or the Cochran Q test, while SPSS performs both.

First, we'll show you how to use Excel to compute the (Cochran) Q statistic, and then find the *p*-value by approximating the distribution of Q by a chi-square variable, using an easy Excel command.

SIDEBAR: WILLIAM COCHRAN

William Gemmell Cochran (July 15, 1909–March 29, 1980) was a prominent statistician; he was born in Scotland but spent most of his life in the United States. He studied mathematics at the University of Glasgow and the University of Cambridge. He moved to the United States in 1939. There, he helped establish several departments of statistics at various universities. His longest spell in any one university was at Harvard University, which he joined in 1957 and from which he retired in 1976. Dr. Cochran wrote several books and many journal articles. "Cochran's Q" tests the hypothesis that two or more "matched sets" (i.e., within-subject design) have the same proportion, or whether the proportions differ. In our setting, the proportion refers to the proportion of people who complete a given task. His test is particularly suitable when the output variable is nominal, which "pass/fail" satisfies. Dr. Cochran showed that his Q statistic is well approximated by a chi-square distribution, and, as you will see, we use this fact to take the value of Q, and turn it into a *p*-value using a simple Excel chi-square command.

So, in this case, we want to test the following hypothesis:

$$H0: p5 = p8$$
vs.
$$H1: p5 \neq p8,$$

where p5 and p8 are the true proportions of successful completions for tasks 5 and 8, respectively, in Table 5.1. (As a reminder: Task 5 involves getting on the waiting list, and Task 8 involves re-registering for a course.) As we have said *ad infinitum,* the true value of this proportion is that which would result if the entire population who could ever be performing the task indeed performed the task. We can sum up the sample results in Table 5.2.

As we see in Table 5.2, task 5 had six successful completions and four failures, while task 8 had five successful completions and five failures.

5.3.1 EXCEL

To perform the Cochran Q test, it is not sufficient to simply provide the values we have in Table 5.2. When we have a within-subject design it is important to know the paired results of the proportions. Consider the pass/fail data for two tasks (in a fictional test) such as in Figure 5.1. The data in columns A and B are not the same as the data in columns E and F, even though in both cases we are comparing a 7/3 pass rate with a 5/5 pass rate.

Table 5.2 Data/Frequencies for Hypothesis Test

Task	5	8
Pass	6	5
Fail	4	5

	A	B	C	D	E	F
1	1	1			1	0
2	1	1			1	0
3	1	1			1	0
4	1	1			1	0
5	1	1			1	0
6	1	0			1	1
7	1	0			1	1
8	0	0			0	1
9	0	0			0	1
10	0	0			0	1
11						

FIGURE 5.1

Two different 7/3 versus 5/5 patterns; Excel.

SIDEBAR: KEEP TRACK OF TASK-COMPLETION PAIRED RESULTS!

The reason the two data sets differ in terms of the appropriate measure of Cochran's Q is subtle, but was true also in the paired t-test of Chapter 3. Even though in both cases it is a 7/3 versus 5/5, in the (A, B) data set, only 2 people differed in their result for the two tasks, persons 6 and 7; the remaining 8 people performed the same way. However, in the (E, F) data set, 8 of the 10 people had a different result. It could have been many different patterns. These differences are relevant when computing the probability that such a result could arise due to luck, basically, the p-value.

In essence, we must know the paired results, and not only the number of passes and fails. This was not true when we had independent samples, but is, unfortunately, true for within-sample/paired data studies.

The moral of the story is to keep track of your task completions/failures during your testing for each participant. This can get a little tricky when you've counterbalanced the tasks to ameliorate a potential "order effect."

Now, let's look at the values in Figure 5.2, which displays the pass/fail pattern you observed during your test.

Now, to perform the Cochran Q test, we need to do various calculations, but doing calculations are what Excel excels at (pun intended!). Here are the steps:

Step (1) Total each column, obtaining the 6 and 5 we knew about from our test data. This is easily done using the SUM command. For column 1, we type "=SUM(A1:A10)," where we enter the command, arbitrarily in cell A12. Then we press enter. Do this similarly for column B. The result is shown in Figure 5.3.

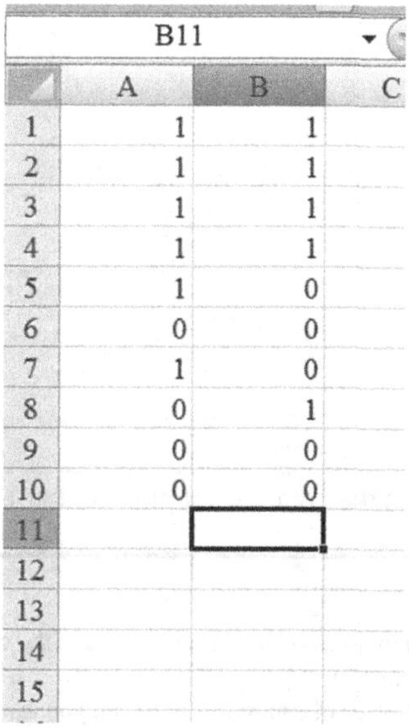

	A	B	C
1	1	1	
2	1	1	
3	1	1	
4	1	1	
5	1	0	
6	0	0	
7	1	0	
8	0	1	
9	0	0	
10	0	0	
11			
12			
13			
14			
15			

FIGURE 5.2

Detailed pass/fail data of our earlier listed two-task hypotheses; Excel.

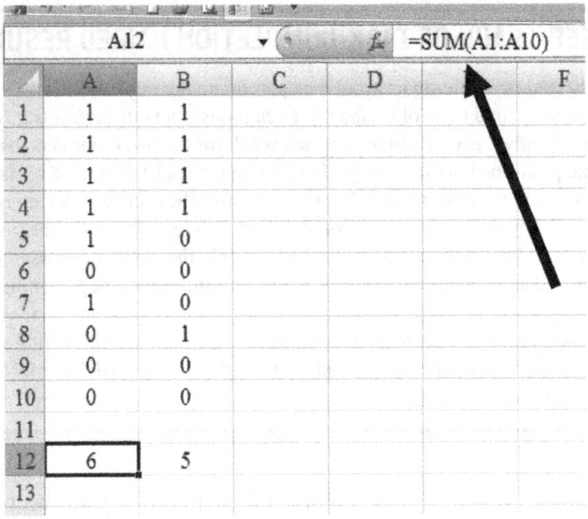

FIGURE 5.3

Finding column sums; Excel.

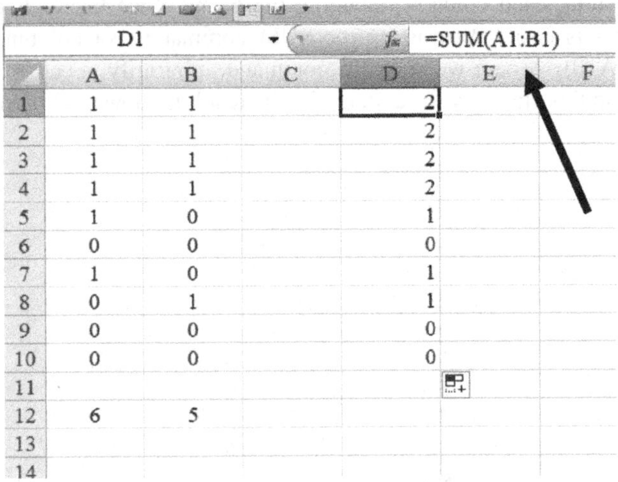

FIGURE 5.4

Finding row sums; Excel. (Note the command in the tool bar.)

SIDEBAR: DRAG IT!

Notice that we have the column totals in cells A12 and B12, and the command we typed in is in the bar at the top (see arrow in Figure 5.3).

But to quickly fill in several types of data series in Excel, you also can select cells and drag the fill handle, pictured here: [□].

To use the fill handle, you select the cells that you want to use as a basis for filling additional cells, and then drag the fill handle across or down the cells that you want to fill.

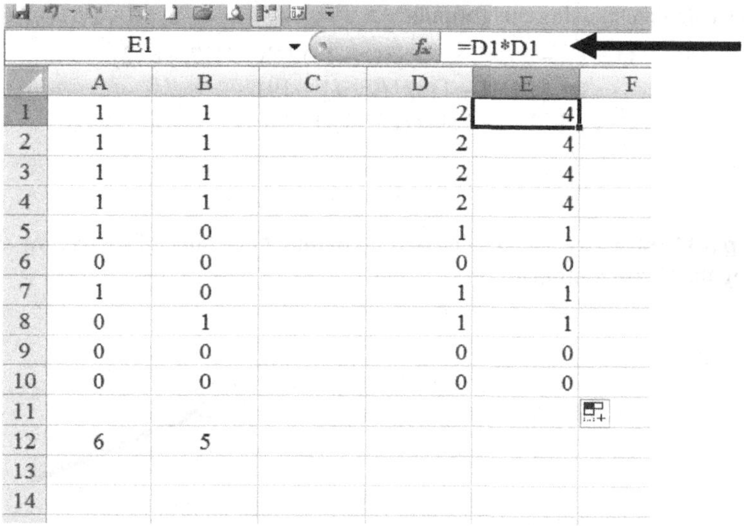

	A	B	C	D	E	F
1	1	1		2	4	
2	1	1		2	4	
3	1	1		2	4	
4	1	1		2	4	
5	1	0		1	1	
6	0	0		0	0	
7	1	0		1	1	
8	0	1		1	1	
9	0	0		0	0	
10	0	0		0	0	
11						
12	6	5				
13						
14						

E1 f_x =D1*D1

FIGURE 5.5

Computing the square of each value in column E into column F; Excel. (Notice the command in the tool bar above.)

Step (2) Next, find the sum of each of the rows. The command for row 1 would be =SUM(A1:B1). We put this arbitrarily in column D. This is done for each row (or "dragged down" for each row), resulting in Figure 5.4.

We now have the column sums and the row sums.

Step (3) Next, form a new column that is the square of column D, that is, the square of each of the row sums. For example, for row 1, type the following in cell E1:

$$= D1 * D1$$

Then press "enter." Complete for each row. See the results in Figure 5.5.

Step (4) Now, add up the values in column D and in column E. For column D, we can write (in cell D12), the command =SUM(D1:D10), and do the same for column E, in cell E12, with the command =SUM(E1:E10). This is shown in Figure 5.6. As a small aside, we actually knew that the sum of column D would be 11 (=6+5).

Step (5) Now, calculate Q, which involves the values in row 12 and the fact that there are two tasks. First, we'll give you the components of the formula and then the formula itself:

- K = number of columns, here = 2
- Values in cells A12, B12, D12, and E12
- $T = A12 + B12$ (here = 6 + 5 = 11)
- $TSSQ = A12^2 + B12^2$ (here = $6^2 + 5^2$ = 36 + 25 = 61)

Now calculate Q using this formula:

$$Q = (K-1) * (K*TSSQ-T^2)/(K*D12-E12)$$
$$= 1 * (2*61-11^2)/(2*11-19)$$
$$= 1 * (122-121)/(22-19)$$
$$= 1/3$$
$$= 0.333$$

Step (6) Now we use the Q value (0.333) to find the *p*-value of the test. We do this by using the Excel command.

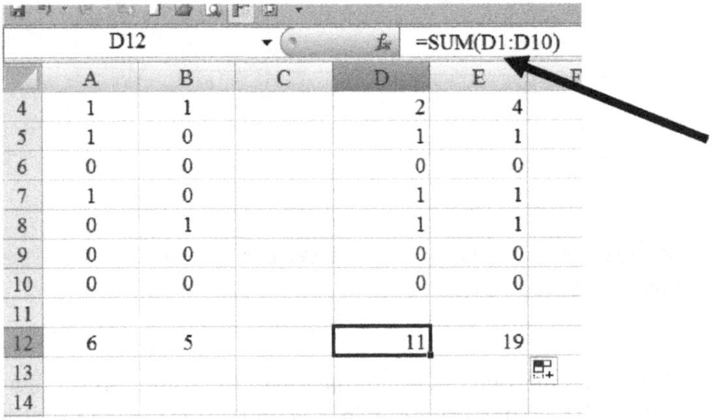

FIGURE 5.6

Calculating the sum of columns E and F; Excel.

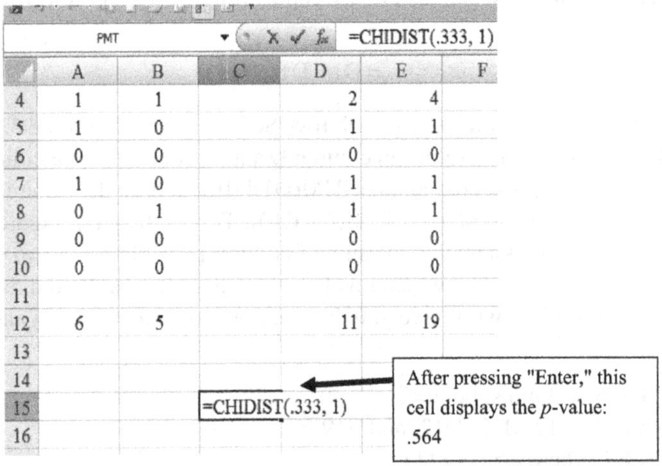

FIGURE 5.7

Setting up to find the *p*-value of the Cochran Q test; Excel.

$$=\text{CHIDIST}\,(Q, K-1)\,\text{or}$$
$$=\text{CHIDIST}\,(0.333, 1).$$

We can implement this command in any cell of Excel; see Figure 5.7 and the arrow in Figure 5.7. (As we noted, the distribution of Q is approximated by a chi-square distribution. And we arbitrarily picked cell C15 in which to put the command.)

Press "Enter" to obtain the p-value of 0.564. Therefore, we accept H0, since $0.564>0.05$. As we have noted, this indicates that we do not have sufficient evidence (it's not even close!) to reject H0.

5.3.2 SPSS

We now present Cochran's Q test in SPSS. First, we enter the data, as shown in Figure 5.8.

SIDEBAR: FINALLY! SOME SPSS AND EXCEL SIMILARITIES

Fortunately, the Cochran Q test requires the data to be entered in SPSS the same way it is entered in Excel. In a sense we're avoiding the usability problem with data entry that we had when we performed the chi-square test in Chapter 4 (which, you may recall, needed the data to be entered as a 30×2 data set.)

From the "Analyze" menu, highlight the menu item "Nonparametric tests," then the submenu "Legacy Dialogs," and finally the sub-submenu "K Related Samples;" see Figure 5.8 and the three arrows in Figure 5.9. Note that we have only two samples, but the Cochran Q test can handle any number, so it is listed under the more general case of "K Related Samples."

12 : Task.5		=su		
		Task.5	Task.8	va
1		1.00	1.00	
2		1.00	1.00	
3		1.00	1.00	
4		1.00	1.00	
5		1.00	.00	
6		.00	.00	
7		1.00	.00	
8		.00	1.00	
9		.00	.00	
10		.00	.00	
11				

FIGURE 5.8

SPSS input for Cochran Q test.

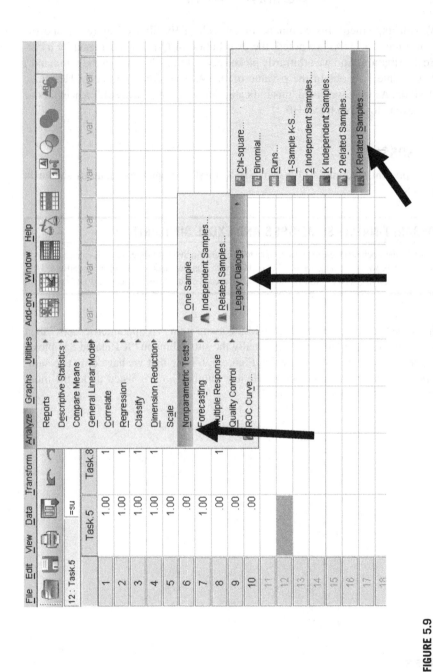

FIGURE 5.9

SPSS Analysis process for beginning the Cochran Q test.

We now arrive at the "Tests for Several Related Samples" dialog box, as shown in Figure 5.10. Check off the small box to the left of "Cochran's Q" (see horizontal arrow in Figure 5.10), and uncheck the small box to the left of "Friedman," which is the default (see vertical arrow in Figure 5.10).

Now we drag over the two "variables" to the "Test Variables" section, as shown in Figure 5.11.

Click on "OK" to obtain our output, as shown in Figure 5.12.

Notice that, of course, we obtain the same value for Cochran's Q (which equals 0.333; see top arrow in Figure 5.12) and the same p-value, which equals 0.564 (see bottom arrow in Figure 5.12) as we did in Excel. As a consequence, we reach the same conclusion of accepting H0, hence concluding that the completion rates cannot be said to differ for the two tasks.

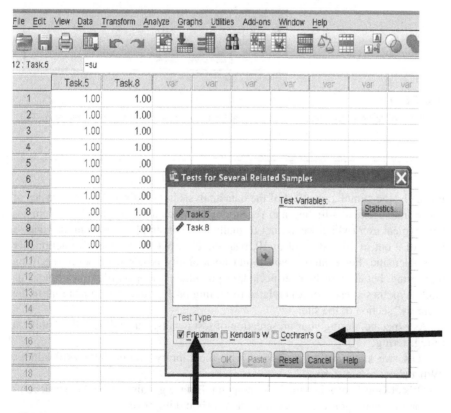

FIGURE 5.10

"Test for several related samples" dialog box; SPSS.

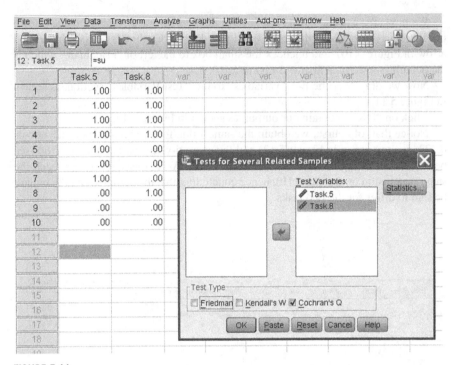

FIGURE 5.11

Test for K related samples dialog box with variables brought over to the test variable box; SPSS.

5.4 MEANWHILE, BACK AT BACKBOARD...

Basically, the cumulative effect of the data analysis has confirmed that the basics of course management—finding and registering for a course—are not a problem for your typical user (which we did not formally test, but simply infer from the success rates of 9 out of 10 and 8 out of 10, respectively), but the tangential functionality is problematic. For example, you found no usability issues whatsoever regarding registering, but at least three suspected, or potential, whoppers (these were not formally hypothesis-tested either) related to finding background course material in the "Library" section of the site.

As expected, during your presentation of test results, Buzzkill is still harping on re-registering:

"OK, we know we've got issues with the Library section," Buzzkill admits. "What about re-registering?"

"It's obviously problematic," you respond. But we got almost the same task completion rate as we got for the waiting list. We should improve both.

"You're telling me the waiting list and re-registering are equally problematic?" Buzzkill asks incredulously.

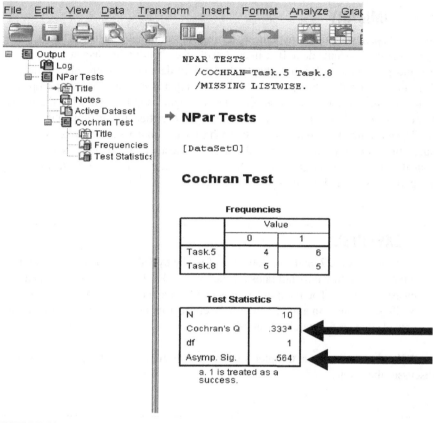

FIGURE 5.12

Cochran test output; SPSS.

"Yes. Not only were the task completion rates almost the same, but the Cochran Q test showed, overwhelmingly, no difference. We got a *p*-value of 0.564, which is obviously way above 0.05."

Buzzkill stares at you blankly. His silence tells you he has no clue what you're talking about. To break the uneasy silence, you make an offer.

"I could run an un-moderated usability test with much larger sample sizes, but there's no guarantee we'll get different results."

"Nah," Buzzkill says, staring at his iPhone. You sense retreat. "I'll get my guys to work on both."

As Buzzkill leaves the conference room. The rest of the attendees give you thumbs-up, and your buddy, Ajay, slaps you on the back:

"That's the first time I've ever seen Buzzkill back down! Wow, that stats stuff blew his mind! Nice work, buddy."

5.5 SUMMARY

In this chapter we studied hypothesis testing for "nominal/categorical" data, more specifically, "pass/fail" data. But, in contrast to the situation in Chapter 4, where we had independent samples, this chapter had paired data or a within-subjects design. This meant that the chi-square test of independence was no longer appropriate. Thus, we introduced the Cochran Q test. We emphasized how knowing the paired responses, and not only the overall pass/fail rates, is critical to performing the analysis. The reasoning behind this is similar to the discussion in Chapter 3 when we introduced the paired t-test and contrasted it with the t-test with independent samples. We considered the Cochran Q test in both Excel (with formulas, since the technique is not part of Excel) and in SPSS, where the Cochran test is available.

5.6 EXERCISE

1. Consider tasks 6, 7, and 8 of Table 5.1. Test the hypothesis that there is no difference in the true pass/fail rates for the three tasks. The design is a repeated measures design. The input in Excel is in a file named Chapter 5.Exercise 1. In SPSS, the input is in a file Chapter 5..Exercise 1.input and the output is in a file named Chapter 5..Exercise 1.output.

   A Word file (file name: Chapter 5.Exercise 1.discussion) is also provided, which discusses the results.

REFERENCES

Cochran, W.G., 1950. The comparison of percentages in matched samples. Biometrika 37, 256–266.
McNemar, Q., 1947. Note on the sampling error of the difference between correlated proportions or percentages. Psychometrika 12, 153–157.

Comparing more than two means: one factor ANOVA with independent samples. Multiple comparison testing with the Newman-Keuls test

6

6.1 INTRODUCTION

As the researcher on a UX team, you are probably frequently asked to compare more than two means. You could be comparing ratings of attractiveness of a specific design across different age brackets. Or, you may be comparing more than two task-completion times from a usability test. Often, the most common scenario of comparing more than two means that a UX researcher confronts is assessing the scores from Likert scales.

A typical Likert scale is a statement to which the respondents rate their level of agreement. Usually a five-point scale is used, and the two ends are labeled.

SIDEBAR: ODD OR EVEN NUMBER OF OPTIONS?

There is some debate whether it is superior to have an even or odd number of choices in a Likert type scale. This debate has been going on for what seems forever. It is the type of issue in the marketing research world about which "reasonable people disagree."

Having an odd number of choices (e.g., 5) gives the responder a midpoint (i.e., 3) to focus on, while an even number gives the user no midpoint (e.g., on a 6-point scale, the midpoint is 3.5). The issue is whether having an able-to-be-chosen midpoint is a good thing or a bad thing.

Continued

SIDEBAR: ODD OR EVEN NUMBER OF OPTIONS?—cont'd

Those who believe it is a good thing argue that being able to focus on a specific midvalue makes it easier for the responder and allows for more accurate assessments.

The proponents of having an even number argue that an odd number of points provides a responder with the ability to not have to commit himself/herself either way, while an even number of choices forces the responder to commit himself/herself to one side of the midpoint or the other—and argue that this is a good thing.

Another thing to consider is this: there is a cognitive bias in human behavior called "anchoring and adjustment" (e.g., Tversky and Kahneman, 1974). This has been demonstrated over and over again and, in essence, says that when people focus on one value, it becomes an "anchor" (whether voluntarily or not, and a specific midpoint, such as a "3" on a 1–5 scale, is an anchor), which retards movement. Thus, a responder does not, on average, move away from the anchor as much as might be chosen were there no anchors. Thus, the extremes are not chosen as much as they should be because responders stay closer to the anchor more than they should.

However, "anchoring and adjustment" applies more when there are a larger number of points among which to choose (e.g., a 7- or 9-point scale). With only 5 points, the "anchoring and adjustment" bias is less prominent, and perhaps, immaterial.

We always use an odd number of points in our scales because we feel that a neutral response is always possible, and denying that kind of neutral choice is akin to "leading the witness"—something we never try to do.

A typical set of end labels is "Strongly Disagree" and "Strongly Agree," like the following:

Strongly Disagree 1 2 3 4 5 *Strongly Agree*

The respondent simply circles (or checks) the number that indicates his/her level of agreement with the statement. Sometimes, an open text field is provided for the respondent to add some comments regarding the score.

In practice, Likert scales (and other types of rating scales, like the System Usability Scale) are a vital part of your UX researcher tool kit. They provide you with quantifiable data about the user's perception of the system, design, ease of task, or anything else, as opposed to what you (or anyone else on your team) think those perceptions are.

In addition, Likert scales can provide vital complementary data that can either corroborate or negate other findings. For example, a post-test ease-of-use rating for a particular task may be 4.6 (on a 5-point scale), and this would complement a task-completion rate of 90%. With these two values, you are probably fairly confident that the task is not problematic for your target audience. Conversely, a post-test ease-of-use rating for a particular task may be 1.2 (on a 5-point scale), and this complements a task-completion rate of (only) 20%. With these two values, you are probably fairly confident you've got a problem on your hands.

In our experience, good ratings of usability usually correlate to good task-completions rates. But if you're using different types of rating scales, all bets may be off. A great example of this is garnering ratings of usefulness, not usability. For example, a post-test usefulness rating for a particular task may be 1.5 (on a 5-point scale), but the task completion rate is 90. The user thought it was easy to complete the task, but there wasn't value in completing the task in the first place!! After all, it may be easy to literally ride a skateboard, but how useful is it when you need to be at work in a half hour and work is 15 miles away?

6.2 CASE STUDY: SOPHISTICATED FOR WHOM?

Let's return to our favorite fashion site, Mademoiselle La La. To refresh your memory, you were hired as the UX researcher at Mademoiselle La La, a high-end online store aimed at urbane women from ages 18–55 years with well-above-average disposable income.

You'll remember that you launched an online survey to determine which new home page design was more sophisticated. Using a t-test for independent samples, you concluded that Design 1—a scene of a young woman sipping a coffee at an outdoor French café, ignoring the adoring eyes of a nearby young man—was considered more "sophisticated" than Design 2, a scene of a young couple snuggling together under one umbrella during a shower, with the Eiffel Tower bisecting a slate-gray sky. Furthermore, you were able to report that the low p-value of 0.023 meant there was a statistically significant difference between the two designs.

So far, so good at your new gig. But a mere week after your presentation, Cinny Bittle, the brash new director of marketing, pokes her head in your office, waving a copy of the latest Forrester report:

"Did you see this? Older boomers spend the most online. We're hosed!"

"Did you see this? Older boomers spend the most online! We're hosed!"

Your head spins with the marketing jargon. "Can you break it down for me?"

She shoots you the "I-can't-believe-you-don't-know-this" look. "Yeah...older boomers, 56–66, spent an average of $367 in the last 3 months, double that of Gen Z, 18–25, at $138. Younger boomers, 46–55, were next at $318, followed by $315 for Gen X, 36–45, closely followed by Gen Y, 26–35, at $311."

"I guess it makes sense," you offer as you copy down the stats. "The older folks are in the prime of their money-making years."

She steps into your office and urgently whispers: "Yeah, but I'm wondering if we're barking up the wrong tree with that new home page design we have. I mean, if only punks think it's sophisticated, don't we have to rethink the strategy?

"Well, we don't know that yet. But keep in mind that our biggest customers are in the 26–45 range, followed closely by the younger boomers, who are ages 46–55. Our styles are a little conservative for the 18–25 crowd, and not conservative enough for the 56–66 crowd. Since sales are low for those 'outlier' brackets, we don't worry about them as much as the others."

Bittle is staring down at her cell, madly texting. You're finished talking but she never looks up. It's obvious she didn't hear what you said, but she persists: "Can we just see which group thinks the design is sophisticated?"

You decide to appease rather than continue the one-way conversation: "Sure, let me slice and dice the survey data by age this time. Then, we can see if there are differences in sophistication by age for the chosen design. Give me the rest of the day and I'll see what I can find out."

"Thanks," she says without a break in the rabid texting. She starts to walk away, never taking her eyes off her phone. "Let me know asap."

You open your Excel file containing the survey data. When you get to the crucial Likert scale about sophistication, "This page makes Mademoiselle La La seem sophisticated"—you start slicing the data to see what the age bracket slices tell you—if anything.

You quickly sort the data by youngest to oldest, using these age brackets:

1. Gen Z, 18–25 years
2. Gen Y, 26–35 years
3. Gen X, 36–45 years
4. Younger boomers, 46–55 years
5. Older boomers, 56–66 years

The data for people in each group are displayed in Table 6.1.

Table 6.1 Data for Five Groups Evaluating "Sophistication" on the 1–5 Likert Scale

Age Bracket 1	Age Bracket 2	Age Bracket 3	Age Bracket 4	Age Bracket 5
18–25 Gen Z	26–35 Gen Y	36–45 Gen X	46–55 Younger boomers	56–66 Older boomers
2	4	4	3	3
3	3	5	4	4
3	3	4	4	3
2	3	4	3	2

(Continued)

Table 6.1 Data for Five Groups Evaluating "Sophistication" on the 1–5 Likert Scale—cont'd

Age Bracket 1	Age Bracket 2	Age Bracket 3	Age Bracket 4	Age Bracket 5
3	4	4	3	3
1	5	5	4	3
3	4	5	4	3
1	5	5	3	2
1	4	4	3	3
4	5	5	2	2
3	5	5	3	3
2	4	4	4	2
2	5	5	3	3
3	4	4	3	3
1	5	5	4	2
1	5	5	3	3
2	5	5	3	4
2	4	4	3	3
2	4	4	2	2
1	5	5	2	2
2	4	5	2	3
3	5	5	2	2
3	4	4	3	3
3	5	2		
3	5	5		
4	5	5		
2				
1				
Mean = 2.25	4.38	4.50	3.04	2.74
n = 28	26	26	23	23
18–25 Gen Z	26–35 Gen Y	36–45 Gen X	46–55 Younger boomers	56–66 Older boomers

Agreement with statement: "This page makes Mademoiselle La La seem sophisticated."
1 = Strongly disagree, 5 = strongly agree.

Staring at the numbers, you're glad to see higher ratings for part of Mademoiselle La La's target audience of 36–45 years. But you're not sure what the other numbers mean. Is there really a statistical difference in sophistication ratings between the older and younger boomers? And what about those "punks," as Bittle calls Gen Z? Is their perception of sophistication really different from those of their grandmothers?

Analysis of variance (ANOVA) to the rescue!

6.3 INDEPENDENT SAMPLES: ONE-FACTOR ANOVA

To put your question into statistical terms, you want to test the hypothesis that differences in perception of sophistication are different for different age-groups. In this kind of scenario, we'll use an independent sample ANOVA to test this hypothesis; the test statistic for ANOVA is the F-statistic.

The samples being independent simply means that each task or design is experienced by different people.

ANOVA can be used in many different situations, but there are often two UX situations when this kind of test is especially appropriate. One case is when we have one task or design and we wish to compare groups of people who differ in some attribute(s). This is the case here: We have five age-groups (brackets), and various people in each age-group providing an evaluation of the same page. The second scenario may be to have a number of groups evaluating a number of different designs or completing different tasks (one group per design or task).

When using ANOVA, it is not important that we have the same number of people evaluating each of the designs, or evaluating the ease-of-use of the different tasks being studied. And the sample sizes do not affect the analysis methodology and workings of the software at all; it would not matter if each age-group consisted of around 3 people or around 3000 people. Of course, the results are more accurate if we have larger sample sizes. (However, if one were allocating people to each design or task, it would be most efficient to split the folks as near as possible to having an equal amount for each design or task.) As can be seen in Table 6.1, we have sample sizes of 28, 26, 26, 23, and 23, respectively.

SIDEBAR: HOW ANOVA IS WORKING UNDER THE HOOD

With more than two means to compare, the calculations are more detailed and complicated, but ultimately, we will get a p-value from the software, which will still "say it all." We have made the conscious decision to not include all these details, but you may be interested in a look under the hood. Read on....

As its name implies, ANOVA computes the variance due to differences between groups, and the variability between individuals within groups. Then, after taking into account the number of columns we have and the sample size of each column, the two variance types are put into ratio to one another. The value of the ratio (called the "F-statistic") determines if we should reject the null hypothesis that all the true column means are equal; the alternate hypothesis is that the true column means are not all equal.

In our example, we examine the differences among the five column (i.e., age-group) means and look at how much they vary from one another. That is done by first computing the mean of all the data, called by the grandiose name of the "grand mean." The grand mean for our data in Table 6.1 is 3.39. Then, each column mean difference from this grand mean is calculated:

Continued

SIDEBAR: HOW ANOVA IS WORKING UNDER THE HOOD—cont'd

$$(2.25 - 3.39) = -1.14$$
$$(4.38 - 3.39) = 0.99$$
$$(4.50 - 3.39) = 1.11$$
$$(3.04 - 3.39) = -0.35$$
$$(2.74 - 3.39) = -0.65$$

These differences add to –0.04, a value near zero, and if we took a weighted average, based on the slightly different sample sizes of the columns, we would get exactly zero (except for any rounding error). But, obviously, the five column means don't have zero difference! So, adding up the differences (with or without using a weighted average) is not a useful way to measure how different the column means are from one another.

Thus, we need to get a bit more inventive in getting a measure of how different the column means are (n.b.: it involves squaring the differences, so that they accumulate, rather than cancel out). After that, we still need to find the right way to "put it all together"—incorporate the differences among the individual data values and the samples sizes used. Oy! Forget it! You don't want any more detail. The only other thing we will mention is that the appropriate test is not a t-test, but what we can mathematically prove is called an "F-test." The F-distribution is a probability curve that does not look like a normal curve—indeed, it's not even symmetric—but it is based on the individual data points following a normal curve, and can be defined in terms of a function of a normal curve.

We repeat that, since the "p-value says it all," some of the even sketchy details we gave you in the last couple of paragraphs are not crucial for you to "master." Of course, this is true as long as you believe what we tell you and show you. Trust us!! It is!!

6.4 THE ANALYSES

6.4.1 EXCEL

First, import your data into Excel. Then go to the "data" column on the main menu of Excel and click on "Data Analysis"—which you have activated as discussed in Chapter 1. Then highlight "Anova: Single Factor" (see arrow in Figure 6.1).

Now, we click on the highlighted command (or the "OK") and consider the dialog box that comes up. Fill in the location of each "variable"—i.e., tell Excel where the data values are located. See Figure 6.2.

Note that we requested that the output be put on a new worksheet (i.e., page!!) that we arbitrarily named "abbyj." See vertical arrow in Figure 6.2.

SIDEBAR: KEEP 'EM TOGETHER IN EXCEL

It can be seen in Figure 6.2 that we have indicated that the input data values are from A1 to E28 (n.b.: We need to use "E28" even though column E has only 23 values, to assure that the 28 values in column A are included—Excel will realize that other columns have fewer data points. See dashed arrow in Figure 6.2.

Keep in mind that in Excel, when conducting an ANOVA, all columns of data need to be contiguous (immediately next to each other). When you type "a1:e28" (you can use either small letters or capital letters), Excel knows that you have data in the block denoted by columns A through E, and whatever rows are filled in. Had there been labels atop each column (such as "age-group 1," "age-group 2," etc., so that the data started in row 2 and ended in row 29—column A ending in row 29), we would have indicated "a1:e29," and checked off "Labels in First Row"—see horizontal (solid) arrow in Figure 6.2.

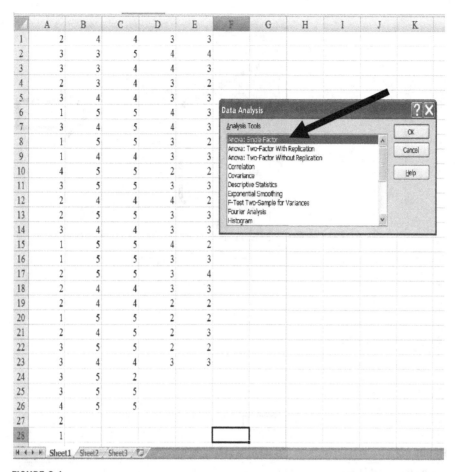

FIGURE 6.1

Opening "Data Analysis" and highlighting desired technique; Excel.

Next, we click on "OK" in the upper right corner (see "thick hollow arrow" in Figure 6.2). This will provide the output shown in Figure 6.3.

We now examine this output in Figure 6.3. The key value on the output, as always, is the "p-value." See arrow in Figure 6.3.

In this output, the p-value = 4.26E-24. As we have noted before, "E" means "exponential" and really means "power of 10." In other words, the p-value = 4.26×10^{-24}, or (with 23 zeros) 0.00000000000000000000000424. Obviously, this is (way) below 0.05; in fact, it's about as close to zero as you'll ever see! So, we reject H0 and go with H1, and thus conclude that there is sufficient evidence to be convinced that the true averages of sophistication evaluation for the five age-groups are not equal.

Now, we know what you may be saying to yourself: "So what? I want to know where the significant differences are!"

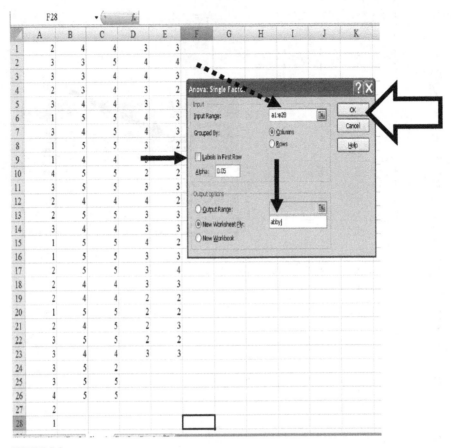

FIGURE 6.2

Opening up and filling in analysis of variance (ANOVA): one factor; Excel.

Well, there's a solution we will describe in Section 6.5 and Section 6.6. In the meantime, we can speculate; based on the means (top part of the output in Figure 6.3—see oval), it would seem that age-groups 2 and 3 have higher true means than the other age-groups, and it is not clear how the other 3 age-groups stack up against one another.

6.4.2 SPSS

Now we illustrate the same ANOVA analysis in SPSS. (If we're importing data from another source (say, Excel), we must cut and paste the data into SPSS. And, as you may recall from Chapter 2, the format of the data in SPSS is different from that of Excel.) The example data input to SPSS is illustrated in Figure 6.4.

Figure 6.4 purposely is showing you the middle of the data, rows 20–42. The data actually consist of 126 rows (since the samples sizes per column are 28, 26, 26, 23,

	A	B	C	D	E	F	G
1	Anova: Single Factor						
2							
3	SUMMARY						
4	*Groups*	*Count*	*Sum*	*Average*	*Variance*		
5	Column 1	28	63	2.25	0.861111		
6	Column 2	26	114	4.384615	0.486154		
7	Column 3	26	117	4.5	0.5		
8	Column 4	23	70	3.043478	0.498024		
9	Column 5	23	63	2.73913	0.383399		
10							
11							
12	ANOVA						
13	*Source of Variation*	*SS*	*df*	*MS*	*F*	*P-value*	*F crit*
14	Between Groups	106.6493	4	26.66232	47.94017	4.26E-24	2.446603
15	Within Groups	67.29515	121	0.556158			
16							
17	Total	173.9444	125				
18							

FIGURE 6.3

Excel output.

23, respectively, which add up to 126). VAR00001 (column 1) is labeled "sophistica-tion." VAR00002 (column 2) is labeled "age_group." You can see that age_group is "1" for the first 28 rows and "2" starting with row 29 and going to row 54 (not visible in the figure). Rows 55–80 are "3," indicating age-group 3, rows 81–103 are "4," and rows 104–126 are labeled "5." (We could not fit all 126 rows in one figure.)

Now, pull down the "Analyze" dropdown, choose "General Linear Model" (hori-zontal arrow), and then on the submenu, "Univariate" (vertical arrow) even though there was no choice here. This is illustrated in Figure 6.5.

After clicking (or "letting go") of Univariate, we see Figure 6.6.

As is always the case for SPSS, and as we have seen, all of the variables are listed on the left. We now drag "sophistication" to the "dependent variable" box and the "age_group" to the "Fixed Factor" box. This is shown in Figure 6.7.

SIDEBAR: A MINI-GLOSSARY OF RELEVANT TERMS THAT YOU NEED TO KNOW!

For the rest of this book, you're going to be reading a lot about terms that you may or may not be familiar with. In addition, statisticians often use different names for basically the same thing when the context changes. Since we think understanding the terms is crucial to understanding the tech-niques we're discussing, we've created a mini-glossary. If you hit a bump in the road, come back here for a refresher.

Continued

SIDEBAR: A MINI-GLOSSARY OF RELEVANT TERMS THAT YOU NEED TO KNOW!—cont'd

- A "*dependent variable*," typically denoted by "Y," is the "quality indicator" we wish to study. Examples we have seen in earlier chapters include the *perceived sophistication level of a design* (Chapter 2) or *the time it takes to post a job* (Chapter 3) and several other quantities throughout the text. In this chapter, the key dependent variable is, again, the *perceived sophistication of a design*. You can think of a dependent variable as an "output variable."

- An "*independent variable,*" typically denoted by "X," is a variable whose impact on the quality indicator (Y) we wish to study. Examples we have seen in earlier chapters includes "design" (Chapter 2), and (again) "design" (Chapter 3). In this chapter, the independent variable is "age group." You can also think of an independent variable as an "input variable."

- The word, "*factor*" is a synonym for "*independent variable*". Whether "independent variable" is used, or "factor" is used, simply depends on the tradition of terminology used when performing different techniques. In this chapter and Chapters 7 and 8, the techniques we shall introduce are all part of the "ANOVA" [Analysis of Variance] family, and the tradition is to use the word "factor." However, as you shall in Chapters 9, 10, and 11, where we shall introduce different types of regression analysis, the tradition is to use "independent variable" instead of "factor."

- *Levels of a factor*: Each factor (or independent variable) has a certain number of "levels." The levels represent the different possibilities for the factor/independent variable. In Chapter 2, there were two levels of the factor/independent variable of "design:" one was the design of the demoiselle drinking the coffee and the second design was the couple under the umbrella embracing near the Eiffel Tower. In Chapter 3, there were also two levels of the factor/independent variable "design:" the Long Scroller and the Wizard. Here, in this chapter, there are five levels for the factor "age:" the 5 age brackets. In general, the levels of a factor may be numerical values or numerical ranges, such as the age groups, or can be non-numerical or qualitative, such as the Chapter 2 designs or the Chapter 3 designs. How many levels a factor has may often determine the technique that is most appropriate for the analysis; this has been and will be discussed as you traverse the chapters.

- *Treatment*: Depending on the tradition of the field of study, sometimes a level of a factor is called a "treatment." This has its roots in the chemical and related fields, but is often used in other fields as a replacement for levels. (Similarly, the dependent variable is often called the "yield," with obvious roots in the agricultural area.) Other esoteric names are sometimes used for these quantities in selected fields.

- *ANOVA* is a technique introduced in this chapter. There can be one factor under study (as in this chapter) or two factors under study (as in Chapters 7 and 8), or a large number of factors under study as in Chapters 10 and 11. However, in Chapters 10 and 11, "factors" are, by custom, referred to as "independent variables."

- Factors can either be **fixed** or **random**. Generally speaking, a factor is **fixed** when the levels of the factor under study are the only levels of interest and are chosen by the experimenter. A classic example would be two or more specific designs that the experimenter wishes to compare, as in Chapter 2. A factor is **random** when the levels under study are a random sample from a larger population and the goal of the study is to make a statement regarding the larger population. A classic example from the field of agriculture would be the level of rainfall; it is what it is whatever Mother Nature delivers! Another example of a random factor is "person," or "participant," when we consider differences among people's opinions and the sample of people used in the study is a random selection from the population of eligible people. (Usually, all participants for any kind of study are considered "random" since they are a random sample from a larger population.) See the sidebar entitled "Fixed versus Random Factors" in Chapter 7 for a deeper dive on this topic, including why it may matter when conducting your analysis!

- *Replication*: When you perform an experiment, you have "replication" when you have more than one data value for at least one combination of factor levels. When there is only one factor,

---

SIDEBAR: A MINI-GLOSSARY OF RELEVANT TERMS THAT YOU NEED TO KNOW!—cont'd

it's a virtual guarantee that you will have replication. For example, you have multiple partici-pants, each providing his/her opinion about the sophistication of different designs; you have replication. In this chapter, we sensibly have more than one person from each age group evaluat-ing the sophistication of designs, and as a consequence we have replication.

However, when there are two or more factors, it is not automatic that you have replication (if you do not have replication, we say you have "no replication"). In Chapter 7, we discuss a two-factor design with no replication. In Chapter 8, we discuss a two-factor design which *does* have replication. In these chapters, we discuss the role of replication, and again, why it may matter when conducting your analysis!

- *Interaction*: When there are two or more factors under study, the factors may have "interaction" between them. The idea of interaction is similar to the notion of "synergy."

  If there is *no* interaction between the (say, two) factors, then each factor is separately having whatever effect it has, if any, on the dependent variable and the effects of the two factors are *additive*.

  However, if the effect of having each of the two factors at a specific level is not simply additive (the sum of the individual effects), then we say that there *is* interaction (or synergy) between them. Whether there is interaction between factors or not can be extremely important, as you will see in Chapters 7 and 8.

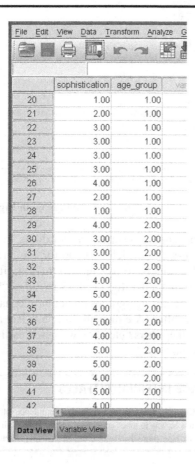

FIGURE 6.4

Data in SPSS format.

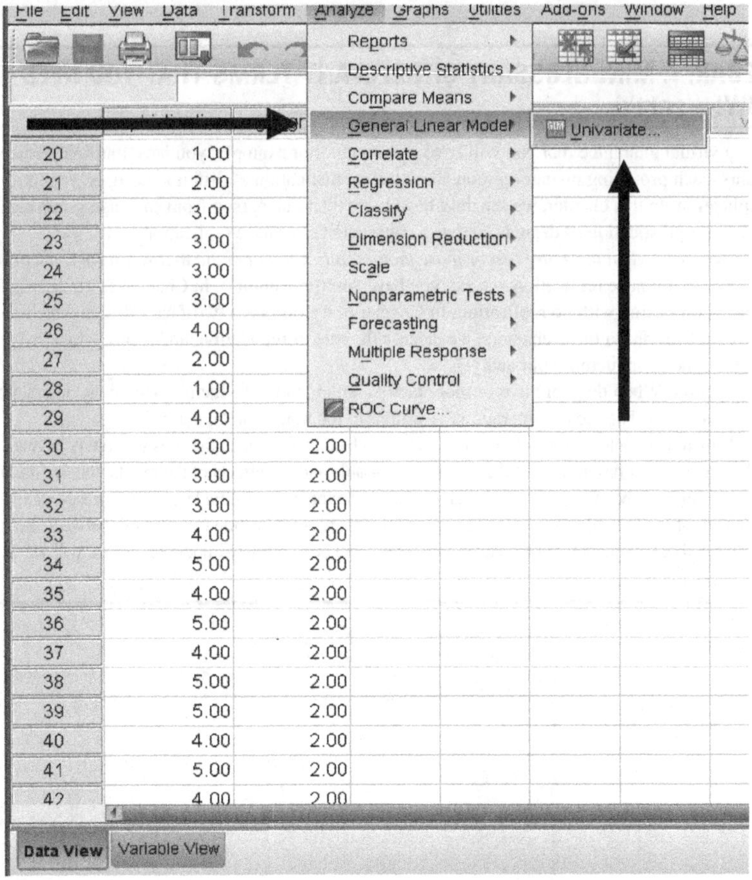

FIGURE 6.5

Beginning to perform the one-factor analysis of variance in SPSS.

We are now ready to click on "OK" (vertical arrow in Figure 6.7). The output is presented in Figure 6.8.

Naturally, we get the same answer as we got doing the analysis with Excel. The key quantity is the p-value, which is 0.000 for age_group in Figure 6.8 (see arrow). Recall that SPSS rounds all p-values to three digits. And we remind the reader (for the last time) that a p-value in SPSS is called "Sig."

So, we conclude that the five age-groups do not have equal true mean sophistication levels. Just how they differ (Are they all different? Are age-groups 2 and 3 the same, but different from the others? etc.). As we noted earlier, the solution will be revealed in Sections 6.5 and 6.6.

SIDEBAR: CONFIDENCE INTERVAL PITFALLS

We saw in the addendum of Chapter 2 that examining whether confidence intervals for the mean of each column overlap or not is not a wise way to reach conclusions about the real difference between means. This is even more true when we have more than two columns, as in this chapter. You've been warned!

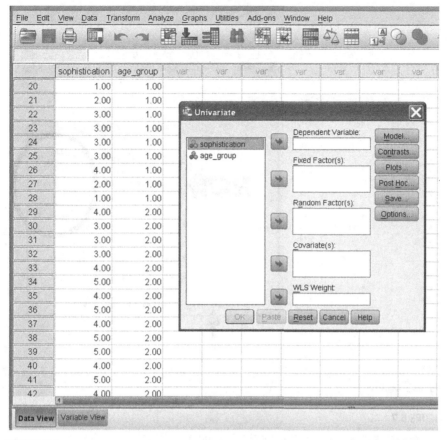

FIGURE 6.6

Univariate dialog box for one-factor analysis of variance; SPSS.

6.5 MULTIPLE COMPARISON TESTING

We indicated earlier in this chapter that when the F-test leads to a rejection of H0, indicating that the true means of each column (e.g., design or age bracket or whatever) are not all the same. However, we still do not know yet the way in which they're not all the same.

For example, for five designs, is the conclusion that all five have different means? Or, is it that four of the five have the same mean but the fifth differs from those four? If so, which one is the different one, and is it larger or smaller than the other four? Or, perhaps the conclusion is that two of the five are the same and different from the other three, the latter three being the same. The possibilities seem endless…but we've got you covered.

SIDEBAR: WE'VE LIGHTENED UP A BIT…

The reader should note that we are being a little bit "loose" and "practical" in our language, rather than using a much more ponderous set of words. Every time we use a phrase like "conclude that they are the same," what is technically the proper phrasing is, "we cannot conclude that they are different." Oy! Continually using this ponderous phrasing would lead the reader to ponder whether to go to sleep (pun intended), or, at best, dilute the flow of the discussion so as to render its meaning less clear and useful.

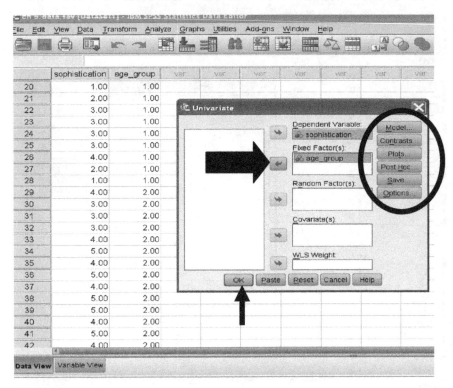

FIGURE 6.7

One-way analysis of variance setup for obtaining output; SPSS.

The most common way to determine which of the column/treatment/design (true) means differ from others is to perform a multiple comparison test. This means, essentially, that you compare every column mean with every other column mean (hence the name— there are multiple comparisons being made). If there are 4 columns, there are 6 combinations of 2 at a time; if there are 5 columns, there are 10 combinations of 2 at a time.

SIDEBAR: WHICH MULTIPLE COMPARISON TEST SHOULD YOU USE?

There are several multiple comparison tests; each has somewhat different properties, with some of them including different assumptions. Also, reasonable people disagree on which is the best of these multiple comparison tests. In fact, most often, the answer will be the same regardless of which test is used (keeping the p-value cutoff point constant, say, at the usual 0.05). Sometimes, different tests will yield slightly different answers, but it would be infrequent to find very different answers.

We have chosen to illustrate how to use only one test, the one we believe is the best choice—the Newman-Keuls test. Sometimes, this test is referred to as the Student-Newman-Keuls test, and is called the "S-N-K" test in SPSS. We will, henceforth, refer to it as the S-N-K test, since SPSS will be critical to our finding the results of the test. It is not that critical for you to dive into the intimate details of the test—although we will give a very brief outline of how it works.

SIDEBAR: DID STUDENT HELP?

William Sealy Gosset (1876–1937) was an English statistician who needed to hide his employment by the Guinness brewery in London in the early 1900s; they didn't want their competitors to know that they were making better beer using statistics. So, Dr. Gosset took the pseudonym "Student" to publish his statistical research.

Apparently, the S-N-K test was based on some earlier work by Student (the "inventor" of the t-test). However, it is uncertain to what degree Student's work contributed to the development of the "S-N-K" test, and whether his name should adorn the test's title.

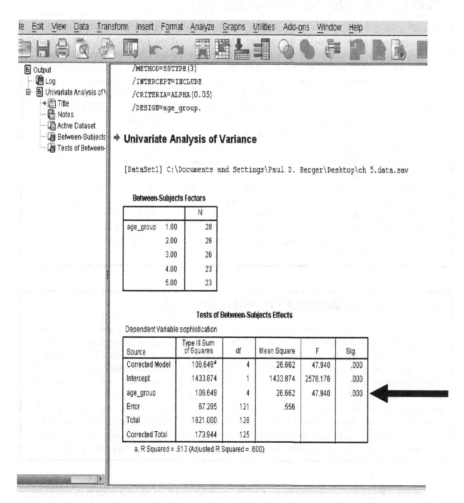

FIGURE 6.8

SPSS output.

Unfortunately, Excel (without an "add-in") does not have the capability to perform the Newman-Keuls (or S-N-K) test. Therefore, our illustration of the test will be solely using SPSS. However, later, we have a sidebar about what you can do using only Excel.

6.6 ILLUSTRATION OF THE S-N-K TEST

All of the S-N-K steps are performed by SPSS, but not all the steps are displayed. (Of course, what is useful for you to know is shown to you.)

SIDEBAR: HOW DOES NEWMAN-KEULS WORK?

Basically, each of the column (sample) means in an S-N-K test is put into increasing order (from the lowest value to the highest value) by the software. Then, using tried and true statistical methods (based on a probability distribution called the "Studentized Range Distribution"), it is determined how far apart the column means need to be so as to constitute a "significant difference." As you might expect, it depends on your input—How many columns do we have? How many data points per column? How much variability is there within columns? What alpha value (usually 0.05) do you choose? (Actually, you are choosing "a," usually to be 0.05, where "a" is called the "overall error rate," and is the probability of making at least one type I error among all the comparison conclusions.)

The S-N-K test recognizes that if there are, for example, five columns, the highest column mean is going to be moderately higher than the lowest column mean, even if the true means of all five columns are the same, while two column means that are adjacent in rank order (i.e., next to each other in the rank order) will, of course, have a smaller difference in sample means than the difference between the extreme columns. So, how far apart two means need to be to constitute a significant difference is dependent on how far apart in the rank order the two means are that are being compared.

As an analogy that should make this point abundantly clear, consider five random 10-year-old boys at a party. If you line up the five boys in increasing height, obviously, the difference between the tallest and shortest boy will be larger than the difference between two boys who are standing next to each other in the lineup.

SIDEBAR: OTHER MULTIPLE COMPARISON TESTS

There is another multiple comparison test, the "Tukey HSD Test," that is very popular—probably used in practice more often than the S-N-K test—but it does not recognize this obvious fact: "How far apart two means need to be to constitute a significant difference is dependent on how far apart in the rank order the two means are that are being compared." Thus, we have decided not to present this test; we believe that it is a test that is inferior to the S-N-K test and is more frequently used than the S-N-K test simply because there are many academic courses that have a "follow-the-leader" mentality and teach the Tukey HSD Test and do not teach the S-N-K test. And, as you will see, right under the S-N-K test option in SPSS is the Tukey HSD test option (called simply "Tukey" in SPSS). If you have interest in exploring the other multiple comparison tests, there are many texts that you can turn to. We are biased and recommend the text written by the authors Berger and Maurer (2002).

When performing an ANOVA in SPSS, such as the one-factor ANOVA illustrated earlier in the chapter, it is very simple to add to the analysis the S-N-K test (as well as many other multiple comparison tests, as you shall see).

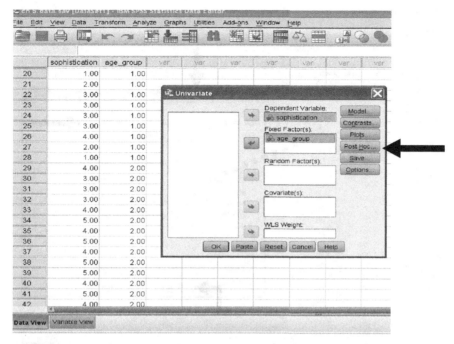

FIGURE 6.9

A repeat of Figure 6.7; SPSS.

For convenience, we redisplay Figure 6.7 (which we now call Figure 6.9), except we do not repeat the circle or other arrows in Figure 6.7. However, we have added an arrow to Figure 6.9.

You will notice that there is a column of choices on the right of Figure 6.9, ranging from "Model" through "Options." First, click on "Post Hoc" (see arrow in Figure 6.9) to arrive at Figure 6.10.

SIDEBAR: POST WHAT?

The term, "post hoc" is Latin and literally means "after this," but is generally translated in context as "after the fact." In a manner of speaking, multiple comparison testing can conceptually be viewed as something we examine "after the fact" of having a significant F-test, to increase our knowledge of what the data's message is.

Note in Figure 6.10 that we have a vertical arrow indicating that we had clicked on Post Hoc. After obtaining the Post Hoc dialog box, we need to bring the factor (age_group) over to the right (see horizontal arrow in Figure 6.10).

You can see in Figure 6.10 that there are several items that can be checked off. One of these is the S-N-K test—see the dashed arrow in Figure 6.10.

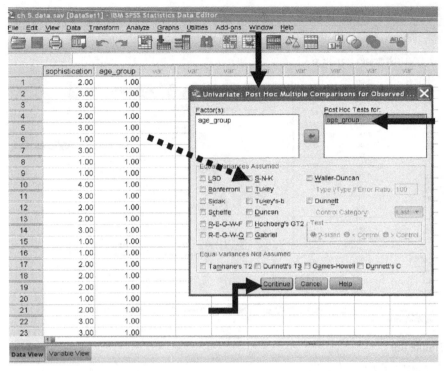

FIGURE 6.10

Post Hoc dialog box; SPSS.

6.7 APPLICATION OF THE S-N-K TO THIS RESULT

You'll remember our F-test results were highly significant with a p-value of 0.000 (see Figure 6.8). Now, we apply the S-N-K test to this result. After clicking on Post Hoc, obtaining Figure 6.10, we then click the S-N-K box (see dashed arrow in Figure 6.10), and then click "Continue" (bent arrow in Figure 6.10). This brings us back to Figure 6.9, and we simply click on "OK." We will get the output in Figure 6.8, but now we will also get the output representing the S-N-K test. The latter is shown in Figure 6.11.

Note that we can identify that the result is, indeed, for the S-N-K test (see arrow in Figure 6.11). We now discuss the interpretation of Figure 6.11.

6.8 DISCUSSION OF THE RESULT

Figure 6.11 displays a table called "Homogeneous Subsets." Basically, this table is telling us that there are three sets of means that are significantly different from one another. First, the true (sophistication) mean of age-group 1 is judged as different from (lower than)

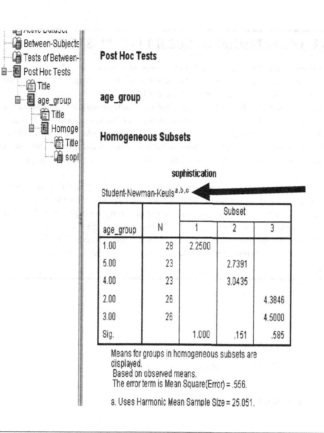

FIGURE 6.11

Output for S-N-K test; SPSS.

the means of the other four columns. The means of age-groups 5 and 4 are judged as the same but higher than that of group 1, but lower than that of groups 2 and 3. Finally, the means of age-groups 2 and 3 are judged to be the same, but higher than the other three age-groups. If the only important issue is finding out if one of the age-group means is higher than all the others, then the last result mentioned above is the relevant result—the true mean of age-groups 2 and 3 cannot be said to be different, but the true mean of those two age-groups can be said to be higher than the true mean of the other three age-groups.

SIDEBAR: SUBSETS: AS FEW AS ONE AND AS MANY AS THE NUMBERS OF MEANS YOU HAVE

The table of Homogeneous Subsets can have more than three subsets (which is what is illustrated in Figure 6.11). Indeed, for five age-groups, there can be five different subsets—this would simply mean that all five means are judged to be different from one another. There might be two subsets, three subsets, or four subsets. Actually, there could be only one subset, but that would mean that the F-test indicated that all the means are the same, and thus, we would not, at least in theory, be examining what the differences are—when the F-test says that there aren't any differences in the first place!!

SIDEBAR: THE POTENTIAL OF SUBSET INCONSISTENCY

This is a "subtopic" that the authors wish they did not have to discuss. The Homogeneous Subsets table can show an inconsistency. Figure 6.11 did not show an inconsistency. But, suppose, for different data, the S-N-K results are shown in Figure 6.12.

In Figure 6.12, the S-N-K results say that there are two subsets of (true) means, subset 1, 2, and 4, and subset 4 and 3. You can see that column mean 4 is in both subsets (see arrow in Figure 6.12)!! This is inconsistent. How can the true mean of column 4 be the same as the true mean of columns 1 and 2 while also being the same as the true mean of column 3, when, at the same time, the true mean of column 3 is different (i.e., in a different subset) from the means of columns 1 and 2?

Sadly, virtually all of the multiple comparison tests allow this possibility to occur. Naturally, you always hope that it does not occur, but if it does, we basically view the mean or means that cause the inconsistency as means whose place in the hierarchy is simply "not clear." In other words, in the above example, we would conclude that the true mean of column 3 is higher than the true mean of column 1 and true mean of column 2, and we would also conclude that the true mean of columns 1 and 2 are not different; finally, we would conclude that it is not clear where the mean of column 4 belongs.

Post Hoc Tests

VAR00002

Homogeneous Subsets

VAR00001

Student-Newman-Keuls[a,b]

VAR00002	N	Subset 1	Subset 2
1.00	6	4.0000	
2.00	6	4.1667	
4.00	6	4.5000	4.5000
3.00	6		4.8333
Sig.		.100	.162

Means for groups in homogeneous subsets are displayed.
Based on observed means.
The error term is Mean Square(Error) = .158.

FIGURE 6.12

An illustration of an inconsistency in the S-N-K results; SPSS.

6.8.1 SUPPOSE THAT YOUR ONLY SOFTWARE AVAILABLE IS EXCEL

SIDEBAR: HOW TO PERFORM MULTIPLE MEANS TESTING IN EXCEL (WITH CAVEATS!)

If you don't have SPSS, you can still do multiple comparison testing in Excel after you've run your ANOVA. You simply run a t-test on the two means you are interested in. Using the example in this chapter, you may be wondering if there really is a statistical difference of mean sophistication ratings between the older and younger boomers. Since these are independent samples, you would use the independent t-test as described in Chapter 2. However, you should be aware that there can be bias induced when you decide on testing various pairs of means, if the choices of which pairs of means to t-test are based on seeing what the values of actual sample means are. This may sound a bit strange, but if you decide on which pairs of means to test before you see any results, that's fine (unbiased!!).

This potential bias is corrected for in the S-N-K test, where all pairs are tested.

However, things get a little more complicated if you want to test more than one pair of means. For example, say you want to perform an independent t-test between older and younger boomers, and then an independent t-test between Gen X and Gen Y—both tests decided to be done before seeing the actual means of the age-groups. When you do this, the probability of making a type I error (or α) increases. After all, if each test has $\alpha = 0.05$, then, because there are two opportunities (i.e., two t-tests) with potential to make a type I error, the probability of making at least one of these errors in the two opportunities to do so is more than 0.05. Without getting too technical, the probability is not exactly, but close to, twice as high. Just think of flipping 10 coins. The chance of 10 heads in a row is about 0.001; however, if you tried the task 500 times, the chances are a lot higher (about 39%) that you get 10 heads in a row *at least once*!!!

To alleviate this problem and retain at approximately 0.05 the probability of making at least one type I error, thus coming closer to duplicating (but not totally duplicating) the logic of the S-N-K test, a good rule of thumb is to choose as a value of α for each t-test you perform a value which is different from 0.05. Instead, you should choose as α for each t-test (0.05 ÷ [the number of t-tests you're performing]). So, in this case of performing two t-tests, you would use 0.025 as the α for each t-test. If you're performing three t-tests, you should divide 0.05 by 3, which is 0.0167, and use 0.0167 as your new alpha for each t-test. And so on.

As we noted, in SPSS, your multiple comparison testing takes care of all the issues alluded to above (potential biases, changing the value of α, etc.), so you don't need to worry about any of these issues. Do you see SPSS in your future?

SIDEBAR: WHY CAN'T I SKIP THE ANOVA STEP?

You may be wondering why you can't skip ANOVA altogether and go right to multiple comparison testing by performing either an S-N-K in SPSS or multiple t-tests in Excel. "ANOVA doesn't tell me exactly how the means differ," you may be saying to yourself. "It tells me only that the population means are either all the same or not all the same. What good is that? I want to know how specific means differ. Why can't I just skip ANOVA?"

The answer in a word, again, is "bias." Suppose that you have several men from each state in the US in a (large) room. If you consider the highest state mean and the lowest state mean, that difference will be relatively large, even when the true mean for each state is the same!! Say, just by chance, the two extreme means are from Louisiana and Idaho. If you do a two-sample t-test on the means of those two states, it will extremely likely be highly significant (because it is the biggest difference among 50 different means!!). Is that a reason to conclude that men from those states

Continued

> ## SIDEBAR: WHY CAN'T I SKIP THE ANOVA STEP?—cont'd
>
> differ in mean height? There have to be two states that have the extreme values of the means, but, assuming all states have the same mean, it is random which ones, and it would almost surely be different for different samples of men. Generalizing that Louisiana and Idaho men differ in mean height, based on this t-test, is ridiculous. If you did conclude that, you'd be guilty of bias (and perhaps stupidity). But that kind of bias can creep into your analysis when you simply eyeball different means, and perform t-tests only on the pairs of means that "look" different, or have large enough differences in sample means that you suspect it to be so.
>
> Performing an ANOVA and doing all the pairwise comparisons (or a subset of comparisons that are chosen to be analyzed before you see the results) eliminates that bias—i.e., it eliminates the increased chance of committing at least one type I error.

6.9 MEANWHILE, BACK AT MADEMOISELLE LA LA...

You'll remember that Cinny Bittle, your new texting-mad marketing manager, got her hand on a Forrester report that claimed older boomers (ages 56–66 years) spend the most online of all generations. Since Bittle was worried that your new home page design was not considered sophisticated by this age bracket, you offered to slice and dice the survey data by age. You were trying to determine if there were different perceptions of sophistication by age, and perhaps appease Bittle. Or at least get her to stop texting on her cell phone for 10 seconds by delivering the results of your analysis.

To refresh your memory, you sorted the data by youngest to oldest, using these age brackets:

1. Gen Z, 18–25 years
2. Gen Y, 26–35 years
3. Gen X, 36–45 years
4. Younger boomers, 46–55 years
5. Older boomers, 56–66 years

Then you calculated the mean for each age bracket, as displayed below in Table 6.2.

Table 6.2 A Refresher on Our Age-Groups and Their Means

Age Bracket 1	Age Bracket 2	Age Bracket 3	Age Bracket 4	Age Bracket 5
18–25 Gen Z	26–35 Gen Y	36–45 Gen X	46–55 Younger boomers	56–66 Older boomers
Mean = 2.25 n = 28	4.38 26	4.50 26	3.04 23	2.74 23

Agreement with statement: "This page makes Mademoiselle seem sophisticated."
1 = Strongly disagree, 5 = strongly agree.

With your basic work out of the way, you performed your ANOVA and S-N-K test, and determined that the means of age-groups 2 and 3 (Gen Y [26–35 years] and Gen X [36–45 years]) cannot be said to be different, but the means of those two age-groups can be said to be higher than the means of the other three age-groups.

This is great news for Mademoiselle La La, since their greatest sales come from the 26–45 years age bracket. In other ones, the customers who are buying the most are the ones who think the new home page is most sophisticated. Following "close on their heels" (we couldn't resist the pun) are the younger boomers (46–55 years), followed by the older boomer and Gen Z groups.

No sooner have you finished your data analysis than Cinny Bittle pops her head in your office. Not surprisingly, she addresses you without raising her head from texting on her iPhone. You're starting to wonder if she's developing carpal tunnel syndrome.

"Got anything yet?" she mumbles, never missing a beat in the texting rhythm.

"As a matter of fact, I do," you reply.

"Cool." She continues to text.

As an experiment, you wait for her to look up. She doesn't.

"Do I need to squeeze it out of your brain?" she admonishes you without lifting her head.

Experiment over. You wind up for the pitch. "I sliced the sophistication rating data by our standard age brackets and calculated the means."

"Keep going..." her texting seems to accelerate.

"Then I performed an ANOVA followed by the Newman-Keuls multiple comparison test...."

"Do you think you're impressing me with the stats mumbo jumbo?" she sarcastically says, keeping up the rhythm.

"Not at all," you reply. "Just trying to be thorough."

"OK, get to the point."

"The means of age-groups 2 and 3, who are the Gen Y and Gen X, cannot be said to be different, but the means of those two age-groups can be said to be higher than the mean of the other three age-groups."

"Ah-ha!" she says smugly as her texting continues. "We're not appealing as much to the older boomers, who spend the most money."

"But our greatest sales come from the 26–45 age bracket. In other words, the customers who are buying the most are the ones who think the new home page is most sophisticated."

Finally, she looks up and glares at you. "How do you know about sales?"

"The Google Analytics conversion rate has consistently shown that our biggest sales come from that group."

She pauses and stares at you. After a pregnant pause, she goes back to texting.

"What about the other age brackets?" You sense retreat.

"That age-group is followed by younger boomers, then older boomers. Gen Z is last."

"I don't care about the punks," she says sarcastically. "They're just trying to pay off their student loans."

"Exactly," you agree. You sense you're starting to reach consensus with someone who's naturally disinclined to consensus. You plow forward.

"Even though the older folks are in the prime of their money-making years and spend the most, our styles appeal to a younger crowd. But the good news is that the 26–45 crowd have plenty of money to burn too."

She's warming to you. "Good point," she says. "We're not Talbots. We're La La. We're hip."

"Right. And the Gen Z's are going after edgier styles."

"But who cares?" she laughs. "They're broke!"

You laugh along. She smiles broadly.

"Well, it looks like we're right where we need to be with that home page design," she says, getting back to her texting. "Can you summarize in a PowerPoint for me? I want to go to Mary with this."

Knowing that Mademoiselle Founder Mary Myers doesn't like to wait for anything, you put forward a tough deadline for yourself. "Sure, I'll get you that by end of day."

"Cool!" she says. "One last thing."

"Yes?" you ask.

"Make sure your executive summary says the customers who are buying the most are the ones who think the new home page is most sophisticated."

"Sure," you reply.

"You did a great job," she says as she leaves your office. "But that's all that Mary will care about." She pauses. "But not me. One of these days you gotta show me how you do that stuff!"

6.10 SUMMARY

In this chapter, we have presented the F-test for testing for differences in means when we have three or more "treatments"/columns (tasks or designs or, as here, age-groups, or whatever we are comparing). We studied one factor, age-group in the illustrative example, and thus, used a technique called one-factor ANOVA. It was assumed that each age-group consisted of different people (here, obvious!!). Thus, we have independent samples (as in Chapter 2). We illustrated its use in both Excel and SPSS.

SIDEBAR: TWO ASSUMPTIONS YOU NEED TO KNOW ABOUT

There are two assumptions (beside having independent samples) that are being made—one is that the sophistication values in any column (age-group) are normally distributed, and the other is that, while the average sophistication may be different for each age-group, the variability of the sophistication values for each age-group is the same. As we mentioned before, these two assumptions are somewhat robust, and modest violations of these assumptions do not materially affect the results. However, we believe that going into detail how to test these assumptions and discussion of how to proceed if the assumptions are materially violated is beyond the scope of the text—and, in truth, in the vast majority of time, it won't matter anyway!!

Also in this chapter, we have introduced the concept of multiple comparison testing to determine when there are more than two means (e.g., designs, tasks, age-groups, etc.) being compared, which means are different or the same as other means. A multiple comparison test is typically analyzed after performing an ANOVA, and when the F-test is significant. In this chapter, the ANOVA was a one-factor ANOVA. In a subsequent chapter, we will discuss applying an ANOVA when two factors are involved.

We also introduced the Newman-Keuls test, sometimes called the S-N-K test, as the authors' choice of the best of several choices of multiple comparison tests. We illustrated it using SPSS (basic Excel does not have the capability to perform the S-N-K test) and discussed the results.

6.11 EXERCISES

1. Consider the case of the time it takes to perform a task and testing whether the true average time it takes for each of four tasks (T1, T2, T3, and T4) is the same. Each person performs only one of the four tasks, so that we have independent samples. Data for the times for each task are in data files in Excel (file name: Chapter 6.Exercise 1.data) and SPSS (file name: Chapter 6..Exercise 1.data). The output in Excel is on sheet 2. In SPSS the output is in a file (file name: Chapter 6..Exercise 1.output). All files are on a Web site indicated in the preface to the text.

   Perform an ANOVA to test whether the (true) average times for the four tasks are equal or not.

   A Word file (file name: Chapter 6.Exercise 1.discussion) is also provided, which discusses the results.
2. For the data in the SPSS file, Chapter 6..Exercise 2.data, perform a Newman-Keuls (S-N-K) test to examine what the differences are among the averages of the four columns. The output will be in an SPSS file named Chapter 6..Exercise 2.output. A discussion of the results will be in a Word file called Chapter 6. Exercise 2.discussion.

REFERENCES

Berger, Paul D., Maurer, Robert E., 2002. Experimental Design: With Applications in Management, Engineering and the Sciences, second ed. Duxbury Press, Pacific Grove, CA.

Tversky, Amos, Kahneman, Daniel, 1974. Judgment under uncertainty: heuristics and biases. Science 185 (4157), 1124–1131.

Comparing more than two means: one factor ANOVA with a within-subject design

7

7.1 INTRODUCTION

As we suggested in Chapter 6, there are probably many times when you are presented with several alternatives and asked which is "best." We also noted that, of course, the word, "best," needs to be clarified, as obviously, "best" can be the highest—for example, satisfaction with a design; other times, "best" might be the smallest—for example, time to complete a task. As a matter of fact, while we hate to be repetitive, we note again that this kind of comparison test may be one of the most common types of jobs you're assigned as a researcher.

Chapter 2 considered comparing two means, with independent samples—for example, the mean satisfaction rating given for two Web designs. We had what we referred to as "independent samples," which meant that different people provided ratings for each design. We discussed reasons why we might not want to have the same person evaluating both designs. In Chapter 3, we considered the same issue of comparing two means, but with the same person evaluating both designs. We referred to that as "paired data." In both cases, we performed a t-test (but different ones!!) to test the hypotheses:

$$H0 : \mu1 = \mu2$$

$$H1 : \mu1 \neq \mu2.$$

A key to Chapters 2 and 3 was that there were, indeed, only two designs (or tasks, or, to be general, "columns") whose means were being compared.

In Chapter 6, we generalized the problem addressed in Chapter 2 to the case of having the means of *more than two* designs, or tasks, or, anything else. We retained the key condition of Chapter 2 of having independent samples—different people evaluating each design, or performing each task, etc. The hypotheses were expanded to (for C columns, for $C > 2$):

$$H0: \mu1 = \mu2 = \cdots = \mu C$$

H1: not all $C\mu$'s are equal

Here, in this chapter, we generalize the problem addressed in Chapter 3 also to the case of having *more than two* designs, or tasks, or anything else, but with the condition of having what is analogous to "paired data," as introduced in Chapter 3. When there are more than two columns whose means are being compared, clearly the word, "paired," doesn't fit the description (grammatically!!), but the idea is the same. Each person evaluates each design, or performs each task. The person "repeats" his/her "measure" for all columns. This is referred to as a "within-subjects" design/experiment, or, is sometimes referred to as a "repeated measures design/experiment."[1] We have the same hypotheses as in Chapter 6:

$$H0: \mu1 = \mu2 = \cdots = \mu C$$

H1: not all $C\mu$'s are equal

But, just as there was the difference in the exact set of commands that you give the software to indicate that you have independent samples versus paired data, the same idea exists here, where, as you shall see, you will use a very similar process to what we used in Chapter 6, but with a modest difference in the software process to indicate that we now have a within-subjects design, instead of Chapter 6's independent samples (or what is sometimes referred to as a "between-subjects design.")

7.2 CASE STUDY: COMPARING MULTIPLE EASE-OF-USE RATINGS AT MADEMOISELLE LA LA

Let's return to our favorite fashion site, Mademoiselle La La. To refresh your memory, you were hired as the UX researcher at Mademoiselle La La, a high-end online store aimed at urbane women from 18-55 years of age with well-above-average disposable income.

You'll remember that you launched an online survey to determine which new home page was more sophisticated. Using a t-test for independent samples, you proved that Design 1—a scene of a young *demoiselle* sipping a coffee at an outdoor French café, ignoring the adoring eyes of a nearby young man—was considered more "sophisticated"

---

[1] We consider the case of independent samples (previous chapter), and the case in which a person sees/tries all "columns." There are more complex cases of within-subject designs that are beyond the scope of this book. For example, if there are six tasks to be performed, there might be a within-subject design in which one person performs three of the six tasks and another person sees the other three of the six tasks. Clearly, we do not have independent data, but the "within-subjects" aspect of the design is more complex than having one person performing all six designs.

than Design 2, a scene of a young couple snuggling together under one umbrella during a shower, with the Eiffel Tower bisecting a slate-gray sky. Furthermore, you were able to report that "the low p-value of 0.023 means we have a statistically significant difference between the two designs. We should launch with Design 1."

So far, so good at your new gig!! But, as soon as you drop a hard copy of the final report on Creative Director Kristen McCarthey's desk, she makes yet another request:

"It's been a long time since we've conducted any kind of testing on the general shopping flow, and in the meantime, we've made some changes. Can you get a test going asap?"

"What's your time frame," you ask?

"Well, I'm meeting Massimo at 3pm Wednesday next week. Is there any way to have results by then?"

You do some quick calculations in your head. It's Tuesday morning, a little over a week until the meeting with CEO Massimo Ranieri.

"Well, if you don't mind me doing half-hour tests, I can do all the testing in one day and just try to report out on the biggest problems."

"Sure, sounds good. Don't make a federal case out of it. Just find the low-hanging fruit."

Because time is tight, you begin the recruit immediately, aiming for a Friday test. Then, you start by performing a heuristic review using the persona of a typical Mademoiselle La La client trying to make a dress purchase. After a morning of studying the site, four potential problem areas pop out: (1) The ability to find the right size of dress, (2) The ability to add the dress to "My Bag" (inexplicably, Mademoiselle uses "My Bag" instead of "shopping cart,") (3) Entering credit card information in the "Checkout" area, and (4) Choosing the best shipping method.

Based on those areas of interest, you start to create the tasks for the test. The tasks seem pretty straightforward, but under the hood, you've carefully crafted each one to either confirm or refute your hypothesis about a usability problem.

Once you've got a first draft of the test script—which also includes your post-task rating scales of ease-of-use—you send it to other members of the UX team as well as the Creative Director. The recruitment is proceeding wonderfully because all you had to do was send out an e-mail blast to current customers, offering them a $100 site-wide credit for a 1-hour in-person usability test. Besides, the Mademoiselle La La brand is pretty hot right now, and most of the hip urbane women are just curious about your cool converted mill space in Boston's South End, and want to check out the place. Who knows? They might be discovered as the next hot Mademoiselle La La model.

The long day of testing on Friday—10 participants, half-hour tests—proceeds very well, albeit in a blur and without your getting a chance to eat lunch. No cancellations, no no-shows, and articulate and thoughtful participants.

When you get to look at the data on Monday morning, your suspicions about usability problems are confirmed, but there are some interesting twists.

Specifically, the completion rate for finding the right size dress is decent, as is the completion rate for adding to "My Bag;" however, entering a credit card and choosing a shipping method are clearly lower than desirable. The completion rates are summed up in Table 7.1.

"OK," you say to yourself. "Checkout in general is problematic. But is the credit card issue better than the shipping problem—or about the same? To round out the picture, your look at your ease-of-use ratings for all of the tasks shown in Table 7.2.

Staring at the numbers, you're glad to see high ratings for the dress size task, and modest ratings for the "My Bag" task, but you are not sure what the other numbers mean. Is there really a difference between the ease-of-use ratings for the credit card

Table 7.1 List of Tasks and Completion Rates

Task #	Verbatim Task	Successful Completions (out of 10 participants)
1	Find the right size for a Valentino pink pleated dress.	8
2	Save the Valentino pink pleated dress to "My Bag."	7
3	Enter your credit card information for purchase of the Valentino pink pleated dress.	3
4	Choose your preferred shipping method for the Valentino pink pleated dress.	2

Table 7.2 Ease-of-Use Ratings of the Four Tasks (1–5 Likert Scale) by the 10 Persons

P = Person	It's Easy to Find the Right Size for a Valentino Pink Pleated Dress	It's Easy to Save the Valentino Pink Pleated Dress to "My Bag"	It's Easy to Enter My Credit Card Information for Purchase of the Valentino Pink Pleated Dress	It's Easy to Choose my Preferred Shipping Method for the Valentino Pink Pleated Dress
P1	4	4	3	2
P2	5	3	3	1
P3	4	4	3	1
P4	5	4	4	2
P5	4	3	3	3
P6	5	4	4	2
P7	3	3	2	2
P8	5	4	3	1
P9	5	4	3	2
P10	5	4	3	2
Mean	4.5	3.7	3.1	1.8

task and the shipping task? Or between the "My Bag" task and the credit card task? It's Monday, right before lunch. You've got to start building your PowerPoint presentation, and you need to know what these ease-of-use ratings mean. Within-subjects ANOVA to the rescue!

7.3 COMPARING SEVERAL MEANS WITH A WITHIN-SUBJECTS DESIGN

In this scenario, you decide to test whether the mean rating of ease-of-use is the same or different for the four different tasks. (The subsequent S-N-K test will specifically compare the credit card task and the shipping task, and will also compare the "My Bag" task and the credit card task.) We would formulate the null and alternate hypotheses accordingly:

- H0: The true mean rating of ease-of-use is the same for the four tasks.
- H1: The true average rating of ease-of-use is *not* the same for the four tasks.

Following the earlier chapters' notation, we might write the hypotheses[2] in a more formal way:

H0: $\mu 1 = \mu 2 = \mu 3 = \mu 4$

H1: The four values of μ are not the same for the four designs.

7.3.1 THE KEY ↜

We'll let you in on a little secret: *when we are studying one factor (e.g., different designs, or different tasks, etc.) using the type of within-subject design (each subject is evaluating all tasks), we "make believe" that we are studying TWO factors.* The first would be the primary factor under study—the design, or the task, or whatever, and the second factor is the person or respondent!! That is, we view the situation as having a template such as that in Table 7.3 (with, let's say, four ratings with six people with each "X" being a data value on the 1–5 Likert scale.)

So, while there is one factor that is of primary interest, the "column factor," *task,* there is also a "row factor"—*respondent*—with each of the six rows representing a different person. Typically, the people comprising the sample are a somewhat random set of people, but who are nevertheless from the same target audience; in this case, women from 18–55 years of age with well-above-average disposable income.

SIDEBAR: "REAL FACTORS" OR NOT?

In this chapter, we do not dive into a discussion of some interesting issues that arise when there are two or more "real" factors being studied. We save that for the next chapter, Chapter 8, in which we will study the effect of two "real" factors, such as *age* and *gender* (e.g., are there differences in ease-of-use rating depending on age *and* gender?)—in a study that, indeed, combines two factors in one study—not unlike what is depicted in Table 7.3, except that the second factor (the "row factor") would be the age or gender factor). It will be called a "two-factor ANOVA."

---

[2] Note that the hypotheses above are the same whether we have independent samples (as in Chapter 6) or repeated measures—a subject evaluates all four designs.

Table 7.3 Template for One-Factor Design with Repeated Measures

	Ease-of-Use Rating for Task 1	Ease-of-Use Rating for Task 2	Ease-of-Use Rating for Task 3	Ease-of-Use Rating for Task 4
Respondent 1	X	X	X	X
Respondent 2	X	X	X	X
Respondent 3	X	X	X	X
Respondent 4	X	X	X	X
Respondent 5	X	X	X	X
Respondent 6	X	X	X	X

So, let's summarize the situation depicted in Table 7.3. We have two factors but one of the factors is a "faux factor" to accommodate a within-subject design. The 4 levels of the factor, "task," are depicted as columns; the 6 levels of the factor, *respondent*, are depicted as rows. (Statistically speaking, we likely have little interest in the effect of the factor, *respondent*, although the routine analysis we will perform will test for its significance.) But, as noted, while the design definitely contains two factors, we can usefully think of it as a "one-factor within-subjects design." That is, the "within-subjects" phrase indicates that we have a second factor, *respondent*, but is not a factor of the same "stature" as the primary factor, in this case, "*task*." Still, the second factor, *respondent*, does need to be taken into consideration in the analysis.

The purpose of the within-subjects/repeated measures design in the example illustrated in the table is to use *only six people* in the study, not 6 × 4 = 24 people, as would be the case if independent samples were needed or desired.

SIDEBAR: FIXED VERSUS RANDOM FACTORS

We introduce the difference between a "fixed" factor and a "random" factor. The distinction contains the underlying rationale for how we tell SPSS what to do, to ensure that the within-subject/repeated measures aspect of the design is properly captured in the analysis that is performed. In UX research, most factors are "fixed," with "person" or "respondent" being a prominent exception.

There are two primary aspects of a factor that determine whether it is referred to as fixed or random. A *fixed* factor is a factor for which (1) the different levels (e.g., designs, tasks) being investigated are chosen by the experimenter (UX person or his/her consultant), and (2) the results will be used to evaluate only the levels (specific designs, tasks) in the experiment. In the UX world, designs and tasks to be tested are, indeed, chosen by the UX person, and results from the, say, four designs or specific tasks cannot advantageously be used to make inferences about other designs or tasks not tested. That is the reason we suggested above that in the UX world, most key factors of interest are *fixed*.

A *random* factor is a factor whose levels are determined randomly, and the results from the testing will be used to make inference about other, usually, intermediate, levels of the factor. A classic example would be the factor, *rainfall*, in an agricultural experiment to study the impact of certain factors on, say, the growth of potatoes. Different pieces of land are available for an experiment, and perhaps one factor under study is the brand of fertilizer used; the brands of fertilizer to be studied are chosen by the agronomist (making "fertilizer" a fixed factor!!), but say the second factor is the amount of rainfall that fell during the two-month period of the study. This is not chosen by the agronomist, but is determined by the "great bell-shaped curve in the sky," and, if the rainfall levels happen to come out 2″, 4″, and 8″ for, say, three pieces of land in the study, the agronomist is likely to interpolate to what might be the potato growth were there 6″ of rainfall. Indeed, *rainfall* is a random factor!! (And, as a separate issue, potato growth may not be a linear function of rainfall, so the interpolation may not be straightforward!!)

Now, we have some good news and some bad news for you bare-bones Excel users.

First the bad news: when considering two factors (even when one of the factors is a faux factor accommodating a within-subject design), bare-bones Excel will perform the analysis only when the two factors are *fixed*. Here, *task* is a *fixed* factor (you chose the tasks you wished to study and cannot usefully infer ease-of-use for other tasks not included in the study), but responder is a *random* factor; the responder set is a random sample of the entire population of those who might have been responders.

Now, the good news: because this specific situation (depicted in Figure 7.3) is a design without *replication* (i.e., each participant provided only one rating of agreement to each statement), we need to assume that there is no *interaction* between the factors. (See the mini-glossary in Chapter 6; we also describe interaction in great detail in Chapter 8.)

Still with us? Here's the cool part: when there is no *interaction* between the factors, the distinction between fixed and random factors *disappears*, and thus, you *can* use Excel for this type of design! Skip ahead to section 7.7 to see how.

7.4 HYPOTHESES FOR COMPARING SEVERAL MEANS

OK, let's get back to work. Let's find out if the average ease-of-use rating for the four tasks is the same by using hypothesis testing.

We remind the reader (again!! But for the last time—we promise!!) that "μ" stands for the true mean, or that which would be the mean if we miraculously were able to average the ease-of-use evaluation of ALL the people who could provide an ease-of-use rating. Who would ever know these values exactly? Only the entity we alluded to near the beginning of the text, in that politically correct way, as the "great normal curve in the sky." Good luck asking him!! (Or, I suppose, him *or her*!!). That is why we agree that do not know these (true) values and possibly never will.

We already know that the sample mean ("X-bar") of each column in the data (i.e., the task's ease-of-use values) is not the same as the true values, and the same "hypothesis testing logic" that we have introduced and repeated (and repeated!!) is with us again—See! We said in Chapter 1 that hypothesis testing techniques will be with us in virtually every chapter!!!!

We also feel compelled to report that if you looked in most statistics/data analysis/data analytics texts, the notation used for the column means of your data when introducing t-tests would be, as you may recall, X-bar, but for whatever reason, when there are more than two column means (i.e., more than two tasks, or designs, or whatever, being compared), the notation for the column means in the majority of cases changes to "Y-bar." It, of course, does not matter whether we call it X-bar, Y-bar, or Chocolate-bar; it is the meaning of the analysis and interpretation of the results that count.

We first present the analysis in SPSS, then later in the chapter in Excel. We begin with SPSS since it can (and does) include the S-N-K (Newman-Keuls) Test.

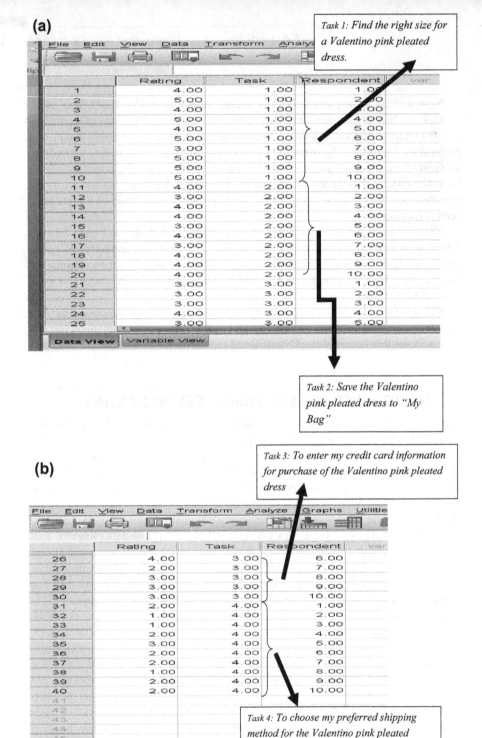

FIGURE 7.1

(a) Data in SPSS format. (b) Continuation of Figure 7.1(a).

7.5 **SPSS ANALYSIS**

Now we illustrate our analysis in SPSS. Our respondent data from Table 7.2, input to SPSS, is illustrated in Figure 7.1(a) and (b). We need two figures to show all 40 data values (i.e., rows of data), since most SPSS screens cannot illustrate all 40 rows at once (unless a "gigantic size" monitor is being used). We need *three* columns, since we "make believe" that we have two factors, the second one being "respondent."

Next, pull down the "Analyze" dropdown, choose "General Linear Model" (horizontal arrow), and then on the submenu, "Univariate" (vertical arrow), even though there was no choice here. This is illustrated in Figure 7.2 and is the same step we used in Chapter 6, when we first introduced ANOVA.

After clicking (or "letting go") of Univariate, we see Figure 7.3.

As is always the case for SPSS, and as we have seen before, all of the variables are listed on the left. We now produce Figure 7.4, drag Rating (column 1) to the "dependent variable" box (recall: the "dependent variable" is, basically, the "output" variable, which is the ease-of-use rating), and the "Task" (column 2) to the "Fixed Factor" box (vertical arrow in Figure 7.4).

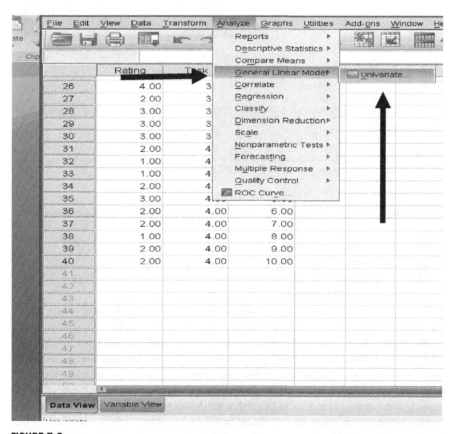

FIGURE 7.2

Beginning to perform the one-factor repeated measures ANOVA in SPSS.

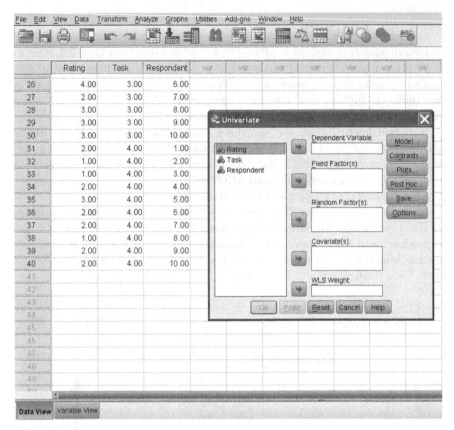

FIGURE 7.3

Univariate dialog box for one-factor ANOVA; SPSS.

The "Respondent" variable goes to the *random factor* box (horizontal arrow in Figure 7.4.)

We are now ready to click on "OK."

The output is presented in Figure 7.5.

The key quantity is the *p*-value for "Task," which is 0.000 in Figure 7.5 (see arrow). Recall that SPSS rounds all *p*-values to three digits.

So, the *p*-value for "task" is way below the 0.05 cutoff point, and we conclude that the mean ease-of-use rating is *not* the same for the four tasks.

We might note that the *p*-value for "people" is 0.081 (see oval in Figure 7.5). This is not below the 0.05 traditional cutoff point, indicating that we conclude that the mean for *each respondent*, averaged across all four tasks, cannot be said to be different (although it is close—the *p*-value is not much above the 0.05 cutoff). This latter point is not of prime interest to us, but it does indicate that we do not have enough evidence to refute that the people, on average, are consistent in their evaluations of the ease-of-use of the four tasks. Of course, this does not indicate directly that each person rates *every* task the

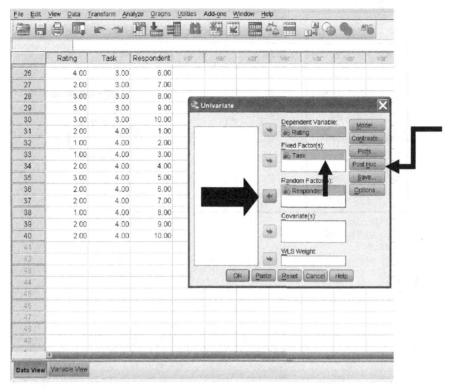

FIGURE 7.4

One-factor within-subject ANOVA setup for illustrative example; SPSS.

same as each other person (although this might be true!!); it indicates, rather, that *averaged across all four tasks*, the respondents cannot be said to be different in their ratings of the tasks. This is likely a good thing (albeit, perhaps not critical), but it suggests that the group of respondents is somewhat homogeneous with respect to their ratings.

7.6 NEWMAN-KEULS ANALYSIS

Now that we have concluded that the ease-of-use averages are *not* the same for the four tasks, it is logical to examine the results of the Newman-Keuls (S-N-K) test, covered in the previous chapter (Chapter 6). The results are displayed in Figure 7.7.

A fast review of how to conduct the S-N-K test: if you go back to Figure 7.4 and click on "*post hoc*" (see bent arrow in Figure 7.4), and then click "OK," you get what is shown in Figure 7.6.

In Figure 7.6, three things were done. First, the factor "Task" was brought over to the right box by highlighting it and clicking on the SPSS arrow, which would be pointing to the right at that point (see horizontal arrow). Second, the "S-N-K"

Dependent Variable:Rating

Source		Type III Sum of Squares	df	Mean Square	F	Sig.
Intercept	Hypothesis	429.025	1	429.025	738.990	.000
	Error	5.225	9	.581a		
Task	Hypothesis	38.875	3	12.958	44.429	.000
	Error	7.875	27	.292b		
Respondent	Hypothesis	5.225	9	.581	1.990	.081
	Error	7.875	27	.292b		
Task*Respondent	Hypothesis	7.875	27	.292		
	Error	.000	0	c		

a. MS(Respondent)
b. MS(Task*Respondent)
c. MS(Error)

FIGURE 7.5

SPSS output for illustrative example.

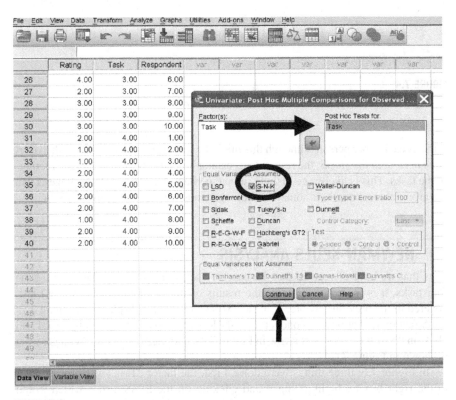

FIGURE 7.6

Preparing for the S-N-K test output; SPSS.

Post Hoc Tests

task

Homogeneous Subsets

ease.of.use

Student-Newman-Keuls[a,b]

task	N	Subset 1	Subset 2	Subset 3	Subset 4
4.00	10	1.8000			
3.00	10		3.1000		
2.00	10			3.7000	
1.00	10				4.5000
Sig.		1.000	1.000	1.000	1.000

Means for groups in homogeneous subsets are displayed.
Based on observed means.
The error term is Mean Square(Error) = .292.

a. Uses Harmonic Mean Sample Size = 10.000.
b. Alpha = 0.05.

FIGURE 7.7

S-N-K results for illustrative example; SPSS.

box (see oval) was checked off. Third, you simply click on "Continue" (see vertical arrow). This brings us back to Figure 7.4, but the output includes not only what is shown in Figure 7.5, but also what is shown in Figure 7.7.

Figure 7.7 indicates that all four (true) means are judged as different from one another!! In other words, the mean ease-of-use rating is concluded to be different for each task. The order is obvious from a simple look at the four means in Figure 7.7.

In order to do the S-N-K test, we needed to undertake a few extra steps in SPSS, compared to what we did in Chapter 6, when we introduced and performed the test using independent samples. When we arrived at Figure 7.4, before using the "Post Hoc" subcommand (see bent arrow in Figure 7.4), which, as Chapter 6 indicated, is a key, but easy, step in how we perform the S-N-K, we need to first click on "Model" (see arrow in Figure 7.8, which figure repeats Figure 7.4).

This produces Figure 7.9.

We now click on "Custom" (see arrow in Figure 7.9), and you will get Figure 7.10. See arrow in Figure 7.10 to note that "Custom" is checked.

We now need to do *three* things. We are sorry that there are so many steps, but it takes longer to explain what to do than to actually do it!!

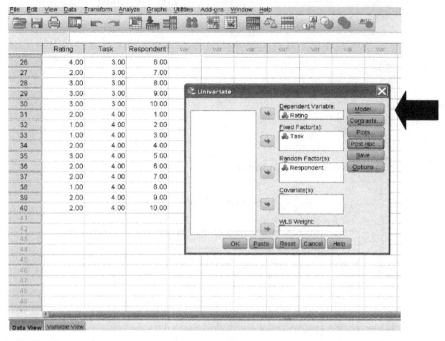

FIGURE 7.8

Clicking "Model" to prepare for S-N-K test; SPSS.

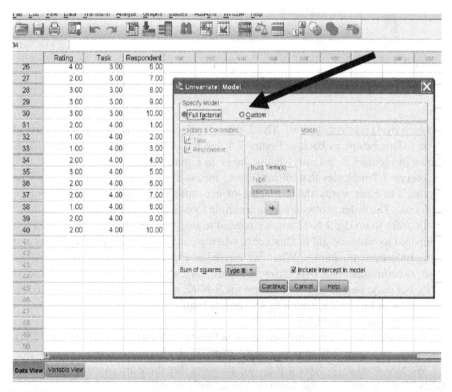

FIGURE 7.9

The "Model" dialog box; SPSS.

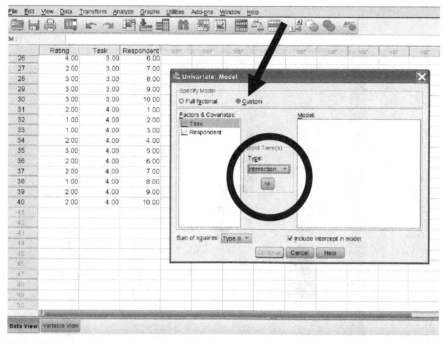

FIGURE 7.10

"Model" dialog box after clicking "custom;" SPSS.

1. Click on "Task" on left, and "drag" it to the model box on the right (see it illustrated in Figure 7.11, by "fat arrow").
2. Look at "type" (see circle in Figure 7.10) and pull down the tab that says "Interaction" (inside of the circle), by clicking on it. This will produce Figure 7.11.

The third thing you must do is to click on "Main Effects" (see bent arrow in Figure 7.11), arriving at Figure 7.12 (see vertical arrow in Figure 7.12), and then click on Continue—see horizontal arrow in Figure 7.12.

After you click on Continue in Figure 7.12, you arrive back to Figure 7.4 (or, equivalently, Figure 7.8) and can now proceed as in Chapter 6 to perform the S-N-K test.

In the next chapter, Chapter 8, we are better equipped to tell you why we need to do these extra steps in this within-subjects design situation.

7.7 EXCEL ANALYSIS

In general, when considering two factors, (bare bones) *Excel will perform the analysis only if the two factors are fixed.* SPSS allows the factors to be either fixed or random. However, when we have a within-subject design of the format of Table 7.3, we have what is referred to as "no replication." In this case, the analysis of variance (ANOVA) is the same whether the row factor is fixed or random. Therefore, the Excel command "Anova: Two-Factor Without Replication" (where one of the factors is "people" or "respondent")

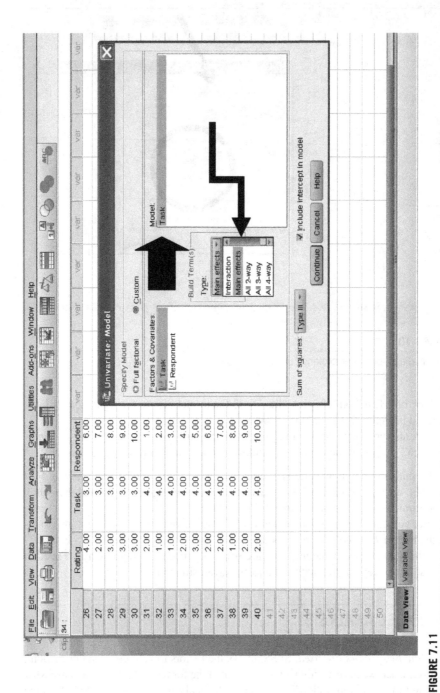

FIGURE 7.11

Dragging over "Task" and pulling down "interaction;" SPSS.

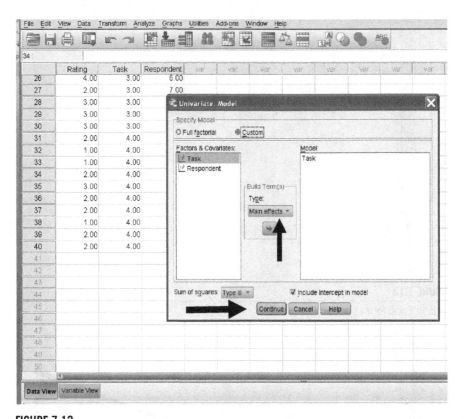

FIGURE 7.12

Clicking on Main Effects; SPSS.

will, in essence, duplicate the within-factor design illustrated in Table 7.3. There is a key assumption being made when there is no replication, and that is there is no "interaction" between the two factors. We describe "interaction" in great detail in the next chapter; for now let us view the lack of interaction between the two factors as simply indicating that the effects of the two factors are "additive"—that is, they combine in a way that simply adds the effects together, without any "synergy." Again, if this is a bit vague, please wait until the next chapter in which we promise to make the ideas about interaction clear.

We illustrate our analysis using Excel and the aforementioned, "Anova: Two-Factors without Replication." In Figure 7.13, we present the data as it is entered onto the Excel spread sheet, looking like the format in Figure 7.3. To recall: we have 10 people rating each of four tasks on the 1–5 Likert scale.

We now go to "Data Analysis" in Excel and down to "Anova: Two-Factor without Replication." See arrow in Figure 7.14.

After we click on that command, we then see the dialog box in Figure 7.15.

It can be noticed in Figure 7.15 that the "Input Range" is filled in with B1:E10 (see vertical arrow in Figure 7.15), and we have arbitrarily asked that the output be placed on a new worksheet named "susan." See horizontal arrow in Figure 7.15.

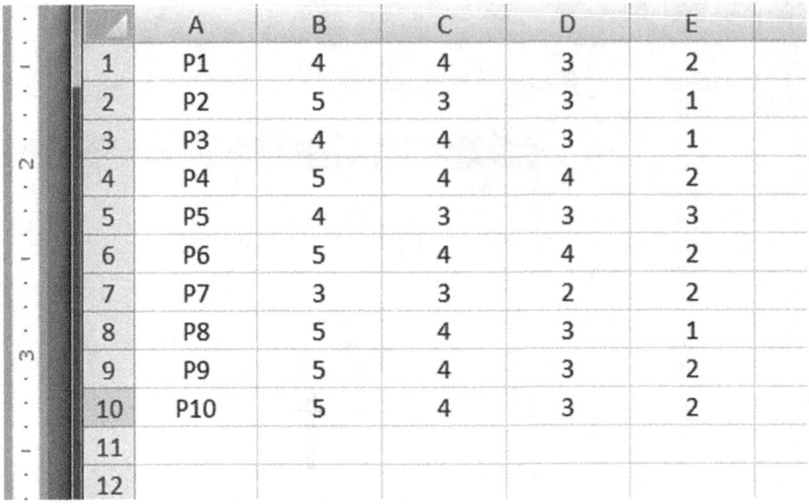

	A	B	C	D	E
1	P1	4	4	3	2
2	P2	5	3	3	1
3	P3	4	4	3	1
4	P4	5	4	4	2
5	P5	4	3	3	3
6	P6	5	4	4	2
7	P7	3	3	2	2
8	P8	5	4	3	1
9	P9	5	4	3	2
10	P10	5	4	3	2
11					
12					

FIGURE 7.13

Data in Excel format.

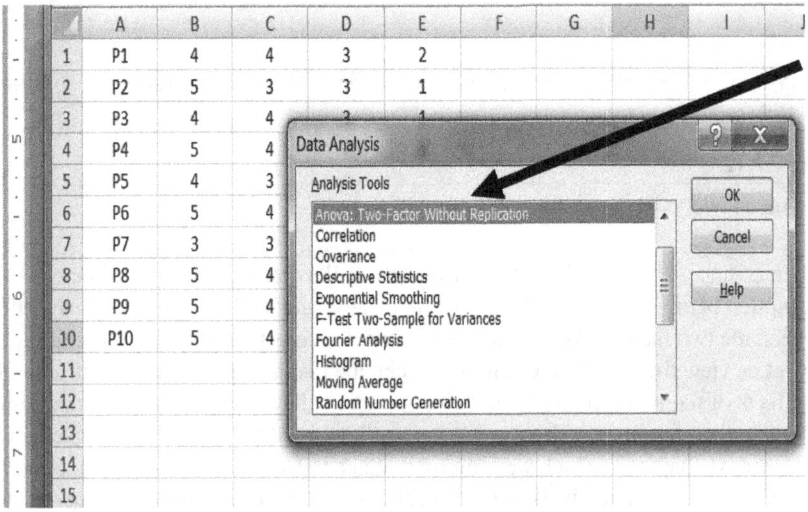

	A	B	C	D	E	F	G	H	I	J
1	P1	4	4	3	2					
2	P2	5	3	3	1					
3	P3	4	4							
4	P4	5	4							
5	P5	4	3							
6	P6	5	4							
7	P7	3	3							
8	P8	5	4							
9	P9	5	4							
10	P10	5	4							
11										
12										
13										
14										
15										

Data Analysis

Analysis Tools

Anova: Two-Factor Without Replication
Correlation
Covariance
Descriptive Statistics
Exponential Smoothing
F-Test Two-Sample for Variances
Fourier Analysis
Histogram
Moving Average
Random Number Generation

OK

Cancel

Help

FIGURE 7.14

Anova: Two-Factor without Replication command in Excel.

We now click the "OK" (upper right of Figure 7.15), and see the output in Figure 7.16.

Of course, the output in Figure 7.16 is exactly the same as we got analyzing the data using SPSS—except that Excel tends to provide my digits (somewhat superfluously).

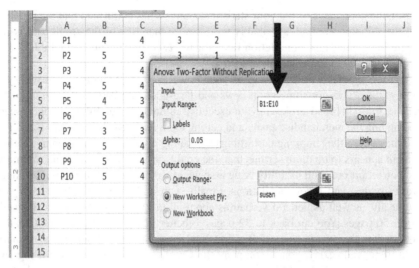

FIGURE 7.15

Dialog box.

	Source of Variation	SS	df	MS	F	P-value	F crit
21	ANOVA						
22	Source of Variation	SS	df	MS	F	P-value	F crit
23	Rows	5.225	9	0.580556	1.990476	0.080691	2.250131
24	Columns	38.875	3	12.95833	44.42857	1.41E-10	2.960351
25	Error	7.875	27	0.291667			
26							
27	Total	51.975	39				
28							

FIGURE 7.16

Excel output for Mm. La La example.

7.8 MADEMOISELLE LA LA: LET'S FIX THE CHECKOUT ASAP!

Now that you've done your statistical analysis, it's time to write your report. It is noon on Monday, and you've got until Wednesday at 3pm to get ready for your presentation. Time is tight.

But, the good news is that your statistical analysis has confirmed that the problem with the shipping method is probably more severe than that of the credit card issue, despite the similar task completion rates for the two issues. You build Table 7.4 to illustrate the added information.

You use this table near the top of your PowerPoint presentation. As usual, you employ the "I've-got-some-good-news-and-I've-got-some-bad-news" angle. (It's tried and true.) In broad strokes in your executive summary, your online shoppers seem to be finding the merchandise easily and getting them fairly easily into "My Bag." But once they get to the shopping cart, things are falling apart. And the shipping method problem appears to be more serious than the credit card problem. After the summary, you then report out each usability issue associated with each task, using screen shots, severity scales, and recommendations. Finally, you add verbatims about each task specifically, as well as general verbatims about all tasks. As usual, your deck swells to over 50 pages. You cut back to 32 pages to better fit in the half hour the Creative Director will give you in front of the CEO. You're ready and confident in the results.

At 3pm Wednesday, you accompany the Creative Director into the mahogany-lined office of the CEO and Milan transplant Massimo Ranieri. You have your laptop, but you have hard copies as well; you have no idea what the projection situation will be inside the inner sanctum. As expected, about a half hour into the meeting, the Creative Director sets you up:

Table 7.4 Table 7.2 Including Statistical Conclusions

Task #	Verbatim Task	Successful Completions (out of 10 participants)	Average Agreement with Ease-of-Use Statement: "It's Easy to...." (all four averages in this column are concluded to be significantly different from each other; i.e., they are all different from one another, beyond a reasonable doubt)
1	Find the right size for a Valentino pink pleated dress.	8	4.5
2	Save the Valentino pink pleated dress to "My Bag."	7	3.7
3	Enter your credit card information for purchase of the Valentino pink pleated dress.	3	3.1
4	Choose your preferred shipping method for the Valentino pink pleated dress.	2	1.8

"Our new UX researcher has some interesting results regarding the shopping cart experience."

"Really?" the CEO muses, focusing on you over his reading glasses. "What do you have?"

"Well, we ran a usability test on the entire shopping experience with 10 target users," you begin, handing the report around. "Everything went fairly well until they got to the shopping cart."

"How so?" the CEO asks. He seems annoyed.

"Well, only 3 out of 10 could enter in their credit card information, and…."

"Accidenti! Only 3 out 10 could enter their credit card info?"

"*Accidenti!* Only 3 out 10 could enter their credit card info?" Ranieri gasps.

"Yes and only 2 out of 10 could use the shipping method dropdown correctly."

The CEO turns to the Creative Director. "It looks like we have some work to do. What problem do we tackle first?"

"Well, when I looked at the posttest ease-of-use ratings between the credit card problem and shipping problem, the shipping problem seemed more serious. The mean rating of ease-of-use for the credit card was 1.8 compared to 3.1 for the credit card problem. I ran an ANOVA and Newman-Keuls test to verify the difference.

"A what? The CEO asks. "I take it that's stats stuff, right?"

"Yes, in a case like this you use a within-subjects ANOVA to determine if there are statistical differences in the first place among the multiple means, then a Newman-Keuls test to determine which means are specifically different from others—i.e., determine the *way* in which the means differ. In this case, all four ratings' means are significantly different from one another."

"English, please?" the CEO says with a laugh. He's warming to you.

"As bad as the credit card problem is, the shipping method problem is likely worse. I'd work on that first. To double check, we should look at our Google Analytics data and see if we're seeing big abandonment in the checkout cart."

The CEO looks at the Creative Director: "Well at least we've got a plan. You're on it?"

"We're on it!"

On the way back to your desk, the Creative Director seems pleased.

"Nice work. That was tough news to report. But you had the goods."

"Thanks. Is he always that grumpy?"

"Are you kidding?" the Creative Director asks. "He was in a great mood, considering. That's the first time I ever saw him laugh!"

7.9 SUMMARY

In this chapter we introduced within-subject designs (or "repeated measures" designs.) The classic description of such a design is to have a factor under study, with several levels (more than two), but have the same person rating the ease-of-use of each task. This is in contrast to the case of having independent samples, in which each person evaluates or rates only one entity—in essence, each person provides only *one* data value. We illustrated the within-subjects design by an example in which we studied one factor (task) having four levels (i.e., four different tasks). Each person provided *four* data values, one for each task under investigation. The measure (or output variable or dependent variable) was ease-of-use evaluation.

We saw that the procedure we used for analysis was ANOVA, even though we needed to be careful to specify what was necessary in telling SPSS what to do, in comparison to the case of independent samples, the latter introduced in Chapter 6. After seeing the results of the analysis, we carried out the S-N-K test introduced in Chapter 6.

7.10 **EXERCISE**

1. For the data in the SPSS file, Chapter 7..Exercise 1.input, perform a one-factor within-subject design analysis. There are four designs being evaluated and six people evaluating each design. Also perform an S-N-K test and discuss the results.
   The output will be in an SPSS file named Chapter 7..Exercise 1.output.
   A discussion of the results will be in a Word file called Chapter 7.Exercise 1.discussion.

Comparing more than two means: two factor ANOVA with independent samples; the important role of interaction

8.1 INTRODUCTION

Chapter 6 introduced simple analysis of variance (ANOVA), where there is one factor or treatment variable, and more than two levels of this factor. In the example used in Chapter 6, the one factor was the age of the person rating the sophistication of a design, and the dependent variable was the sophistication rating (on a 1–5 Likert scale). There were five age groups, or five levels of the factor.

Now suppose we wish to determine if the sophistication rating varies not only with the age of the respondent, but also with the *gender* of the respondent. Now we have two factors. How should we proceed?

Two-factor ANOVA to the rescue.

SIDEBAR: THE DANGER OF SEQUENTIAL TESTING

Hopefully, you've planned your study well enough so you've collected the data for all the factors you want to consider in your posttest analysis. But invariably, there will be times where you don't collect the data on all the factors that may have an impact on your dependent variable.

For example, you launch a survey that attempts to quantify inequality of pay between males and females for the same job. In the demographic section of your career survey you, of course, collect data on gender; you then test whether there is a difference in pay between the genders. However, you did not collect data on highest level of education completed. After the results are in, it dawns on you that level of education would possibly be a useful factor, since it can also affect pay; if the two genders have a large difference in highest educational level completed, this could be the key factor in explaining any discrepancy in pay between males and females.

What to do? Well, we could conduct another survey. This time, we would collect data on the factor: highest level of education completed, as well as pay, and test whether this factor affects pay.

Continued

> **SIDEBAR: THE DANGER OF SEQUENTIAL TESTING—cont'd**
>
> This "sequential testing" process occurs frequently in practice. However, there are many reasons why this is an unwise path forward. The key reason is simply that the conclusions you reach from two separate one-factor ANOVA studies *may be incorrect!*
>
> Consider this example: suppose we are examining sophistication ratings, as we did in Chapter 6, in which the one factor under study was age. Suppose further that for some age groups, females rate a design as more sophisticated than do males, but for other age groups, males rate the sophistication level to be higher than do females. In other words, it is possible that, *averaged over all the ages*, males and females give about the same sophistication ratings, so it looks like gender has no effect on sophistication rating, and, *averaged over both genders*, perhaps all the age groups get about the same sophistication rating, so it appears that there is no difference there either.
>
> But you would be missing that fact that for some ages, there is a large gender gap in rating in one direction, while for other ages, there is a large gender gap in the other direction!! A prudent experiment would allow for the measurement of this possibility, which we (and much of the rest of the world!) refer to as *interaction*. We will discuss this notion at length later in the chapter.

8.2 CASE STUDY: COMPARING AGE AND GENDER AT MADEMOISELLE LA LA

Let's return yet again to our favorite fashion site, Mademoiselle La La. To refresh your memory, you were hired as the UX researcher at Mademoiselle La La, a high-end online store aimed at urbane women from ages 18–55 years with well-above-average disposable income.

In Chapter 6, you'll remember that Cinny Bittle, your director of marketing, got her hand on a *Forrester* report that claimed older boomers (aged 56–66) spend the most online of all generations. Since Bittle was worried that your new home page design was not considered sophisticated by this age bracket, you offered to slice and dice the survey data by age. You were trying to determine if there were different perceptions of sophistication by age. To refresh your memory, you sorted the data by youngest to oldest, using these age brackets:

1. Gen Z, 18–25
2. Gen Y, 26–35
3. Gen X, 36–45
4. Younger boomers, 46–55
5. Older boomers, 56–66

Then you calculated the mean for each age bracket, as displayed in Table 8.1.

With your basic work out of the way, you performed your ANOVA analysis and Student-Newman-Keuls (S-N-K) test, and you determined that the means of age groups 2 and 3 (Gen Y [26–35] and Gen X [36–45]) cannot be said to be different, but the means of those two age groups can be said to be higher than the means of the other three age groups.

Table 8.1 Means and Sample Size for the Different Age Groups

Age Bracket 1	Age Bracket 2	Age Bracket 3	Age Bracket 4	Age Bracket 5
18–25 Gen Z	26–35 Gen Y	36–45 Gen X	46–55 Younger boomers	56–66 Older boomers
Mean = 2.25 n = 28	4.38 26	4.50 26	3.04 23	2.74 23

Agreement with Statement: This page makes Mademoiselle seem sophisticated.
1 = Strongly disagree, 5 = Strongly agree.

Which is great news for Mademoiselle La La, since their greatest sales come from the 26–45 age bracket. In general, the customers who are buying the most are the ones who think the new home page is most sophisticated.

After some initial skepticism, Bittle was happy with the results and stated that it "looks like we're right where we need to be with that home page design." You provided Bittle with a summary of the results, which she took to Mademoiselle La La Founder Mary Flynn Myers.

The morning after you delivered the results to Bittle, you step into the elevator and run smack dab into Bittle. This time, she's clutching an iced pumpkin *macchiato* in one hand and her iPhone in the other, still managing to text!

"Good morning!" she says, as her thumb continues to pound the phone. "Mary liked your research results regarding age differences, but she has another request." She leans in and whispers: "I think it's silly, but you have to appease your boss, ya know."

"Of course," you reply good-naturedly.

"She wants to have the data sliced by gender too. She thinks there's a fundamental difference between how different age brackets of men and women perceive sophistication, and she wants to verify."

"Ah, potential interaction effects; interesting," you respond.

"Interwhat?" she says before she takes a large gulp of her *macchiato*.

"I can look at the individual effect of age, the individual effect of gender, plus the simultaneous effect of both."

"Good. I'm sure it's a colossal waste of time," she says, stepping off on her floor. "I mean, seriously, over 75 percent of our clients are females. What's the point? But she's the boss. Can I have results by end of day?"

"You got it!"

Getting back to your desk, you open up your spreadsheet, but this time you display gender information. See Table 8.2, which includes not only the responder's *age*, but also his/her *gender*.

We will later analyze the data in Table 8.2.

Table 8.2 Data on Age and Gender for Five Groups Evaluating "Sophistication" on the 1–5 Likert Scale

18–25	26–35	36–45	46–55	56–66
2F	4F	4F	3F	3F
3M	3F	5F	4F	4F
3M	3F	4F	4F	3F
2F	3F	4F	3M	2M
3M	4F	4F	3M	3F
1F	5F	5F	4F	3F
3M	4F	5F	4F	3F
1F	5F	5F	3M	2M
1F	4F	4M	3M	3F
4M	5F	5F	2M	2M
3M	5F	5F	3F	3F
2F	4F	4M	4F	2M
2F	5F	5F	3F	3M
3M	4F	4M	3F	3F
1F	5F	5F	4F	2M
1F	5F	5F	3M	3F
2F	5F	5F	3M	4F
2F	4M	4M	3F	3F
2F	4M	4M	2M	2M
1F	5F	5F	2M	2M
2F	4M	5F	2M	3F
3M	5F	5F	2M	2M
3M	4M	4M	3F	3F
3F	5F	2M		
3F	5F	5F		
4M	5F	5F		
2F				
1F				

Agreement with Statement: This page makes Mademoiselle seem sophisticated.
1 = Strongly disagree, 5 = Strongly agree.

8.3 INTERACTION

When we study two or more factors simultaneously, we need to deal with the potential of interaction. Interaction is the primary—but not the only—reason why we should not perform separate one-factor analyses when studying two or more factors.

There are two different ways of looking at, or measuring, interaction. Ultimately, they produce the same value and reduce to the same conclusion. But they differ by how to practically define interaction in the most intuitively understandable way.

8.3.1 INTERACTION—DEFINITION 1

Consider the following two-by-two table, Table 8.3, where the two rows stand for the length of a Web page (Shorter, Longer), the two columns stand for the shading (black and white, multicolored), and the values in the cells are the *mean satisfaction rating* (using the 1–5 Likert scale) of the design by a large number of respondents, with independent samples—each person sees only one of the four (combinations) designs.

Let us assume for the moment that there is no error in the means in the cells. This is similar to saying that each cell mean is the mean of "a million" responders, so that the sample means (the ones in the cells) are only itsy-bitsy, teeny-weeny, virtually invisible amounts different from the respective true μ values.

We can see in Table 8.3 that if we start in the upper left-hand corner, we gain 0.4 in rating (3.9−3.5=0.4) if we hold the shading at Black and White and go from shorter to longer page. If we hold length constant at shorter, and move to the right, we see that we gain 0.8 (4.3−3.5=0.8) going from black and white to multicolored. What if we move from upper left to lower right (where there is now a question mark)—(i.e., shorter, black and white, to longer, multicolored)?

Do we obtain a mean rating of 4.7? This would be taking the original 3.5 and adding the 0.4 for longer length and adding the 0.8 for multicolored shading, getting 3.5+0.4+0.8=4.7.

This may sound odd, but in this case we'd say that we have *no* interaction. Adding both boosts to the design—longer and multicolored—has an effect on ratings that is simply *additive*. Strictly speaking, there is no interaction effect. This leads to our first definition of interaction:

> **Interaction** = *degree of difference from the sum of the separate effects.*

If the value in the lower right-hand cell (longer, multicolored) is 4.7, there is no interaction. If the value were, for example, 4.5, we would say we have *negative interaction* (even though 4.5 would be the largest value in the table). If the value were 4.85, we would say that we have *positive interaction*.

Table 8.3 2 × 2 Table of Ratings of Length and Shading of Pages

	Black and White	Multicolored
Shorter	3.5	4.3
Longer	3.9	?

SIDEBAR: INCREASE SHELF SPACE, PROMOTION, OR BOTH?

To illustrate an interaction effect, let's pick a simple supermarket example. Suppose that we double the shelf space we allocate to apples and increase sales by 30%. It is no surprise that increasing shelf space increases sales! Now suppose that we increase our promotion of the apples from none to a "standard promotion—if we promote" (e.g., signs all over the supermarket indicating that brand of apples is now available), and sales increase 40%. It is not surprising that increasing promotion increases sales! Both of these types of increases were predictable and, while not satisfying what might be called hard science, have been verified time and time again in the world of marketing.

Now, what if we both double the shelf space and increase the promotion from none to standard promotion. Will we get an increase of 70%, which is the sum of the individual increases (30%+40%)? Or will we get a sales increase, for example, of only 60% (less than the sum of the separate increases—some cannibalization occurred)? Or, will we get an increase of, say, 80% (more than the sum of the separate effects—some reinforcement occurred)?

The answer is that *we don't know*—until we try it (at least) a few times!!! Most often, there are really no hard and fast rules for predicting interaction effects. This illustrates the fact that often, we know virtually for sure what the direction of the result will be when changing the level of an individual factor, such as shelf space or promotion, but do not know what the value of an interaction effect will be—will the result from the two boosts provide an increase of 60% or 70% or 80%, or what? Unless, amazingly, this particular combination was studied a lot in the past, and it was published (not proprietary), how would anyone know? This is all the more reason that an experiment cannot afford to ignore potential interaction effects.

8.3.2 INTERACTION—DEFINITION 2

Take a look at Table 8.4. Again, the two rows stand for the length of a Web page (shorter, longer), and the two columns stand for the shading (black and white, multicolored), and the values in the cells are the *mean satisfaction rating* (using the 1–5 Likert scale) of the design by a large number of respondents, with independent samples.

Now, the number in the bottom right cell in Table 8.4 is 4.9. And now, there *is* interaction, since the value is not equal to (but, in this case, exceeds) 4.7.

What is the effect of changing from a length of shorter to longer? Well, if we use a shading of black and white, the effect is +0.4 (i.e., going from 3.5 to 3.9); however, if we use a shading of multicolored, the effect is +0.6 (going from 4.3 to 4.9). So, what is the effect? The answer is that *it depends on the shading!* At shading=black and white, it's +0.4, while at shading=multicolored, it's +0.6. *This leads us to the second definition of interaction:*

> **Interaction**=If the effect of changing the level of one factor *depends* on the level of another factor, we have **interaction** between the factors.

Table 8.4 Alternate 2 × 2 Table of Ratings of Length and Shading of Pages

	Black and White	Multicolored
Shorter	3.5	4.3
Longer	3.9	4.9

Table 8.5 2 × 2 Table with Extreme Interaction and No Other Effect!!

	Low	High
Low	3.4	3.9
High	3.9	3.4

From Table 8.4, we just demonstrated that the effect on the rating of satisfaction of the design by changing the level of length depends on the level of shading (+0.4 or +0.6, for a difference of +0.2). If we go the other way, we get the same +0.2. What is the effect of changing the shading from black and white to multicolored? If we have length=shorter, it's +0.8 (going from 3.5 to 4.3); if we have length=longer, it's +1 (going from 3.9 to 4.9).

It is no coincidence that the difference between +0.8 and +1 is also 0.2. And, indeed, the difference between 4.9 and 4.7 (the latter value indicative of no interaction) is also +0.2. *The bottom line here is that we should always conduct an experiment that tells us if we have a significant interaction effect between two factors when there are multiple factors*[1]. *However, as we noted in Chapter 7, we need to have replication or else need to assume that there is no interaction. Happily, we do have replication in this example; each [age, gender] combination occurs more than once.*

SIDEBAR: AN EXTREME CASE OF (NEGATIVE) INTERACTION

In an extreme case, you could have data such as in the ratings in Table 8.5, in which we use two generic factors, and for each we have levels that are called "low" and "high."

The overall effect of the row factor is *zero* (each row averages the same: 3.65) and the overall effect of the column factor is *zero* (each column averages the same: 3.65). But there is something else going on: *we have gigantic (negative) interaction!!* The lower right cell has a mean of 3.4, *not* the sum of the horizontal and vertical increases of 0.5, which would result in 4.4.

8.4 WORKING THE EXAMPLE IN SPSS

We illustrate two-factor ANOVA using SPSS.

SIDEBAR: EXPERIMENTAL DESIGN TO OVERCOME THE LIMITS OF EXCEL

To perform ANOVA with Excel, the data have to be comprised in a way that is extremely restrictive. You need to have the same number of people of each age group and need the same number of males and females in each age group! That is not even close to what we have in our example; we have a different number of people in different age groups (sample sizes by age group, respectively, are 28, 26, 26, 23, 23), and we have *nowhere close* to the same male/female split for each age group (males are, respectively, by

Continued

---

[1] There are possible "three-way" and higher order interactions, but they are usually assumed to be zero or negligible. Discussion of these interactions is beyond the scope of the text. For further discussion of these higher-order interactions, we recommend the Berger and Maurer text referenced at the end of Chapter 6.

SIDEBAR: EXPERIMENTAL DESIGN TO OVERCOME THE LIMITS OF EXCEL—cont'd

age group, 9/28, 4/26, 7/26, 11/23, 9/23). And, let us not forget another Excel restriction mentioned in Chapter 7. All factors must be fixed factors—although that is usually the case in UX applications, except for the aforementioned "within-subjects" or "repeated measures" designs discussed in Chapter 7.

The only recourse you have if you are using Excel is to "sort" the data and arrive at the restrictive conditions required. For example, if you examine Table 8.2, you will note that each age group has at least four males and four females (age group 2 has only four males). So, you can get to the conditions needed by Excel by considering eight people in each age group, four males and four females. You should choose the four males (in the other age groups), and the four females in all the age groups, randomly. You would now have five age groups and two genders and each of the 10 combinations ("cells") contains the same number of people: four.

However, it is worth discussing this point a bit more. The above paragraph assumes that the data have already been collected. There was an effort to make the sample size in each age group the same or nearly so (as they are); *no attention was paid to gender*. Indeed, you were *unlucky* that the minimum number of males in any column was only 4, so that meeting the requirements for Excel leads to using only 40 (10 age/gender combinations times 4) of the 126 data points. Nobody likes to "waste" data!! Had there been, for example, eight males in group 2, and that was the minimum number of males in any of the five age groups, then you would have been able to use 80 (10 combinations of 8 data points each) of the 126 data points.

That brings us to the issue of "designing" the data set. If you had realized earlier that gender was important, and had a budget for roughly the same number of data points—126, then perhaps you could have *chosen* to have 10 combinations of 12 people each, thus utilizing 120 data points. Of course, this supposes that you have the ability to control the age and gender mix of your participants in the study, and are OK with the potential added expense of carefully arranging the participant mix to be balanced in this way. This idea of "designing" your sample is a precursor of the entire field of "design of experiments," a subject that is beyond the scope of this book, but is a worthy topic. If you wish to follow up on this topic, we recommend the text, *Experimental Design, with Applications in Management, Engineering and the Sciences*, by Berger and Maurer (2002), referenced at the end of Chapter 6.

First we'll display our original data of sophistication and age from Chapter 6.

Remember that we actually have 126 rows of data and Figure 8.1 is showing only some of them (since they would not all fit on one screen shot).

We now add a column of data reflecting gender. We will use "0" for male and "1" for female. (Which two numbers we use, and which gender gets which number, does not matter, as long as you remember [or write it down!] which number means which gender.) This is shown in Figure 8.2.

Again, rows 20–42 out of the 126 rows are showing. We now pull down "Analyze" and go again to "General Linear Model" and sub menu "Univariate," as shown in Figure 8.3 (see arrows).

The resulting dialog box, "Univariate," is shown in Figure 8.4.

We now bring "Sophistication," our dependent measure, over to "Dependent Variable," and bring both of our factors over to "Fixed Factors." The age and gender variables are clearly "fixed factors"—neither will (in fact, can't!!) be extrapolated or interpolated—there are no other genders, and there are no age groups of interest beside the five being studied, and there are no gaps between any of the age groups. This produces Figure 8.5.

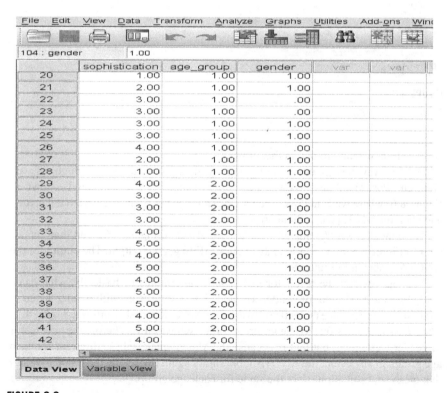

FIGURE 8.1

SPSS input from Chapter 6, with only one factor: AGE.

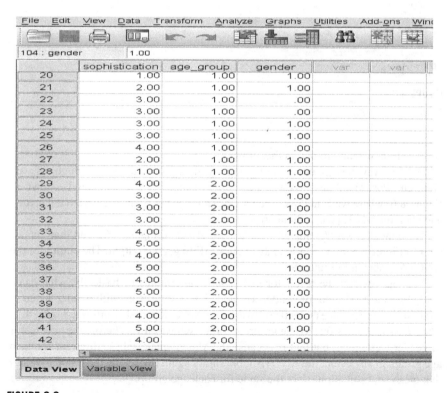

FIGURE 8.2

Data with two factors ready for SPSS analysis.

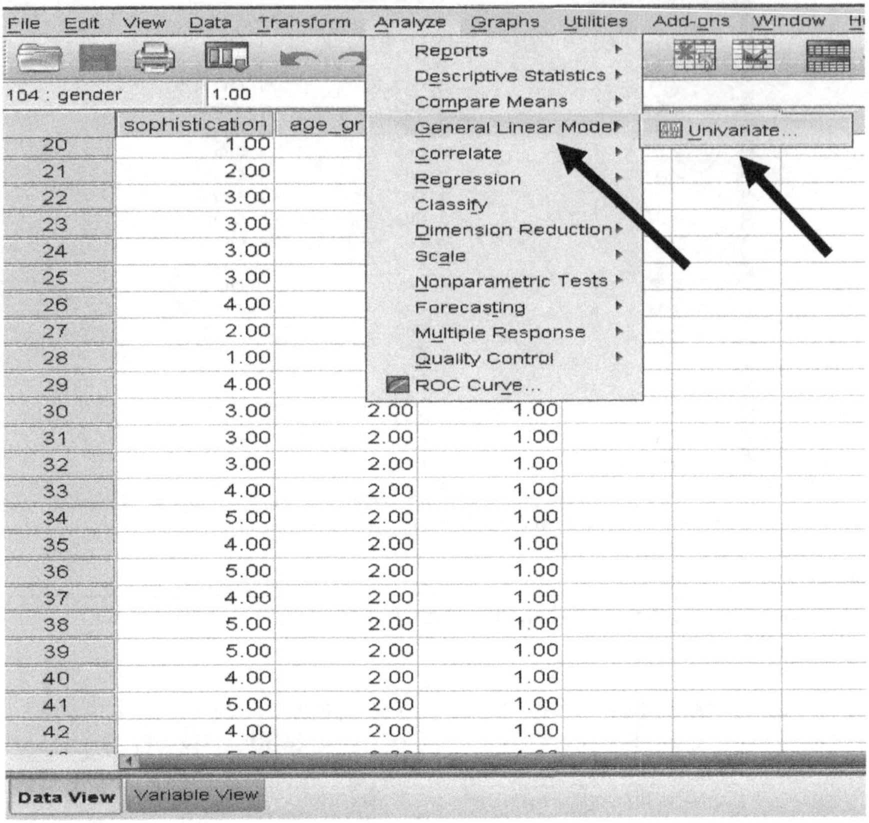

FIGURE 8.3

Preparing for SPSS analysis.

We are now ready to obtain the output.

(By the way, just to anticipate finding significant differences, we might as well click on "Post Hoc," and ask for the results of the S-N-K tests. This is shown in Figure 8.6, where we bring over the two variables to the right [see horizontal arrow] and click on S-N-K [see vertical arrow].)

We now click on "Continue" (see dashed arrow in Figure 8.6), and that gets us back to Figure 8.5, and we are ready to click OK to get our output. The output for the ANOVA is shown in Figure 8.7.

You can see that the result for *age-group (generation)* is, basically, what came out before the new factor of gender was added. It is significant with p-value listed as 0.000, meaning a p-value that is 0.000 to three digits (see top; dashed arrow in Figure 8.7). The sums-of-squares due to age group is *not* the same as it was before the new factor of gender was added, but that is because the Male/Female split is different for each age group. In any event, the ANOVA table shows again (by seeing the 0.000 p-value) that mean sophistication is not the same for each age group.

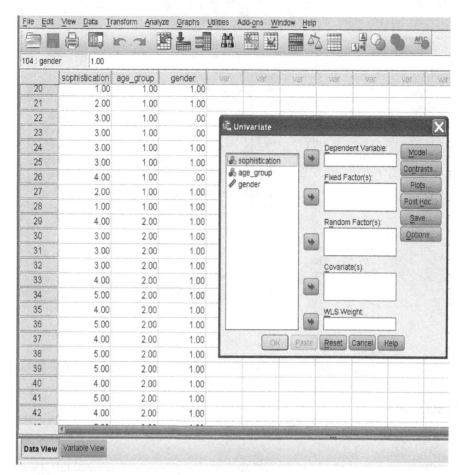

FIGURE 8.4

Univariate dialog box in SPSS.

The result for *gender* is also highly significant, with *p*-value listed as 0.000 (see bottom; dashed arrow in Figure 8.7). This indicates that we conclude that mean sophistication is not the same for each gender. It turns out that Mademoiselle La La Founder Mary Flynn Myers was right after all, despite the protest by Cinny Bittle.

Now, if we examine the S-N-K test for age groups, we find the same result as in Chapter 6 (where we first performed the S-N-K test). The true (sophistication) mean of age group 1 is judged as different from the mean of each of the other four columns; also, the means of age groups 5 and 4 are judged to be the same, but both higher than that of group 1; finally, the means of age groups 2 and 3 are judged to be the same, but both higher than that of the other three age groups.

Now, let us look at the output for the S-N-K test for gender. This is shown in Figure 8.8.

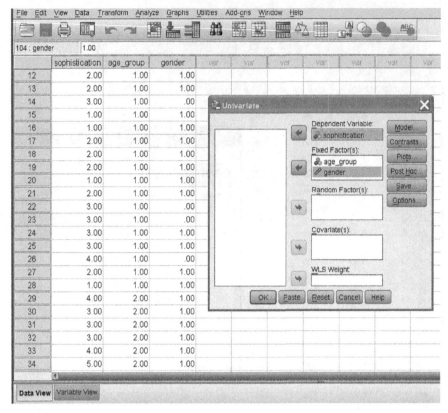

FIGURE 8.5

Preparing to run the two-factor ANOVA in SPSS.

We are playing a bit of a statistical joke here. Did you guess in advance that it was coming? There are only two genders, and their means were judged to be significantly different by the F-test. There is no further notion of how they are different! There are only two sample means, and the difference between them is judged to indicate that the true means are not the same.

That's the end of the story about gender alone, except of course, for the actual difference itself. For the males ($n=41$), the average sophistication is 2.95, while for the females ($n=85$), it is 3.60. It appears that women gave higher ratings of satisfaction than males, aggregated over all the age groups. But an S-N-K test on gender has nothing to add to the story. Indeed, you need at least three levels of the factor for any multiple comparison test to add to the knowledge provided by the F-test; if there are only two means, and we conclude from the ANOVA (F-test) that they differ, what else can be said (beside the direction of the difference)? Nothing!

Now, let's consider the interaction effect. This is also significant (see solid arrow in Figure 8.7), with p-value $= 0.000$. It is not useful from a practical viewpoint to try to express the meaning of the interaction in terms of definition 1: that the total difference is not equal to the sum of the two separate differences.

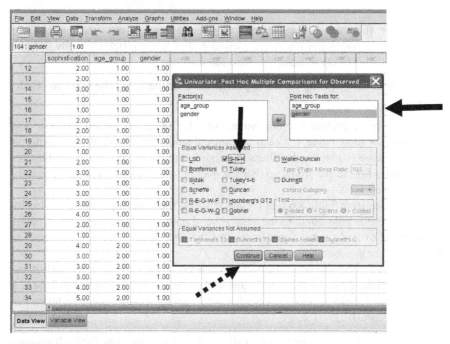

FIGURE 8.6

Asking for the S-N-K tests; SPSS.

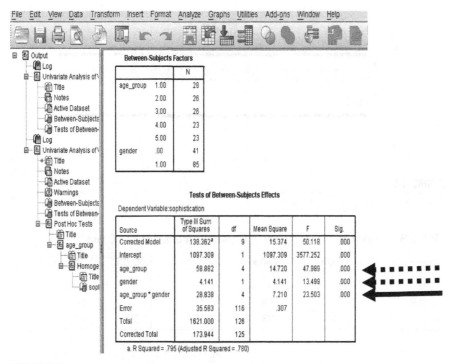

FIGURE 8.7

ANOVA output for our two-factor analysis; SPSS.

However, there are two basic ways to tell the story of this interaction. Each one uses the second definition we alluded to earlier in the chapter. Simply put, the description that is likely to make the most sense is this:

The effect of *age group* on the sophistication rating is not the same for each gender.

By way of supporting that statement, consider Table 8.6, which shows us the mean sophistication rating for each age group/gender combination. In looking at Table 8.6, please remember that there are slightly more than twice as many females (85) as males (41) in the study, so that the overall means are dictated quite heavily by the female means.

We can see from Table 8.6 that for the females, the general pattern indicated by the S-N-K results holds, and, indeed, the general pattern of female means is consistent with the overall means. You can see that the rank order of the female means is the same as for the overall means.

However, for the males it differs. The youngest age group rated the sophistication very differently from the females and higher than age groups 4 and 5. That is a reversal of the female pattern. This is what we meant by what we bolded a bit earlier (which we repeat):

The effect of *age group* on sophistication rating is not the same for each *gender*.

Warnings

Post hoc tests are not performed for gender because there are fewer than three groups.

FIGURE 8.8

S-N-K "result" for gender; SPSS.

Table 8.6 Means for Each Age Group/Gender Combination and Overall

Age Group:	1–25	26–35	36–45	46–55	56–66
Male	3.20	4.00	3.71	2.55	2.11
Female	1.72	4.45	4.79	3.50	3.14
Overall	2.25	4.38	4.50	3.04	2.74

Actually, we can describe the practical meaning of the interaction another way (we said earlier that there were two ways to do so). That second way is:

The effect of *gender* on sophistication rating is not the same for each *age group*.

8.5 MEANWHILE, BACK AT MADEMOISELLE LA LA...

You'll remember that Cinny Bittle was sceptical about Mademoiselle La La Founder Mary Flynn Myers' hypothesis that there's a fundamental difference between perceived sophistication by men and women. Bittle thought your analysis was going to be a "colossal waste of time," but asked you to proceed anyway, to appease Myers.

It turns out Myers' hunch was a good one. Using a two-factor ANOVA, you were able to determine that the effect of *gender* on sophistication rating is not the same for each *age group*. In fact, there is a reversal of sophistication ratings between genders for some age groups. The youngest male age group rated the sophistication higher than the same age group for females, but male ratings were lower than female ratings for the higher age groups. This makes sense for Mademoiselle La La, since the company doesn't offer much in the way of older men's attire. Its limited offerings for men target men between the ages of 18 and 45 years.

No sooner have you finished your analysis when you run into La La Founder Mary Flynn Myers as you cross the grand atrium of company headquarters. She's dressed to the nines, sporting a beautifully cut Armani skirt suit. She recognizes you, smiles and stops to chat.

"Good morning," she says with a smile. "I'm glad I ran into you because I was wondering about the status of your latest research. Do you have an update?"

"Yes, I was just finishing up."

"Great," she beams. "I'm all ears!"

"Well, we initially determined that there were clearly differences in perception of sophistication by age."

"Right," she smiles. "So how did you proceed?"

"I ran a two-factor ANOVA on the data we originally collected from the survey."

"Ah, ANOVAs," she sighs with a smile. "I remember them from grad school. Don't remember the 2-factor part though. What's that?"

You're thrilled that she has some basic understand of what's coming. You already like her, so you try very hard to not sound too professorial.

"We were looking at the two factors of age and gender and their impact on perception of sophistication. Whenever you look at two factors simultaneously, you need to deal with the potential of interaction."

"Interesting. Keep going."

"The 2-factor ANOVA showed that sophistication rating is different by gender, and the gender differences are not the same for each age group."

"With statistical significance?" she asks.

"Absolutely. The *p*-value for the age-gender interaction was way below 0.05."

"Well done," she says. She's warming to you. "So what exactly are the differences?"

You hand her a hard copy of the table that displays means for each age group/gender combination. "There's a reversal of sophistication ratings between genders. The youngest male age group rated the sophistication higher than the youngest female age group, but lower than the females for the higher age groups."

"Fascinating," she says looking at the table. "This is good news, because we've been building up our young men's collection, while pushing styles for older women. Sales are up, so I think we've hit our sweet spot. This data confirms that we're on the right track for both genders."

You smile broadly. "Great," you reply. "I can get the full report to Cinny by noon tomorrow."

"I think she's intimidated by your statistical *savoir-faire*."

"Oh, don't bother," she says, waving her hand in the air. She leans in, partially covers her mouth, and whispers: "This is tremendous work, but Cinny doesn't really grasp this kind of thing, and actually gets flummoxed when I spend too much time asking about your research."

"Oh?" you ask, trying to retain objectivity.

She leans in, puts her hand up to mouth and whispers: "I think she's intimidated by your statistical *savoir-faire*. Let's just keep it between us. Deal?"

"Deal!"

"Thanks again," she says as she leaves. "The board is gonna love this!"

SIDEBAR: REPLICATION: THE GOOD, THE BAD AND THE... "PENALTY".

The issue of replication and the role it plays in our ability to measure interaction effects is important to understand.

We have gone out of our way to separate the two-factor design, as covered in this chapter, from the situation in Chapter 7, where you have two factors, but one of them is simply, "respondent" (or, equivalently, "participant"), which can be considered a "faux factor."

If the two factors are ones that do *not* include "participant" (a random level factor as discussed in Chapter 7), which is the case in this chapter – Age and Gender are the two factors – it is very likely you *will* have replication, and not just one data point for each combination.

For example, with 5 age groups and 2 genders (using the data from this chapter), it would hard to imagine having only two respondents for each age group – one male and one female. Thus, there is replication. Indeed, in a case not involving "respondent" as a factor, the "no replication" situation is very unlikely to arise.

However, when you have two factors and one *is* "respondent" (making it a within-subjects design), and you have only one "real" factor, then you will *not* have replication.

This is what occurred in the previous chapter, Chapter 7, when you needed to perform a few added steps, clicking on "Model" and then "Customization." Basically, you were telling SPSS that there was no interaction between "person" and "task." This was necessary because *there is, indeed, no replication in that example – for any individual participant and task combination, there was only one data value.*

Here's the bottom line:

If you do not have replication, you must assume no interaction with two fixed-level factors.

Why is this important? Well, first of all, you need to tell the software whether or not there is interaction so that the software will perform the analysis correctly.

But there's another reason: there may be what we call an "analysis penalty." That is, in running an experiment with no replication (for example, because you want to save time and money) means you MUST assume that there is no interaction.

Why is that a "penalty"? Well, there might indeed be an interaction effect between the factors, but you MUST assume that there is no interaction, and there is no way to know if the "no interaction" assumption is "doing you in!" You can think of the situation as analogous to the old saying, "There's no free lunch." ☺

But here's the good news: you can comfortably assume no interaction when one of the factors is "respondent." And that's indeed the case with the standard "within-subjects" usability test described in Chapter 7.

Nevertheless, as noted, you still need to tell the software there is no interaction. The way you do this is to repeat the process as we discussed in Chapter 7, illustrated by Figures 7.8 through 7.12 and the accompanying text.

Continued

> ### SIDEBAR: REPLICATION: THE GOOD, THE BAD AND THE..."PENALTY".—cont'd
>
> You will get output that does not include any measure of interaction and tests each of the two factors in the correct way under this no-interaction assumption.
>
> In the within-subject design in Chapter 7, we needed to do this to obtain the S-N-K analysis; after all, in that within-subjects design, there was no replication – as we noted, for each combination of person and task, there was, and can be, only one data point.

8.6 SUMMARY

In this chapter, we have introduced the studying of the impact of two factors on the dependent measure/dependent variable. This necessitated the introduction of the very important idea of *interaction effects*. These are joint effects that may impact the dependent measure (in our core example, Sophistication Rating) in a way that is not additive and may play a key role in explaining how different factors impact the dependent measure. The two factors, individually, are not necessarily the only important forces at work.

8.7 EXERCISE

1. Consider the situation where you have three age groups and four designs, and wish to test whether (1) the true average sophistication rating is the same for each design, (2) the true average sophistication rating is the same for each age group, and (3) the two factors have (nonzero) interaction. You have independent samples, as each person evaluates only one of the four designs (and each person obviously belongs to only one age group). There are two people (replicates) for each age/design combination, thus having 3*4*2 = 24 data values. Data for the sophistication ratings for each design are in data files in SPSS (file name: Chapter 8..Exercise 1.data). The output in SPSS is in a file (file name: Chapter 8..Exercise 1.output). All files are on a Web site indicated in the preface to the text.

    Perform an ANOVA to test whether the (true) average sophistication ratings are equal or not for the four designs, equal or not for the three age groups, and whether there is an age*design interaction effect.

    A Word file (file name: Chapter 8.Exercise 1.discussion) is also provided, which discusses the results.

Can you relate? Correlation and simple linear regression

9

9.1 INTRODUCTION

Making sense of data, as we have noted, is a required skill for any UX researcher. No matter what the data values are or how you got the data, you're the one who's responsible for making sense of the data. Your other team members may casually watch you conduct a usability test or two, but you are on the hook for interpreting the results. Perhaps just as importantly, everyone (including top brass) wants to know what your recommendations are based on your findings. Although rarely explicitly stated, you know what those execs are thinking: "You told me what you observed; now tell me what to do to increase my bottom line."

Of course, we've already discussed lots of ways to analyze data to gain meaning through statistical inference (hypothesis testing and confidence intervals) methods. But, what about using data to determine the *relationship* between quantities, in order to garner even more meaning? More specifically, how does the value of one variable change when the value of another variable changes? Furthermore—and here comes perhaps one of the most important concepts for not just UX, but all social and behavioral researchers—how can we *predict* the value of one variable from the knowledge of the value of another variable?

Enter the wonderful world of regression analysis.

9.2 CASE STUDY: DO RECRUITERS REALLY CARE ABOUT BOOLEAN AT BEHEMOTH.COM?

Let's return to our favorite employment Web site, Behemoth.com, where you were hired as usability researcher. As we mentioned in Chapter 3, Behemoth.com is aptly named, because it's one of the largest job search engines in the world, with over a million job openings at any time, over 1 million resumes in the database, and over 63 million job seekers per month. Behemoth has over 5000 employees spread around the world.

You'll also recall from Chapter 3 that one of the main sources of Behemoth's income is from employers and recruiters who (1) post jobs on the site and (2) buy access to its enormous database of resumes to search for good candidates to fill those jobs.

You'll recall from Chapter 4 that you had to deliver the cold, hard facts about "Novix" to UX Director Hans Blitz: despite spending 80 million dollars on the new search, the current Behemoth search performed better than the new one in a head-to-head comparison usability test.

To put it mildly, Hans was shocked. But bad news doesn't get any better with age, so he quickly scheduled a meeting with Joey Vellucci, CEO, to break the news. You were glad you didn't have to be in the meeting, although a "fly-on-the-wall" perspective might have been interesting.

Strolling into work one morning, you spy Hans enjoying a cigarette in "smoker's alley," the only place where the few remaining Behemoth workers who smoke can indulge. It's behind the old mill, where 19th century workers brought in the raw materials for the looms, and where finished textiles were loaded onto trains. Hans sees you walking by and motions for you to come over for a chat.

"Well, Joey didn't go ballistic like I expected, but he's pretty annoyed and wants more answers pronto."

"Hmmm…what kind?"

"Well, first of all, he's curious about why our recruiting clients are complaining about our current search if our current search engine does better than Novix."

"Well, just because we did better than Novix doesn't mean that our current search is perfect."

"*You* tell him that," Hans offers with a chuckle. "He did raise some interesting points, though."

"Such as?" you ask.

"He looked at your report and was baffled that recruiters kept talking about the missing Boolean search; the big selling point that the Palo Alto guys kept hammering was that you don't need a Boolean with Novix, and that was supposed to be a *good* thing."

"Yeah," you admit. "It's a valid point. But what we found out is that a lot of the recruiters are really creatures of habit who have been using their same complex Boolean strings for a long time. You take that away from them and it's like taking a juicy T-Bone from a hungry dog. As a consequence, the lack of Boolean search capability may decrease adoption of the Novix search engine."

Hans' mood suddenly goes dark, and he glares at you with disdain: "Prove to me we spent 80 million getting rid of something our clients want!"

"Prove to me we spent 80 million getting rid of something our clients want!"

You're briefly taken aback, but decide to suppress the immediate urge to reply that UX should have been given the opportunity to run usability tests *before* the Novix purchase. You opt to utilize a more proactive approach: "Well, we could conduct an online usability study on our current search engine. We'll use an unmoderated study to get the sample sizes much higher than we would get with a standard usability test."

"OK," Hans says slowly and cautiously. "And?"

"After folks have used the search for a while, we could ask all the participants to rank their perception of usefulness with the different search fields, along with their likelihood to adopt the search engine. Then, I can calculate the correlation coefficient between the usefulness of the ability to perform a Boolean search and likelihood of adoption of the search engine, and perform some simple regression."

Hans hesitates: "I have no idea what you just said, but it sounds feasible. When can we have the results?"

"Well, it'll take some time to get the test together and screen for the right participants. After the results come in, we'll do the number crunching. Give me 2 weeks."

"Ok, but no more than 2 weeks right? Bad news doesn't get any better with time." He throws down his finished butt, stomps on it, turns abruptly on his heels and leaves in a huff.

Again, you're off to the races to get answers for Hans and to alleviate his Boolean angst. Realizing that you need higher sample sizes to make a convincing case for your results, you decide to go with an unmoderated online test of the current Behemoth search engine. The e-mail invite goes out to about 300 recruiters who are regularly searching for candidates. After answering some basic eligibility questions, they are carefully screened to disqualify any current Behemoth customers; you want newbies who've never used the engine before.

All the respondents are tasked with finding good candidates for the same three requisitions: (1) A Java Developer with at least 5 years experience, a bachelor's degree from MIT, a maximum salary requirement of $95,000 per year, willing to relocate, who is looking for a full-time position; (2) A Web Designer with skills using Axure, Photoshop, and Illustrator within 25 miles of San Diego, with an Active Confidential Security Clearance; and (3) A Business Analyst who has previously worked at Oracle, an average length of employment of no less than 1 year, with a resume dated no earlier than 2013, willing to travel up to 50% of the time.

After completing the tasks of finding candidates for the three positions, the respondents are asked about overall satisfaction with the search engine. In addition, they are specifically asked to rate their perception of usefulness for each of the fields in the search engine, on a scale of 1–5, where 1 = not at all useful and 5 = extremely useful. Table 9.1 shows the 15 specific search engine components respondents are asked to rate.

At the very end of the survey rating, you insert the moment of truth question: "Imagine that this search engine is available to you at no cost to find qualified candidates using the candidate databases you currently employ. Rate your likelihood of adopting this candidate search engine on a scale of 1–5, where 1 = not at all likely and 5 = extremely likely."

With everything in place, you launch the online study. After a week, you check into your online test tool. You're happy to find 233 responses. However, there were 36 incompletes, and another 17 who you have to disqualify for suspicious looking activity (mostly in the form of overly quick task completion times). You end up with 180 bona fide test responses. You download the Excel spreadsheet containing the rating scales of the search engine components.

Time to roll up your sleeves. The first thing you want to establish, of course, is the perceived value of Boolean search, and its correlation with likelihood of adoption.

SIDEBAR: GET THOSE SAMPLE SIZES UP! UNMODERATED REMOTE USABILITY TESTING

Unmoderated remote usability testing is a low-cost and effective technique for collecting task-based usability data. As a consequence, the technique has experienced great growth in recent years by UX professionals.

Unmoderated remote usability tests allow you to:

- Collect data easily and efficiently.
- Find the right participants.
- Conduct studies on a limited budget.
- Test users in their natural environment.
- Test internationally without traveling.
- Validate or define lab-based research.
- Achieve statistical significance when comparing designs, identify areas of a Web site that need improvement, and conduct competitive benchmarking studies.

Those are the advantages, but how does it work? In a nutshell, the participant receives an e-mail invitation to participate in the study, and clicks on the link to begin. He/she is taken to a Web site where he/she is asked to complete a series of tasks. During task completion, data are being collected on a wide range of variables, like task completion rates, time to complete the tasks, pages visited, data entered, etc. Once finished, the participant is asked a series of questions regarding satisfaction on several different variables. In our case with Behemoth, the participant is asked to rate the usefulness of specific components of the search engine.

For an outstanding introduction and how-to guide on online usability studies—including planning, designing, launching, and data analysis—we heartily recommend *Beyond the Usability Lab: Conducting Large-Scale Online User Experience Studies*, by Bill Albert, Tom Tullis, and Donna Tedesco (Morgan Kaufmann, 2010). The book shows you how to use commercial tools, like User Zoom and Loop 11, but also offers discount approaches that can yield perfectly good results.

Table 9.1 The 15 Search Engine Components

1. Ability to search by job title
2. Ability to search by years of experience
3. Ability to search by location
4. Ability to search by schools attended
5. Ability to search candidates by date of updated resume
6. Ability to search candidates by level of education
7. Ability to search by skills
8. Ability to search candidates by average length of employment at each company
9. Ability to search candidates by maximum salary
10. Ability to search candidates by job type he/she is looking for: full time, part time, temporary/contract, per diem, intern
11. Ability to search candidates by companies in which they have worked
12. Ability to search candidates by willingness to travel. (Expressed as "no travel ability required," "up to 25%," "up to 50%," "up to 75%," "up to 100%")
13. Ability to search candidates by willingness to relocate
14. Ability to search candidates by security clearance. (Active Confidential, Inactive Confidential, Active Secret, Inactive Secret, Active Top Secret, Inactive Top Secret, Active Secret/SCI, Inactive Top Secret/SCI)
15. Ability to perform a Boolean search

9.3 THE CORRELATION COEFFICIENT

The "correlation coefficient" reflects the relationship between two variables. Specifically, it measures the strength of a straight-line relationship between two variables, and also tells you the direction of the relationship, if any. It is a numerical value that ranges between −1 and +1 and is typically denoted by "r":

$$-1 \leq r \leq +1$$

The absolute value of the correlation reflects the strength of the relationship. So, a correlation of −0.80 indicates a stronger relationship than +0.70.

There is an arithmetic formula to compute the correlation coefficient, but you should simply use Excel or SPSS to compute it for you. (We will show you how to do this later in this section.)

Let's first consider a small example before we dive into the Behemoth.com data set. Say that we have two variables: (1) Assessment of how sophisticated a Web design is, and (2) Amount of experience buying products online. We will assign the sophistication assessment as the output variable, "Y," and the amount of experience as the input variable, "X." It is common to use Y to notate the output variable and X to notate the input variable.

The correlation coefficient, "r," measures the relative degree to which a straight line fits the data. Let's consider the six "scatter plots" in Figure 9.1, and discuss them in light of the value of r.

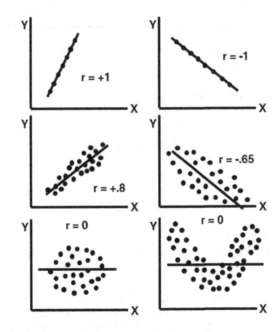

FIGURE 9.1

Scatter plots of Y and X data.

The top left plot has all the data points exactly on a straight line, and the straight line has a positive slope. With real data, we would never see such an exact relationship; we present it only for illustration purposes. The value of r is +1. This value is the maximum value r can take on. And, the fact that the slope of the line is positive ensures that the sign of r is positive (i.e., +). Now, if you look at the top right plot, the relationship is also perfect—the data values are all right on the line. But, the line is downward sloping. The value of r, correspondingly, comes out −1. The "1" indicates that the fit to a straight line is perfect, while the "−" sign indicates, indeed, that the line is downward sloping.

This illustrates a useful property of r; while the numerical value of r tells us about how well the data fit a straight line (referred to as the [relative] *strength* of the relationship), its sign tells us the *direction* of the relationship, if any. A + value of r indicates a positive relationship—as one variable goes up, the other variable also goes up; as one variable goes down, the other variable also goes down. (You may also see this relationship described as a "positive" or "direct" correlation.)

A − [minus] value of r indicates an "inverse" relationship—as one variable goes up, the other goes down, and vice versa. (You may also see this relationship described as a "negative or "indirect" correlation.) A value of zero for r (or, as a practical matter, right near it) indicates that the two variables are unrelated linearly, and this is illustrated in the bottom left scatter plot; you can see that there is no indication at all of a relationship between the variables. The best-fitting line[1] is horizontal—indicating zero slope, the equivalent of no linear relationship. Whenever the best-fitting line has zero slope (i.e., is horizontal), the value of r is zero, and vice versa.

If we look at the middle left plot, the data values are not right on the line that goes through the values, but it will, intuitively, give you a pretty accurate value of Y from inputting the value of X into the equation of the line. The line might be, for example, $Y = 0.2 + 1.07X$, and when you plug in the value of X, the Y that comes out will be pretty close to the actual Y value for most all the data values. Without specific data, we cannot provide the exact value of r, but it might be in the neighborhood of +0.8; the line clearly has a positive slope. (The "r = 0.8" listed for this plot in Figure 9.1 is just a rough estimate by the authors when looking at the data.)

Let's compare this plot with the middle right plot. It should be clear to the reader that the fit to a straight line is not as good as the plot on the left—the data values are not as tightly clustered around the line as in the middle left plot—and also, the line best-fitting the data is downward sloping. Since the fit is less good, the value of r is lower, say, 0.65 (again, an estimate based on the authors' view at the data). Also, it is negative, reflecting the negative slope of the straight line best-fitting the data.

The final plot among the six is the bottom right plot. The purpose of that plot is to dramatically illustrate a key point that r is measuring the relative strength of a

---

[1]We will more precisely define "best-fitting line" later in the chapter.

straight-line fit. Clearly, there is a relationship, perhaps somewhat strong, between Y and X in the bottom right plot. But, it is a "U-shaped" curve. A straight line does not do a good job *at all* of fitting that data. The best-fitting line would be horizontal, or very close to it, and the value of r would, correspondingly, be equal to or very close to zero. After all, what does Y do as X increases? For the first half of the X's, Y goes down; for the second half of the X's, Y goes up. We might say that, *on average*, Y *does not do anything*—hence the zero slope of the best-fitting line and a value of r of zero.

Remember, if a line has a slope of zero (and is, thus, horizontal), it means that as X changes, Y does not change at all. After all, if a line is Y = 4 + 0*X, with its zero slope, no matter what X you plug in, the Y stays the same—indeed, Y is totally unaffected by X; that is why we noted earlier that a zero value for r indicates that there is no linear relationship at all between the two variables.

9.3.1 EXCEL

We will now describe how to find r using Excel. We will analyze the real-world Behemoth.com data a bit later. Let us use our limited data set to illustrate the finding of the correlation, r, using Excel. Suppose we have the five data points in Table 9.2 (which we can envision coming from respective 5-point Likert scales).

For the most part, when X is larger, Y is larger, so we would expect a positive value for r.

First we open Data Analysis in Excel and identify "Correlation." See the arrow in Figure 9.2. Then we click "OK." This gives us the Correlation dialog box, shown in Figure 9.3.

We enter the (input) data range (see vertical arrow in Figure 9.3), and, we ask the output to be on a page arbitrarily named "paul" (see horizontal arrow in Figure 9.3). After we click "OK," we get the answer—the correlation between the two variables—as shown in Figure 9.4.

Figure 9.4 tells us that the correlation, r, equals +0.895. We noted earlier that we anticipated a positive value, and, indeed, we do get a positive value. Notice that in Figure 9.4, the top right cell is empty. That is because the correlation coefficient between two variables is the same, regardless of which is the "Y" and which is the "X." In other words, the correlation between the Column 2 variable

Table 9.2 Illustrative Data

X	Y
5	4
4	4
2	1
3	3
4	3

and the Column 1 variable (noted as 0.895144) is the same as the correlation between the Column 1 variable and the Column 2 variable. Also note that we have a value of 1.0 as the correlation between each variable and itself!! This is always the case and, of course, it makes perfect sense that a variable is perfectly correlated with itself.

Now we present finding r using SPSS.

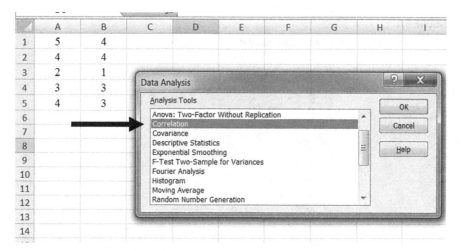

FIGURE 9.2

Data analysis with correlation highlighted; Excel with illustrative data.

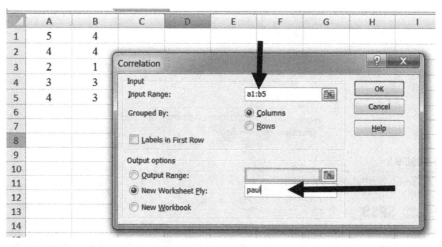

FIGURE 9.3

Correlation dialog box; Excel with illustrative data.

	A	B	C
1		*Column 1*	*Column 2*
2	Column 1	1	
3	Column 2	0.895144	1
4			
5			

FIGURE 9.4

Correlation output; Excel with illustrative data.

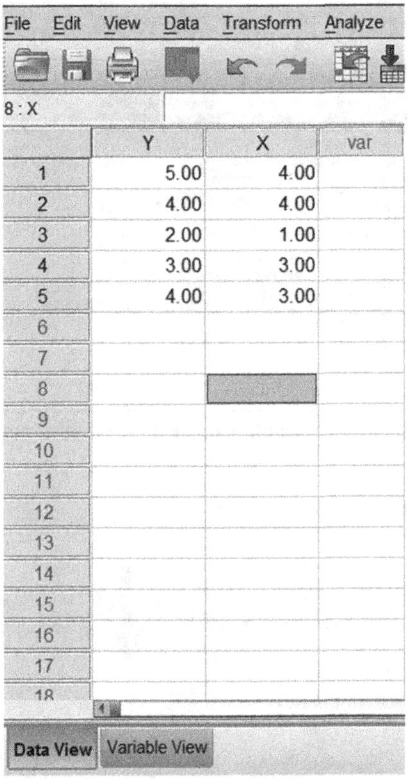

File	Edit	View	Data	Transform	Analyze

8 : X

	Y	X	var
1	5.00	4.00	
2	4.00	4.00	
3	2.00	1.00	
4	3.00	3.00	
5	4.00	3.00	
6			
7			
8			
9			
10			
11			
12			
13			
14			
15			
16			
17			
18			

Data View   Variable View

FIGURE 9.5

SPSS with illustrative input data.

9.3.2 SPSS

Figure 9.5 shows the same limited data set in SPSS. You can see in the figure that we used "Variable View" to change the variable names to Y and X. Of course, the Y values are what they are and the X values are what they are; however, it does not matter if the Y column is typed in to the left of the X column (as in Figure 9.5) or to the right of the X column.

SIDEBAR: THE COEFFICIENT OF DETERMINATION (R-SQUARED)

Since this is the first example in which we found r for an actual data set (albeit, a small one!), we now introduce another interesting idea, one that helps interpret the actual value of r.

If we compute r^2, we get $(0.895*0.895) = 0.801$. The quantity, r^2, is called the "coefficient of determination," even though, often, it's referred to as simply the "r^2."

We can give a very useful interpretation to the 0.801. Based on the data, we estimate *that 80.1% of the variability in Y (i.e., the degree to which all the Y values are not the same) can be explained by the variability in X (i.e., the degree to which all the X values are not the same).* In loose terms, we might say that X is estimated to explain about 80.1% of Y, and if X were held constant, Y would vary only 19.9% as much as it varies now.

In our example, Y = assessment of how sophisticated a specific design is, and X = amount of experience buying products online. So, in that context, an r of 0.895, and r^2 of 0.801, we would say that we estimate that about 80% of the variability in the respondents' opinions about how sophisticated the design is can be explained by how much experience a respondent has had buying online products. By the way, in this type of context, 80% would nearly always be considered a pretty high value!

We now pull down "Analyze" (we noted earlier in the book that "Analyze" is always how we begin a statistical analysis of any kind), highlight "Correlate," and go to the submenu item, "Bivariate." See arrows in Figure 9.6.

The term "bivariate" means correlation between *two* variables. The other choices are more complex, and are beyond the scope of this chapter.

After we click, we get the "Bivariate Correlations" dialog box, as shown in Figure 9.7. The word, "Correlations," is plural, since if your data set had, for example, three variables/columns (say, Y, X1, X2), the output would give you the correlation between each of the three pairs of variables; (Y, X1), (Y, X2), (X1, X2). Here, with only two variables, we will get, of course, only one correlation value (not counting the "1's"—the correlation of a variable with itself).

In Figure 9.7, we need to drag the Y and X over to the right-side box called "Variables." There is no need to change the defaults, including the check next to "Pearson" (see sidebar).

SIDEBAR: KARL PEARSON

What we are finding is, technically, the *Pearson* correlation coefficient, named after the mathematician and biometrician (i.e., bio-statistician), Karl Pearson (1857–1936). He was born Carl Pearson, but changed his name purposely and officially to Karl, since he was a fervent fan of Karl Marx.

In 1911 he founded the world's first university statistics department at University College, London. In addition to his work on the correlation between variables, Dr. Pearson also headed up the work on the chi-square test we worked with in an earlier chapter. We noted that it was called the "Pearson chi-square test."

Another claim to fame, although he didn't know it at the time, was that when the 23-year-old (http://en.wikipedia.org/wiki/Albert_Einstein) Albert Einstein started a study group, the Olympia Academy, he suggested that the first book to be read was Karl Pearson's *The Grammar of Science*.

Dr Pearson had two daughters and a son. His son, Egon Pearson, became a prominent statistician in his own right, and succeeded his father as head of the Applied Statistics Department at University College. Egon Pearson, along with Jerzy Neyman, another prominent statistician, developed the basics of hypothesis testing as we know it today (improving ideas that had been earlier considered by Karl Pearson).

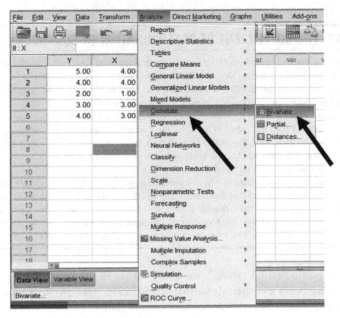

FIGURE 9.6

Asking SPSS to find a bivariate correlation; illustrative data.

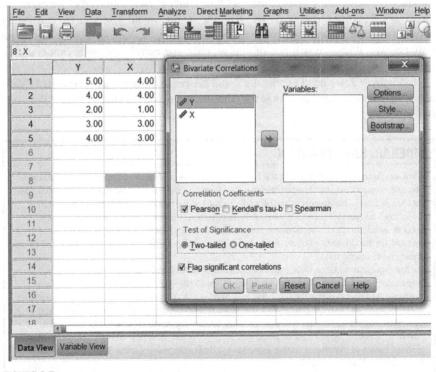

FIGURE 9.7

Bivariate Correlations dialog box; SPSS with illustrative data.

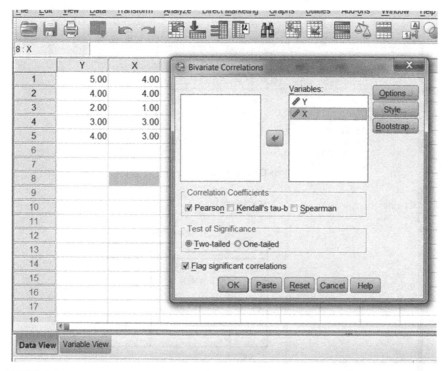

FIGURE 9.8

Variables brought over to Variables dialog box; SPSS with illustrative data.

In addition, we might as well see if the r, that we find, is statistically significant, and if so, have it flagged. (This is essentially testing our old friend the null hypothesis. H0 is that the true value r [often referred to as "ρ"] is 0, vs. ρ ≠ 0. Refer to Chapter 1 for a brushup on hypothesis testing.) Again, these are the default options in the bottom portion of the "Bivariate Correlations" dialog box in Figure 9.7.

Figure 9.8 shows the variables brought over to the "Variables" dialog box.

We now click on OK, and get the output shown in Figure 9.9.

Of course, we get the same answer we got when doing the problem in Excel. However, the SPSS output provides even more value: it tells us that the 0.895 value of r is *statistically significant* (based on a significance level of 0.05), because (1) the asterisk on the 0.895 value tells us that, and, (2) the *p*-value = 0.04, which, indeed, is less than 0.05. (Recall that the *p*-value is always notated as "Sig." in SPSS.)

9.3.3 CORRELATION APPLICATION TO BEHEMOTH.COM

You'll recall that Hans Blitz told you to prove to him that Behemoth spent $80 million getting rid a feature that clients actually wanted.

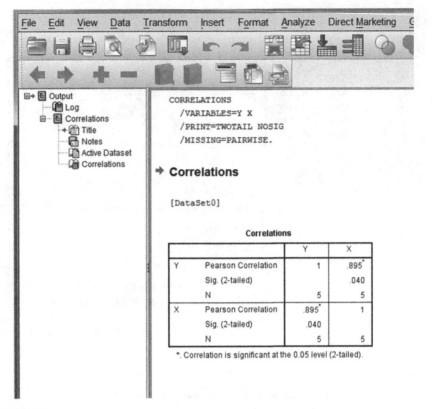

FIGURE 9.9

Correlation output; SPSS with illustrative data.

As a consequence, two of the columns of data you collected during the unmoderated usability test were the Likelihood of adoption (of the search engine) and the assessed usefulness of the Ability to perform a Boolean search, each rated on a 1–5 Likert scale, as mentioned earlier.

Therefore, we have 180 rows of data for these two variables (as we do for all of the data). Figure 9.10 displays the first 26 rows of data in Excel. Also, we should take note of the fact that the first row on the spreadsheet is taken up with the column labels.

As we noted, there are 180 data values in rows 2–181. When we open "Data Analysis" and then "Correlation," we have what is shown in Figure 9.11.

We show you Figure 9.11 specifically since it illustrates the use of a column label (i.e., title). Note how we entered the location of the input data: A1–B181, since there are 180 rows of data. We then check the box that asks whether we have a label in row 1. We do, and thus, we check that box; see arrow in Figure 9.11. Excel now knows to consider rows 2–181 as actual data rows.

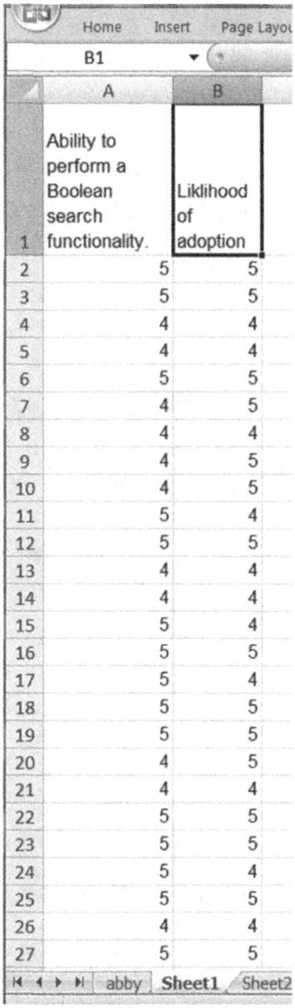

	A	B
1	Ability to perform a Boolean search functionality.	Liklihood of adoption
2	5	5
3	5	5
4	4	4
5	4	4
6	5	5
7	4	5
8	4	4
9	4	5
10	4	5
11	5	4
12	5	5
13	4	4
14	4	4
15	5	4
16	5	5
17	5	4
18	5	5
19	5	5
20	4	5
21	4	4
22	5	5
23	5	5
24	5	4
25	5	5
26	4	4
27	5	5

Home
Insert
Page Layou
B1
abby
Sheet1
Sheet2

FIGURE 9.10

Behemoth.com data in Excel.

Our output is in Figure 9.12.

We can see that the correlation coefficient is +0.449 (the "+" sign is no surprise!). What this tells us is that a higher sense of usefulness of Boolean search capability is associated with an increased likelihood of adoption of the search engine. (If we performed this using SPSS, we would find that the *p*-value of r is 0.000 to 3 digits [actually, for those who care: 0.000000000247] and is thus highly statistically significant.)

Furthermore, we can say that the responder's opinion about the usefulness of the ability to perform a Boolean search, by itself, explains slightly over 20%

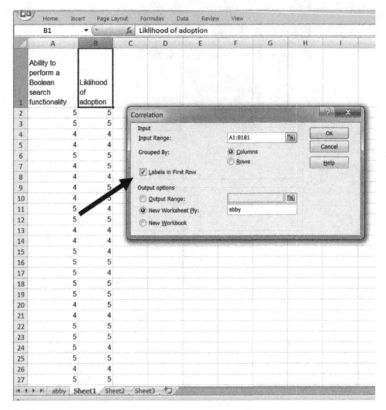

FIGURE 9.11

Correlation dialog box for Behemoth.com data; Excel.

	A	B	C
1		*Ability to perform a Boolean search*	*Liklihood of adoption*
2	Ability to perform a Boolean search	1	
3	Liklihood of adoption	0.449452745	1
4			
5			
6			

FIGURE 9.12

Correlation output for Behemoth.com data; Excel.

(0.449*0.449 = 0.202 or 20.2%) of the variability among the responders of their indicated likelihood to adopt the search engine.

The values of r and r^2 indicated the strength of the (linear) relationship between the two variables. This is certainly important, but we also need to determine what the specific relationship is between the two variables. So, we now introduce Regression Analysis, which will determine the best fitting slope and intercept of this linear relationship based on the data. Using the scenario from this chapter, it will tell us, for example, how much an increased assessment of the usefulness of the ability to perform a Boolean search, say by one unit, will increase the likelihood of adoption of the search engine.

Onward!

9.4 LINEAR REGRESSION

The fundamental purpose of regression analysis and correlation analysis is to study the relationship between a "dependent variable" (which can be thought of as an *output* variable) and one or more "independent variables" (which can be thought of as *input* variables). In this chapter, we will have one independent variable— this form of regression is called "simple regression"; in the next chapter, we will have several input/independent variables (i.e., X's)—this will be called "multiple regression."

Let's return to the illustrative data set we used in the correlation section. This data set is shown in Table 9.2, but, for convenience, we repeat it in Table 9.3. We will illustrate the principles of regression analysis using this data set and then apply the methodology to the Behemoth.com data.

We traditionally refer to the "Y" as the *dependent variable*, and the "X" as the *independent variable*. In fact, you shall see that SPSS uses those terms.

Let us consider a straight-line (i.e., "linear") relationship between the two variables in Table 9.3. We usually start off considering a straight-line relationship first, unless the (Y, X) graph of the data points (similar to the graphs in Figure 9.1) strongly indicates that the relationship is clearly curved. The graph of the data in Table 9.3 is in Figure 9.13. The graph in Figure 9.13 is referred to as a "scatter diagram."

It is evident that a straight line fits the data pretty well, and that there is no meaningful indication of curvature. In Figure 9.14, we add a line that, intuitively, fits the data well.

Thus, we can pretty safely consider a straight-line relationship between X and Y, and not be concerned about more complex relationships. In fact, let us

Table 9.3 Illustrative Data

Y	X
5	4
4	4
2	1
3	3
4	3

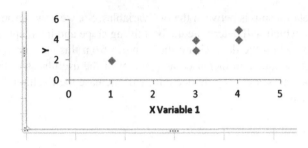

FIGURE 9.13

Scatter diagram.

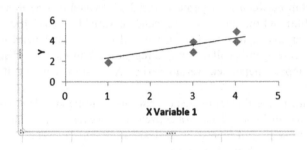

FIGURE 9.14

Adding to the scatter diagram a line that, intuitively, fits well.

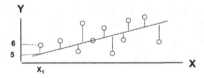

FIGURE 9.15

Illustration of the least-squares definition of "best."

determine the "best-fitting" line to the data (which, surely, will be close to the line drawn "by eye" by the authors in Figure 9.14, but likely will not be identical to it).

But hold on! We cannot find the "best-fitting line" without deciding how to define "best-fitting." Well, in about 99.99% of the cases you would encounter, "best-fitting" is defined as the *least-squares line.* This is the line that minimizes the sum (for all the data values) of the squared differences between the actual Y value and the predicted Y value from using the line. Put another way, it is the line that best fits the actual scores and minimizes the error in prediction, using this criterion. This is illustrated in Figure 9.15.

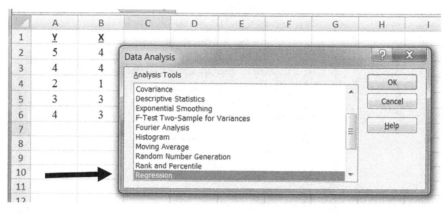

FIGURE 9.16

Regression command within data analysis; Excel with illustrative data.

To calculate this line, the vertical differences from the dots to the line are first squared and summed. For example, at X_1, the line predicts 5, but the actual data value equals 6, for a difference of 1. It can be proved that the least-squares line is unique. In other words, there cannot be a tie for which line is the least-squares line. Perhaps more importantly, Excel and SPSS will find it for us.

First, let's begin by providing our notation[2] for the formula for a simple regression least-squares line:

$$Yc = a + b * X$$

where:

- **"Yc"** is the predicted ("computed") value of Y based on a known value of X,
- **"b"** represents the slope of the line,
- **"a"** represents the intercept, or the point at which the line crosses the Y-axis (sometimes called the "Y-intercept").

There are some very tedious mathematical formulas you can use to calculate the slope and intercept of the least-squares line (sometimes called the "regression line"), but both Excel and SPSS will save you lots of time and headaches. Let's start with Excel.

9.4.1 EXCEL

To do a regression analysis in Excel (and what we have been doing for all statistical analyses in Excel) we first open "Data Analysis." Then, we scroll down to "Regression." See Figure 9.16, with the arrow pointing to the command.

---

[2] There is no standard notation for this least-squares line. If you looked at 10 statistics/predictive analytics/data analysis texts, you might see five or six different notations for the slope and intercept.

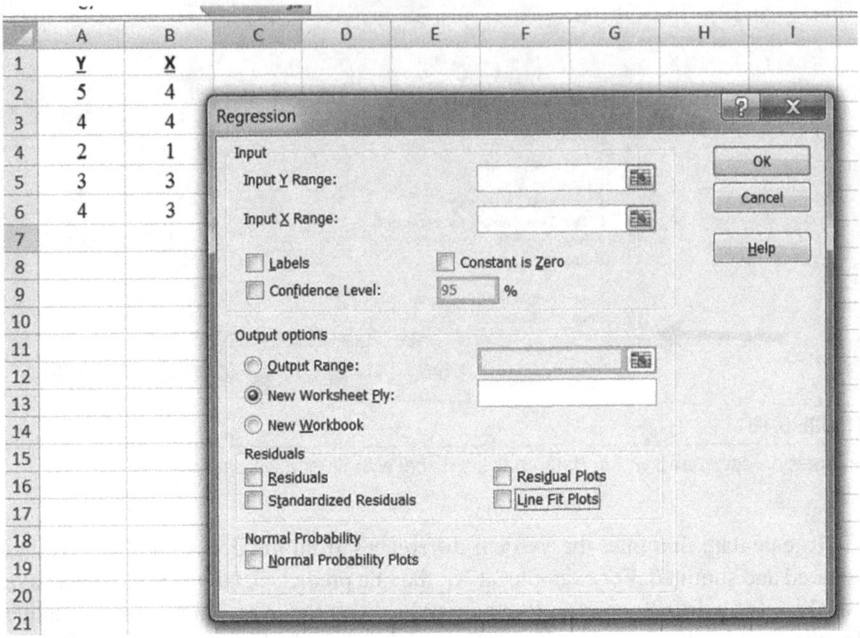

FIGURE 9.17

Regression dialog box; Excel with illustrative data.

We click on "Regression," and get the dialog box shown in Figure 9.17.

We enter the location of the Y variable data and the location of the X variable data, and enter an arbitrary name of a new worksheet: "JARED." That brings us to Figure 9.18.

Note that we checked "Labels" and listed the data as (a1:a6) and (b1:b6), even though there are no data values in row 1.

We now click "OK," and find the output in Figure 9.19.

There is a lot to digest in Figure 9.19. But let's take it step-by-step, and you'll be fine.

First, we note the least-square (best-fitting) line by examining the circled column in the bottom left of the figure; the intercept is 1.1 and the slope is 0.833. (The intercept is labeled "intercept" and the slope is labeled by "X" [row 18 in Figure 9.19], which is standard notation in all statistical software. Since there can be more than one X, the label is to indicate which X the slope pertains to.) It is understood that the value (in this case: 0.833) is the slope of the X listed. Our line, thus, is:

$$Yc = 1.1 + 0.833 * X.$$

The slope of 0.833 means that for each unit increase in X (i.e., X goes up by 1), we predict that Y goes up by 0.833. If X is 0, then our prediction for Y is 1.1, since that's our intercept.

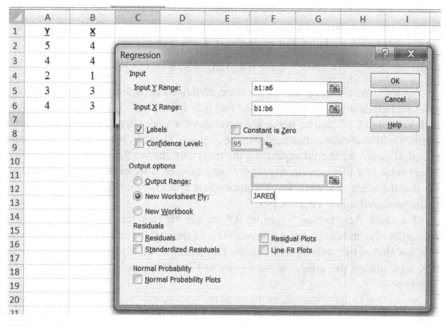

FIGURE 9.18

Filling in the Regression dialog box; Excel with illustrative data.

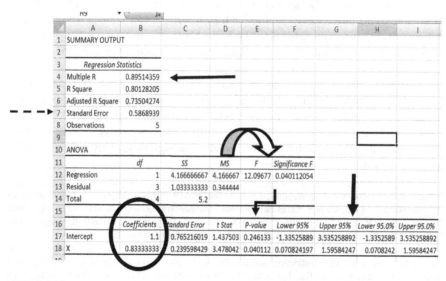

FIGURE 9.19

Regression analysis output; Excel with illustrative data.

OK, here's where things really get interesting. If we have a value of X, we can insert it into the equation for the line, and compute Yc, the value of Y that is predicted for the value of X we input. For example, if X = 3, we predict that Y is

$$1.1 + 0.833\,(3) = 3.599$$

But wait, there's more! Check out the correlation coefficient, which is 0.895 (see solid horizontal arrow in Figure 9.19,[3] labeled "Multiple R"). This is a reasonably high value (and, of course, is the same value we found when we did a correlation analysis with these same data earlier in the chapter). Loosely, but pragmatically interpreted, it means we should expect, for the most part, the predicted value of Y and the actual value of Y to be reasonably close to one another. If we examine the data set, we see that the average of the (two) Y values when X = 3 is 3.5, which, indeed, is close to the predicted value, Yc, of 3.599.

If we look right below "Multiple R," we see "R Square," which equals 0.801. As earlier, this indicates that a bit over 80% of the variability in Y (i.e., how come Y is not always the same!!) is due to the fact that X is not always the same. Indeed, if X were always the same, the variability in Y would be only about 20% as much as it is now.

In addition to the least-squares line and the correlation coefficient (and its square, r^2, the coefficient of determination), there are a few other noteworthy values in the output of Figure 9.19.

If you look at the bottom right of the output (see vertical arrow), you see a 95% confidence interval for each of the coefficients (i.e., intercept and slope[4]). Let's take them one by one.

Our best estimate of the intercept is 1.1; however, a 95% confidence interval for the true value of the intercept is −1.34 to 3.54. However, we can see that the intercept is not significant, since its *p*-value is 0.24 (see the bent arrow in Figure 9.19). Therefore, we cannot rule out that its true value equals zero. Quite often, however, the intercept is not a quantity that, by itself, is of great value to us.

Now let's look at the confidence interval for the slope. Keep in mind that the slope is crucially important; whether it's zero or not directly indicates whether the variables are actually related. Here, we get a value for the slope of 0.833. The 95% confidence interval of the true slope is 0.071 to 1.596. Its *p*-value (0.040) is below the traditional 0.05 benchmark value. Therefore, at significance level equal to 0.05, the slope is statistically significant.

---

[3] The reader will note that the correlation is labeled "Multiple R." This is simply reflecting oversimplification (sloth?) on Excel's part. Excel did not want to bother writing *simple R* when there is only one X, and *multiple R* when there is more than one X, and decided to just write *multiple R* no matter how many X's there are. We obviously weren't involved in the usability testing. ☺

[4] The reader may note that the confidence intervals for the intercept and for the slope are each written twice! This, again, is simply reflecting laziness on Excel's part. You can specify a confidence level other than 95%, and if you do, Excel gives that confidence interval to you, but also, automatically, gives you the confidence interval for 95%. If you do not specify another confidence level (and one virtually never does so), Excel gives you the confidence interval for the 95% default and then gives you the automatic one for 95%.

So, we now can formally conclude that the two variables are, indeed, linearly related.

SIDEBAR: EXCEL'S WEIRD LABEL FOR THE *P*-VALUE FOR THE F-STATISTIC

We want to add that the middle section of the output, the ANOVA table (you saw ANOVA tables in several earlier chapters), gives you a *p*-value also, relative to the F-statistic. You can see the F-statistic value of 12.097 (see curved arrow in Figure 9.19); its *p*-value is just to the right of it and equals 0.040. But, wait a moment!!!! *This value is exactly the same as the* p-*value for the slope!!*

For reasons unknown to the authors, Excel calls the *p*-value for the F-statistic "Significance F," but we assure you that this is the *p*-value (and should be called *p*-value!!). Any time we are running a simple regression (recall: this means there is only one X variable), the *F-statistic will have the same* p-*value as the* p-*value for the slope (t-test),* and provide exactly the same information content. In fact, in writing up a report on the results of a simple regression, you would not want to separately discuss the two *p*-values, since it would be a redundancy. In the next chapter, Chapter 10, the *p*-value for the F-statistic and that for the slope will have different values and will mean different things.

There is one final thing that we wish to impart about the output in Figure 9.19, and that is the "Standard Error," as listed in row 7 in the top section of the output (see dashed horizontal arrow in Figure 9.19). Its value equals 0.587, and its notation is often: Sy.x. This is a key value for finding a confidence interval for a prediction, often a very important thing to find. In essence, this is the standard deviation estimate of the error of a prediction if we had the correct regression line. However, we do not have the exact correct regression line (finding which, in theory, would require infinite data!!). However, if the sample size is reasonably large (say, at least 25), and we are predicting for a value of X that is near the mean of our data, we can, as an approximation, use the standard error value as if it were the overall standard deviation of the prediction. With this caveat, the formula for a 95% confidence interval for a prediction is

$$Yc \pm TINV\ (0.05,\ n{-}2)\ *\ Sy.x,$$

where "*n*" is the sample size (in this example, $n = 5$) and TINV is an Excel command that provides a value from the t-distribution. The first value (i.e., 0.05) reflects wanting 95% confidence—it would be 0.01 for 99% confidence, 0.10 for 90% confidence, etc.; the second value, $(n{-}2)$, is a degrees-of-freedom number—you really don't need to know the details/derivation of why that value is what it is—it is easy to determine, since you know the value of *n*, the sample size, and hence, you obviously know the value of $(n{-}2)$. For our earlier example, where we predicted a value of Yc to be 3.599, a 95% confidence interval for what the value will actually come out *for an individual person* is:

$$3.599 \pm TINV\ (0.05,\ 3)\ *\ (0.587)$$

$$3.599 \pm (3.182)\ *\ (0.587)$$

$$3.599 \pm 1.865$$

or
$$(1.734\ to\ 5),$$

with the realization that we cannot get a value that exceeds 5.

If we determine the actual value for the confidence interval, using the relatively complex formula, we would get 1.339 to 5, a bit wider, but not that different, even though, after all, n is only 5. In a real application, in which n is not so small (such as in the Behemoth.com data set, in which $n = 180$), the difference from the theoretically true confidence interval will be very much smaller, and virtually for sure, the difference will be immaterial. Indeed, the difference is not that big *even with our sample size of only 5!*

This confidence interval for what will actually occur in an individual case when $X = 3$ is wider that you might like, but that is because, as we have noted, it is based on only five data values. If we had pretty much the same results for $n = 30$, the interval would be much more precise, around 2.45 to 4.75.

9.4.2 SPSS

Figure 9.20 shows the same sample data in SPSS. We have already gone into "Variable View" to label the columns Y and X.

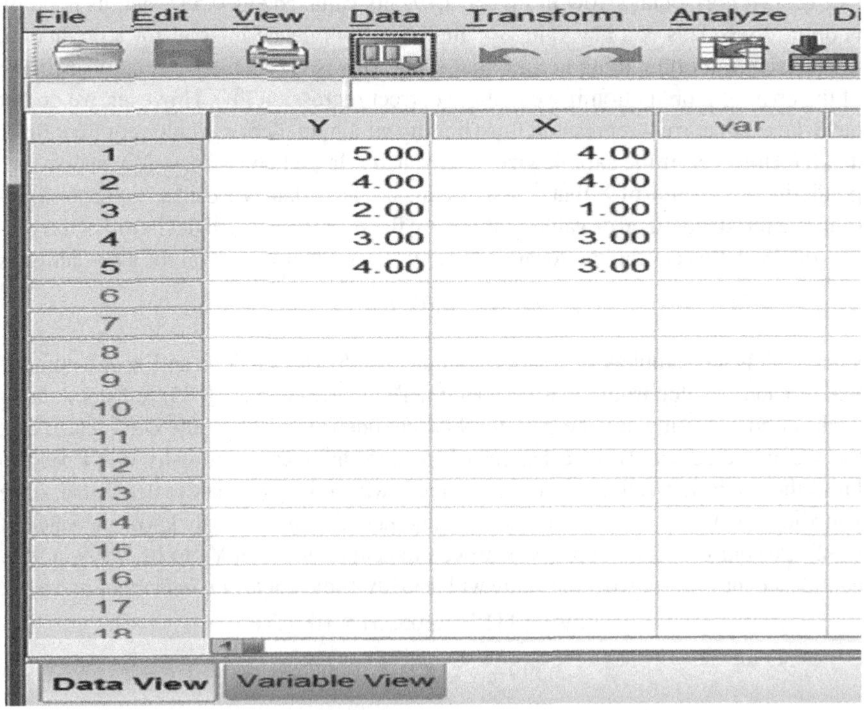

FIGURE 9.20

SPSS template for illustrative data regression analysis.

We now pull down "Analyze," and go to "Regression," and then "Linear," as shown in Figure 9.21 (see arrows).

After we click/let go of "Regression/Linear," we get the dialog box shown in Figure 9.22.

We now drag "Y" over to the "Dependent" rectangle, and X to the "Independent" rectangle. (We weren't kidding you when we said that you needed to become familiar with the terms "dependent variable" and "independent variable"!) This is shown in Figure 9.23 (see arrows).

We are now ready to click "OK" and obtain our output. The output is shown in Figure 9.24.

The output has exactly the same values that the Excel output had, although it does not have the confidence intervals for the coefficients, but they're easy to determine. See Sidebar coming up. The coefficients are circled; notice that SPSS calls the intercept the "constant." That's fine, and we point it out only to illustrate how each

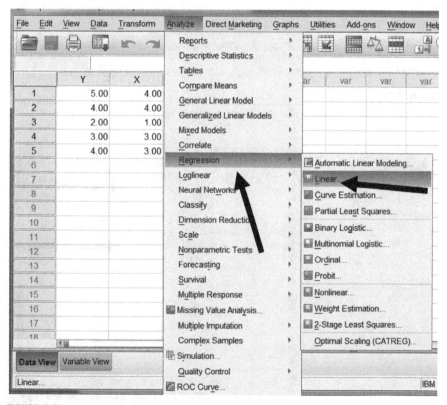

FIGURE 9.21

Accessing linear regression in SPSS; illustrative data.

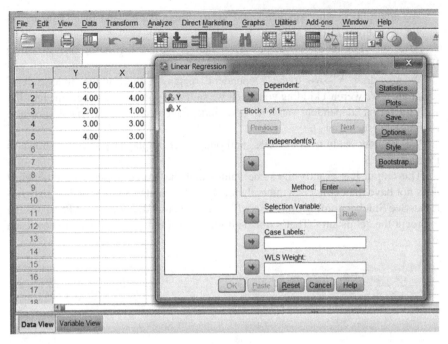

FIGURE 9.22

The Linear Regression dialog box; SPSS with illustrative data.

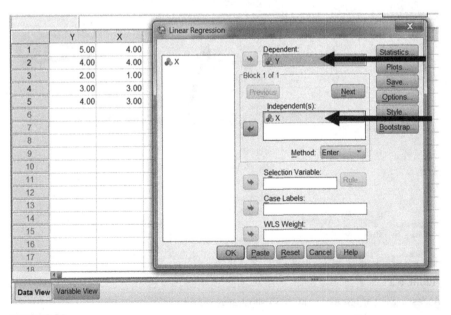

FIGURE 9.23

Getting ready to receive the linear regression output; SPSS with illustrative data.

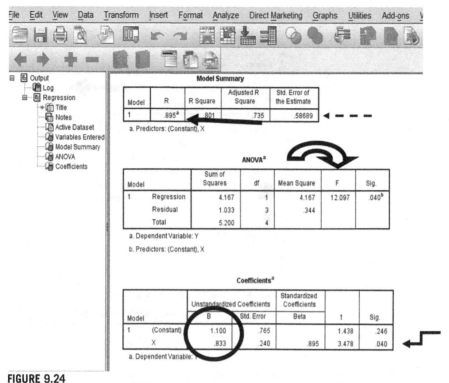

FIGURE 9.24

Linear regression output; SPSS with illustrative data.

statistical software package often uses slightly different (but still "sensible") names for selected quantities. We have also added the same types of arrows that are in Figure 9.19, so you will easily see the correspondence between the Excel and SPSS outputs.

SIDEBAR: CONFIDENCE INTERVALS FOR INTERCEPT AND SLOPE IN SPSS

If you want the confidence intervals for the intercept ("constant") and slope to be displayed in SPSS, follow these instructions:

Go back to Figure 9.23, and click "Statistics," as in Figure 9.25 (see horizontal arrow), and then click "Confidence intervals" under the "Regression Coefficients" section (see vertical arrow in Figure 9.25).

Finally, click "Continue" (see dashed arrow in Figure 9.25), which takes you back to Figure 9.23.

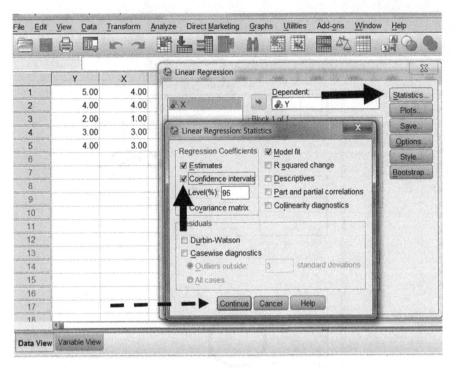

FIGURE 9.25

Extra command in SPSS to obtain confidence interval for intercept/constant and slope; illustrative data.

Now the output looks like Figure 9.26, the same as in Figure 9.24, except for the added confidence intervals for the intercept and slope, as circled in Figure 9.26. The values, of course, are the same values we obtained in the Excel output.

9.5 LINEAR REGRESSION ANALYSIS OF BEHEMOTH.COM DATA

OK, we're finally ready to apply our linear regression technique to the 180 data points of the Behemoth.com data (see Figure 9.10). Applying the same steps we used for the sample data to the Behemoth data, we get the results shown in Figure 9.27.

We can see that, of course, the correlation is the same as it was in the correlation analysis section: 0.449.

The best-fitting (i.e., least-squares) line is (see circle in Figure 9.27):

$$Yc = 2.456 + 0.460 * X$$

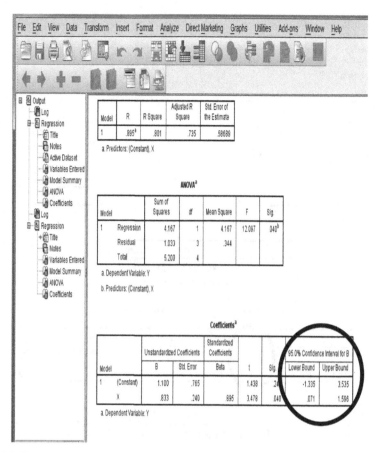

FIGURE 9.26

Augmented SPSS output; illustrative data.

So, for each unit increase in the perceived usefulness of the ability to do a Boolean search, there is a corresponding increase of 0.46 (on the 5-point Likert scale) of "Likelihood of Adoption" of the search engine. A person who gives a 5 for usefulness of the ability to do a Boolean search has a predicted value of about 4.76 on the 5-point scale of likelihood to adopt the search engine.

A confidence interval for this value, using the methodology described in the previous section, is 3.85 to 5.00. A person who gives a 4 for the usefulness of doing the Boolean search has a predicted value of 4.30 for likelihood of adoption of the search engine. A confidence interval for this value is 3.39 to 5.00. We would, of course, prefer narrower intervals, but we must remember that we are using only one X variable in the prediction process, and while the r^2 is about 20%, which is often very good

	A	B	C	D	E	F	G	H	I
1	SUMMARY OUTPUT								
2									
3	*Regression Statistics*								
4	Multiple R	0.449452745							
5	R Square	0.20200777							
6	Adjusted R Square	0.197524667							
7	Standard Error	0.465465764							
8	Observations	180							
9									
10	ANOVA								
11		*df*	*SS*	*MS*	*F*	*Significance F*			
12	Regression	1	9.762586607	9.762587	45.05982	2.46748E-10			
13	Residual	178	38.56519117	0.216658					
14	Total	179	48.32777778						
15									
16		*Coefficients*	*Standard Error*	*t Stat*	*P-value*	*Lower 95%*	*Upper 95%*	*Lower 95.0%*	*Upper 95.0%*
17	Intercept	2.456157279	0.315493032	7.78514	5.5E-13	1.833569372	3.0787452	1.833569372	3.078745186
18	Ability to perform a Boolean search	0.460378724	0.068583641	6.712661	2.47E-10	0.32503708	0.5957204	0.32503708	0.59572036 8
19									

FIGURE 9.27

Linear regression output for Behemoth.com data; Excel.

(i.e., high) for just one X variable, there is still 80% of the variability ($1-r^2 = 0.8$) unaccounted for.

The *p*-value of the slope is 0.000; thus, the slope is highly significant; remember that the value "2.47E-10" actually means 0.000000000247 as the notation indicates that we should move the decimal point 10 places to the left. It is, of course, the same *p*-value we found much earlier when we analyzed the correlation. This very low *p*-value indicates that there is virtually no doubt that there is a positive linear relationship between the *usefulness of the Ability to do a Boolean search, and the Likelihood of Adoption of the search engine. Furthermore, the r-square value of 0.202 means we estimate that the former, by itself, explains more than 20% of the responder's choice for the Likelihood of Adoption of the search engine query.*

The results are the same, of course, in SPSS. See Figure 9.28.

Model Summary

Model	R	R Square	Adjusted R Square	Std. Error of the Estimate
1	.449[a]	.202	.198	.46547

a. Predictors: (Constant), VAR00001

ANOVA[a]

Model		Sum of Squares	df	Mean Square	F	Sig.
1	Regression	9.763	1	9.763	45.060	.000[b]
	Residual	38.565	178	.217		
	Total	48.328	179			

a. Dependent Variable: VAR00002

b. Predictors: (Constant), VAR00001

Coefficients[a]

Model		Unstandardized Coefficients		Standardized Coefficients	t	Sig.
		B	Std. Error	Beta		
1	(Constant)	2.456	.315		7.785	.000
	VAR00001	.460	.069	.449	6.713	.000

a. Dependent Variable: VAR00002

FIGURE 9.28

Linear Regression output for Behemoth.com data; SPSS.

9.6 MEANWHILE, BACK AT BEHEMOTH

The statistical analysis complements your qualitative findings perfectly. The recruiters complained mightily that the Novix search engine had eliminated Boolean searching; now you find that a higher sense of usefulness of Boolean search capability is associated with an increased likelihood of adoption of the search engine that contains a Boolean capability—with statistical significance! Recruiters want Boolean, and they're more likely to use your engine if you have it. Killing Boolean was a mistake—and a costly one.

You send the results to Hans in an e-mail, and within a minute, he pops his head in your cube.

"You sure 'bout all this stats stuff?"

"Yes, but I can walk you through the details if you like."

"Nah. But do me a favor; put it all in a nice, sharp Powerpoint. Max 5 pages. Bullets for everything. Keep the stats jargon to a minimum, but give enough details so Joey will think you know what you're talking about."

"Sure, how's early afternoon tomorrow?"

"Perfect, I've got my running 1pm meeting with him tomorrow. Maybe the Chianti he likes during lunch will defuse the inevitable explosion!"

9.7 SUMMARY

In this chapter, we have introduced correlation and regression analysis. Both of these techniques deal with the relationship between a "dependent variable" or output variable that we label "Y," and an "independent variable" or input variable that we label "X."

The correlation, r, is a dimensionless quantity that ranges between −1 and 1, and indicates the strength and direction of a linear relationship between the two variables; the (hypothesis) test of its significance is also discussed. We also note that the coefficient of determination, r^2, has a direct interpretation as the proportion of variability in Y explained by X (in a linear relationship).

We consider example scatter diagrams (graphs of the X, Y points) and discuss how they correspond with the respective values of r. We also demonstrate in both Excel and SPSS how to obtain the correlation.

Regression analysis quantifies the linear relationship between Y and X, by providing a least-squares line from which we can input a value of X and obtain a predicted (best estimate) value of Y, using the line's corresponding slope and intercept. We note how to perform a regression analysis in both Excel and SPSS, and discuss various confidence intervals of interest, as well as hypothesis testing to decide if we should conclude that there truly is a linear relationship between Y and X "beyond a reasonable doubt." In each case—correlation and regression—our illustrations use a small data set that is easier for the reader to follow, and then we apply the technique to the prototype real-world data from Behemoth.com.

9.8 ADDENDUM: A QUICK DISCUSSION OF SOME ASSUMPTIONS IMPLICIT IN INTERPRETING THE RESULTS

When we perform "statistical inference" (more or less, for us, confidence intervals, and hypothesis testing) in a correlation or regression analysis, there are three theoretical assumptions we are technically making.

One assumption, called "normality," says that if we hold X constant at any (and every) value, and were to look at many values of Y at that X value, the Y values would form a normal distribution.

A second assumption, called "constant variability" (or often by the ugly word, "homoscedasticity," which is said to mean "constant variability" in Greek [and sometimes, it is spelled with the first "c" being a "k"]), says that the normal curves for each X have the same variability (which as we might recall from Chapter 1, means equally tall and thin/short and fat curves) for all values of X. For this to be exactly true, it is often a bit dubious.

However, these two assumptions are referred to as "robust." Essentially, this means that if the two assumptions are "moderately violated," it does not materially affect the results of the analysis. In the world of user experience data, it is unlikely that any assumption violations are sufficiently large to affect the results materially. There are ways to test these assumptions, but they are well beyond the scope of this chapter.

The third assumption, called "independence," is that the data points are independent. This is a more critical assumption (because it is not robust), but is usually the easiest to avoid violating. If each respondent provides one row of data and there is no connection between the respondents/data points, the assumption is generally satisfied fully.

Overall, the majority of people who perform correlation and regression analyses do not worry much about these assumptions, and in the vast majority of cases, there is no problem with concluding an accurate interpretation of the results. Still, if the results arrived at seem to very much belie common sense, perhaps somebody familiar with these assumptions should be called upon for consultation.

9.9 EXERCISE

1. Consider the Excel data in the file "Chapter 9.Exercise 1," which has 402 data points on Y (column A) and X (column B).
   a. Run a correlation analysis. Is the correlation significant at $\alpha = 0.05$? What percent of the variability in Y is explained by the linear relationship with X?
   b. Run a regression analysis. What is the least-squares line? What do you predict Y to be when X = 4?
   c. Repeat parts (a) and (b) using SPSS and the data in the file named "Chapter 9..Exercise 1.data." The output is in a file named "Chapter 9..Exercise 1.output."

The answers are in a Word file named, "Chapter 9.Exercise 1.ANSWERS."

Can you relate in multiple ways? Multiple linear regression and stepwise regression

10

10.1 INTRODUCTION

When there is more than one independent variable (X), we call the regression analysis by the term "multiple regression." With one X, we referred to the regression analysis in the previous chapter as "simple regression." Using Excel or SPSS, we generate the best-fitting (least-squares) line,[1] as we did in the previous chapter. This line would be, say with seven X's:

$$Yc = a + b1 * X1 + b2 * X2 + b3 * X3 + \cdots + b7 * X7.$$

Finding this line by hand would be prohibitive, so statistical software *must* be used unless you are a mathematics prodigy, and even then we would use the software!! (For simple regression, statistical software *should* be used, but doing it by hand with a calculator would be feasible, although not preferred, if the number of data points were not exceedingly large.)

10.2 CASE STUDY: DETERMINING THE IDEAL SEARCH ENGINE AT BEHEMOTH.COM

Let's return to our favorite employment Web site, Behemoth.com, where you were hired as usability researcher. Behemoth is one of the largest job search engines in the world, with over a million job openings at any time, over 1 million resumes in the database, and over 63 million job seekers per month. Behemoth has over 5000 employees spread around the world.

You'll recall from Chapter 4 that you had to deliver the hard, cold facts about "Novix" to your creative director, Hans Blitz: despite spending $80 million on a new search engine, your current one still performed better than the new one in a head-to-head usability test.

You'll also recall from Chapter 9 the UX Director Hans Blitz challenged you to prove to him that Behemoth spent 80 million getting rid a feature that clients actually wanted: the ability to perform a Boolean search.

---

[1] Actually, in multidimensions, it would not be, literally, a "line." It would be a plane or hyperplane. However, for simplicity, we shall continue to call it the least-squares *line*.

As a consequence, you ran an unmoderated usability study with recruiters searching for candidates with the current Behemoth search engine. After recruiters used the search for a while, each participant was asked to rank their perception of the usefulness of the different search engine fields. At the end, they were asked to rate their likelihood to adopt the search engine. With the data in hand, you calculated the correlation coefficient between the ability to perform a Boolean search and likelihood of adoption of the search engine, and performed simple regression.

The results were dramatic. Your correlation coefficient of +0.449 between the capability to perform a Boolean search and likelihood of adoption of the search engine told you that a higher sense of utility of Boolean search capability is associated with an increased likelihood of adoption of the search engine. Furthermore, the very low p-value showed that there is no doubt that there is a positive linear relationship between the ability to do a Boolean search and the likelihood of adoption of the search engine. Lastly, the r^2 value of 0.2 meant that you estimate that the capability of performing a Boolean search, *by itself,* explains more than 20% of the responder's choice for the likelihood of adoption of the search engine query.

Bottom line: recruiters want Boolean, and they're more likely to use your search engine if you have it. Despite what the Palo Alto hipsters told Joey, killing Boolean in the new Turbo Search was a mistake—and a costly one.

All of which blew Hans' mind. As requested by Hans, you summarized the findings in a 5-page PowerPoint deck that he took to Behemoth CEO Joey Vellucci. But that was Tuesday; now it's Friday afternoon and you haven't heard a thing about their meeting. Suddenly, he pops his head into your cube as he's racing out of the office for a long weekend.

"Hey there," he says. "Sorry I never got back to you. It's been a crazy week."

"No worries," you say. "How did the meeting with Joey go?"

"I won't sugar-coat it; it was ugly," he sighs, plopping down in your extra office chair.

"Sorry to hear that, Hans."

"Well, he wasn't angry with UX, but he's *furious* with the Palo Alto dudes."

"Yeah, I can understand," you say, trying to maintain objectivity.

"But he did have a parting shot for UX."

"Really?" you ask.

"At one point, he kind of got red in the face and said 'Why doesn't UX come up with their own frickin' ideal search engine since they keep findings problems all the time in the usability lab?' (He thinks you and all the other UX researchers are a bunch of doom and gloomers, sort of like Agnew's 'nattering nabobs of negativism'.)"

This time you chuckle at the Watergate-era reference. "Well," you respond, "We find problems. It's the nature of the beast. But…I've got an idea."

"Shoot!"

"Well, in the test we just finished, we had people rank their perception of usefulness with the different search fields, along with their likelihood to adopt the search engine. By analyzing the data, we can figure out which combination of search fields will maximize likelihood of adoption."

"Wow! How are you going to do that?" Hans asks incredulously.

"Ah, that's where the fun begins. We'll run stepwise multiple regression and determine the best model to increase adoption."

Hans hesitates. "I have no idea what you just said, but it sure sounds cool. When can we have the results?"

"Give me a couple of days to crunch the data. How's next Tuesday?"

"Sounds good!" he says as he stands up. "One last thing though."

"Yes?"

"This time I'm going to bring you into see Joey to present. When I presented your PowerPoint last time, he kept asking me stats questions I couldn't answer. You up for it?"

Despite the sudden surge of adrenaline, you calmly reply, "Sure, I wouldn't mind finally meeting him."

"Oh, you'll meet him alright," Hans chuckles as he throws his laptop over his shoulder. "Will you *ever* meet him! Have a great weekend!"

10.3 MULTIPLE REGRESSION

In this section, we shall introduce a small data set example using multiple regression and use it to explain various aspects of the techniques and interpretation of its output. In this small example, we have a Y and three X's, and a sample size of $n = 25$. In this data set, Y represents the time it takes to complete a Major Task (in seconds) and the three X's represent the time it takes the respondent, respectively, to complete three component tasks. The goal is to determine which skills/types of knowledge have more bearing on the ability to complete the Major Task. Later in the chapter, we shall apply multiple regression analysis to the Behemoth.com data set with its "Y" and 15 independent variables (X's) and sample size of $n = 180$.

10.3.1 EXCEL

The data set of tasks times in seconds is shown in Table 10.1.

SIDEBAR: KEEP 'EM TOGETHER IN EXCEL

One important thing that needs to be mentioned is that in Excel, it is critical that all of the X's be contiguous (i.e., in adjacent columns—columns right next to each other); this will not be necessary in SPSS. Indeed, the first three columns, A, B, and C, display the three X's, and they are, obviously, contiguous—right next to each other.

As when we performed a simple regression, we open "Data Analysis" to "Regression," getting the dialog box in Figure 10.1.

Note that we inputted the Y (dependent variable) range as D1 to D26, accounting for the label in the first row. For the X (independent variables) range, we inputted A1:C26. (By doing this, Excel knows that we have X's in columns A, B, and C. The input process would not work if the three X columns were not next to each other [i.e., "contiguous"],

Table 10.1 Multiple Regression Data for Illustrative Example; Excel

	A	B	C	D	E
1	P-task 1	P-task 2	P-task 3	Major Task	
2	80	105	89	86	
3	79	109	100	78	
4	81	113	103	94	
5	73	105	93	74	
6	75	112	90	78	
7	75	104	86	71	
8	70	99	76	56	
9	96	122	104	114	
10	86	120	107	102	
11	85	97	99	97	
12	70	100	90	62	
13	93	111	110	124	
14	76	110	91	92	
15	78	95	80	69	
16	89	109	111	109	
17	82	111	110	107	
18	80	103	104	98	
19	87	118	112	125	
20	88	110	97	97	
21	75	79	92	80	
22	71	105	87	65	
23	94	101	105	98	
24	73	90	82	76	
25	95	95	106	113	
26	77	115	85	81	
27					

seth **Sheet1** Sheet2 Sheet3

per the sidebar. The dependent variable column [column D in Figure 10.1] need not be next to the X columns, but it is natural to input the data so that it is. Notice also that we are asking for the output to be in a sheet arbitrarily called "seth" [see arrow in Figure 10.1].)

After clicking on OK, we see the output in Figure 10.2. There is a lot to discuss about the output.

First, note that the value of r^2 is 0.877 (see horizontal arrow in Figure 10.2). This says that the three X's as a group explain about 87.7% of the variability in Y. In essence, the three X's explain about 87.7% of the reason that the value of Y comes out what it does. In a context such as this one, that is a relatively high value for r^2!

We mentioned in Chapter 9 that the t-test and the F-test for the single X variable yielded exactly the same results, and that this was evidenced by the same p-value. However, when performing a multiple regression, the results of the F-test and the t-test are not the same and have different meanings.

Here, the F-test has a p-value of 1.03197E-09 (see vertical *solid* arrow in Figure 10.2); this means in "Excel speak" $1.03197*10^{-9}$, which, in turn, equals 0.00000000103197. Remember that Excel refers to the p-value of the F-test as "significance F." This is very close to zero—it's about one in a billion! In multiple regression, what this is saying is that *beyond any reasonable doubt*, the three X's *as a group* do provide predictive value about Y.

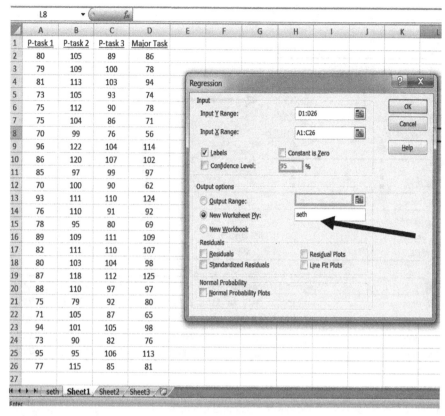

FIGURE 10.1

Regression dialog box in Excel; illustrative example.

SIDEBAR: *F*-TEST: THE TEST OF THE OVERALL MODEL

In multiple regression, the *F*-test is testing:

HO: The X's **as a group** do not help you predict Y.

H1: The X's **as a group** do, indeed, help you predict Y.

In other words, the *F*-test is testing whether all of the independent variables together help us predict the dependent variable (Y).

But here's an important heads-up: the *F*-test tells us we are getting predictive value about Y, but *says nothing about which of the X's are providing this predictive value*. At this point, it could be all of three X's, any two of the three X's, or only one of the three X's. In fact, this is why the *F*-test is referred to as the "Test of the Overall Model."

To address the issue of which X's are giving us the predictive value (which surely is, logically, the next step in the analysis), we need to examine the t-test for each of the X variables, as explained below.

By the way, if the *F*-test had not been significant (i.e., its *p*-value > 0.05), you would basically stop your analysis (and lament the fact that none of the X's are of any value to you in predicting Y).

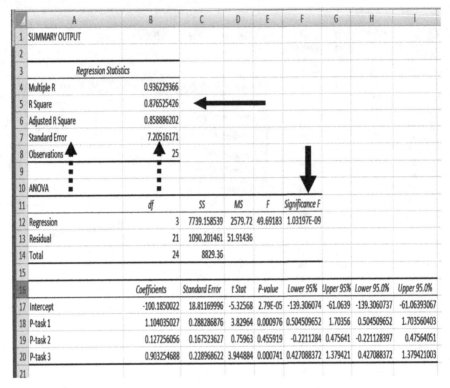

	A	B	C	D	E	F	G	H	I
1	SUMMARY OUTPUT								
2									
3	*Regression Statistics*								
4	Multiple R	0.936229366							
5	R Square	0.876525426							
6	Adjusted R Square	0.858886202							
7	Standard Error	7.20516171							
8	Observations	25							
9									
10	ANOVA								
11		*df*	*SS*	*MS*	*F*	*Significance F*			
12	Regression	3	7739.158539	2579.72	49.69183	1.03197E-09			
13	Residual	21	1090.201461	51.91436					
14	Total	24	8829.36						
15									
16		*Coefficients*	*Standard Error*	*t Stat*	*P-value*	*Lower 95%*	*Upper 95%*	*Lower 95.0%*	*Upper 95.0%*
17	Intercept	-100.1850022	18.81169996	-5.32568	2.79E-05	-139.306074	-61.0639	-139.3060737	-61.06393067
18	P-task 1	1.104035027	0.288286876	3.82964	0.000976	0.504509652	1.70356	0.504509652	1.703560403
19	P-task 2	0.127256056	0.167523627	0.75963	0.455919	-0.2211284	0.475641	-0.221128397	0.47564051
20	P-task 3	0.903254688	0.228968622	3.944884	0.000741	0.427088372	1.379421	0.427088372	1.379421003
21									

FIGURE 10.2

Multiple regression output; Excel with illustrative example.

So, we now know that we are getting predictive value, but we don't know from where. Let us now examine the t-test for each X variable.

We have three X variables and thus, have three t-tests. For convenience, the p-value for each variable is displayed in Table 10.2 (a portion of Figure 10.2).

We can see that two of the variables, P-task 1 (component task 1) and P-task 3 (component task 3), are significant, each with a p-value < 0.05—in fact, each has a p-value that is *way* below 0.05, being less than 0.001! On the other hand, the variable, P-task 2, is not significant, having a p-value of 0.456, way above 0.05.

Table 10.2 *P*-Value for Each X Variable; Excel with Illustrative Example

X Variable	P-Value
P-task 1	0.000975612
P-task 2	0.455919008
P-task 3	0.000741126

Interpreting these results involves a bit of a subtle point. When a t-test is performed in a multiple regression, what is being tested is whether the particular X adds incremental value to the prediction of Y. The formal hypotheses for a given X variable in a multiple regression are:

H0: Variable X is NOT helping you predict Y, *above and beyond (i.e., incremental to) the other variables in the regression equation.*
H1: Variable X is, INDEED, helping you predict Y, *above and beyond (i.e., incremental to) the other variables in the regression equation.*

In other words, we are *not* testing simply whether the X variable helps us predict Y in a vacuum. Whether a particular X is found significant (i.e., when we reject H0, and thus conclude that the X variable *does* add incremental value) may depend on which other variables are in the regression equation. Pretty cool (or subtle!!), right?

So, what this means in the above example is that component tasks 1 and 3 each gives us incremental value in the prediction of Y; each *p*-value is below 0.05. Another way to look at it is that each of those two variables is needed for the best prediction of Y. Furthermore, the coefficient of each variable is positive (1.10 for component task 1 and 0.90 for component task 3), indicating that for each of these two component tasks, the higher the time required, the higher the time required for the Major Task (Y).

However, for component task 2, we ACCEPT H0, and conclude that knowing the completion time for component task 2 *cannot* be said to add to our knowledge base about Y; in other words, once we know the times for component tasks 1 and 3, **we do not gain anything additional by knowing the time for component task 2.**

But why is component task 2 not useful? There are two possibilities. First, it is possible that the time a person takes for component task 2 is simply not related to the time a person takes for the Major Task.

But, there is another possibility. Perhaps, the time a person takes for component task 2 *is* related to the time a person takes to complete the Major Task, and would help us predict the time a person takes for the Major Task, *if it were the only information we had.* But once we know the time the person takes to perform component tasks 1 and 3, the knowledge of the time the person takes to complete component task 2 is *redundant.*

As we've said, the time for component task 2 does not add *incrementally* to our knowledge base about how long it takes for the person to complete the Major Task. Thus, *we do not need X2 in the equation.* As a consequence, we are better off dropping that variable and performing a multiple regression with only component tasks 1 and 3.

If there are a larger number of variables, and more than one of them were not significant (as was P-task 2), determining which variables are saying what about Y is somewhat challenging. However, there is a special technique, called "stepwise regression," that we shall discuss in a later section and which is extremely useful.

SIDEBAR: TIME TRAVELING?

You might notice that the intercept is −100.185. In theory, it means that if a person took 0 time for each component task, his/her time would be predicted to be −100.185 for the Major Task. This is, of course, silly—and impossible.

This is not a scene from *Star Trek*, where time is going backward, represented by negative numbers. Even if the person took 10 seconds for each component task, his/her predicted time for the Major Task would be negative. But it's reasonable to ask—why is this happening?

Take a look back at the data (Table 10.1). Is there a single person for whom the component task times are anywhere near (0, 0, 0)? or, even (10, 10, 10)? **No.**

The moral of the story? *It is not a wise idea to try to predict Y for values of X that are not anywhere near your X data values.* Most of the time, you will get results that are nonsensical.

10.3.2 SPSS

In SPSS, performing a multiple regression is not very different from performing a simple regression. (The columns of all the variables can be anywhere—and the X's do not need to be in columns that are contiguous.) In Figure 10.3, the same data are shown in SPSS format. By going into "Variable View" (see arrow in Figure 10.3), the columns are given the names of the variables. (After obtaining the names you wish, you then go back to "Data View," as displayed in Figure 10.3.)

SIDEBAR: PICKY SPSS WHEN IT COMES TO NAMES OF VARIABLES

As an aside, it might be noted that SPSS is a bit fussy about what names are given to variables. You are not allowed to have spaces, nor dashes, so "P-task 1" (what we wanted to name the first variable to be consistent with its name in the Excel file) was not allowed. You'll notice we've purged all "nonkosher" addenda in the headers.

As we did in the last chapter, for simple regression, we pull down "Analyze," go to "Regression," and then submenu "Linear." This is shown in Figure 10.4 (see arrows).

Clicking gets us to Figure 10.5, the "Linear Regression" dialog box.

We now drag over *Major Task* to the "Dependent" box and all three independent (X) variables to the "Independent(s)" box. (The latter can be done one variable at a time, or, holding down the shift key, all three P-task X variables can be highlighted and dragged over together.)

After the variables are in their respective boxes, as shown in Figure 10.6, we now click on "OK" to obtain our output in Figure 10.7.

Of course, you get the same output as you saw in the Excel output, except that in SPSS most of the values are provided to only three decimal places (which is certainly sufficient!!). For example, the r^2 is the same 0.877, as shown in the top section of the SPSS output.

As you have just seen, there was very little difference in SPSS between running a simple regression and a multiple regression. It's only a matter of whether one

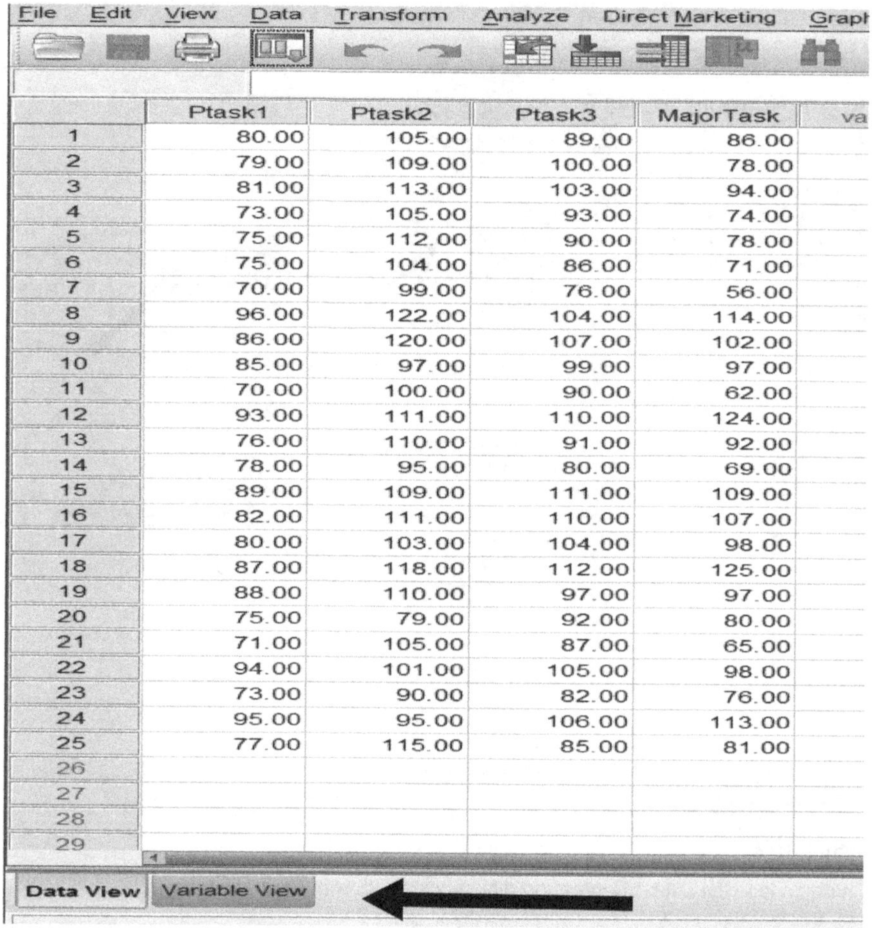

	Ptask1	Ptask2	Ptask3	MajorTask	va
1	80.00	105.00	89.00	86.00	
2	79.00	109.00	100.00	78.00	
3	81.00	113.00	103.00	94.00	
4	73.00	105.00	93.00	74.00	
5	75.00	112.00	90.00	78.00	
6	75.00	104.00	86.00	71.00	
7	70.00	99.00	76.00	56.00	
8	96.00	122.00	104.00	114.00	
9	86.00	120.00	107.00	102.00	
10	85.00	97.00	99.00	97.00	
11	70.00	100.00	90.00	62.00	
12	93.00	111.00	110.00	124.00	
13	76.00	110.00	91.00	92.00	
14	78.00	95.00	80.00	69.00	
15	89.00	109.00	111.00	109.00	
16	82.00	111.00	110.00	107.00	
17	80.00	103.00	104.00	98.00	
18	87.00	118.00	112.00	125.00	
19	88.00	110.00	97.00	97.00	
20	75.00	79.00	92.00	80.00	
21	71.00	105.00	87.00	65.00	
22	94.00	101.00	105.00	98.00	
23	73.00	90.00	82.00	76.00	
24	95.00	95.00	106.00	113.00	
25	77.00	115.00	85.00	81.00	
26					
27					
28					
29					

Data View | Variable View

FIGURE 10.3

Input data in SPSS format; illustrative example.

variable or several variables are dragged over to the "Independent(s)" box in Figures 10.5 and 10.6.

OK, now let's build the regression equation. Suppose that we want to predict the time it would take a person to perform the Major Task, given his/her times for the component tasks were:

$$\text{P-task } 1 = 80$$

$$\text{P-task } 2 = 100$$

$$\text{P-task } 3 = 100$$

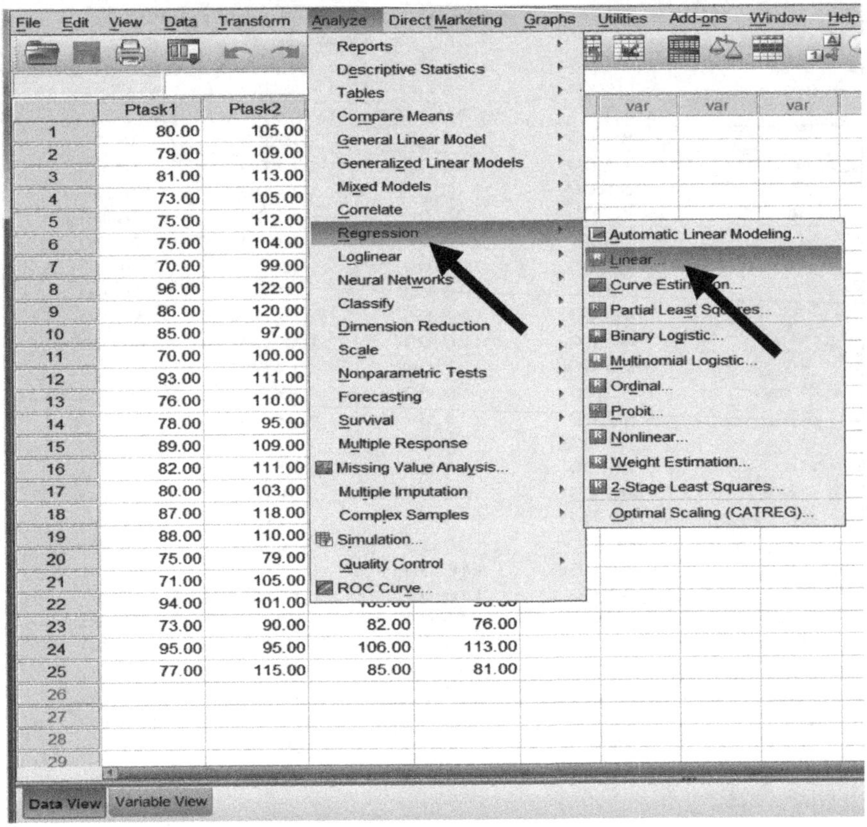

FIGURE 10.4

Commands to the Linear Regression dialog box; SPSS with illustrative example.

Using the circled coefficients in Figure 10.7, we produce the following least-squares line (see values in the oval in Figure 10.7):

$$Yc = -100.185 + 1.104 * Ptask1 + 0.127 * Ptask2 + 0.903 * Ptask3$$
$$= -100.185 + 1.104 * 80 + 0.127 * 100 + 0.903 * 100$$
$$= -100.185 + 88.32 + 12.7 + 90.3$$
$$= 91.135$$

Your best estimate for the time it would take the person to perform the Major Task, given the component task times of 80, 100, and 100, respectively, is 91.135 seconds.

10.4 A CONFIDENCE INTERVAL FOR THE PREDICTION

Of course, whenever a prediction is made, be it through simple regression or multiple regression, it is important to find a confidence interval for the prediction.

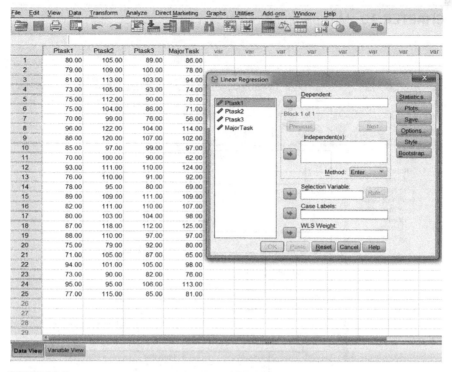

FIGURE 10.5

The Linear Regression dialog box; SPSS with illustrative example.

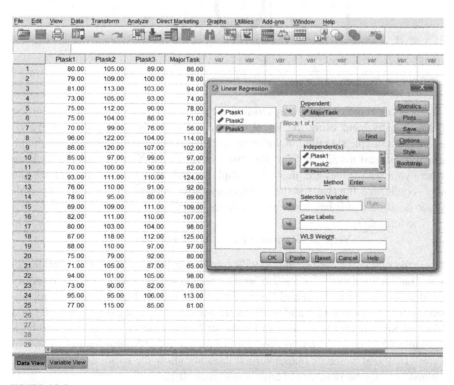

FIGURE 10.6

All ready to click "OK" to obtain output; SPSS with illustrative example.

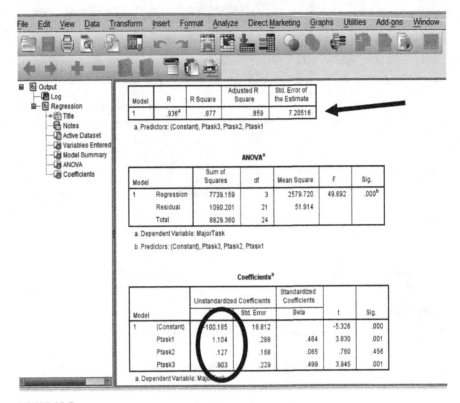

FIGURE 10.7

SPSS output; illustrative example.

There are some complex ways to find the exact 95% confidence interval for the prediction, by hand using the Excel output, or by simply using SPSS. However, assuming a sample size used in the regression that is not very small (a rule of thumb might be at least $n=25$), and for predicting values of the X or X's not too far from where your data values are, there is a simple formula that provides an approximate 95% confidence interval for the prediction—close enough for virtually any real-world decision that is based on the confidence interval.

The formula is

$$Yc \pm 2*(\text{Standard Error of the Estimate})$$

where the value, "2," corresponds to 95% confidence. If you wanted 99% confidence, you would replace the "2" with "2.6" and for 90% confidence with "1.65." The really good news is that the "Standard Error of the Estimate" is obtained from the regression output, in both Excel and in SPSS. In Figure 10.7, you can see it in the first block of SPSS output (see arrow in Figure 10.7); the value is 7.205. If you go back to Figure 10.2, the Excel output, you can see the same 7.205 value, called "Standard Error" by Excel, since its output format does not allow the entire expression to be written out (see the two *dashed* arrows in Figure 10.2).

OK; so, for the example in the previous section, we computed Yc to be 91.135, which is our best estimate of the time it would take a person to complete the Major Task, given he/she required 80, 100, and 100 seconds, respectively, for the three component tasks. That, of course, does not mean that an individual person with component task times 80, 100, and 100 seconds, will require *exactly* 91.135 seconds for the Major Task. After all, we have sampled and based our estimate on a random sample of $n=25$, not a sample of a *zillion*.

More importantly, even if we had infinite data, which would make 91.135 the *true mean time* for the Major Task for people with component task times of 80, 100, and 100 seconds, the fact is: if we examined a bunch of people with component task times of 80, 100, and 100 seconds, they would all have different times to complete the Major Task!! Hence, there is the need for a confidence interval for how long it would take an individual person with these component task times to complete the Major Task. A 95% confidence interval for that time is

$$91.135 \pm 2 * (7.205)$$

or

$$76.725 \text{ to } 105.545$$

In other words, there is a 95% chance (or, equivalently, probability 0.95) that the interval, 76.725–105.545 seconds will contain the time an individual person requires to complete the Major Task, if his/her time for the component tasks are 80, 100, and 100 s, respectively.

10.5 BACK TO BEHEMOTH.COM

Now, let's get to our Behemoth.com data.

In an unmoderated usability test, 180 recruiters used the Behemoth.com candidate search engine to search for job candidates. All the respondents were tasked with finding good candidates for the same three requisitions: (1) A Java Developer with at least 5 years experience, a bachelor's degree from MIT, a maximum salary requirement of $95,000 per year, willing to relocate, who is looking for a full-time position; (2) A Web Designer with skills using Axure, Photoshop, and Illustrator within 25 miles of San Diego, with an Active Confidential Security Clearance; and (3) A Business Analyst who has previously worked at Oracle, an average length of employment of no less than 1 year, with a resume dated no earlier than 2013, willing to travel up to 50% of the time.

After completing the tasks of finding candidates for the three positions, the respondents were asked how likely they are to adopt the search engine. In addition, they are specifically asked to rate their perception of usefulness for each of the fields in the search engine, on a scale of 1–5, where 1 = not at all useful and 5 = extremely useful. Table 10.3 shows the 15 specific search engine components respondents are asked to rate (this table is listed also in Chapter 9).

These 15 variables are now our 15 X's (independent variables) in a multiple regression analysis, with the dependent variable, Y, being the **likelihood the respondent would adopt the search engine**. (The actual question was, "Imagine that this search

Table 10.3 The 15 Search Engine Components (as depicted in Chapter 9)

1. Ability to search by job title
2. Ability to search by years of experience
3. Ability to search by location
4. Ability to search by schools attended
5. Ability to search candidates by date of updated resume
6. Ability to search candidates by level of education
7. Ability to search by skills
8. Ability to search candidates by average length of employment at each company
9. Ability to search candidates by maximum salary
10. Ability to search candidates by job type he/she is looking for: full time, part time, temporary/contract, per diem, intern
11. Ability to search candidates by companies in which they have worked
12. Ability to search candidates by willingness to travel. (Expressed as "no travel ability required," "up to 25%," "up to 50%," "up to 75%," "up to 100%")
13. Ability to search candidates by willingness to relocate
14. Ability to search candidates by security clearance. (Active Confidential, Inactive Confidential, Active Secret, Inactive Secret, Active Top Secret, Inactive Top Secret, Active Secret/SCI, Inactive Top Secret/SCI)
15. Ability to perform a Boolean search

engine is available to you at no cost to find qualified candidates using the candidate databases you currently employ. What is your likelihood of adopting this candidate search engine on a scale of 1–5, where 1=not at all likely and 5=extremely likely?")

Now, let us see *which of the 15 variables seem to be important* in influencing a responder's likelihood to adopt the search engine, and *how much, overall, the 15 variables tell us* about the responder's likelihood of adoption of the search engine.

Figure 10.8 displays the 16 variables in the study (15 X's and the Y), and the first 10 data points (11 rows, including the label row) out of the 180 data points in total in an Excel spreadsheet. The names of the variables have, in some cases, been abbreviated to save space. The full name of each variable is in Table 10.3.

To run the full multiple regression using Excel, we do what we have done before, with *labels* box checked, the Y range being P1:P181, and the X range being A1:O181. The output is in Figure 10.9.

Let us now discuss this output. (We purposely left off a few columns on the right-hand side of the output that had to do with confidence intervals for the coefficients, so we could show you the more important parts of the output on one page with a bigger font size.)

First of all, you can note that the multiple r^2 = 0.493 (see horizontal arrow in Figure 10.9). So, all of the variables together explain about 49.3% of the differences in Y from responder to responder.

We might next note that the F-test is highly significant. The p-value is 1.37E-17 (see circle around the p-value of the F-test), which, as we noted earlier, indicates $1.37*10^{-17}$; this, of course, is very close to zero.

Ability to search by job title	Ability to search by years of experience	Ability to search by location	Ability to search by candidates by schools attended	Ability to search candidates by date of updated resume	Ability to search by candidates by education level	Ability to search by skills	Ability to search candidates by average length of employment at each company	Ability to search candidates by maximum salary	Ability to search by candidates by job type his/she is looking for.	Ability to search candidates by companies at which they have worked.	Ability to search candidates by willingness to travel	Ability to search candidates by willingness to relocate	Ability to search candidates by security clearance.	Ability to perform a Boolean search functionality.	Y Likelihood of adoption
2	5	5	5	2	4	1	4	4	5	4	4	4	4	5	5
5	5	4	5	4	4	3	4	3	5	5	3	3	4	5	5
5	4	5	5	3	2	1	3	3	2	3	2	2	2	4	4
3	4	5	5	3	3	1	3	3	3	4	3	2	3	4	4
5	5	5	5	3	3	3	4	2	4	4	4	4	5	5	5
5	5	4	4	2	3	3	4	4	4	4	3	3	3	4	5
4	4	5	4	3	2	5	3	2	2	3	3	2	3	4	4
5	5	5	4	3	3	3	5	2	3	4	2	3	4	4	5
5	4	5	4	4	3	3	5	4	4	4	3	4	3	4	5
4	4	5	4	3	2	5	4	2	3	3	2	3	4	5	4

FIGURE 10.8

Behemoth.com data for 15 X's and the Y using Excel.

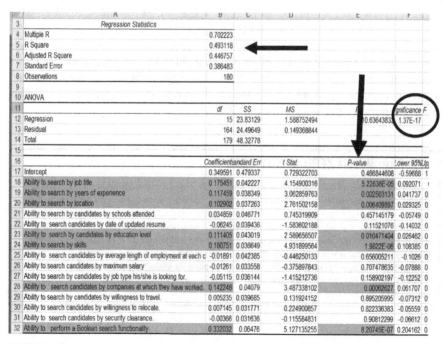

FIGURE 10.9

Output for multiple regression for Behemoth.com; Excel.

Now, note that of the 15 independent (X) variables, 7 of them are significant. We know this by examining the *p*-values. The significant variables are highlighted in the *p*-value column of Figure 10.9; see vertical arrow in Figure 10.9. Each highlighted *p*-value is less than 0.05.

The significant variables (i.e., those with a *p*-value < 0.05) are (in the order listed in the output):

Ability to search by job title
Ability to search by years of experience
Ability to search by location
Ability to search candidates by education level
Ability to search by skills
Ability to search candidates by companies in which they have
worked
Ability to perform a Boolean search

This means that these seven variables provide incremental/unique predictive value about Y, the respondent's **likelihood to adopt the search engine**, beyond a reasonable doubt. Let us take the liberty, for the moment, of calling these variables "the big 7." This does not mean that the other variables of the 15 are unrelated to Y, but rather, that none of the other variables, by themselves, add incremental (unique) predictive value about Y. However, there can be subtlety that is discussed in the "Nonsignificant but Useful Variables" sidebar.

Now, if we run a regression using only "the big 7" X variables, the regression analysis yields an r^2 value of 0.469 (46.9%), *only slightly* under the 0.493 (49.3%) we had with all 15 variables. This might surprise you, but this slight reduction always occurs. That is, even though the other eight variables are not significant, each does produce at least a tiny bit of r^2. Indeed, we have eight variables (all not significant) which are adding only about 2.4% in total to the overall r^2 value, which is an average of three-tenths of a percent each (i.e., 0.3%)!!

SIDEBAR: WHEN ZERO IS NOT ZERO

Remember that even if the r^2 of an X with Y is really zero, or incrementally adds zero, given it is real data and (of course) not *infinite* data, a variable's r^2 will not come out exactly zero, but will be some small value (e.g., 0.3%).

If we pick two variables that we *know* are unrelated, and, hence, have a true r^2 value of zero, with real data (and, obviously, less than infinite data!!), we will *not* get an r^2 of exactly zero when we analyze the data. It will be some (very likely small) positive value, since a squared value cannot be negative. This logic harkens back to the logic of hypothesis testing in general, as discussed way back in Chapter 1, where we noted that means and other values from a sample do not come out exactly the respective true value.

SIDEBAR: NONSIGNIFICANT BUT USEFUL VARIABLES

It is possible that some of the *nonsignificant* variables belong in the final conclusion about important variables to help us predict Y. How can that be, if they, indeed, are not significant?

The answer is that perhaps two (or more) of the nonsignificant variables are providing exactly the same, *useful*, information. Since each provides the same information, neither of the two variables adds anything *unique*, and thus, both variables would show up as not significant. Regression analysis can be pretty subtle!!

With this added complexity, what do we do? We certainly do not want to do a "zillion" regression analyses among the eight nonsignificant variables—even if you limited yourself to two at a time, there would be 28 different regressions. A simple illustration might help explain the paradox of nonsignificant variables that are still useful. Imagine three X's in total:

X1 provides information content 1–10 (out of 100 units of information that exist),
X2 provides information content 11–20, and
X3 provides information content 1–20.

Any one of the X's could be left out without harm to the overall units of information we have: 20. If X1 is left out, you still have information content 1–20 in total, provided by X2 and X3 (in fact, by X3 alone); if, instead, X2 is left off, you still have information content 1–20 in total, provided by X1 and X3 (in fact, by X3 alone); if X3 is left out, you still have information content 1–20 in total, provided by X1 and X2.

Therefore, the t-test, which evaluates each variable, one at a time, would not find any of these three variables useful at all (i.e., none of the three variables adds anything that can't be gotten from the other two) and thus, *will find all three variables not significant*. Yet, you want X3, or second best, X1 and X2, in your equation to maximize the number of units of information you have in the equation.

Interestingly, you would have a "hint" that something like this might be occurring, because, in this case, with only the three aforementioned variables, the *F*-test, the test of the overall model, *would be significant*, since it would identify that having the three variables is, beyond a reasonable doubt, better than having no variables at all!!

However, in our 15-variable problem, this help (from the *F*-test) is not forthcoming, since the *F*-test will be significant whether the subtlety among a few of the nonsignificant variables exists or not; the *F*-test will be significant just due to the existence of "the big 7" variables.

So, what do we do? Well, luckily, there is good news that there is a technique purposely developed to address this issue, called *stepwise regression*, which we mentioned before and will discuss in the next section. However, stepwise regression is not available in the bare-bones Excel. (Several add-ins to Excel (such as XL Miner) provide it, but the basic Excel does not have the capability to do it.) If you have SPSS, you're covered.

OK, now let's present our multiple regression analysis using SPSS. The data (first 18 rows out of the 180 data points) are shown in Figure 10.10. We already used *Variable View* to relabel the variables into X's and Y.

The SPSS dialog box for Linear Regression is shown in Figure 10.11.

The dependent variable is noted as Y. The independent variables are X1 through X15, even though you can see only X1, X2, and X3. If you scroll down, you would see all 15 X's. We are ready to click on "OK," and obtain our output, which is displayed in Figure 10.12. (However, please note in Figure 10.11 the "Method:" Enter

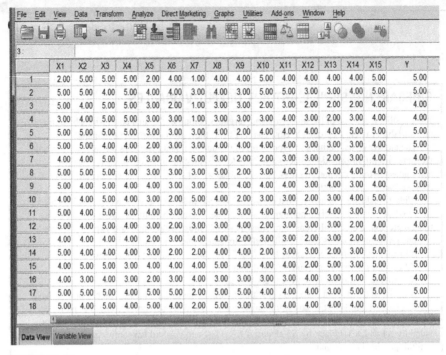

FIGURE 10.10

Behemoth.com data in SPSS format.

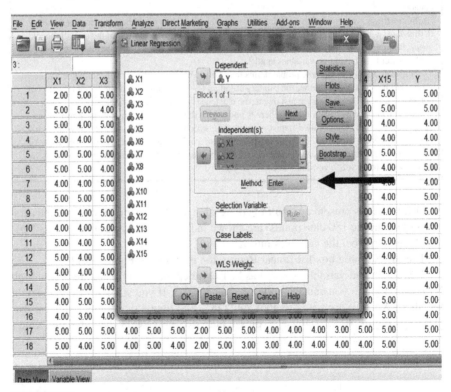

FIGURE 10.11

The Linear Regression dialog box in SPSS; Behemoth.com.

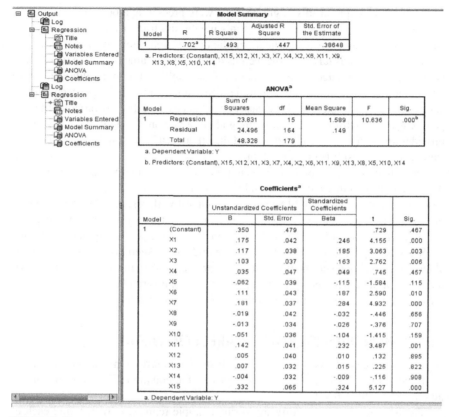

FIGURE 10.12

SPSS output for Behemoth.com data.

(see arrow in Figure 10.11). We have not discussed "Method" before, and have left the method as "Enter," the default. In the next section, this will be an issue of note.)

The results, of course, are the same as we obtained from the Excel software, except, as noted in previous chapters, for most everything in SPSS being rounded to three digits. We get the same "big 7" as significant variables in the regression model.

10.6 STEPWISE REGRESSION

Stepwise regression is a variation of regular multiple regression that was invented to specifically address the issue of variables that overlap a lot in the information they provide about the Y. We noted above that when variables overlap a lot in what they tell us about Y, it is possible that two, or more, variables that are *not statistically significant* may nevertheless be important in the prediction process.

A classic example of this might be if we were predicting a person's weight (Y), and two of the variables were the person's height and his/her pant length. Clearly, each of these variables is a significant predictor of weight; nobody can deny that on average, if a person is taller, he/she weighs more. If we assume that these two X variables are 99% correlated (to the authors, a reasonable assumption, although we've never done an actual study!!), the multiple regression results would find each of these variables not significant! That is because, given that each of the two variables (height, pant length) are telling us the same thing about a person's weight, neither variable provides *unique* (i.e., "above and beyond the other variables") predictive value, and, statistically, the result is the correct one.

Obviously, what we really want is to retain one of the two variables in our predictive equation, but we do not need both variables. If you remove both variables from the equation, you would be harming yourself with respect to getting the best prediction of a person's weight that you can. In fact, if these were the only two variables under consideration, and you drop them both, you would have nothing!!

Stepwise regression deals with this issue and would keep one of these two variables, whichever one was the tiniest bit more predictive than the other, and would bar the other variable from being in the equation. The one variable of the two that is in the equation is clearly significant, both statistically and intuitively.

10.6.1 HOW DOES STEPWISE REGRESSION WORK?

As silly as it sounds to say, we are saying it: stepwise regression works in steps!

It picks variables one at a time to enter into the equation. The entire process is automated by the software.

The first step is for the software to run a simple regression with Y and each of the X's available. These regressions are run "internally"—you do not see (nor wish to see!) that output; the software picks the variable with the highest r^2 value. Then it displays (as you'll see) the results of this one ("winning") regression.

In step 2, stepwise regression runs (internally) a bunch of new regressions; each regression contains two X's, one being the winner from step 1, and every other X. So, for example, if there are six X's to begin with (X1, X2, X3, X4, X5, X6), step 1 involves six simple regressions. Now let's assume that X3 has the highest r^2, say, 0.35, and is, thus, considered the "winner." In step 2, 5 regressions would be run; they would involve two X's each, and all would include the X3. Ergo, the new step 2 regressions would be Y/(X1 and X3), Y/(X2 and X3), Y/(X4 and X3), Y/(X5 and X3), and finally, Y/(X6 and X3). Next, which pair of X's *together* has the highest r^2 is identified. Imagine the overall r^2 with X3 and X6 is the highest, say, 0.59. This two-variable regression would be displayed on the output.

Onward to step 3. Four regressions are run that contain X3 and X6 and each *other* variable eligible (X1, X2, X4, and X5). Again, the highest overall r^2 of the four regressions would be identified and that variable would enter the equation. And so forth—the process continues.

This may sound daunting, but don't forget that it is all automated by the software; one click and you're done! Based on some other features of Stepwise Regression (see sidebar), when you examine the last step of the stepwise regression process, you are guaranteed that all variables in the equation are variables that you want in the equation (i.e., are significant), and there are no other variables out there that you are missing out on—no other variables out there that you would want in the equation (that would be significant if they entered). You can't do better than this!!!

SIDEBAR: THE BEAUTY (AND CONTROVERSY) OF STEPWISE

The Beauty

There are a few added features that are critical to the stepwise regression technique being the great technique we believe it is. They are built into the process. We list them below:

1. At each step where the stepwise process is deciding which variable is the best one to add into the equation, a check is made to determine if the variable would be significant with a t-test if it is entered into the equation. If the best variable is not significant (via the t-test), the variable *does not enter the equation* and the stepwise process ends. Thus, only significant variables are allowed to enter the equation. (Of course, if the best variable to enter the equation is not significant, then all the rest of the variables would also be not significant if they entered the equation.)

2. As we just discussed, only significant variables are allowed to enter the equation. However, a variable can be significant as it enters the equation (say X2), and later, as other variables enter the equation, the variable, X2, *can lose its significance*. This can happen because each new variable that enters the equation adds unique information (or it would not be allowed to enter the equation), but also can, at the same time, duplicate information provided by X2, thus taking away some of X2's uniqueness and significance. If a variable loses too much of its uniqueness, it may no longer be significant, and the stepwise process boots out the variable! Thus, the stepwise process has a built-in process that will delete any variable that does not retain its significance.

   So, the bottom line beauty of the stepwise regression process is that when you examine the outcome of the stepwise regression process (i.e., the results at the last step):

   a. All variables in the equation will be significant.

   b. It is guaranteed that there are no other variables that would be significant if they entered the equation.

The Controversy

There are folks who are not big fans of stepwise regression. One key reason is that the r^2 value may be inflated due to chance. For example, if you have 10 X's, and none of them correlates at all with the Y, then theoretically, the overall r^2 should be zero. However, there are 10 "opportunities" for "false r^2" to enter the analysis. When the stepwise algorithm picks the best variable first—which is the one with the highest r^2—the value of that r^2 will be the highest of 10 different "false r^2 values," and thus, even though that first equation has only one X variable, the r^2 will surely be inflated beyond what one would expect if there were only one X variable to begin with (i.e., a simple regression).

An analogy may help explain this phenomenon. If you flipped one coin 10 times, you expect on average to get 5 heads, but could easily get 6 or 7. The chance of getting more than 7 (i.e., 8 or 9 or 10) heads out of 10 is only about 5.5%. However, suppose that we flipped a *dozen coins* 10 times each, and picked, as our result, the number of heads that was *maximum (i.e., the highest of the 12 results)*. Given that there are now 12 "opportunities" to get 8 or 9 or 10 head, the odds are about 50% (actually, 49.1%) that at least *one* of the coins would give a result of 8 or 9 or 10 heads. So, for one coin, the chance of getting 8 or more heads is 5.5%, but for 12 coins, the chance of such a result occurring at least once is 49.1%—a *big* difference. The 49.1% value can be said to be *inflated*, since it does *not* represent the chance of 8 or 9 or 10 heads out of 10 flips of *one coin*, even though you can pick up that one coin and say, *truthfully*, that you flipped that particular coin 10 times and got a result of at least 8 heads.

Continued

SIDEBAR: THE BEAUTY (AND CONTROVERSY) OF STEPWISE—cont'd

This criticism, which extends to possibly getting variables in the equation in a stepwise process that really don't belong in the equation (e.g., the X that, just by chance, had the inflated value of r^2), is a legitimate one. However, if the sample size is at least 10 times the number of X's, the chance of a material misleading result is greatly minimized. In our example, the ratio is 12 to 1 (i.e., 180 data points for 15 X's), and it is unlikely that our results are incorrect in any material way.

In spite of the possible inflation aspect of performing a stepwise regression, we believe that it is the best available technique to use in a multiple-regression-analysis situation when confronted with a several X variables (say, at least three), with every chance of high correlation among the X's. We add the caveat that we embrace the 10:1 rule of thumb—i.e., you should try hard to have a sample size at least 10 times the number of eligible X's in the analysis.

10.6.2 STEPWISE REGRESSION ANALYSIS OF THE BEHEMOTH.COM DATA

We remind the reader that, sadly, bare-bones Excel (and bare-bones StatsPlus for Mac) does not accommodate stepwise regression.

So, we perform a stepwise regression using SPSS.

Let's start by repeating Figure 10.11, now labeled Figure 10.13.

We have the data in the background, and we have pulled down "Analyze" and highlighted "Regression" and then "Linear." We dragged over Y to the "Dependent"

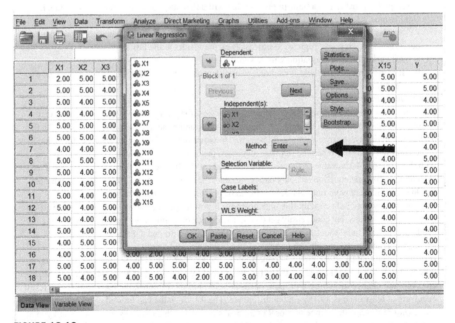

FIGURE 10.13

Getting ready for an SPSS stepwise regression analysis; Behemoth.com.

box, and X1 through X15 to the "Independents(s)" box (even though you would have to scroll through them to see them all.) Now we deviate from simply clicking "OK," which would get us the output we obtained earlier in Figure 10.12.

Now, here's the key 🗝⟶ to performing stepwise regression versus regular multiple regression: We need to change what is labeled in the Linear Regression dialog box as "Method" (see arrow in Figure 10.13). When we pull down that menu, we obtain the circled options that are displayed in Figure 10.14:

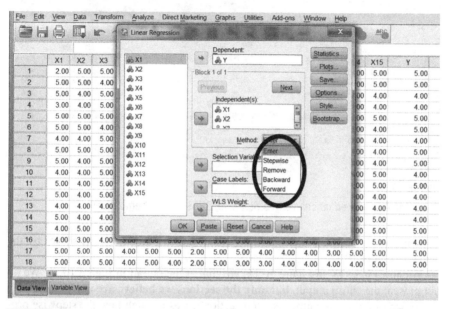

FIGURE 10.14

The different linear regression *methods* available; SPSS.

SIDEBAR: WHAT ARE THOSE OTHER METHODS, ANYWAY?

As you see in Figure 10.14, there are other choices, beside *Stepwise*. We do not believe that there is any merit in choosing *Forward*; that is equivalent to *Stepwise*, except that once a variable is in the equation, it cannot be deleted. We believe that the deletion provision of Stepwise is something you should normally want. The choice, *Remove*, is basically *Stepwise* in reverse. You start with an equation with ALL the eligible variables and keep removing the least significant variable at each stage, until all the variables left are significant and then the process stops; however, it may occur that a variable that is removed ends up back in the equation, perhaps becoming significant after other variables have left the equation—the counterpart of a variable in *Stepwise* that enters the equation, but later gets deleted. General wisdom suggests that *Remove* is equally good as *Stepwise*, but *Stepwise* is more well known and is far more popular. The two methods often yield the same final equation (and it is this last step result that matters!!), or an equation that is quite similar, and, in cases where the final equation is not the same, the predictions resulting from the two equations (i.e., from the two methods) would usually be nearly the same. *Backward* is *Remove* without the option of bringing back a variable that becomes significant after leaving the equation—analogous to the relationship of *Forward* to *Stepwise*.

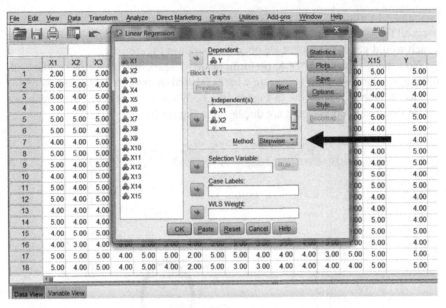

FIGURE 10.15

Linear regression *method* changed to *Stepwise*; SPSS with Behemoth.com.

Click on "Stepwise," and it will appear in the "Method" box, as shown by the arrow in Figure 10.15.

We now click OK in Figure 10.15, arriving at the output in Figure 10.16. We do not present the entire output, **but only the sections we believe are useful to you.**

As we examine the output, the top section traces through how the stepwise process proceeded. Significant variables were entered into the equation in the order X15, X7, X11, X1, X3, X2, X6 (the same 7 X's that earlier comprised "the big 7" were significant) and the r^2 values increased at each step from 0.202 (a value we have seen before, the r^2 between Y and X15 [ability to perform a Boolean search]), up to 0.469 (see the circled r^2 values in the top section of Figure 10.16). Recall that variables 1, 2, 3, 6, 7, 11, and 15 are, respectively:

Ability to search by job title
Ability to search by years of experience
Ability to search by location
Ability to search candidates by level of education
Ability to search by skills
Ability to search candidates by companies in which they have worked
Ability to perform a Boolean search

Now, the bottom section tells you the equation at each step. However, it is really only the last step that counts!! We can see that the equation of the last step is (see the rectangle in the lower section of Figure 10.16):

Model Summary

Model	R	R Square	Adjusted R Square	Std. Error of the Estimate
1	.449[a]	.202	.198	.46547
2	.542[b]	.294	.286	.43916
3	.598[c]	.357	.346	.42016
4	.634[d]	.402	.388	.40633
5	.661[e]	.437	.421	.39531
6	.679[f]	.461	.442	.38802
7	.685[g]	.469	.447	.38628

a. Predictors: (Constant), X15

b. Predictors: (Constant), X15, X7

c. Predictors: (Constant), X15, X7, X11

d. Predictors: (Constant), X15, X7, X11, X1

e. Predictors: (Constant), X15, X7, X11, X1, X3

f. Predictors: (Constant), X15, X7, X11, X1, X3, X2

g. Predictors: (Constant), X15, X7, X11, X1, X3, X2, X6

Model		Unstandardized Coefficients B	Std. Error	Coefficients Beta
1	(Constant)	2.456	.315	
	X15	.460	.069	.449
2	(Constant)	2.210	.302	
	X15	.402	.066	.393
	X7	.196	.041	.308
3	(Constant)	1.979	.294	
	X15	.333	.065	.325
	X7	.190	.039	.299
	X11	.160	.038	.261
4	(Constant)	1.370	.330	
	X15	.337	.063	.329
	X7	.178	.038	.279
	X11	.143	.037	.234
	X1	.153	.042	.215
5	(Constant)	.950	.346	
	X15	.333	.061	.325
	X7	.176	.037	.276
	X11	.125	.037	.204
	X1	.162	.041	.228
	X3	.120	.036	.190
6	(Constant)	.668	.354	
	X15	.320	.060	.313
	X7	.174	.036	.273
	X11	.130	.036	.212
	X1	.158	.040	.221
	X3	.104	.036	.164
	X2	.099	.036	.157
7	(Constant)	.528	.363	
	X15	.311	.060	.304
	X7	.177	.036	.278
	X11	.121	.036	.197
	X1	.153	.040	.214
	X3	.106	.036	.168
	X2	.106	.036	.168
	X6	.055	.034	.092

FIGURE 10.16

Relevant stepwise regression output for Behemoth.com; SPSS.

SIDEBAR: HOLD ON! WHAT HAPPENED TO THE HIGHER R SQUARE I HAD WITH GOOD OLD-FASHIONED MULTIPLE REGRESSION?

We might recall that the value of r^2 was 0.493 when we used all 15 variables, most of which were not significant. Now we have a value of "only" 0.469.

We reiterate what we noted earlier: What you need to realize is that the 0.493 is a bit misleading in that it includes the sum of a bunch of small values added to the r^2 based on variables that really cannot be said to add value to predicting Y. When we eliminate all these small "fake" additions to r^2, we end up with 0.469, or 46.9%. If this sounds subtle, we sympathize, but do not apologize. Regression analysis is a fairly complex topic and has many subtle areas, most of which, fortunately, you do not have to be concerned with.

$$Yc = 0.528 + 0.311 * X15 + 0.177 * X7 + 0.121 * X11 + 0.153 * X1 + 0.106 * X3$$
$$+ 0.106 * X2 + 0.055 * X6,$$

or, if we order the variables by subscript,

$$Yc = 528 + 0.153 * X1 + 0.106 * X2 + 0.106 * X3 + 0.055 * X6 + 0.177 * X7$$
$$+ 0.121 * X11 + 0.311 * X15.$$

In other words, this equation says that if we plug in a person's value for X1, X2, X3, X6, X7, X11, and X15, we get our best prediction for what the person will put for Y, the likelihood on the 5-point scale that he/she will adopt the search engine. For example, if we arbitrarily assume a person gives a "4" to each of the seven X's in the equation, the Yc comes out 4.64. Of course, an individual responder cannot respond 4.64, since the value chosen must be an integer. The right way to think of this is that if we had a large number of people who answered "4" for each of the variables, the **mean response** for the Y, *likelihood to adopt the search engine*, is predicted to be 4.64.

We want to add one more piece of potentially useful information about interpreting the bottom portion of Figure 10.16. You will notice that there is a column (right-hand-most column shown in the bottom portion of Figure 10.16) called "Coefficients Beta." In a stepwise regression, where there is relatively little overlap among the X variables in the equation (remember: the way [and a strength] of how stepwise regression works is that if there were a lot of overlap between two variables, one of the two variables would not be in the equation!), the magnitude of these "Beta values" roughly (not exactly, but likely close enough) reflect, in some sense, the relative importance of the variables. Here, the order is:

Ability to perform a Boolean search
Ability to search by skills
Ability to search by job title
Ability to search candidates by companies in which they have worked
Ability to search by location
Ability to search by years of experience
Ability to search candidates by level of education

This order is reasonably close to the order that is considered by many to be the true order of importance. Of course, these results are based on a sample, and not the total population, so you should not expect that the order would come out "perfectly."

The top two are what are considered by most to be the top two, although many would change their order. The third and fifth on the list above would be most folks' choice for the next most important two. The last one on the list would be most folks' choice of the least important of these "big 7."

10.7 MEANWHILE, BACK AT BEHEMOTH.COM

The results are reassuring, because the variables identified by both your multiple and stepwise regression analyses dovetail perfectly with the fields you've seen recruiters rely on during your traditional usability testing in the Behemoth lab.

On the other hand, the fact remains that CEO Joey Vellucci is furious that he spent $80 million on Novix which did worse than your current search engine in your recent usability testing. In addition, Joey's challenge to UX to come up with "their own frickin' ideal search engine" seems like more of a caustic dare than an encouraging set of marching orders. You decide that your presentation has to be bulletproof.

You begin by clearly defining the study goals. On your "Demographics" slide, you make sure that everyone understands your participants were representative of real end-users. You present the step-by-step methodology used and the verbatim tasks that all participants were asked to complete. Then, you deliver the high-level findings, keeping in mind you'll probably get no more than 15 minutes face time with Joey. Then you get into the detailed findings. You insert all the relevant charts and tables. You make it abundantly clear that your sample size of 180 makes the regression techniques viable.

For your recommendations, you produce a wireframe that illustrates the user interface for a new search home page. Your new design shows a two-tiered system; a "basic search" includes the top seven variables identified as significant in your regression analysis. If desired, the user can click on "Advanced" search to reveal the remaining eight variables; even though they were not statistically significant, they nevertheless might be useful for certain recruiters looking for a very specific set of qualifications.

No sooner do you spell-check your PowerPoint deck than you see the familiar Outlook meeting from Hans pop up on your screen: "Tuesday, July 15. 10am. Present Regression Results to Mr. Vellucci."

You quickly accept the meeting invite, and blast an instant message to Hans:

"My presentation is ready. How much time will I have?"

Hans responds: "15 minutes max; he's flying out to Palo right after your presentation."

"Got it," you shoot back.

It's about 5:30 on Monday night. You print out a copy of the presentation to take home and reread. You gotta be ready!

The next morning at 9:45, you make the long trek from the Behemoth Usability Lab to the elevators at the end of the floor, where you run into Hans, waiting impatiently for the elevator to arrive.

"Hey there; everything ready?"

"Yes, I have my laptop with the presentation, but I also made some hard copies of the deck in case we don't have time to project."

"Good call," he says, stepping into the elevator and grabbing a copy from your stack. "Joey prefers hard copy of everything." He flips through the deck. "Are you confident of these findings and recommendations?"

"Yes, they all make sense given what I've seen in the lab over the past year."

"OK," he says, still flipping through the deck. "One word of caution: Keep it brief. Let the data do the talkin'. He respects that and his brain contains a well-tuned nonsense detector."

"Got it."

You step off the elevator, and Joey's secretary stares at you impassively. "Can I help you?"

"We have a 10 o'clock with Mr. Vellucci."

She glances at her computer. "Yup, I see you guys in here. He's waiting for you; step right in. He's anxious to get you guys in and out because he's got to catch a flight at noon."

Vellucci's office is a combination of old world charm and modern chic, with two luxurious sofas in the anteroom that leads to his desk. Behind his opulent desk, a panoramic window provides a sweeping view of the old mill town where *Behemoth* makes its home. Vellucci is on the phone, berating someone, but he sees you and Hans enter. He waves you in, motioning for to take seats on the sofas.

"Look, I already give you my answer!" he yells into the phone. "Now you've got to execute!" He hangs up the phone, stands up, and comes out from behind his desk to sit next to you on the couch. During the entire movement, his eyes remain fixed on you, ignoring Hans.

"So, you're the Boolean fanatic, eh?"

"Well, not exactly, sir. Let's just say I'm fanatic about good data", you say, passing him your PowerPoint deck.

"That's not what I heard" he defiantly replies, flipping through the pages of the report. "I heard you think our search should be one big Boolean box; sort of like Google but with the ability to do insanely-long Boolean stringing." He looks up. "Is this an accurate assessment of your findings, or is there some kind of evil spin going on here?"

Sir, I'm not sure how you obtained that impression," you reply quietly but with confidence. "But allow me to describe the research I conducted."

"Ah! A diplomat as well!" Vellucci exclaims with a sardonic chuckle, looking over at Hans. "This is one slick researcher", he says, pointing to you. But Hans has your back; he stares at Vellucci impassively. Sensing support form Hans, he turns back to you and quiets down. "Alright, alright..waddya got?"

"We ran an unmoderated usability study with recruiters searching for candidates for specific jobs using our current search engine—not the Novix search engine. After recruiters used the search for a while, we asked each participant to rank their perception of usefulness of the different search fields, along with their likelihood to adopt the search engine."

"Okay," he says slowly, rifling through the deck. "Keep going, I'm listening."

"Then we analyzed the data, and determined which combination of search fields positively affected the likelihood of adoption of the search engine they had just used."

"Really?" he says, looking over his reading glasses. "Sounds like magic."

"No, just stepwise multiple regression."

Velluci look up at Hans. "Do you follow any of this?"

"Hmm…not exactly. My college stats class was a long time ago."

"Yeah, me too," he agrees. "But I have some questions."

"Sure," you reply with a grin.

"What's your sample size?"

"180."

"All bonafide professional recruiters who had never used our current search?"

"Yes."

"And they rated Boolean as the most useful field?"

"Yes, it had the highest positive correlation with likelihood of adoption."

"OK…," he says. "And where is this so-called ideal search engine you've been able to identify?"

"It's on page 11. Basically, we have the most important fields on the Basic Search, with the less important fields on the Advanced Search."

"How can 'advanced' be less important?" he says, with more than a hint of sarcasm, as he studies the design.

"Good point," you reply calmly. "It's been standard practice on the Web for a while. You call esoteric fields, "Advanced," and hide them in a pop-up. It sounds better than, "Esoteric.""

"You got that right," he chuckles. But he turns more serious. "How confident are you of these findings?"

"Well, you always need a sample size of at least 10 per independent variable to have confidence in the stepwise regression results. Since there were 15 fields, we were more than covered with 180. And all the p-values of the fields we've included in the Basic Search are way below 0.05."

Joey uses the under-the-throat "cut" sign. "Answer the question."

"Yes," you state.

"Good", he states. "It's refreshing when I get a straight answer around this place once in a while." He pauses, then holds up your report in one hand while pointing to it with his other hand. "But let me ask you something."

"What's that?" Hans asks, trying to stay relevant in a conversation that is above his head. Velluci ignores him and stares at you.

"Why didn't one of my clown VPs ask UX to do this kind of great research before I spent a boatload?"

"Why didn't one of my clown VPs ask UX to do this kind of great research *before* I spent a boatload?"

Surprised, you stare blankly at Vellucci, frantically trying to decide whether the question is rhetorical. After what seems like an eternity, Vellucci senses your discomfort and breaks the silence.

"Well, here's what you're going to do," he states emphatically. "If you hear of *any* new acquisition that hasn't passed muster with UX, march right in here and let me know." He stares at you with steely eyes: "You do *not* need any appointment; just come on in and give me the data. Deal?"

"Deal!" you say solemnly.

Vellucci gets up quickly, grabs his suit coat, and starts striding toward the exit. As he passes his secretary's desk, he points back to you and Hans, still sitting on the couches.

"Dorothy, please get these folks some complimentary Red Sox tickets. They deserve them." He turns to you and Hans one last time before he steps into the hall. "I know it's hard to tell, but I really do appreciate this kind of work. Thanks again!"

10.8 SUMMARY

In this chapter we introduced multiple and stepwise regression. We illustrated multiple regression with a small data set and then applied it to the real-world prototypical problem at Behemoth.com. That led naturally to stepwise regression, a technique that is a variation of multiple regression, very specifically oriented toward finding the best model/equation in a world of many variables which invariably have patterns of overlap of information about Y, the dependent variable, which are difficult to see and understand. Stepwise regression is guaranteed to result in an equation that has only significant variables and guarantees that it does not miss any variables that, if included, would be significant.

10.9 EXERCISE

1. Consider the Excel data in the file "Chapter 10.Exercise 1," which has 250 data points. The first 12 columns represent the evaluation of a search engine on 12 respective attributes. The 12 attributes are not measured on the same scale. Attribute 1 is a 0,1 scale (whether a respondent is able to fully fulfill some tasks using the search engine). The other Attributes are on a scale of 0–50 or 0–100, some a function of actual results by the responder, and some a subjective evaluation by the responder. Some of the attributes are "negatively scaled," so that a lower number is superior.

   a. Run a multiple regression with "Overall Satisfaction" as the dependent variable and attributes 1–12 as the 12 independent variables. Which attributes are significant at alpha = 0.05?

   b. What percent of the variability in Y is explained by all 12 attributes?

   c. Using SPSS and the data file named "Chapter 10..Exercise 1.data," run a stepwise regression with the default values for variables to enter and be deleted. The output is in a file named "Chapter 10..Exercise 1.output." Which attributes are in the stepwise regression model at the last step? What percent of the variability in Y is explained by the variables that are in the stepwise regression model at the last step?

   The answers are in a Word file named "Chapter 10.Exercise 1. answers."

Will anybody buy? Logistic regression

11.1 INTRODUCTION

Logistic regression is an extension of "regular" linear regression. It is used when the dependent variable, Y, is categorical. We now introduce *binary logistic regression,* in which the Y variable is a "Yes/No" type variable. We will typically refer to the two categories of Y as "1" and "0," so that they are represented numerically. However, the two categories can be virtually anything, such as "adopted the search engine vs. did not adopt the search engine" or "completed a task vs. did not complete a task" or, in the world of general database marketing, "responded to an offer (i.e., made a purchase) vs. did not respond to the offer." In these situations, regular linear regression (whether simple or multiple) is not appropriate.

It should be noted that the goal of binary logistic regression is the same as in the two previous chapters—to find the best fitting, simplest model, to understand the relationship between the Y and the X's, and to be able to reach appropriate statistical conclusions. Not only does binary logistic regression allow you to assess how well your set of variables predicts your categorical dependent variable and determine the "goodness-of-fit" of your model as does regular linear regression, but also it provides a summary of the accuracy of the classification of cases, which helps you determine the percent of predictions made from this model/equation that will be correct.

But, once we account for the difference between regular linear regression, which assumes that Y is continuous (and, for our purposes, bell-shaped), and logistic regression, which assumes that the Y is a set of categories (only two categories, if we are discussing *binary* logistic regression), the logistic regression process follows the same general principles as used in regular linear regression.

Binary logistic regression was used originally only in epidemiologic research, but is now routinely used in many fields, including general business and marketing. Its use has mushroomed in the past two decades. A classic early application was in finance, where a "1" stood for "person paid back the loan," and a "0" stood for "person defaulted on the loan."

SIDEBAR: WHY CAN'T I USE REGULAR REGRESSION?

Regular linear regression models (whether simple or multiple) are not appropriate for binary responses for a couple of reasons. First, the assumptions that underlie them are violated to too large an extent. For example, one of our assumptions in Chapters 9 and 10 is that if we had a bunch of data values with the same set of X's, the Y's would form a bell-shaped (normal) curve. Here, the Y "curve" would be not even close to that, being just a set of 1's and a set of 0's—two vertical lines on a graph. In addition, some of the theory of binary logistic regression differs from regular linear regression; for example, the best fitting line is not chosen by the criterion of least squares.

If we *did* find the least-squares regression line when the Y data that yielded the line is 1 and 0, there's a possibility that the resulting Yc can actually be greater than 1 or less than 0. Both of these are theoretically meaningless, since we interpret Yc as the probability of obtaining a 1. Thus is another reason we use logistic regression, which does not allow a Yc outside of the (0,1) range.

11.2 CASE STUDY: WILL ANYBODY BUY AT THE *CHARLESTON GLOBE*?

You've just been hired as a UX researcher at the CharlestonGlobe.com, a subscription-based Web site affiliated with the *Charleston Globe*, a newspaper based in Charleston, Massachusetts.

The *Charleston Globe* has a long and noble history, established in 1862, garnering no fewer than 38 Pulitzer Prizes since 1966. When the Internet changed everything in the early 1990s, the *Globe* hopped on the bandwagon early, creating CharlestonGlobe.com, a free, albeit stripped-down, version of the paper in 1995. Then fast forward to 2011, and the new owners decided to gamble on subscription-based Web site, CharlestonGlobe. com, where the entire contents of print version are posted behind a paywall.

The new site is slick; its response design automatically adapts its layout to your device's screen size, whether you're using a laptop, tablet, smartphone, or just about any Web-reading device you can imagine. The site also contains every single word of the paper version along with some "premium content." Current paper subscribers are given free access to CharlestonGlobe.com, but all others must break out their credit cards and plop down $3.99 a week.

And that's the rub, because very few Charlestonians—or anybody else—are breaking out their credit cards. The numbers are abysmal, and it's got the new owners scratching their heads.

Their game plan seemed to make sense at the time. With the inevitable decline of paper subscriptions, and with an ever-increasing percentage of Americans getting their news online at free sites like CNN.com and Googlenews.com, the new owners thought they had a solution custom-built for the current trend: an online version of the paper that was convenient, comprehensive, and accessible everywhere—without the hassle of recycling.

Now they're wondering where they went wrong and have turned to the Digital Product team to figure it out. After all, your group produces and runs the site, so you should be able to diagnose and rectify the problem. It doesn't really matter to the new owners that American news consumption has been altered more in the past 10 years that since the advent of television, and that just about every mass media company is trying to figure out what to do about abysmal network news ratings, reduced print subscriptions, and anemic revenue. They just want you to figure out a way to stop the cash bleed–because if you can't, they're pulling up stakes and leaving town pronto.

You've been barely at your job for a week, when creative director Denise Dangle calls an all-hands meeting in her office to relay the new owner's angst. Dangle, trained as a librarian in the 1970s, has suddenly been thrust into a position of authority, despite not really having a handle on the reality of news consumption in the new millennium. She's brusque, impatient, and exudes a "don't confuse me with the facts" vibe that drives everybody nuts whenever they have to deal with her. But this time, she seems especially irritated.

"Okay, look, we're in trouble here, and nobody has given one solitary good idea how to get these subscriptions up." She glares around the room. "What do I have to do? Break out the 'We have to work this weekend' card?"

Nick Bonovich, a recent transplant from *The New York Times,* clears his throat and raises his hand.

"Thank God," Dangle sighs. "Yes, Nick?"

"What about credibility?" Bonovich asks.

"What about it?" Dangle implores. She's getting irritated.

"We had a bunch of research done at the *Times,* and credibility was often cited as a main reason for renewals."

"You think you have a corner on credibility just because it's the mighty *Times*?" Dangle asks incredulously. "The *Globe* has been around since the Civil War. If we weren't believable, we wouldn't have made it into the twentieth century, let alone the twenty-first."

A hush falls over the room. Dangle's eyes travel around the conference room and land on you.

"How 'bout our new UX researcher? Any ideas?"

"Well, willingness to pay for news has typically been correlated to demographic factors, like age, income, and education," you state.

Dangle stares at you. "Right and…." She waves her hands in the air impatiently, motioning you to keep going.

"But for digital subscribers, these kinds of traditional predictors obviously aren't telling us the full story about consumer behavior."

Dangle perks up: "So?"

"We can launch an online survey that probes current news consumption, willingness to pay for online news, and what attributes of an online news experience would have the most impact of the respondent's willingness to pay for digital news content."

"Hmmm," Dangle muses, "Interesting."

You have an opening; you plunge forward.

"We'll still gather the demographic stuff, but the survey will really try to get at what content and attributes of that content would impact willingness to buy."

"What about credibility?" Nick asks.

"Yup, we'll get respondents to rank the impact perceived credibility has on willingness to buy."

You can feel consensus growing, but Dangle rolls her eyes.

"The credibility question is a waste of time, but go ahead, if you insist, Nick." She turns to you: "Aren't you forgetting something?" she asks.

"You mean the 'Is there any kind of news experience you'd be willing to pay for' question? Don't worry; it will be there. For those who answer 'yes,' we'll probe further and get respondents to rank impact on willingness to buy on different content and attributes."

"Well, I hope this so-called research isn't a colossal waste of time!"

"OK," Dangle says cautiously. "I *think* it's a plan. Don't forget to add the 'how much would you spend' question. When can we see some results?"

"Well, I have to construct the survey, post it in various forums online, and then process the results. Two weeks should do, soup to nuts."

"I love it!" Nick says. "Wow, we'd really impress the new owners if we could crack this one!"

Dangle waves off Bonavich, indicating she believes he's just spouted nonsense. She's still sceptical. Tapping her hands together using her fingertips, she delivers her parting shot, glaring at you: "Well, I hope this so-called research isn't a colossal waste of time."

"Nothing ventured, nothing gained, right?" you reply good-naturedly.

Dangle utters something under her breath as she heads out the door, but you don't catch it.

At least you have some marching orders.

11.3 LOGISTIC REGRESSION

In this section, we introduce details of *binary* logistic regression. This is the regression method we use when the Y (dependent) variable is a categorical variable with *two* categories. If the Y variable is categorical with more than two categories (e.g., willing to buy, not sure, not willing to buy), we refer to the analysis as *multinomial* logistic regression; we are covering only the case of *binary* logistic regression. Your independent variables can be either categorical or continuous, or a mix of both.

For the dependent variable, we adopt the "1" and "0" notation, where "1" stands for one category and "0" stands for the other category. Traditionally, if the two categories are analogous to "buy" versus "didn't buy," we usually let the "1" stand for the "buy," or positive result, and the "0" for the "not buy," or negative result. Given this customary choice of notation, the predicted Y, which we have been notating by Yc, stands for *the predicted probability that the result is a "1."* And, of course, a probability must be between 0 and 1 (or, 0–100%), by definition. In a "regular" simple linear regression, our regression line is

$$Yc = a + b * X.$$

Our logistic model is a complicated expression, but results in an equivalent regression line,

$$Yc = a + b * X.$$

However, the Yc is no longer itself, the probability that the result is a "1." Instead, it is the natural logarithm of the odds of obtaining a "1." (See the sidebar.)

SIDEBAR: THE BINARY LOGISTIC REGRESSION MODEL

Let P(E) stand for the probability that an event, E, occurs. The *odds* of event E occurring is defined as

$$P(E)/(1 - P(E)).$$

The odds is a numerical value that ranges from 0 to ∞ (infinity). The natural log (LN) of the odds

$$LN\{P(E)/(1 - P(E))\}$$

ranges from $-\infty$ to ∞, the same range that holds for a value of Yc in "regular" linear regression in previous chapters.

We specify that

$$LN\{P(E)/(1 - P(E))\} = a + b * X. \tag{11.1}$$

In binary logistic regression, with just one X variable (assumed in this discussion for ease of explanation), a predicted P(E) is actually Yc. If we replace P(E) in Eqn (11.1) with Yc, we have

$$LN\{Yc/(1 - Yc)\} = a + b * X, \tag{11.2}$$

and if we work backward from Eqn (11.2), we arrive at the ugly-looking expression:

$$Yc = e^{a + b * X}/(1 + e^{a + b * X}). \tag{11.3}$$

However, as ugly as the expression in Eqn (11.3) is, Yc is easily able to be computed for any X we have, once we determine the values of "a" and "b."

You can note that Yc in Eqn (11.3) is a value from 0 to 1, *exactly what is appropriate for a probability*. When (a + b * X) is very negative, $e^{a + b * X}$ is very near 0, and Yc is near 0, since we have what is, in loose terms, Yc = (0/(1 + 0)) = 0. When (a + b * X) is very large and positive, $e^{a + b * X}$ is a very high number, say, 1,000,000, and we have, in loose terms, Yc = (1,000,000/1,000,001), a value close to 1.

If we let

$$Y*c = LN\{Yc/(1 - Yc)\}, \tag{11.4}$$

we have a familiar-looking expression,

$$Y*c = a + b*X. \tag{11.5}$$

Of course, when we find Y*c in Eqn (11.5), we can then compute Yc by Eqn (11.4), or better, have the software do it for us!!

So, in essence, we have a linear regression equation,

$$Y*c = a + b*X,$$

or, if there are several X's,

$$Y*c = a + b1*X1 + b2*X2 + b3*X3 + ...$$

But, this time, we cannot find the "a" and the "b" using the least-squares criterion, as we did in Chapters 9 and 10. Instead, we need to use a different method, called "maximum likelihood estimation." While the criterion of least squares chooses the values of "a" and "b" that minimize the sum of squared differences between the actual Y and predicted Y, Yc, the criterion of maximum likelihood estimation, finds values of "a" and "b" that *maximize the probability of obtaining the sample data you actually have*. The good news is that the fact that the criterion used to find the "a" and "b" is a different criterion from least squares doesn't complicate your life; SPSS simply finds the "a" and "b" for you using that criterion. (Sadly, basic Excel does not have logistic regression capability, but some Excel plug-ins, like XLMiner and paid versions of StatPlus, do.)

It should also be noted that even though $Y*c = a + b*X$ is linear, Yc itself is not linear, as can be seen in Eqn (11.3) above. Indeed, we noted that Yc ranges from 0 to 1, and a graph of the Yc is in Figure 11.1. It clearly is not a straight line (although, in theory, a straight line would be a special case of the curve in the figure). The horizontal axis is $(a + b*X)$ and the vertical axis is $Yc = e^{a+b*X}/(1 + e^{a+b*X})$.

SIDEBAR: WHY NOT USE THE CRITERION OF LEAST SQUARES?

Remember that we are not using Y, itself, as a linear function of X. We are using the natural logarithm of the odds as a linear function of X. This expression, $LN\{Y/(1 - Y)\}$ (which mirrors the expression in Eqns (11.1) and (11.2)), is problematic when Y = 0 or 1. When Y = 0, we have LN(0), which is undefined (it heads to $-\infty$); when Y = 1, we have LN(1/0), which is undefined (it heads to ∞). In other words, when Y is a (0, 1) variable, the values that need to be used by the software to find the least-squares line are undefined, so the least-squares line cannot be found. So, we must find another criterion to define "best." In fact, without the bell shape of the Y's for a given X (earlier discussed), the very desirable properties of the least-squares line, even if you could find it, would not hold true. The maximum likelihood criterion is eminently sensible—it results in the "a" and "b" that most highly agree with the data you have.

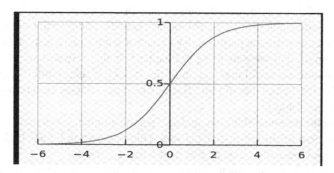

FIGURE 11.1

A graph of the binary logistic regression line.

11.4 LOGISTIC REGRESSION USING SPSS

To demonstrate performing logistic regression with SPSS, we'll use small sample size for the example. Then we will introduce the CharlestonGlobe.com data set and discuss the results.

Suppose that we are interested in examining the relationship between the ability to successfully complete task 9 of the Backboard LMS Co., as listed in Chapter 5, and the number of courses a student has taken that have used a "Backboard-type" system. Task 9 was listed as

Table 11.1 Data for Illustrative Binary Logistic Regression Analysis

Person Number	Y (Successful or Not)	X (No. of Past Courses with Backboard-Type System)
1	1	8
2	1	7
3	0	5
4	0	3
5	0	3
6	0	4
7	1	6
8	0	5
9	1	6
10	0	4
11	0	7
12	0	4

> *You're currently taking a course called "Analytics for Decision Making." You turned in you first homework assignment, but never got the graded assignment back from the professor. You're wondering if anyone else did. What's the quickest way to ask all of your classmates without resorting to email?*

and, if you look back at the usability test results in Chapter 5, you will see that only 2 of the 10 participants who attempted the task actually completed it successfully.

Now, for demonstration purposes, let's create a sample of 12 respondents, totally different from the data we were using in Chapter 5. In this case we have not only data for successful/unsuccessful completion of the task (1 = successful, 0 = unsuccessful), but also for the number of past "Backboard-type" courses each respondent has completed. See Table 11.1.

We enter the data into SPSS. We include "person number," even though it will not explicitly be part of the regression analysis. This is shown in Figure 11.2, and note that we entered "variable view" to give names to the columns.

In Figure 11.3, we pull down "Analyze," go to "Regression," and then go to sub-menu item, "Binary Logistic" (see arrows in Figure 11.3).

When we click, we arrive at the (Binary) "Logistic Regression" dialog box, as seen in Figure 11.4.

In Figure 11.5, we drag over "success_not" to the "Dependent" rectangle (see vertical arrow in Figure 11.5), and the one X, "num_courses" to the "Covariates" rectangle (see horizontal solid arrow in Figure 11.5). Note that in this technique, the X's are called "Covariates." For all practical purposes, you can simply think of "Covariates" as "Independent Variables."

For now, we simply click "OK," arriving at our SPSS output, as shown in Figure 11.6.

The top section of output in Figure 11.6 is analogous to overall fit and r^2 in "regular" linear regression. Most noteworthy are the values of "r^2;" we put quotes around the term,

---

SIDEBAR: COX, SNELL, NAGELKERKE: WHO ARE THESE GUYS ANYWAY?

We are familiar with the r^2 in regular linear regression; it indicates our estimate of the proportion of variability in Y accounted for by X (or the X's in multiple linear regression). But, when the Y variable is categorical, we cannot compute an r^2 value that has the same meaning. So, there are approximation methods used to compute this proportion of variability. We'll go over the most common here.

Perhaps the most well known is the Cox and Snell R-square. It can be extremely useful, but there's a caveat: Its maximum value is 0.75 with a categorical Y (as we have in our example).

The other SPSS R-square measure for a categorical Y is the Nagelkerke R-square. This is an adjusted version of the Cox and Snell R-square that expands the range to be 0 to 1. Of course, just like when examining an r^2 for regular linear regression, we cannot clearly define what is a high value for these pseudo-R-square values. As we noted in Chapter 9, it depends on the specific application. We conclude discussion of this section of the output by stating that for you, the UX person, this is likely the least important of the three sections of output, a fact that differs from the usual case in regular linear regression.

In terms of a hypothesis test that is easy to understand and somewhat in the spirit of an F-test, we recommend the Hosmer-Lemeshow test, which is exemplified later.

---

	person_num	success_not	num_courses	var
1	1.00	1.00	8.00	
2	2.00	1.00	7.00	
3	3.00	.00	5.00	
4	4.00	.00	3.00	
5	5.00	.00	3.00	
6	6.00	.00	4.00	
7	7.00	1.00	6.00	
8	8.00	.00	5.00	
9	9.00	1.00	6.00	
10	10.00	.00	4.00	
11	11.00	.00	7.00	
12	12.00	.00	4.00	
13				
14				
15				
16				
17				
18				
19				
20				
21				
22				
23				
24				
25				
26				

Data View | Variable View

FIGURE 11.2

Data entered into SPSS; illustrative example.

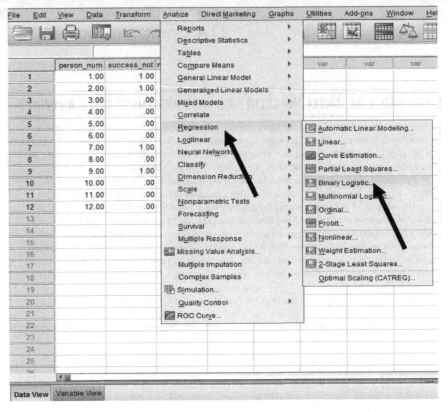

FIGURE 11.3

Pull-down menu commands for binary logistic regression; SPSS with illustrative example.

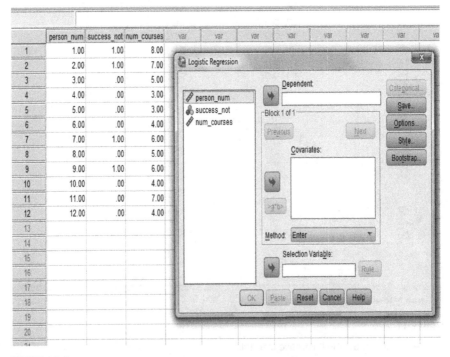

FIGURE 11.4

The Logistic Regression dialog box; SPSS with illustrative example.

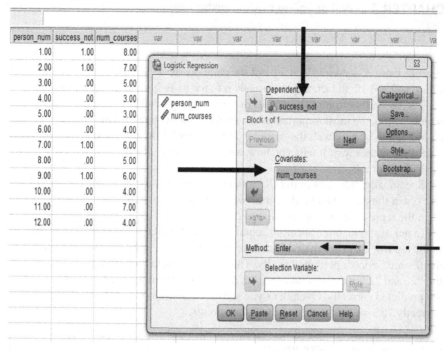

person_num	success_not	num_courses	var	var	var	var	var	var	var	va
1.00	1.00	8.00								
2.00	1.00	7.00								
3.00	.00	5.00								
4.00	.00	3.00								
5.00	.00	3.00								
6.00	.00	4.00								
7.00	1.00	6.00								
8.00	.00	5.00								
9.00	1.00	6.00								
10.00	.00	4.00								
11.00	.00	7.00								
12.00	.00	4.00								

FIGURE 11.5

Variables dragged over to appropriate places; SPSS with illustrative example.

Model Summary

Step	-2 Log likelihood	Cox & Snell R Square	Nagelkerke R Square
1	7.789[a]	.464	.645

a. Estimation terminated at iteration number 6 because parameter estimates changed by less than .001.

Classification Table[a]

			Predicted		
			success_not		Percentage Correct
Observed			.00	1.00	
Step 1	success_not	.00	7	1	87.5
		1.00	2	2	50.0
Overall Percentage					75.0

a. The cut value is .500

Variables in the Equation

		B	S.E.	Wald	df	Sig.	Exp(B)
Step 1[a]	num_courses	1.617	.902	3.215	1	.073	5.037
	Constant	-9.776	5.382	3.299	1	.069	.000

a. Variable(s) entered on step 1: num_courses.

FIGURE 11.6

SPSS output for binary logistic regression; illustrative example.

because these *R*-square values are not the same as the r² we are accustomed to from Chapters 9 and 10. In fact, they are usually referred to as "pseudo-*R*-square measures."

The second section of the output in Figure 11.6 is called a *Classification Table*, which is often the most important and useful part of the output. This provides us with an indication of how well the model is able to predict the correct category for each case. Put another way, it tells you how well the X (or, multiple X's) predicts whether the Y is a 1 or a 0.

Specifically, the rows in the Classification Table tell us the actual number of 1's and 0's in the data (which, of course, we know already), while the columns tell you what the regression process *predicts* is the case.

In our example, there are eight actual observed 0's (the sum of the "7" and the "1" in the top row), and seven of them are predicted as 0's—so 87.5% (seven of eight) of the 0's are, indeed, predicted as 0's. There are four actual observed 1's (the sum of the "2" and "2" in the second row), but only two of them are predicted as 1's—50% are predicted correctly. Overall, as you see in the bottom row of the table, we predict correctly 75% of the (in this case) 12 data points.

SIDEBAR: THE CUTOFF POINT

By the way, unless we change a setting (and we do not suggest you do that), if the predicted probability of a 1 is at least 0.5, the software predicts/classifies the result as a "1," while if the predicted probability is less than 0.5, the software classifies the result as a "0." In fact, this 0.5 "cutoff point" is noted right below the classification table.

Should predicting 75% of the cases correctly be considered "good"? Of course, as a practical matter, it depends on the real-world situation. However, in the abstract, statistically speaking, we can reason this way: If you were guessing whether each of the 12 participants successfully completed the task, given *no information at all* about these people (just a code number!!), how many would you guess correctly? 75%? We doubt it!! So, are you going to take your chances or use logistic regression? Of course, it's a rhetorical question.

SIDEBAR: JUST MAX 'EM OUT AND BE A PRO: CMAX AND CPRO CRITERIA

Well, you can get 8 of the 12 (67%) correct by predicting all 12 people to be unsuccessful (i.e., 0's). This is called the "Cmax" criterion, and you cannot guarantee a higher percentage of correct predictions by using any other strategy. The strategy is to predict everyone to be in the category with the highest frequency!! If the data had consisted of 25 people, for example, and 15 had been "1's," with 10 being 0's, then the highest frequency category would be 1's, and you could guarantee 60% correctly predicted (100*(15/25)). The binary logistic regression process resulted in 75% predicted correctly. It's always nice if the regression results predict a higher percent correct than the Cmax criterion!

However, there are some cautions that need to be mentioned. First, with a sample size of only 12, it turns out that the 75% is really not statistically significantly higher than 67%, so the fact that 75% exceeds 67% is not that impressive—primarily due to the small sample size; these results based on a sample size of 120 (instead of 12) would be statistically significant at the traditional 0.05 significance level.

SIDEBAR: JUST MAX 'EM OUT AND BE A PRO: CMAX AND CPRO CRITERIA—cont'd

Secondly, some people believe that this Cmax criterion is too strict; they argue that a more realistic criterion is one called "Cpro," which would be, in our example, $(8/12)^2 + (4/12)^2 = 0.56$, or 56%. The logic of Cpro is that it is not realistic to predict everybody to be in the highest frequency category. So, the issue is phrased as follows: "How many would be guessed correctly if you had to allocate 8 people of the 12 to 0's, and 4 to 1's—that is, insisting that the prediction includes an allocation that duplicates the proportions in the actual data?" It turns out that the answer to this question is to add up the squares of the two proportions. (It turns out that 75% is also not statistically significantly above 56% either, due to the small sample size of 12; however, it's a close case, since the p-value is about 0.089, not that much above 0.05.) Perhaps, the quickest and easiest guideline we can give you would be to be happy if (1) for a sample size of at least 25, your results exceed Cmax, or (2) for a sample size of at least 100, your results beat Cpro by at least 0.08.

The third/bottom section—Variables in the Equation—is extremely useful. It gives you information about the incremental contribution of each of the predictor variables, using the Wald test. (It is analogous to the t-test results of regular linear regression.) Scan down the label Sig. and look for values less than 0.05; these are the variables that contribute significantly to the predictive power of the model above and beyond the other variables in the model.

In this case, it turns out that "num_courses" is not quite significant at the traditional value of 0.05. The p-value, as you can see, is 0.073 (see arrow in Figure 11.6), a bit over 0.05.

SIDEBAR: THE SHIFTING "CONSTANT" IN SPSS

The authors always find it interesting that the output has the "Constant" listed *below* the slope of the X variable(s); in regular linear regression, as you saw in Chapters 9 and 10, the "Constant" is listed first, *followed* by the slope of the X variable(s). It's not a big deal, but we'd like to ask the designers at SPSS: Why? For consideration, we offer guideline 11.2 from the "Research-Based Web Design and Usability Guidelines" from the United States Department of Health and Human Services:

"Ensure that the format of common items is consistent from one page to another."

11.4.1 COMPUTING A PREDICTED PROBABILITY

Now, using the results from the first column of the Variables in the Equation, we can note the best fitting line of the model:

$$Y*c = -9.776 + 1.617*X.\qquad(11.6)$$

We often wish to find Yc, the predicted probability of obtaining a "1" for various X values. So, if we take the first X data value of 8, and plug it into Eqn (11.6) above, we get

$$Y*c = -9.776 + 1.617*8$$
$$= 3.16.$$

Recall that this is *not* Yc, but Y*c. If we find the exponentiation of this value (i.e., we use our calculator to find $e^{3.16}$),[1] we obtain 23.57.

The last step in finding Yc (the actual predicted probability you wish to find) is to solve the equation:

$$Y_c/(1 - Y_c) = 23.57.$$

Solving this equation: $Yc = 23.57 * (1 - Yc)$
$$Yc = 23.57 - 23.57Yc$$
$$24.57 * Yc = 23.57$$
$$Yc = 0.96.$$

So, for a person who completed eight previous courses that used a Backboard-type system, we predict that the probability is 0.96 that he/she would complete the task successfully. Or we can think of it this way: If we have a large number of people who completed eight previous courses that used a Backboard-type system, we would expect about 96% of them to complete the task successfully.

For a person who had completed five courses that used a Backboard-type system, the probability of completing the task successfully can be computed similarly to be about 0.16. As we just noted, the probability is 0.96 for X=8. It is 0.82 for X=7, 0.48 for X=6, 0.16 for X=5, and 0.04 for X=3. You can see that the curve is pretty steep (the values change a lot as X changes) when we are near the middle of our data values. Indeed, if you go back and look at Figure 11.1, you will see that between the middle values (−2 to 2 in the figure), the curve is somewhat steep, while at the ends (between −6 and −2 and also between 2 and 6) the curve is somewhat flat.

11.4.2 SOME ADDITIONAL USEFUL OUTPUT TO REQUEST FROM SPSS

11.4.2.1 The Hosmer and Lemeshow goodness-of-fit test

One way to assess the goodness-of-fit of the binary logistic model to the data you have is to request from SPSS the output for the Hosmer and Lemeshow test. (By the way, SPSS states in their documentation that the Hosmer-Lemeshow test is the most reliable test of model fit available in SPSS.) It uses the chi-square distribution that we have encountered in Chapter 4. Basically, a *poor* fit is indicated by a significance value less than 0.05. Ergo, to support a model we want a value *greater* than 0.05. Now there's a twist, eh?

---

[1] The symbol "e" stands for a constant that arises frequently when dealing with logarithms and other quantities. It has a value of approximately 2.718. The constant is, in mathematical terms, the same type of constant as the much more familiar "π," approximately 3.14, that we learn about in high school, the ratio of the circumference of a circle to its diameter.

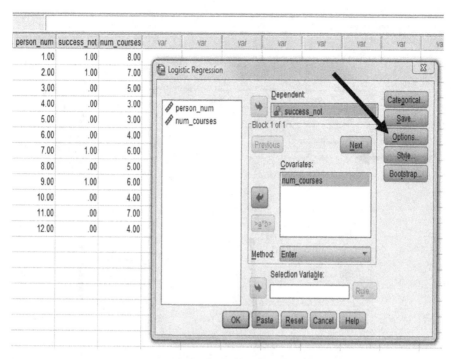

person_num	success_not	num_courses	var	var	var	var	var	var	var	va
1.00	1.00	8.00								
2.00	1.00	7.00								
3.00	.00	5.00								
4.00	.00	3.00								
5.00	.00	3.00								
6.00	.00	4.00								
7.00	1.00	6.00								
8.00	.00	5.00								
9.00	1.00	6.00								
10.00	.00	4.00								
11.00	.00	7.00								
12.00	.00	4.00								

FIGURE 11.7

A repeat of Figure 11.5; SPSS with illustrative example.

It can be requested in SPSS by going back to Figure 11.5, repeated here as Figure 11.7, and clicking on "Options" (see arrow in Figure 11.7).

We see the "Logistic Regression: Options" dialog box in Figure 11.8.

We clicked the box for the "Hosmer-Lemeshow goodness-of-fit" (see horizontal arrow in Figure 11.8) and then clicked "Continue" to return us to Figure 11.7 (see vertical arrow in Figure 11.8). Now, in addition to the output in Figure 11.6 (that we discussed), we also obtain additional output that includes what is shown in Figure 11.9.

So, we earlier noted the twist: usually, the focus in hypothesis testing is to see if we obtain a low p-value (less than 0.05); here, the key is to note if we obtain a high p-value. Obtaining a "high" p-value means *we do not have evidence to reject that the logistic regression model fits the data well*. Here, we have a p-value of 0.388; that is nowhere near 0.05, and would be generally considered a "high" p-value. Thus, we can conclude that this model is a good fit.

11.4.2.2 Finding the predicted probability of a "1" for each data point

Quite often, we wish to find the predicted probability of getting a "1" (here, completing the task successfully) for several of the X values. In the previous section, we showed how to compute these predicted values. While it is not really difficult, it can

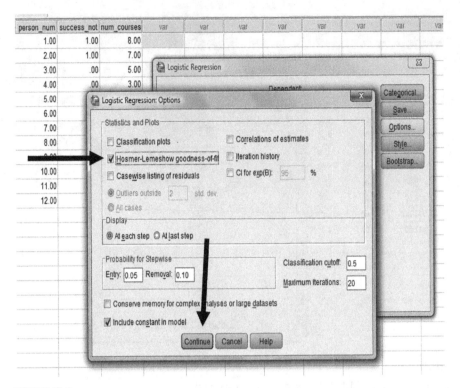

FIGURE 11.8

The Logistic Regression: Options dialog box; SPSS with illustrative example.

Hosmer and Lemeshow Test			
Step	Chi-square	df	Sig.
1	4.134	4	.388

FIGURE 11.9

The Hosmer and Lemeshow test output; SPSS with illustrative example.

be very tedious, and likely unworkable for a large data set. Luckily, we can simply ask SPSS to find the predicted value for all of the X's.

If you go back to Figure 11.2, you see that it is our first figure for this numerical example and consists of the two key columns of data, "success_not" (the Y variable) and "num_courses" (the X variable), as well as a column not used formally in the analysis, "person_num."

Now, refer back to Figure 11.7 for reference. This time, instead of clicking on the "Options" button, click on "Save" (see oval in Figure 11.10). This results in displaying the "Logistic Regression: Save" dialog box shown in Figure 11.10 (see horizontal arrow in Figure 11.10).

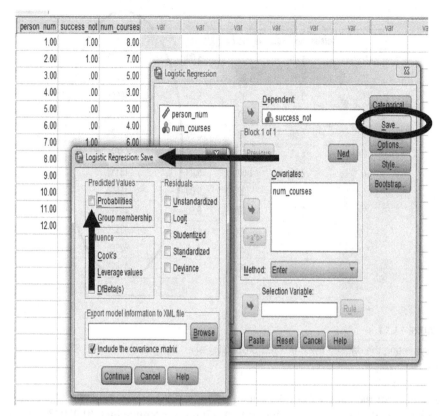

FIGURE 11.10

The Logistic Regression: Save dialog box; SPSS with illustrative example.

We now click on "Probabilities" in the top left part of the dialog box (see vertical arrow in Figure 11.10). Now clicking "Continue" puts us back to Figure 11.7, where we click "OK," as we did earlier.

You can see in Figure 11.11 that along with our three columns of original data, we now have a new column, "PRE_1"—"prediction of a 1" (see oval in Figure 11.11). This new column represents the predicted probability that each person will be a "1," or will successfully complete the task.

You can note that for row 1 of Figure 11.11, which has X (num_courses) = 8, you see a probability of 0.95923. This is consistent with what we computed in the earlier section as 0.96. For X = 5, which corresponds with both rows 3 and 8, the probability is given as 0.15548, again, consistent with our result in the section of 0.16. In both cases, the only difference is miniscule, involving rounding error.

You can see in Figure 11.11 that we have obtained the predicted probability for each X value in our data set. What if we want to predict the probability of a "1" for a value of X that is *not in our data set*? How do we do that? Well, in the current

	person_num	success_not	num_courses	PRE_1
1	1.00	1.00	8.00	.95923
2	2.00	1.00	7.00	.82366
3	3.00	.00	5.00	.15548
4	4.00	.00	3.00	.00720
5	5.00	.00	3.00	.00720
6	6.00	.00	4.00	.03526
7	7.00	1.00	6.00	.48115
8	8.00	.00	5.00	.15548
9	9.00	1.00	6.00	.48115
10	10.00	.00	4.00	.03526
11	11.00	.00	7.00	.82366
12	12.00	.00	4.00	.03526
13				
14				

FIGURE 11.11

Augmenting the data by the predicted probability of a "1" for each row; SPSS with illustrative example.

example, all the values from 3 through 8 are in the data set. And, for X = 3, the probability of a "1" is very small (0.0072) and for X = 8 quite high (0.95023), and it would not seem that fruitful to worry about what happens when X = 2 or 9. However, for the sake of introducing the technique, suppose that we decide that we do wish to know the predicted probability when X = 9. What do we do?

Obviously, there is no data value with X = 9. Here's the trick. We enter the 9 for X as an additional data value, *but do not enter any value of Y*. We see this in Figure 11.12; see the arrow where we added the "9." The one thing we know is that the resulting predicted probability will be higher than the 0.95203 for X = 8.

When we now click on the "Save" option, and then click on "Probabilities" and then "OK," we arrive at Figure 11.13, which not only gives us the predicted probability of a "1" for the actual X data values, but also gives us the answer for X = 9 (see arrow in Figure 11.13).

In other words, since we added an X value, but did not enter a corresponding Y value, the logistic regression analysis ignores the "9" for purposes of doing the analysis (and hence, the resulting equation, etc., do not change), but the analysis does give us a predicted probability of getting a "1," since this predicted value does not depend on the specific Y value.

You can see in Figure 11.13 that our predicted probability for X = 9 is 0.99163. By the way, we wish to mention again that if you take a quick look way back at Figure 11.1, you can see that at the "end points" of the graph (left or right!!), the rise

person_num	success_not	num_courses	var
1.00	1.00	8.00	
2.00	1.00	7.00	
3.00	.00	5.00	
4.00	.00	3.00	
5.00	.00	3.00	
6.00	.00	4.00	
7.00	1.00	6.00	
8.00	.00	5.00	
9.00	1.00	6.00	
10.00	.00	4.00	
11.00	.00	7.00	
12.00	.00	4.00	
		9.00	

FIGURE 11.12

Adding a fictitious data value for X to determine the predicted probability of "1;" SPSS with illustrative example.

person_num	success_not	num_courses	PRE_1	v
1.00	1.00	8.00	.95923	
2.00	1.00	7.00	.82366	
3.00	.00	5.00	.15548	
4.00	.00	3.00	.00720	
5.00	.00	3.00	.00720	
6.00	.00	4.00	.03526	
7.00	1.00	6.00	.48115	
8.00	.00	5.00	.15548	
9.00	1.00	6.00	.48115	
10.00	.00	4.00	.03526	
11.00	.00	7.00	.82366	
12.00	.00	4.00	.03526	
.	.	9.00	.99163	

FIGURE 11.13

Getting a predicted probability of a data value not in our data set; here: X=9; SPSS with illustrative example.

in the curve is not very steep, and that is consistent with the difference from $X = 8$ to $X = 9$ being relatively small (roughly 0.96 to 0.99), while the curve rises far more steeply near the "middle" of the data values, and correspondingly, from $X = 5$ to $X = 6$ engenders a much larger increase (roughly 0.16 to 0.48).

11.5 CHARLESTONGLOBE.COM SURVEY DATA AND ITS ANALYSIS

You'll recall that in an attempt to determine what kinds of online news content consumers would be willing to pay for, you launched an online survey. The survey probed on current news consumption, willingness to pay for online news, and what attributes of an online news experience would have the most impact of the respondent's willingness to pay for digital news content.

Your survey began with demographic questions of age, gender, income, and level of education. On a hunch that there might be a correlation between print subscribers and online use, you added a question about whether the participant has a print subscription.

Then, the meat of the survey: participants were offered seven attributes of online news content, and each participant was asked to rate each attribute's impact on his/her willingness to pay for online news content. (Each participant was asked to rate each one on a scale of 1–5, where 1 = not at all impactful to 5 = extremely impactful.) The attributes were as follows:

- Strong credibility
- Unique local content not available on local newspaper sites
- In-depth analysis of national stories
- In-depth analysis of international stories
- In-depth analysis of business stories
- Strong sports content
- Strong arts content

You then asked how much a participant was willing to pay per month for online news, using a dropdown of different denominations. Finally, the survey posed the crucial question, "Is there any kind of online news experience that you would be willing to pay for?" as a "yes" or "no" response.

In total, the survey launched with 14 questions. You ran it on various news forums and communities.

After 1 week, you assess the responses. After some serious cleaning of the data, you end up with a sample size of 203 usable responses. The questions and response options and how they were coded are listed in Table 11.2.

After you imported and recoded your data into SPSS, you're ready to perform the logistic regression. The first 20 lines of the 203 rows of data are displayed in Figure 11.14.

Our primary objective at the moment is to find out how to predict who is willing to pay for some kind of news online. In other words, variable 14 (see Table 11.2 or column 14 (right-hand most column) in Figure 11.14) is our Y (dependent variable). Since it is a yes/no variable, our regression analysis will be binary logistic regression.

Table 11.2 Questions and Coding in the CharlestonGlobe.com Survey

Question	Measured	Coded	Comments
1. Gender	Male/Female	1 = Male 0 = Female	
2. Highest education level achieved	High school diploma Associate's degree Bachelor's degree Master's degree Doctorate	1–5 in the order listed	This assumes an interval scale, which may not be exactly true, but evidence indicates that there is unlikely to be any change in the conclusions by analyzing a monotonic scale such as this as an interval scale.[1]
3. Income per year	Seven categories (in thousands of dollars) <30, 31–60, 61–90, 91–120, 121–160, 161–200, >200	Numbered 1–7	This also assumes an interval scale, and evidence is even stronger that there is unlikely to be any change in the conclusions by analyzing this monotonic scale as an interval scale.
4. Age	Years of age	Actual number of years	
5. Are you a subscriber to a print newspaper?	Yes/No	Yes = 1 No = 0	
6. Please rate the impact that the following attributes have on *your willingness to pay for online news content.* Please use a scale of 1–5, where 1 = not at all impactful and 5 = extremely impactful. *Unique local content not available on local newspaper sites.*	1–5 Likert scale, 1 = Not at all impactful 5 = Extremely impactful	1–5 as checked off	
7. *Strong credibility*	Same Likert scale	1–5 as checked off	
8. *In-depth analysis of national stories*	Same Likert scale	1–5 as checked off	
9. *In-depth analysis of international stories*	Same Likert scale	1–5 as checked off	
10. *In-depth analysis of business stories*	Same Likert scale	1–5 as checked off	

(Continued)

Table 11.2 Questions and Coding in the CharlestonGlobe.com Survey—cont'd

Question	Measured	Coded	Comments
11. *Strong sports content*	Same Likert scale	1–5 as checked off	
12. *Strong arts content*	Same Likert scale	1–5 as checked off	
13. What is the maximum you would be willing to pay on a monthly basis for access to CharlestonGlobe.com?	Eight categories, in dollars: 0, 1–4, 5–9, 10–15, 16–20, 21–25, 26–30, >30	None of the categories above 1–4 had a sufficient frequency to stand alone, nor did they in total. So, 0 was coded 0, and anything >0 was coded 1.	
14. Is there any kind of online news experience that you would be willing to pay for?	Yes/No	Yes = 1 No = 0	

[1]*Further discussion of scale types and interval-scale assumptions are beyond the scope of the text. Further elaboration can be found in any Marketing Research text.*

However, before running and analyzing the regression, we first consider a couple of issues of interest to Denise Dangle and others at *The Charleston Globe*.

First, let's examine the results of question 13: "What is the maximum you would be willing to pay on a monthly basis for access to *CharlestonGlobe.com*?" The frequency distribution for that question is shown in Table 11.3.

We can see in Table 11.3 that the frequency of responses above $4/month is quite sparse, and, indeed, none of the categories above $4 has sufficient frequency to be a "stand-alone category." In fact, if we add them all up (i.e., from third through eighth categories), we find a total of only 21 responses. A rule of thumb (from database marketing studies) for a stand-alone category is to have at least 25 people. The reason for this is that for a categorical variable, if the frequency is too small, the results you get may be unreliable. Therefore, we coded the variable for regression-analysis purposes at 0 and 1, where "0" indicates the person is willing to pay *nothing* for CharlestonGlobe.com, and a "1" indicates the person is willing to pay something for CharlestonGlobe.com.

Next, we consider the relationship of great interest to Nick Bonovich: the possible correlation between the importance of *Strong Credibility* and *Willingness to pay something for an online news experience*. We performed a chi-square test of independence with the two variables. The results are shown in Figure 11.15.

Nick was right! The chi-square results indicate a strong relationship between the variables—indeed, the *p*-value is 0.000 (see horizontal arrow in Figure 11.15). A careful look at the frequencies (top section of output) indicates that the direction of the relationship is that "the more impactful the issue of strong credibility, the more likely to be willing to pay for an online news experience." In addition, we can also see from

	Gender	Education	Income	Age	p_newspaper	Local	Credibility	National	International	Business	Sports	Arts	Pay_for_CGlobe	Pay_for_news
1	.00	1.00	4.00	40.00	.00	.00	1.00	2.00	5.00	2.00	2.00	5.00	.00	.00
2	1.00	3.00	3.00	52.00	.00	1.00	5.00	5.00	1.00	4.00	2.00	1.00	1.00	1.00
3	.00	2.00	3.00	23.00	.00	.00	3.00	4.00	2.00	2.00	2.00	1.00	.00	.00
4	.00	2.00	6.00	23.00	.00	.00	2.00	3.00	5.00	2.00	2.00	1.00	.00	.00
5	.00	1.00	5.00	24.00	.00	1.00	2.00	2.00	2.00	2.00	2.00	2.00	.00	.00
6	.00	4.00	3.00	55.00	.00	4.00	5.00	2.00	3.00	4.00	2.00	2.00	1.00	1.00
7	.00	3.00	7.00	59.00	.00	5.00	2.00	3.00	2.00	5.00	2.00	2.00	1.00	1.00
8	.00	4.00	4.00	44.00	.00	5.00	4.00	1.00	4.00	5.00	2.00	2.00	1.00	1.00
9	.00	4.00	3.00	26.00	.00	5.00	3.00	2.00	3.00	3.00	2.00	2.00	1.00	1.00
10	1.00	4.00	4.00	43.00	.00	4.00	3.00	2.00	3.00	4.00	2.00	2.00	.00	1.00
11	.00	3.00	5.00	30.00	.00	5.00	4.00	4.00	5.00	3.00	2.00	2.00	.00	1.00
12	.00	4.00	1.00	44.00	.00	4.00	4.00	2.00	1.00	4.00	2.00	1.00	.00	1.00
13	.00	3.00	4.00	45.00	.00	5.00	4.00	3.00	3.00	2.00	2.00	3.00	.00	1.00
14	.00	3.00	2.00	47.00	.00	5.00	5.00	1.00	5.00	2.00	2.00	1.00	.00	1.00
15	1.00	1.00	7.00	25.00	.00	1.00	3.00	2.00	3.00	5.00	2.00	2.00	1.00	.00
16	.00	2.00	3.00	23.00	.00	1.00	1.00	2.00	3.00	2.00	2.00	2.00	1.00	.00
17	.00	2.00	1.00	18.00	.00	1.00	2.00	2.00	2.00	1.00	2.00	2.00	1.00	.00
18	.00	2.00	6.00	19.00	.00	2.00	4.00	1.00	1.00	2.00	2.00	3.00	.00	.00
19	.00	3.00	7.00	21.00	.00	2.00	3.00	2.00	2.00	2.00	2.00	4.00	.00	.00
20	1.00	1.00	7.00	22.00	.00	2.00	3.00	2.00	3.00	2.00	2.00	4.00	.00	.00

FIGURE 11.14

CharlestonGlobe.com data in SPSS.

Table 11.3 Frequency Distribution of Question 13

Category ($/month)	Frequency
0	79
1–4	103
5–9	7
10–15	4
16–20	1
21–25	3
26–30	2
>30	4
Total	203

Figure 11.15 that about 83% (a total of 169, the sum arrived at by adding the individual numbers contained in the black oval in Figure 11.15) of the respondents indicated that strong credibility was at least "3" on the 1–5 scale (1 = not at all impactful, 5 = extremely impactful) in a decision to pay for an online news experience.

We now perform and discuss the binary logistic regression analysis. The output is displayed in Figure 11.16.[2]

First, observe the "pseudo-R-square" values at the top of the figure. The Cox & Snell R Square is 0.523 and the Nagelkerke R Square is 0.703. If we were to interpret the Nagelkerke R Square as an r^2 value in a regular multiple linear regression, the 0.703 would indicate that we estimate that about 70% of the variability in Y (whether or not a person would pay for some type of online news experience) is associated with the variables in the equation. In loose terms, we estimate that these 13 X variables explain 70% of whether a person answers "Yes" or "No" to the question. So far, so good.

Credibility * Pay_for_news Crosstabulation

Count

		Pay_for_news		Total
		.00	1.00	
Credibility	1.00	10	0	10
	2.00	22	2	24
	3.00	39	10	49
	4.00	9	6	15
	5.00	37	68	105
Total		117	86	203

Chi-Square Tests

	Value	df	Asymp. Sig. (2-sided)
Pearson Chi-Square	50.015[a]	4	.000
Likelihood Ratio	56.847	4	.000
Linear-by-Linear Association	48.398	1	.000
N of Valid Cases	203		

a. 1 cells (10.0%) have expected count less than 5. The minimum expected count is 4.24.

FIGURE 11.15

Chi-square test for strong credibility versus willingness to pay for online news; SPSS with CharlestonGlobe.com.

[2] The formal process for performing this analysis indicates that you should take steps to tell SPSS which of the X variables are (0,1) or "categorical"-type variables. We believe that this is best not done, as long as you are very clear which category got a 1 and which got a 0, and that you understand that a positive coefficient indicates that, everything else equal, a "1" for that X increases the probability that Y = 1 and a "0" decreases this probability, and that it is the reverse if the coefficient of the X is negative. We believe that identifying these details in SPSS adds more confusion than benefit.

Model Summary

Step	-2 Log likelihood	Cox & Snell R Square	Nagelkerke R Square
1	126.293[a]	.523	.703

a. Estimation terminated at iteration number 6 because parameter estimates changed by less than .001.

Classification Table[a]

Observed			Predicted		
			Pay_for_news		Percentage Correct
			.00	1.00	
Step 1	Pay_for_news	.00	106	11	90.6
		1.00	14	72	83.7
	Overall Percentage				87.7

a. The cut value is .500

Variables in the Equation

		B	S.E.	Wald	df	Sig.	Exp(B)
Step 1[a]	Gender	-.291	.489	.354	1	.552	.748
	Education	.614	.197	9.726	1	.002	1.848
	Income	.175	.131	1.783	1	.182	1.191
	Age	-.032	.017	3.486	1	.062	.969
	p_newspaper	2.876	.651	19.535	1	.000	17.741
	Local	.597	.234	6.512	1	.011	1.817
	Credibility	.579	.226	6.587	1	.010	1.784
	National	-.385	.203	3.607	1	.058	.680
	International	-.121	.189	.413	1	.521	.886
	Business	1.157	.278	17.329	1	.000	3.179
	Sports	-.124	.214	.337	1	.562	.883
	Arts	-.268	.169	2.517	1	.113	.765
	Pay_for_CGlobe	-.597	.625	.912	1	.339	.551
	Constant	-7.790	1.764	19.497	1	.000	.000

FIGURE 11.16

Output for CharlestonGlobe.com binary logistic regression; SPSS.

SIDEBAR: HOW HIGH IS HIGH?

It is difficult, if near impossible, to say whether you should consider 70% to be a high or not-so-high value of an r^2, since that issue is so context dependent, and there is little previous work in the public domain to compare the 70% to. As we noted in the previous two chapters, there are situations when 70% would be viewed as fabulous (e.g., trying to predict who will buy and who will not buy in a catalog marketing endeavor), while in other situations when it clearly is not high enough to use the results to strong advantage. Still, the authors' instinct in this case is that it is decently high.

Next, move down the figure to the Classification Table (middle section). It tells you that this regression analysis predicts 87.7% of the case correctly (see oval in Figure 11.16). Specifically, the vast majority of the people who answered "No" to the question whose answer is our "Y" (Is there any kind of online news experience that you would be willing to pay for?) are correctly predicted (90.6%), and the vast majority of those who answered "Yes" were predicted correctly (83.7%—72 correctly predicted, 14 incorrectly predicted). As noted, overall, we have 87.7% predicted correctly. This 87.7% fares *very* favorably with both the Cpro and Cmax values. (See earlier sidebar on Cmax and Cpro.) There are 107 "0's" (No) and 86 "1's" (Yes) as values of Y. The values are the row totals in Figure 11.16 ($106 + 11 = 117$ and $14 + 72 = 86$). Thus, 117 is the frequency of the largest group:

$$\text{Cmax} = 117/203 = 0.576 = 57.6\%$$

$$\text{and Cpro} = (117/203)^2 + (86/203)^2 = 0.512 = 51.2\%.$$

If a hypothesis test were performed to see if the 87.7% is statistically significantly higher than the 57.6%, the result is significant with *p*-value < 0.001, leaving little doubt that the equation classifies beyond any reasonable doubt better than random chance, using even Cmax, the higher benchmark, as the baseline.

The third section of the output tells us an even richer story. By examining the "Sig." column, you can see that there are five significant variables, i.e., five of the *p*-values are below 0.05. We've listed them with their respective *p*-value and coefficient sign in Table 11.4.

OK, now you're ready to make some really powerful predictions based on empirical evidence. Since all the coefficients of these significant variables are positive, we can conclude that, everything else being equal,

- a person who is of the opinion that "unique local content not available on local newspaper sites" is more impactful on his/her likelihood of paying for an online new experience is indeed more likely to be willing to pay for an online news experience;
- a person who subscribes to a print newspaper is more likely to be willing to pay for an online news experience;
- a person who is of the opinion that having *Unique Local Content Not Available on a Local Newspaper Site* is more impactful in making a decision about his/her likelihood of paying for an online news experience is more likely, indeed, to be willing to pay for an online news experience;

Table 11.4 The Significant Variables in the Multiple Regression; CharlestonGlobe.com

- Education (*p*-value = 0.002 + coefficient)
- p_newspaper (*p*-value = 0.000 + coefficient)
- Local (*p*-value = 0.011 + coefficient)
- Credibility (*p*-value = 0.010 + coefficient)
- Business (*p*-value = 0.000 + coefficient)

- a person who is of the opinion that having *Strong Credibility* is more impactful in making a decision about his/her likelihood of paying for an online news experience is more likely, indeed, to be willing to pay for an online news experience; and
- a person who is of the opinion that having *In-depth Analysis of Business Stories* is more impactful in making a decision about his/her likelihood of paying for an online news experience is more likely, indeed, to be willing to pay for an online news experience.

The other 8 of the 13 X variables are not significant, although two are close: age (p-value = 0.062) and national (p-value = 0.058).

Of course, you're very excited that the model fared well, and that so many of your variables have an impact on its success.

But, before blurting out these findings to anyone who will listen, you need to do one more thing—we need to perform a *stepwise (binary logistic) regression*. Why? As we noted in Chapter 10, it is possible that two (or rarely, but possibly, more than two) of the nonsignificant variables in the multiple regression are highly overlapping, masking the real significance of both of them. The stepwise regression will reveal if this is the case and provide a more accurate accounting of which variables are really significant.

11.5.1 STEPWISE REGRESSION ANALYSIS OF THE CHARLESTONGLOBE.COM DATA

To perform stepwise regression, we have to return to a previous step, when we chose the "Method" dropdown in SPSS. This is shown in Figure 11.17 (see oval in Figure 11.17). As you can see, there are various options available.

The option that is most similar to the "Stepwise Regression" command of Chapter 10 is "Forward: LR." This is the option you should use. The "LR" stands for "Likelihood Ratio," a term involved in the process of using the "maximum likelihood" criterion as discussed earlier in the sidebar on page 275.

After we click on "Forward: LR" and then "OK," you get the stepwise output shown in Figure 11.18.

Let's begin with the "Variables in the Equation" section at the bottom of the output. You can see in the third (bottom) section that there were five steps. (To brush up on stepwise regression, refer back to Chapter 10.) As we noted in discussing stepwise regression in Chapter 10, where it was first introduced, it is only the last step that really matters. In this case, it is step 5. In step 5, there are still five variables, same as in the earlier multiple regression. But there are major differences in the output.

First, the *Unique Local Content Not Available on a Local Newspaper Site* has dropped out of the regression model. What do we make of that? Well, regression analysis (linear or logistic) is a complex technique, with different patterns of overlap when different sets of variables are in the equation. As a consequence, different p-values and different benchmarks have to be overcome to be significant at 0.05. (If we forced it to enter as a sixth variable, its p-value would be 0.113, which is, of course, not less than 0.05, which is why it did not enter; still, 0.113 is not considered that much above 0.05.)

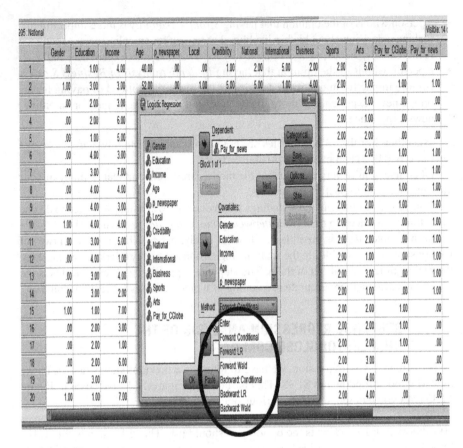

FIGURE 11.17

The logistic regression dialog box with "Method" pulled down; SPSS with CharlestonGlobe.com.

Another difference between the binary logistic multiple regression and binary logistic stepwise regression results is the difference of the coefficient for the "Subscriber to Printed Newspaper" variable. It's gone down from 17.7 to 10.7 (rounded). However, the *p*-value has remained 0.000 (which, we recall means 0.000 to three digits). Obviously, this variable is still a very strong predictor. Our enthusiasm for this predictor is still extremely high.

The final noteworthy point is that the stepwise results have thrown us an interesting curve. You'll notice the "national" coefficient is significant (*p*-value = 0.033) and is negative! (Remember, column B displays the *slope* of the linear equation, when the Y*c is the LN (natural log) of the odds. When B is negative, it means that increasing that X will decrease the LN of the odds (Y*c), which will, in turn, *decrease* the odds, which, in turn, will decrease the probability of willingness to pay. Review pages 281 and 282 for how the probability is determined.) This suggests also that there is a negative impact on willingness to pay for an online news experience

Model Summary

Step	-2 Log likelihood	Cox & Snell R Square	Nagelkerke R Square
1	194.133[a]	.334	.449
2	163.310[a]	.428	.575
3	150.466[b]	.463	.622
4	143.963[b]	.480	.645
5	139.101[b]	.492	.661

a. Estimation terminated at iteration number 5 because parameter estimates changed by less than .001.

b. Estimation terminated at iteration number 6 because parameter estimates changed by less than .001.

Classification Table[a]

			Predicted		
			Pay_for_news		Percentage Correct
	Observed		.00	1.00	
Step 1	Pay_for_news	.00	101	16	86.3
		1.00	31	55	64.0
	Overall Percentage				76.8
Step 2	Pay_for_news	.00	98	19	83.8
		1.00	17	69	80.2
	Overall Percentage				82.3
Step 3	Pay_for_news	.00	102	15	87.2
		1.00	19	67	77.9
	Overall Percentage				83.3
Step 4	Pay_for_news	.00	103	14	88.0
		1.00	19	67	77.9
	Overall Percentage				83.7
Step 5	Pay_for_news	.00	105	12	89.7
		1.00	18	68	79.1
	Overall Percentage				85.2

Variables in the Equation

		B	S.E.	Wald	df	Sig.	Exp(B)
Step 1[a]	Business	1.263	.173	53.067	1	.000	3.537
	Constant	-5.054	.708	51.023	1	.000	.006
Step 2[b]	p_newspaper	2.411	.481	25.107	1	.000	11.150
	Business	1.046	.181	33.275	1	.000	2.846
	Constant	-4.880	.742	43.258	1	.000	.008
Step 3[c]	Education	.552	.161	11.720	1	.001	1.737
	p_newspaper	2.566	.505	25.827	1	.000	13.011
	Business	.983	.191	26.461	1	.000	2.674
	Constant	-6.339	.942	45.255	1	.000	.002
Step 4[d]	Education	.584	.171	11.638	1	.001	1.793
	p_newspaper	2.341	.524	19.962	1	.000	10.389
	Credibility	.500	.199	6.285	1	.012	1.648
	Business	.814	.195	17.486	1	.000	2.256
	Constant	-7.727	1.178	43.057	1	.000	.000
Step 5[e]	Education	.627	.177	12.509	1	.000	1.872
	p_newspaper	2.369	.533	19.725	1	.000	10.689
	Credibility	.521	.204	6.545	1	.011	1.683
	National	-.397	.186	4.553	1	.033	.672
	Business	.912	.207	19.450	1	.000	2.489
	Constant	-7.119	1.216	34.286	1	.000	.001

FIGURE 11.18

Stepwise (Forward: LR) regression output; SPSS with CharlestonGlobe.com.

if the person views *In-Depth Analysis of National Stories* as very impactful in the decision. So, how do we interpret this? Carefully, in a word. But it's safe to say that increasing the amount of in-depth analysis of national news will not increase likelihood of adoption. If folks were asked what the regular news networks such as CNN and MSNBC News do well, many would respond that they cover national news very well. Therefore, the negative coefficient of "national" may be reflecting that this coverage is not lacking, and is readily available for free, so if it is a person's primary interest, he/she would not be as inclined to pay for an online news experience.

11.5.2 DUE DILIGENCE COMPARING STEPWISE RESULTS TO REVISED BINARY REGRESSION RESULTS

It can be useful to compare the last step of the stepwise analysis to yet another (binary logistic) regression analysis in which we enter only the five variables that were deemed significant in the original binary logistic multiple regression. This result is in Figure 11.19, where we've entered *only* the significant variables we identified in the original regression model.

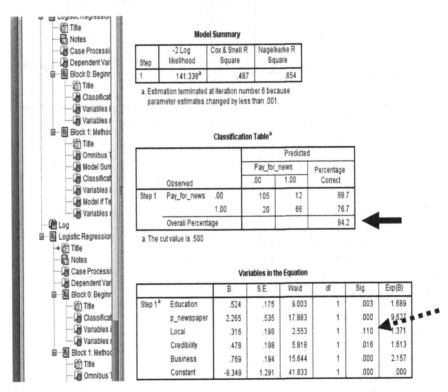

FIGURE 11.19

Multiple regression analysis with only the five significant variables in the multiple regression shown in Figure 11.16; SPSS with CharlestonGlobe.com.

Surprisingly, "Local" is not significant in the above regression analysis, although it is fairly close (p-value $= 0.110$; see dashed arrow).

Now compare the top two sections of this regression with the top two sections of the last step of the stepwise regression analysis depicted in Figure 11.18.

If we go up to the second section of output, we can see that in the last step of the stepwise regression analysis, we have 85.2% of the people correctly classified. In the multiple regression with the five original significant variables, this value is 84.2% (see arrows in Figures 11.19 and 11.18). This is a somewhat negligible difference, especially when we remember that these values are estimates based on 203 people, and not exact values we would get with the entire population of people that CharlestonGlobe.com can solicit. Both of these percentage values are only marginally below what we get using all 13 values (Figure 11.16), 87.7%.

If we move up to the top section of output, we see the same pattern. In the stepwise regression, we have the two pseudo-R-square values of 0.492 and 0.661 for step 5, and 0.487 and 0.654 in the multiple regression with the original five significant variables. Clearly, there is not much difference between the sets of values, and both are marginally below the 0.523 and 0.703 we obtain in Figure 11.16 using all 13 variables.

What's the takeaway? Ultimately, very similar conclusions are to be reached from the original multiple regression and the stepwise regression. However, the stepwise regression has decreased somewhat the importance of *Unique Local Content Not Available on a Local Newspaper Site.*

11.6 IMPLICATIONS OF THE SURVEY-DATA ANALYSIS RESULTS—BACK TO CHARLESTONGLOBE.COM

Looking over the final results from your stepwise regression (step 5 of Figure 11.18), we can revise our main conclusions that were garnered as a result of the original binary logistic model. Here are the revised (and final) conclusions:

1. A person with higher educational level is *more* likely to be willing to pay for an online news experience.
2. A person who subscribes to a print newspaper is *more* likely to be willing to pay for an online news experience than a person who does not subscribe to a print newspaper.
3. A person who is of the opinion that having *Strong Credibility* is more impactful in making a decision about his/her likelihood of paying for an online news experience is *more* likely to be willing to pay for online news experience.
4. A person who is of the opinion that having *In-Depth Analysis of Business Stories* is more impactful in making a decision about his/her likelihood of paying for an online news experience is *more* likely to be willing to pay for an online news experience.
5. A person who is of the opinion that having *In-Depth Analysis of National Stories* is more impactful in making a decision about his/her likelihood of paying for an online news experience is *less* likely to be willing to pay for an online news experience.

Thus, the results describe two (identifiable) main characteristics of people likely to pay for online news content: higher educated ones with a subscription to a printed newspaper. A pivot toward these types of folks in the *CharlestonGlobe.com*'s marketing endeavors will probably yield better results than what they're getting right now.

The results also indicate that CharlestonGlobe.com should fill its gated online news site with highly credible in-depth analysis of business stories to increase likelihood of people buying a subscription to the site. Adding in-depth national news will likely not help to increase paying customers. Adding unique local content will not hurt, and may well help (although we are not so sure of its help, as we are regarding highly credible in-depth analysis of business stories).

Now you believe you have a compelling story to tell—and one that will help increase online subscribers to CharlestonGlobe.com. It's time to present the results to the team.

11.6.1 THE RESULTS ARE IN: SHOWTIME AT CHARLESTONGLOBE.COM

You build your PowerPoint presentation carefully; you start with goals, methodology (including samples size and data collection), and move quickly to a high-level summary. Then you move into the analysis. Trying to not sound too professorial, you describe the basics of logistic regression and stepwise regression. Since your output is awash in numbers, your screens include large red ovals that show the critical numbers. Your recommendations are to the point, but not overly pedantic. Even though they carry the weight of a solid sample size and equally solid statistical analysis, your recommendations are suggestions, not mandates.

You're finally ready, so you send out the meeting invite to everyone on the team. Most team members accept immediately, but Denise Dangle accepts the meeting request only an hour before the actual presentation. This is yet another example of Dangle's standard passive-aggressive techniques.

Everyone is silent during the first couple of slides, which outline goals and methodology. But, the room comes to life during the high-level findings.

"The data suggest that people who are likely to pay for online news content are higher educated and have a subscription to a printed newspaper. A pivot toward these types of folks in the *CharlestonGlobe.com*'s marketing endeavors will probably yield better results than what we're getting right now."

"A printed newspaper?" Dangle gasps.

"Yes," you say, calmly bracing for a fight. "As a matter of fact, print subscribers are about 2.6 times more likely than a non-print subscriber to buy online news when we assume that the other four variables are at their averages."

"But why in the world would you want an online version when you've already got a printed newspaper?" Dangle implores with a caustic laugh. She looks around the room for support. But meeting attendees ignore her, staring at your slides.

"Remember, we weren't asking about an online version of the *Globe*. We were asking about an online news *experience*. We kept the dependent variable vague, but used the independent variables to ascertain what that experience should be."

"Hmmm…was there an answer to my question in there?" Dangle says, staring down at her iPad.

You plunge forward, ignoring the barb: "Consider this: We already know that older folks in general are higher consumers of news than younger ones. The networks figured that out a long time ago. Ever notice how many 'old folks' ads, like 'Cialis,' appear during the *CBS Evening News*?"

"Look," Dangle interrupts, "Nobody gets their news from TV anymore."You remain cool: "Well, the ratings have definitely dropped in the past 20 years. But, it doesn't erase the fact that older folks are usually more interested in news than younger ones." "*Globe* demographics have always been older."

"OK, OK," Dangle says impatiently. "Keep going."

It's time for you to start wrapping up: "OK. Older folks want news, and we know from our printed subscription data that older folks are much more prone to have a printed subscription. We also know that older folks are usually better educated on the whole."

Dangle is getting flustered: "Where are you going with this?"

It's time to cut to the chase. "The folks who are willing to pay for online news content are news junkies. And news junkies are older, highly educated, and still get a printed paper in the morning."

The room is quiet. Finally Nick Bonovich breaks the silence.

"What about credibility?"

"Your hypothesis was right, Nick," you smile. "The *p*-value for that independent variable was 0.01 with a positive coefficient. If they're gonna pay for online news, it's got to be highly credible."

Stacy Souley, the affable business analyst, pipes up.

"But what about the actual content?"

"Good question," you answer. "We asked about a wide range of news content: national, international, business, sports, arts, and unique local stories."

Dangle looks up from her iPad. "And?"

"In-depth analysis of business stories was the only variable that moved the needle."

Stacey nods in agreement: "Makes sense. Folks will actually pay for great business analysis. Think of Bloomberg and Morningstar."

Dangle is still skeptical. "What about international? The *Globe* has had foreign bureaus since World War I and we've won at least 10 Pulitzers on international coverage."

"It's a real strength of the *Globe*," you acknowledge. "But this study doesn't offer any evidence of people willing to pay extra for it." You pause and offer an explanation. "I think there are simply too many online international options available for free. Same with sports, arts, national. To some extent, the jury is still out on local."

"OK," Dangle says with a smirk. "You're saying we create a business site with strong credibility and leave it at that?"

"Well, no," you reply. "Keep in mind that we had folks rate several variables' impact on 'willingness to pay'; nothing was rated in isolation. You can't just pull out the variable with the strongest coefficient and highest significance. The results are only meaningful within the context of the entire study about an online news experience. And other variables came close to significant, like unique local content and arts content. Last, an alpha of 0.05 is pretty rigorous. I could redo the regression with an alpha of 0.10 and...."

"OK, OK," Dangle interrupts, motioning you to stop. "You've done your homework. And God knows this stats stuff makes my head spin." She looks directly at you: "Do me a favor. Trim down your preso to no more than five pages. I'll schedule a meeting with Mark." As she gets up to leave, she offers the first compliment of your tenure: "Thanks. Good stuff."

As Dangle shoots down the hall, Nick comes up and offers his hand in congratulations.

"Wow. You, my friend, are presenting to CEO Mark Munzer. Spectacular! You might have just saved CharlestonGlobe.com from the digital graveyard."

11.7 SUMMARY

In this chapter we introduced binary logistic regression. The key to its use is that the dependent variable, Y, is a Yes/No-type (i.e., two possibilities) categorical variable. We discussed how the technique works, and then went through a small example in detail, using SPSS (Basic Excel does not accommodate binary logistic regression). Next we addressed the CharlestonGlobe.com data, which had 13 independent variables (called "covariates" by SPSS), and performed a multiple binary logistic regression analysis, followed up by a stepwise binary logistic regression analysis (the Method is labeled "Forward: LR" by SPSS). We then interpreted and discussed the results.

11.8 EXERCISE

1. Use the SPSS data set from the previous chapter, "Chapter 10..Exercise 1.data," to run a binary logistic regression. The dependent variable (unused in the exercise in Chapter 10) is to be the variable labeled "Purchase" (right-hand-most column in the data set). It represents whether the responder feels that he/she is more likely than not to purchase the search engine ("1"), or is more likely not to purchase it ("0"). The output is in a file, "Chapter 11..Exercise 1.output."
   a. Which attributes are significant?
   b. What percent of the cases, overall, are predicted correctly?
   c. What percent of the "1's" are predicted correctly?
   d. Repeat parts a, b, and c, performing a stepwise regression analysis (using the "Forward: LR" option).

   The solutions are discussed in a Word file, "Chapter 11.Exercise 1.answers."

Addendum: For Mac Excel Users

INTRODUCTION

We are well aware of the fact that some UX departments run exclusively on Macintosh computers. Thus, we have included this addendum for you Mac folks out there who want to use the techniques described in this book.

The biggest immediate difference you will notice between the PC and Mac versions of Excel is the absence of the Analysis Toolpack in the Mac version. As a consequence, some of the more advanced statistical features (like ANOVA) are missing from out-of-the-box Excel 2011 for Mac.

However, these advanced features are easily accessible for free by downloading StatPlus from AnalystSoft at http://www.analystsoft.com/en/products/statplusmacle/.

Nevertheless, keep in mind that many of the techniques described in this book (and perhaps the ones you will use the most) are available *without* the StatPlus download. Thus, we will walk you through the out-of-the-box techniques first by displaying screenshots from the basic Excel 2011 for Mac. Then, we will switch to the StatPlus screen shots when needed.

CHAPTER 1
SECTION 1.2.1: FINDING THE PROBABILITIES OF COMPLETION TIMES OR SATISFACTION LEVELS, OR ANYTHING ELSE, ON A NORMAL CURVE

We will use the sample data from the chapter and section to illustrate the process.

Step 1: Select "Function" from the "Insert" dropdown to access the formula builder:

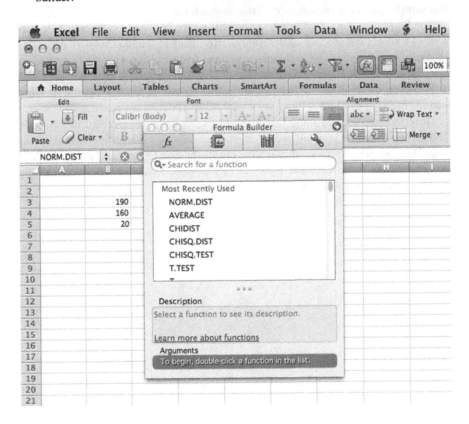

Step 2: Search for the "NORMDIST" Excel command, and double-click on "NORMDIST" option to open the "NORMDIST" formula builder:

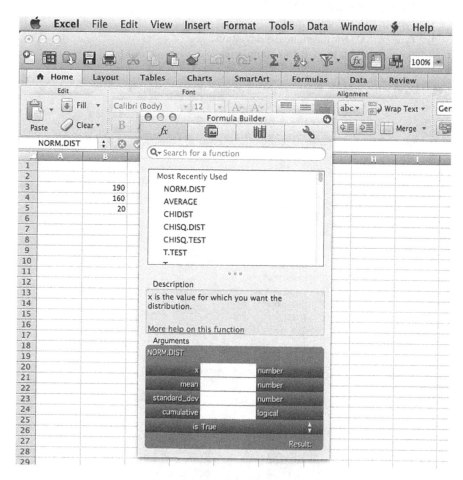

Step 3: Enter the appropriate values for the NORMDIST formula builder. Using the illustrative data from Chapter 1:

- Type in "190" for the "X."
- Type in "160" for the mean.
- Type in "20" for the standard deviation.
- Type in "1" for the left-tail cumulative.

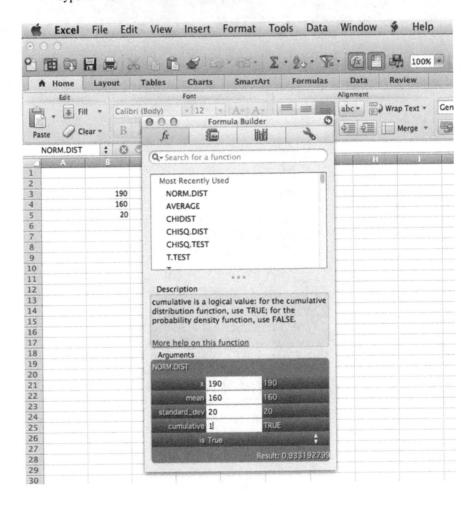

Step 4: Find the *p* value as soon as all the fields are entered correctly (in this case, the *p* value is 0.93,319,279).

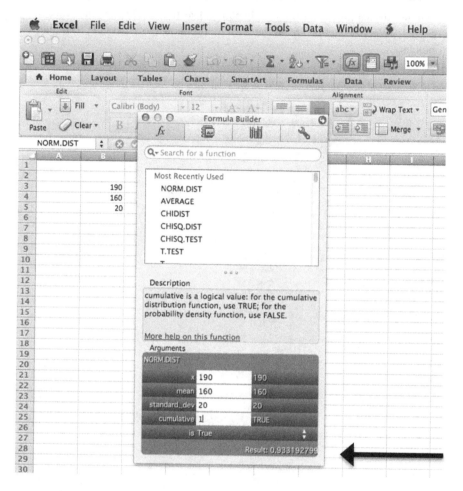

SECTION 1.2.2: FINDING COMPLETION TIMES OR SATISFACTION LEVELS, OR ANYTHING ELSE, ON A NORMAL CURVE

We will use the sample data from the chapter and section to illustrate the process.

Step 1: Select "Function" from the "Insert" dropdown to access the formula builder:

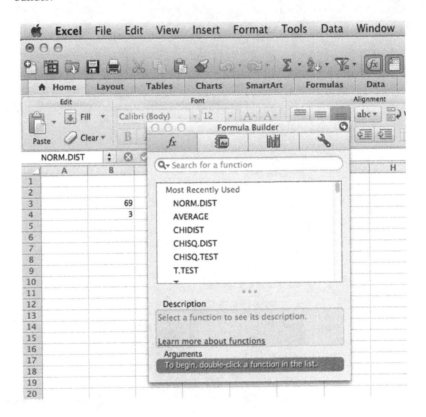

Step 2: Search for the "NORMINV" Excel command, and double-click on "NORMINV" option to open the "NORMINV" formula builder:

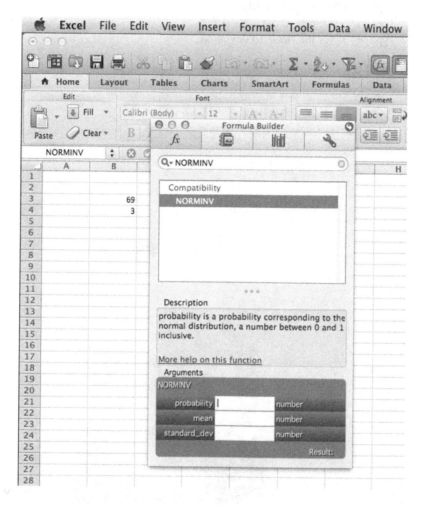

Step 3: Enter the appropriate values for the NORMDIST formula builder. Using the illustrative data from Chapter 1:

- Type in ".025" for probability.
- Type in "69" for the mean.
- Type in "3" for the standard deviation.

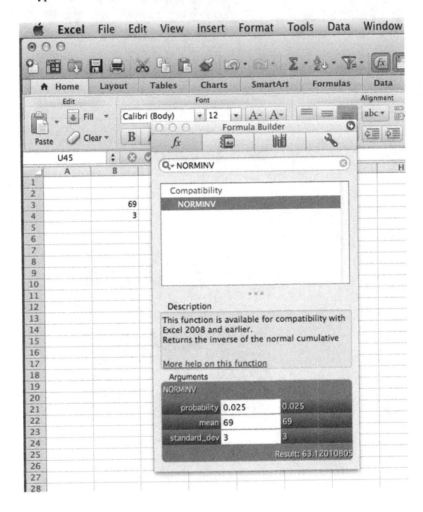

Step 4: Find the x value as soon as all the fields are entered correctly (in this case, the x value is 63.12,010,805).

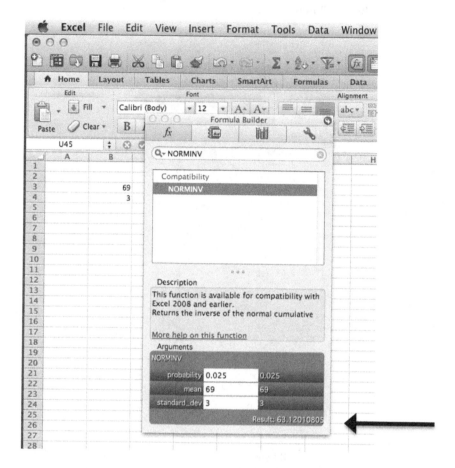

As per the instructions of 1.2.2, repeat filling out the formula builder using a probability of 0.975. In this case, 95% of the user task completion times will be between about 63 s and 75 s.

SECTION 1.3.2: FINDING A CONFIDENCE INTERVAL

We will use the sample data from the chapter and section to illustrate the process.

We will demonstrate two different ways to find a confidence interval, using (1) standard Excel 2011 and (2) Excel StatPlus.

Standard Excel 2011

First, you will need to calculate the standard deviation of the data for which you want to calculate a confidence interval.

Step 1: Place the cursor in a cell directly beneath the column of data for which you want to calculate a confidence interval. Right click within the cell. From the dropdown, click on "Insert Function."

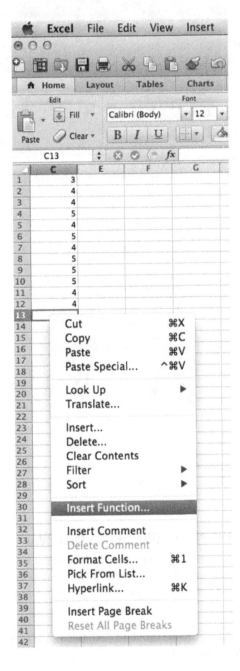

Step 2: Search for the "STDEV.S," Excel command, and double-click on "STDEV.S" option to open the "STDEV.S" formula builder:

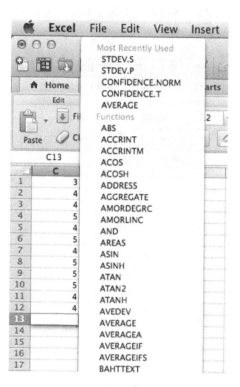

The STDEV.S formula appears in your selected cell:

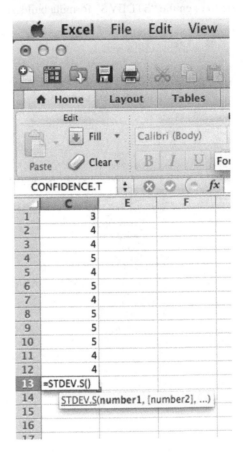

Step 3: Select the column of data for which you want to calculate your standard deviation.

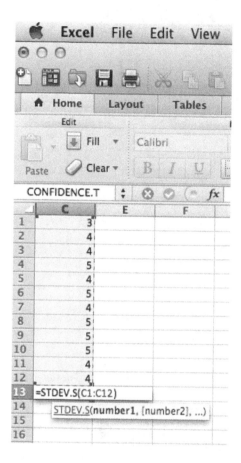

Step 4: Use the RETURN key to generate your standard deviation:

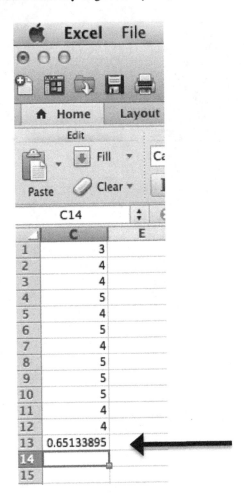

Step 5: Repeat steps 1 and 2 to access the formula for the "CONFIDENCE.T" command:

Step 6: Enter the appropriate values for the CONFIDENCE.T formula.
- Type in ".05" for alpha (this is the typical setting, but you can use others).
- Click directly on the cell containing your standard deviation to fill in the standard deviation part of the formula.
- Type in your sample size. In this case, it is 12.

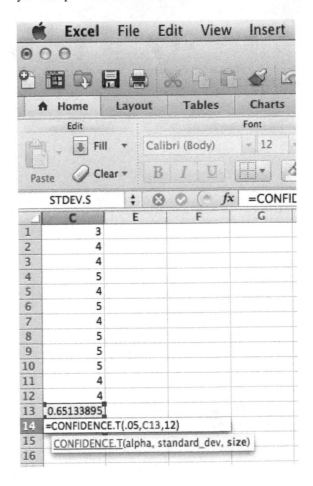

Step 7: Use the RETURN key to generate your error:

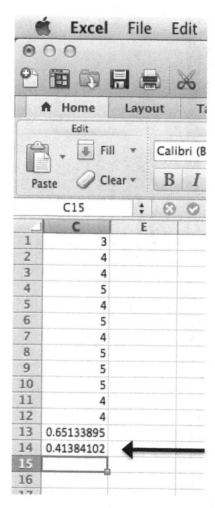

As noted in the text, Excel refers to this number as the "confidence level." More commonly, it is referred to as "error" or "margin of error." Add and subtract the "error" to your mean to calculate the confidence interval (it is also the number you will need when you are adding error bars to any means you have charted).

StatPlus

Step 1: If you have not done so already, download StatPlus from http://www.
analystsoft.com/en/products/statplusmacle/.

Step 2: Open StatPlus. From "Statistics" dropdown, select "Descriptive Statistics":

You will arrive at this dialog box. Click on the cell selector.

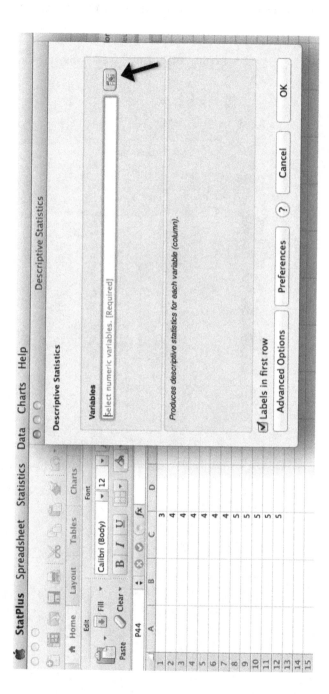

Step 3: You will be returned to the spreadsheet in regular Excel. Select and copy the data:

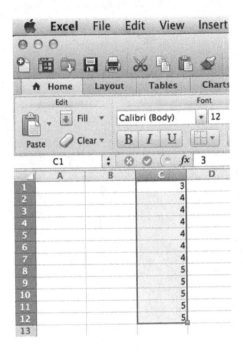

Step 4: Renew StatPlus as your active working window. The cells containing the data you want to analyze should already be inserted into the correct field on the Descriptive Statistics variable dialog box. If not, paste the selected data cells into the Descriptive Statistics variable dialog box. Then, click "OK."

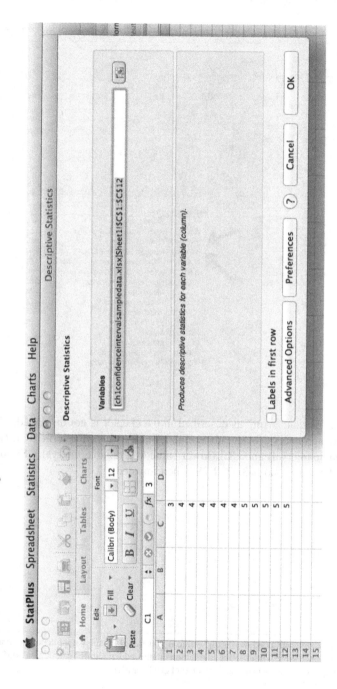

Step 5: Your descriptive statistics results are displayed:

	A	B	C	D	E	F
1	Alpha value (for confidence interval)	0.05				
2		Variable #1 (Var1)				
3	Count	12	Skewness	-0.3818		
4	Mean	4.33333	Skewness Standard Error	0.58177		
5	Mean LCL	3.91949	Kurtosis	2.32653		
6	Mean UCL	4.74717	Kurtosis Standard Error	0.91655		
7	Variance	0.42424	Alternative Skewness (Fisher's)	-0.43866		
8	Standard Deviation	0.65134	Alternative Kurtosis (Fisher's)	-0.33673		
9	Mean Standard Error	0.18803	Coefficient of Variation	0.15031		
10	Minimum	3.	Mean Deviation	0.55556		
11	Maximum	5.	Second Moment	0.38889		
12	Range	2.	Third Moment	-0.09259		
13	Sum	52.	Fourth Moment	0.35185		
14	Sum Standard Error	2.2563	Median	4.		
15	Total Sum Squares	230.	Median Error	0.06803		
16	Adjusted Sum Squares	4.66667	Percentile 25% (Q1)	4.		
17	Geometric Mean	4.28576	Percentile 75% (Q2)	5.		
18	Harmonic Mean	4.23529	IQR	1.		
19	Mode	4.	MAD	0.5		
20						

Notice that "error" as described in the chapter is not displayed.[1] However, your confidence interval is already defined. StatPlus uses the term UCL (lower value of a reliable interval) and UCL(lower value of a reliable interval.). So in this case, our confidence interval is 3.92–4.75 (when rounded).

[1] However, you will need the "error" value if you want to display confidence intervals on a bar chart. To determine "error", refer to the instructions in this addendum for calculating confidence intervals—including the "error"—using standard Excel 2011 for Mac.

CHAPTER 2
SECTION 2.5.1: COMPARING TWO DESIGNS: INDEPENDENT T-TESTS

We will use the sample data from the chapter to illustrate the process.

Step 1: Select "Function" from the "Insert" dropdown to access the formula builder. Search for "T-TEST":

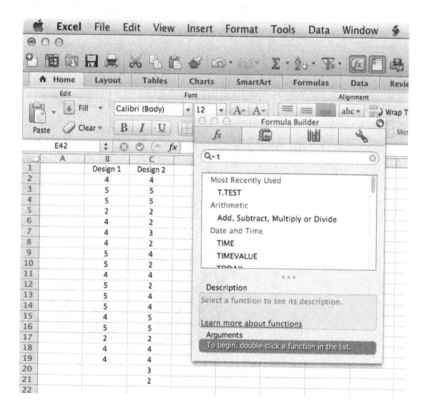

Step 2: Double-click on "T-TEST" to access the "T-TEST" formula builder:

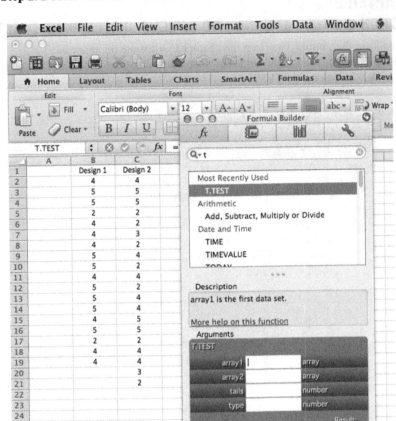

Step 3: Enter the appropriate values for the independent samples t-test:
- Click directly in the array fields to select the values from the two different columns of data.
- Type in "2" for the number of tails.
- Type in "2" for type. If type equals 2, T-TEST in Excel performs a two-sample equal variance (homoscedastic) test. This is also known as an independent samples t-test.

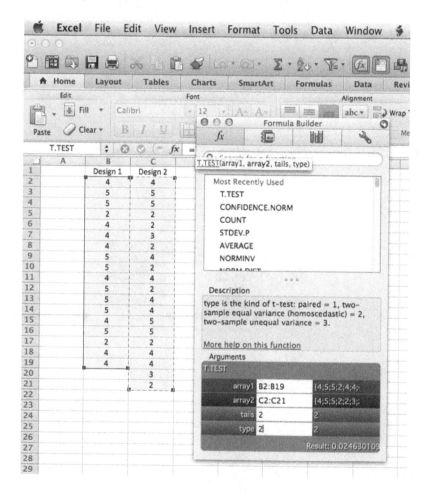

Step 4: Find the *p* value as soon as all the fields are entered correctly (in this case, the *p* value is 0.024,630,109).

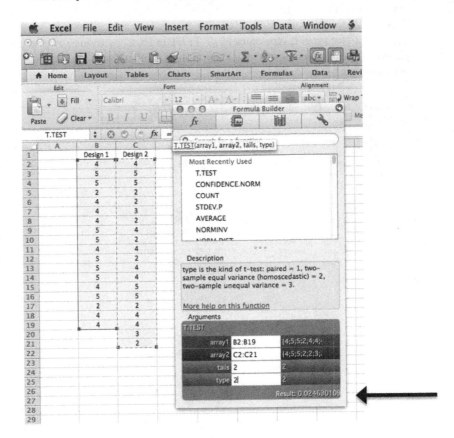

CHAPTER 3
SECTION 3.4.1: COMPARING TWO DESIGNS: PAIRED T-TESTS

We will use the sample data from the chapter and section to illustrate the process.

Step 1: Select "Function" from the "Insert" dropdown to access the formula builder:

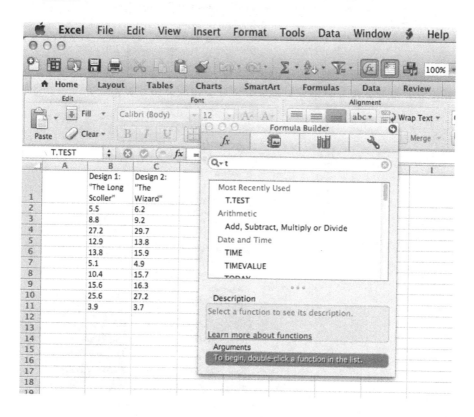

Step 2: Double-click on "T-TEST" to access the T-TEST formula builder:

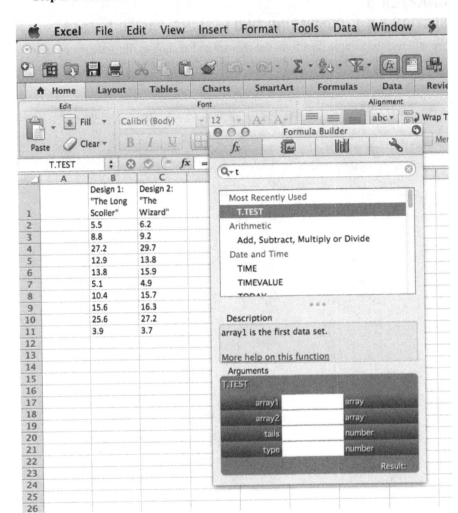

Step 3: Enter the appropriate values for the paired samples t-test:
- Click directly in the array fields to select the values from the two different columns of data.
- Type in "2" for the number of tails.
- Type in "1" for type. If type equals 1, T-TEST performs a paired test.

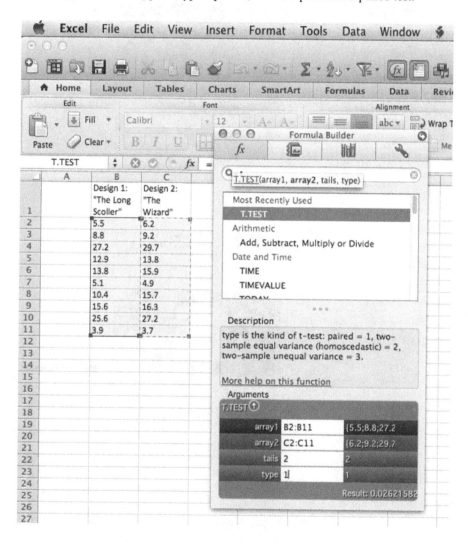

Step 4: Find the *p* value as soon as all the fields are entered correctly (in this case, the *p* value is 0.02,621,587).

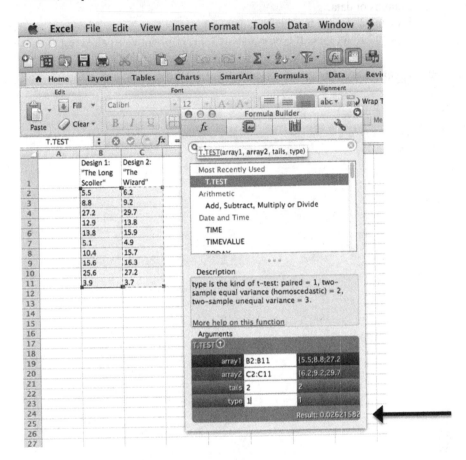

CHAPTER 4
BINOMIAL-RELATED HYPOTHESIS TESTING USING INDEPENDENT SAMPLES

We will use the sample data from the chapter and section to illustrate the process.

Step 1: Construct your actual range and expected range for the data you are analyzing. See Section 4.3.1. for details.

Step 2: Select "Function" from the "Insert" dropdown to access the formula builder:

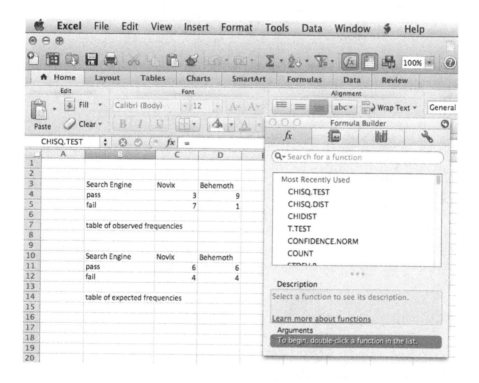

Step 3: Double-click on "CHISQ.TEST" to access the CHISQ.TEST formula builder:

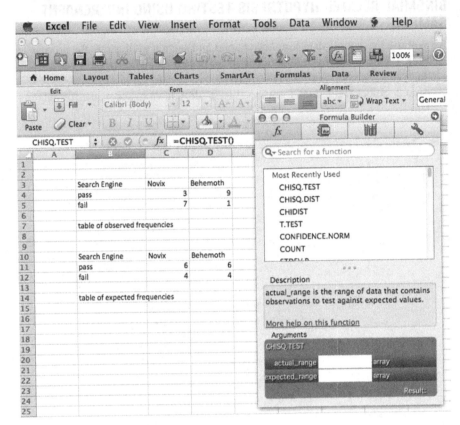

Step 4: Enter the appropriate values for the chi-square test:
- Enter the observed frequencies in the "actual range" field.
- Enter the expected frequencies in the "expected range" field.

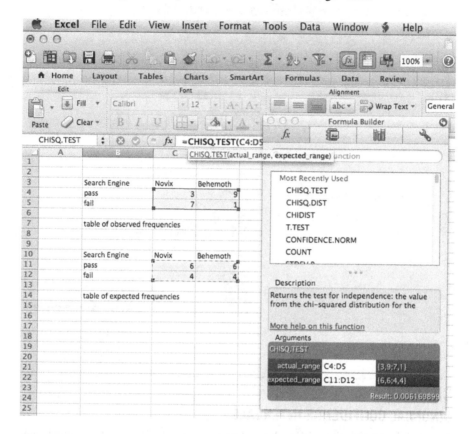

Step 5: Find the *p* value as soon as all the fields are entered correctly (in this case, the *p* value is 0.006,169,899).

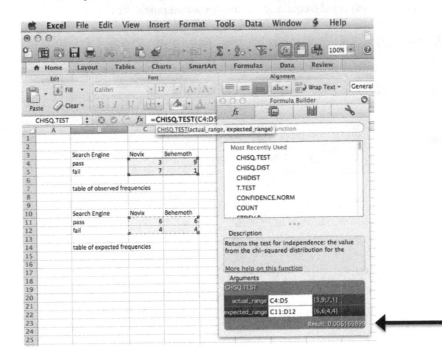

CHAPTER 4
BINOMIAL CONFIDENCE INTERVALS

As noted, Excel (for either PC or Mac) does not have a built-in module for calculating binomial confidence intervals. Consult Section 4.5 for calculating binomial confidence intervals, or simply use Table 4.9 to determine binomial confidence intervals for samples sizes from 1 to 15.

CHAPTER 5
SECTION 5.3.1: BINOMIAL-RELATED HYPOTHESIS TESTING USING PAIRED DATA

We will use the sample data from the chapter and section to illustrate the process.

Step 1: Calculate your "Q" for your collected data per the instructions in Section 5.3.1 (for this tutorial, we will use 0.333 as "Q" as per Section 5.3.1).

Step 2: Select "Function" from the "Insert" dropdown to access the formula builder:

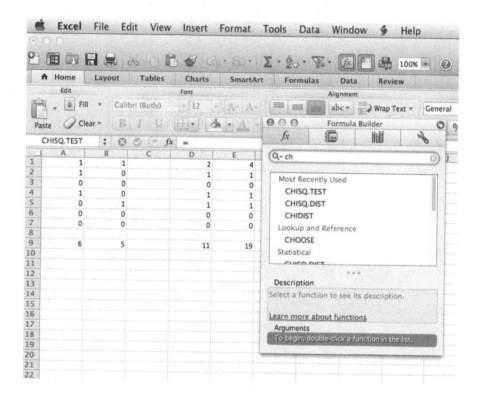

Step 3: Double-click on "CHIDIST" to access the CHIDIST formula builder:

Step 4: Enter the appropriate values for the CHIDIST test:

- Enter the "X" number or "Q".
- Enter the degrees of freedom. (The degrees of freedom value is simply the number of columns (tasks) minus 1. We refer to it as (K-1) in Chapter 5, since that is the notation used by Cochran.)

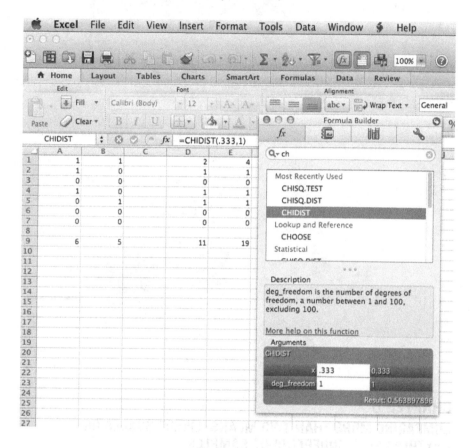

Step 5: Find the *p* value as soon as all the fields are entered correctly (in this case, the *p* value is 0.563,897,895).

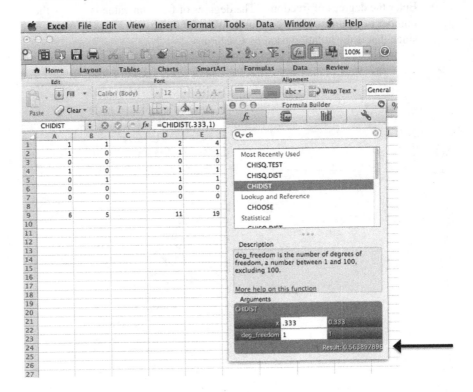

CHAPTER 6
COMPARING MORE THAN TWO MEANS: LIKERT SCALES OR ANYTHING ELSE! INDEPENDENT SAMPLES

We will use the sample data from the chapter and section to illustrate the process.

Step 1: If you have not done so already, download StatPlus from http://www.analystsoft.com/en/products/statplusmacle/.

Step 2: Open StatPlus. From "Statistics" dropdown, select "Analysis of Variance" and then "One-way ANOVA."

StatPlus Spreadsheet Statistics Data Charts Help

macexamplechapter6.xlsx

Menu	Submenu
Basic Statistics and Tables	
Analysis of Variance (ANOVA)	**One-way ANOVA (simple)...**
Design of Experiments	One-way ANOVA (with post-hoc tests)... ⌥A
Regression	One-way ANOVA [Group variable] (with post-hoc tests)... ⌥⇧A
Nonparametric Statistics	**Two-way ANOVA...**
Time Series/Forecasting	Three-way ANOVA...
Survival Analysis	Mixed Treatment by Subjects ANOVA...
Power Analysis/Sample Size	Mixed ANOVA with Two Treatments...
	Within Subjects ANOVA...
	Discriminant Function Analysis...
	General Linear Model (GLM)...

Home Layout Tables
Edit
Paste Fill Clear Calibri (Body) B I U

C30

	A	B	C	D	E	F	G
1	2	4	4	3	3		
2	2	5	5	4	4		
3	3	3	4	4	3		
4	3	4	4	3	2		
5	3	4	4	3	3		
6	1	5	5	4	3		
7	3	4	5	3	3		
8	1	5	5	4	2		
9	1	4	4	4	3		
10	3	5	5	2	2		
11	3	5	5	3	3		
12	2	4	5	4	3		
13	3	4	4	3	3		
14	3	4	5	3	2		
15	1	5	5	4	3		
16	1	5	5	3	3		
17	2	5	5	3	4		
18	2	4	4	2	3		
19	2	4	4	2	2		
20	1	5	5	2	2		
21	4	4	5	2	2		
22	3	5	5	2	2		
23	3	4	4	3	3		
24	3	5	4	3			
25	3	5	5	2			
26	4	2	5	5			
27	2		5	5			
28	1						
29							

You will arrive at this dialog box. Click on the cell selector.

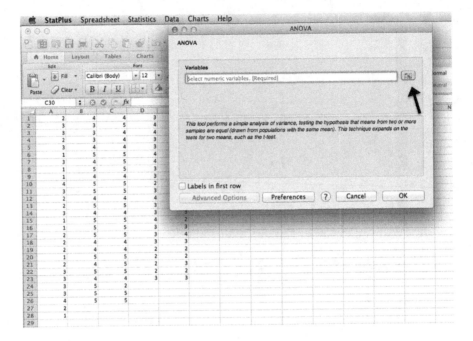

Step 3: You will be returned to the spreadsheet in regular Excel. Select and copy the data:

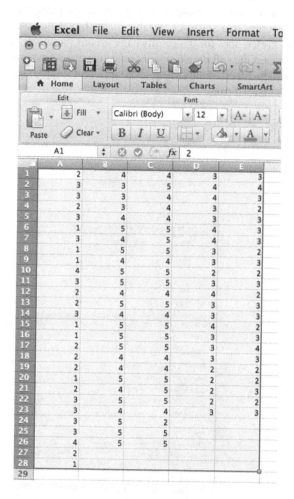

Step 4. Renew StatPlus as your active working window. The cells containing the data you want to analyze should already be inserted into the correct field on the Descriptive Statistics variable dialog box. If not, paste the selected data cells into the Descriptive Statistics variable dialog box. Click on "Preferences to chose your preferences for the results page (in this particular case, notice that we have instructed the software to ignore missing values since we have highlighted a complete block of data, despite the different sample sizes). Then, click "OK" on both dialog boxes.

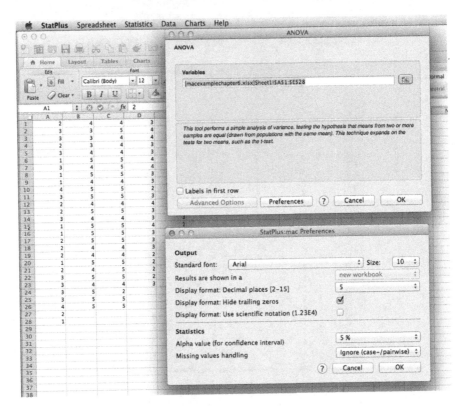

Step 5: Your descriptive statistics results are displayed, including your p value, labeled "p-level" in StatPlus:

N.B. You will notice we ended up with a slightly different p value using StatPlus than the PC version of Excel. The PC value was 4.26E-24. Of course, this is an extremely low value with an exponential of −23 (in other words, 23 zeros and 0.426 all after the decimal point), The result we are seeing using the StatPlus (0E+0) is also an extremely low p value, with a value of 0 with a multiple zero exponential. Practically speaking, both versions of Excel are delivering identical values—as close to zero as you will ever see—so we reject HO.

CHAPTER 7
COMPARING MORE THAN TWO MEANS: WITHIN-SUBJECTS (PAIRED) DESIGN

We will use the sample data from the chapter and section to illustrate the process.

Step 1: If you have not done so already, download StatPlus from http://www.analystsoft.com/en/products/statplusmacle/.

Step 2: StatPlus requires that you arrange your data differently than what is accepted in the PC version of Excel. Basically, you must arrange all the data in columns—by dependent variable and by the different factors. Thus Table 7.2 should be reformatted this way:

	A	B	C
	Participant	Question	Rating
1	1	1	4
2	1	2	4
3	1	3	3
4	1	4	2
5	2	1	5
6	2	2	3
7	2	3	3
8	2	4	1
9	3	1	4
10	3	2	4
11	3	3	3
12	3	4	1
13	4	1	5
14	4	2	4
15	4	3	4
16	4	4	2
17	5	1	4
18	5	2	3
19	5	3	3
20	5	4	3
21	6	1	5
22	6	2	4
23	6	3	4
24	6	4	2
25	7	1	3
26	7	2	3
27	7	3	2
28	7	4	2
29	8	1	5
30	8	2	4
31	8	3	3
32	8	4	1
33	9	1	5
34	9	2	4
35	9	3	3
36	9	4	2
37	10	1	5
38	10	2	4
39	10	3	3
40	10	4	2

Step 3: Open StatPlus. From "Statistics" dropdown, select "Analysis of Variance" and then "Two-way ANOVA."

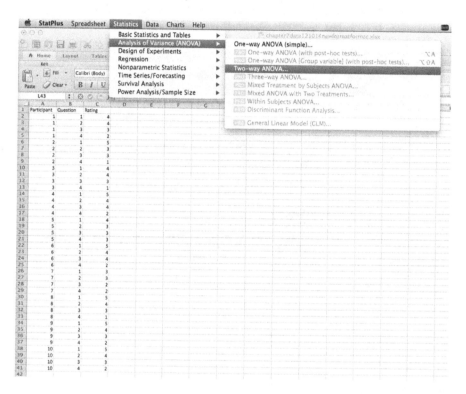

You will arrive at this dialog box:

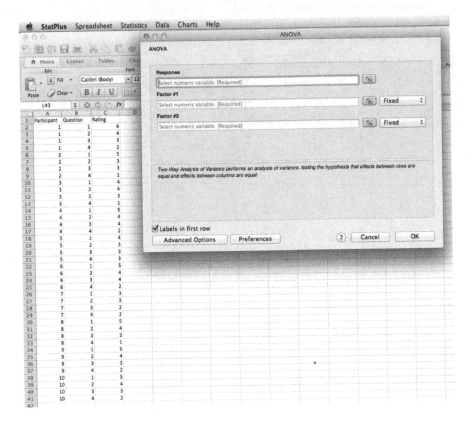

Step 4: In the Response box, enter the cell range for the dependent variable. In this case, that is all of the ratings that were collected from the test participants. Click on the icon to the right of the Response box, which will take you back to the regular Excel spreadsheet. Select all of the ratings data:

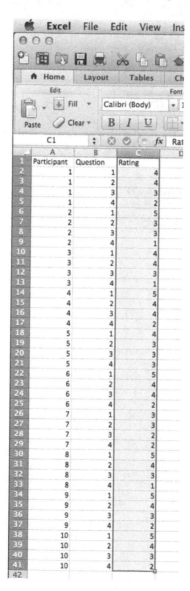

Step 5: Reactivate StatPlus. Your dependent variables have been inserted into Response box:

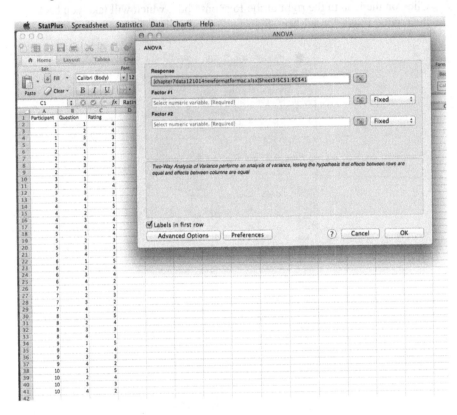

Step 6: In the Factor #1 box, enter the cell range for the first independent variable. In this case, the first independent variable is "Participant." Click on the icon to the right of the Factor #1 box, which brings you back to the spreadsheet, and select A1–A41. Your participant data has now been inserted in the Factor #1 box.

Step 7: Repeat Step 6 for all independent variables.

Step 8: Return to the Two-Way ANOVA dialog box and do the following:

- Make sure the "Labels in First Row" have been checked if your included them in your data selection. In this case, we did.
- On the Advanced Options dialog box, make sure "No Interactions" is checked:

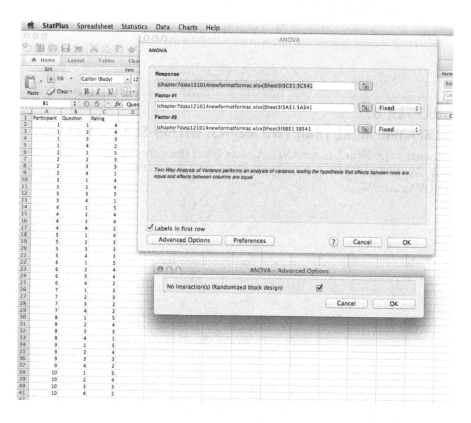

Step 9: Click OK in both ANOVA dialog boxes. The results appear in a new page, and the output is extensive. Scroll down until you find the ANOVA table, and find your *p* value:

60	Question		2	10		3.7	0.23333	0.48305		
61	Question		3	10		3.1	0.32222	0.58765		
62	Question		4	10		1.8	0.4	0.63246		
63										
64	**ANOVA**									
65	*Source of Variation*	*SS*	*d.f.*	*MS*		*F*	*p-level*	*F crit*	*Omega Sqr.*	
66	*Factor #1 (Participant)*	5.225	9	0.58056		1.99048	0.08069	2.25013	#N/A	
67	*Factor #2 (Question)*	38.875	3	12.95833		44.42857	0.	2.98035	#N/A	
68	*Within Groups*	7.875	27	0.29167						
69	*Total*	51.975	39	1.33269						
70										
71										
72				**Comparisons among groups (Factor 2 - Question)**						
73	*Scheffe contrasts among pairs of means*									
74	*Group vs Group (Contrast)*	*Difference*	*Test Statistics*	*Critical value (5%)*	*Accepted?*					
75	1 vs 2	0.8	3.31231	2.92493	accepted					
76	1 vs 3	1.4	5.79655	2.92493	accepted					
77										

CHAPTER 8
COMPARING MORE THAN TWO MEANS: WITHIN-SUBJECTS DESIGN

As noted, to perform 2-factor ANOVA using Excel (for either PC or Mac), your data may have to be severely compromised. Consult Section 8.4 for performing 2 factor ANOVAs in SPSS.

CHAPTER 9
CORRELATION

We will use the illustrative data from Section 9.3.1 to illustrate the process.

Step 1: Select "Function" from the "Insert" dropdown to access the formula builder; then search for the "CORREL" Excel command:

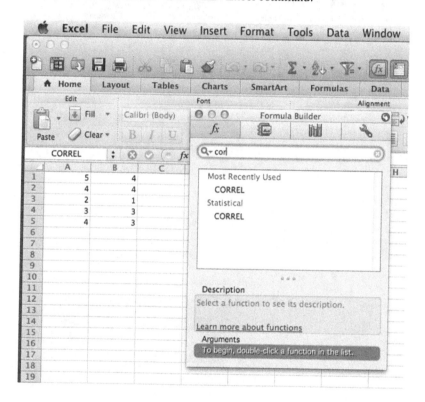

Step 2: Double-click on "CORREL" option to open the "CORREL" formula builder:

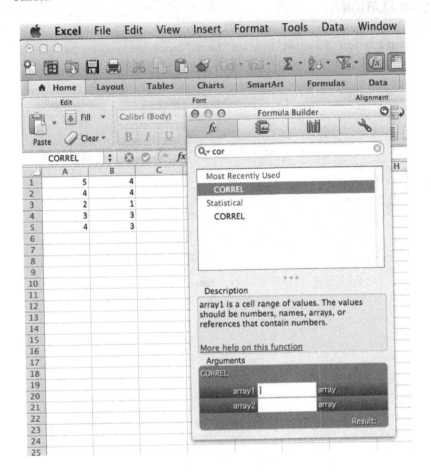

Step 3: Enter the appropriate values for the CORREL formula builder. Click directly into the first array box and then highlight your data; repeat for the second array box:

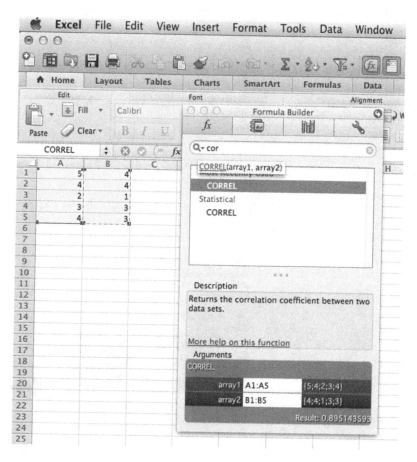

Step 4: Find the r as soon as all the fields are entered correctly (in this case, the r is 0.895,143,593).

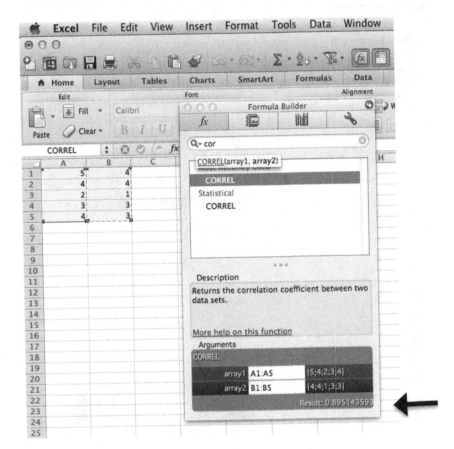

CHAPTER 9
SIMPLE REGRESSION

We will use the sample data for Section 9.4 to illustrate the process.

Step 1: If you have not done so already, download StatPlus from http://www.ana lystsoft.com/en/products/statplusmacle/.

Step 2: Open StatPlus. From "Statistics" dropdown, select "Regression" and then "Linear Regression."

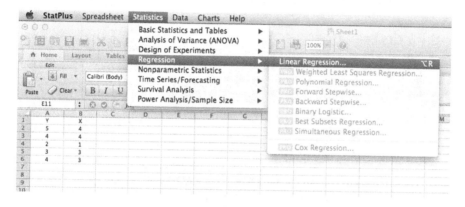

Step 3: You will arrive at this Linear Regression dialog box. Click on the icon next to the dependent variable box:

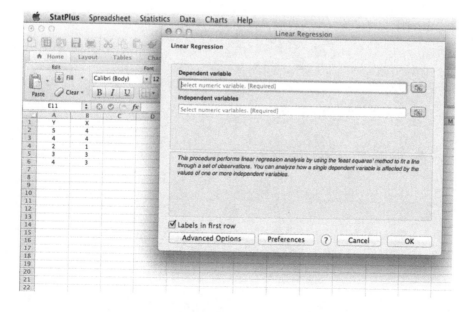

Step 4: You will be returned to the spreadsheet in regular Excel. Select and copy the dependent variable data. Navigate back to StatPlus, and your correct dependent data has been inserted in the correct position. Repeat this process for your independent variables.

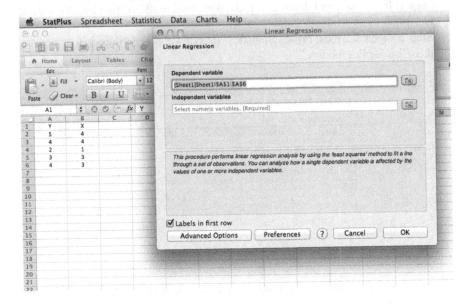

Step 5: Once your variables have been entered:
- Click on "Labels in first row" if you have selected your label names (in this case we have).
- Click on "Residual Plots" and "Line Fixed Plots" in the Advanced Options dialog box if you would like to see your data charted.
- Click "OK" on both dialog boxes.

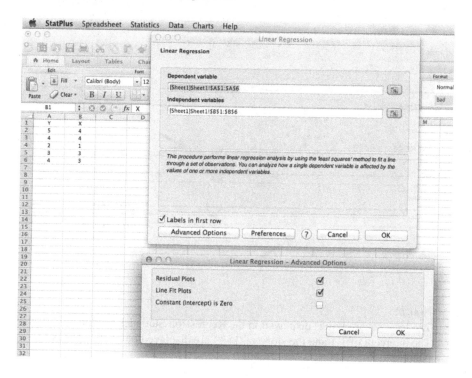

Step 6: The results are displayed on a new page; here is the top half of the page.

| | Excel | File | Edit | View | Insert | Format | Tools | Data | Window | | Help |

```
B2        fx
```

	A	B	C	D	E	F	G	H
1				Linear Regression				
2								
3	**Regression Statistics**							
4	R	0.89514						
5	R Square	0.80128						
6	Adjusted R Square	0.73504						
7	S	0.58689						
8	Total number of observations	5						
9				Y = 1.1000 + 0.8333 * X				
10								
11	**ANOVA**							
12		d.f.	SS	MS	F	p-level		
13	Regression	1.	4.16667	4.16667	12.09677	0.04011		
14	Residual	3.	1.03333	0.34444				
15	Total	4.	5.2					
16								
17		Coefficients	Standard Error	LCL	UCL	t Stat	p-level	H0 (5%) rejected?
18	Intercept	1.1	0.76522	-1.33526	3.53526	1.4375	0.24613	No
19	X	0.83333	0.2396	0.07082	1.59584	3.47804	0.04011	Yes
20	T (5%)	3.18245						
21	LCL - Lower value of a reliable interval (LCL)							
22	UCL - Upper value of a reliable interval (UCL)							
23								

Notice:

- The least square line is displayed in the Regression Statistics section.
- The intercept of 1.1 and the slope of 0.833 are displayed below the ANOVA table.

To see the charts associated with this regression analysis, scroll down the page.

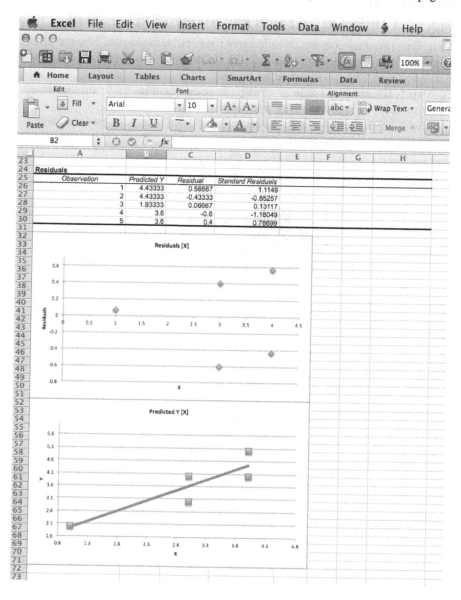

CHAPTER 10
MULTIPLE LINEAR REGRESSION AND STEPWISE REGRESSION

Basic Excel StatPlus does not provide a tool for stepwise regression. However, Basic Excel StatPlus does accommodate multiple linear regression. We'll use the sample data for section 10.3.1 to illustrate the process.

Step 1: If you haven't done so already, download StatPlus from http://www.anal ystsoft.com/en/products/statplusmacle/.

Step 2: Open StatPlus. From "Statistics" dropdown, select "Regression" and then "Linear Regression".

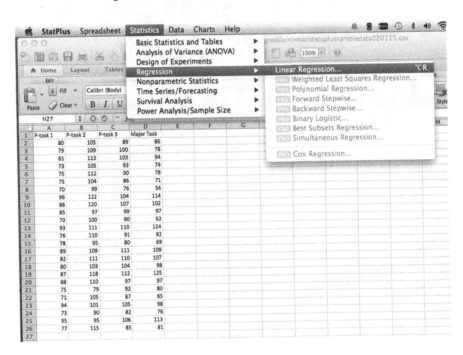

Step 3: You'll arrive at this Linear Regression dialog box. Click on the icon next to the dependent variable box:

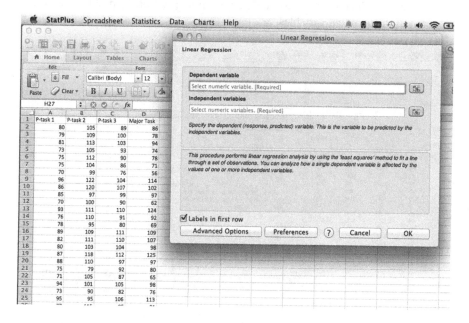

Step 4: You'll be returned to the spreadsheet in regular Excel. Select and copy the dependent variable data. Navigate back to StatsPlus, and your correct dependent variable data has been inserted in the correct position. Repeat this process for your independent variables.

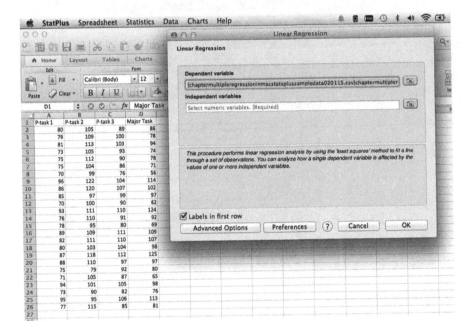

Step 5. Once your variables have been entered:

- Click on "Labels in first row" if you've selected label names. (In this case we have.)
- Click on "Residual Plots" and "Line Fixed Plots" in the Advanced Options dialog box if you'd like to see your data charted.
- Click "OK" on both dialog boxes.

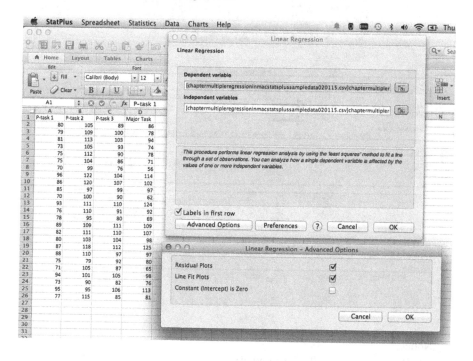

Step 6: The results are displayed on a new page; here's the top half of the page.

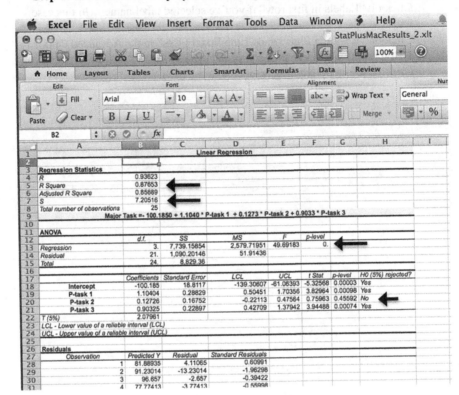

Notice:

- The R Square value is 0.877(rounded).
- The Standard Error is 7.20516.
- The p-value of the F test is 0 (to several digits).
- The three p values for each variable are displayed. P-task 1 and 3 are significant, but P-task 2 is *not* significant.

CHAPTER 11
MULTIPLE LOGISTIC REGRESSION

Basic Excel StatPlus does not have a built in module for calculating logistic regression. Consult Section 11.4 for calculating logistic regression using SPSS.

Index

Note: Page numbers followed by "b," "f," and "t" indicate boxes, figures, and tables respectively.

Printed in the United States
By Bookmasters